Africa's Grand Walk to Greatest Tomorrow

ABISAI TEMBA

Gotham Books

30 N Gould St.
Ste. 20820, Sheridan, WY 82801
https://gothambooksinc.com/

Phone: 1 (307) 464-7800

© 2023 *Abisai Temba*. All rights reserved.

No part of this book may be reproduced, stored in a retrieval system, or transmitted by any means without the written permission of the author.

Published by Gotham Books (November 15, 2023)

ISBN: 979-8-88775-420-8 (P)
ISBN: 979-8-88775-421-5 (E)

Because of the dynamic nature of the Internet, any web addresses or links contained in this book may have changed since publication and may no longer be valid.

The views expressed in this work are solely those of the author and do not necessarily reflect the views of the publisher, and the publisher hereby disclaims any responsibility for them.

TABLE OF CONTENTS

ACRONYMS AND ABBREVIATIONS 1

DEDICATION...4

ACKNOWLEDGEMENT.. 5

1 BACKGROUND AND INTRODUCTION 8
2 DEFINING AFRICA AND ITS FEATURES 20
3 THE HISTORICAL PERSPECTIVE OF AFRICA 53
4 AFRICA'S TRADE PATTERN IN THE MEDIEVAL TIME......................... 74
5 SLAVERY AND SLAVE TRADE AROUND AFRICA 89
6 IMPACT OF EUROPEAN INDUSTRIAL REVOLUTION ON AFRICA 109
7 THE HORRIFIC TRANSATLANTIC SLAVE TRADE 121
8 ZANZIBAR: THE SLAVE TRADE HUB OF EASTERN AFRICA 137
9 CONTEMPORARY SLAVE TRADE IN AFRICA 151
10 EUROPE SPONSORS EXPLORATION OF AFRICA 167
11 H.M. STANLEY AND KING LEOPOLD III ALLIANCE 191
12 THE TIME OF IMPERIALISM IN AFRICA.. 204
13 SPECIAL PROJECTS FOR PROMOTION OF IMPERIALISM 234
14 PROCESS TO COLONIALIZATION OF AFRICA 251
15 THE START OF MISSIONARY WORK IN AFRICA 272
16 CROSSING THE CHASIM TO POLITICAL INDEPENDENCE 294
17 RACISM: PROMOTER OF SOCIAL DISINTEGRATION 309
18 DARK SKIN: A SCAPEGOAT 332

19 ARICA'S FUTURE IN THE HANDS OF AFRICA 345

20 AFRICA'S CHALLENGES 355

21 SELECTING PRIORITIES OUT OF PRIORITIES 385

22 CRITICAL DRAWBACKS 404

23 THE NEED TO BE STRONG AND SAIL ON 427

24 AFRICA YESTERDAY, TODAY AND TOMORROW: 433

25 GOVERNANCE ISSUES IN AFRICA 476

26 THE NEW PARTNERSHIP FOR AFRICA'S DEVELOPMENT (NEPAD) .. 487

27 THE AFRICAN INTEGRATION- THE SOLE VIABLE PATH 494

ACRONYMS AND ABBREVIATIONS

AD: Anno Domini

AU: African Union

ADB: African Development Bank

ACS: American Colonialization Society

AVC: Agricultural Value Chains

CE: Common Era

BCE: Before Common Era

CENSAD: The Community of Sahel-Saharan States

CMFB: Co-operative Micro Finance Bank

COMESA: Common Market for Eastern and Southern Africa

CFS: Congo Free State

COVID 19: Corona Virus Disease 2019

District Micro Finance Bank

DRC: Democratic Republic of Congo

EAC: East African Community

ECCAS: Economic Community of Central African States

ECOWAS: Economic Community of West African States

EFT: Electronic Fund Transfers

GDP: Gross Domestic Product

GM: Genetically Modified

HIV/AIDS: Human Immunodeficiency Virus/ADS

IMF: International Monetary Fund

ICT: Information and Communications Technologies

IGAD: Inter-Governmental Authority on Development

ILO: International Labour Organization

KM: Kilometres

LDC: Less Developed Countries

LRA: Lord's Resistance Army

MDG: Millennium Development Goals

MP: Member of Parliament

OECD: Organization of Economic Cooperation and Development

OAU: Organization of African Unity

PE: Private Equity

PEC: Private Equity Capital

PRC: People's Republic of China

PNG: Papua New Guinea

R&D: Research and Development

REC: Regional Economic Community

RMFB: Regional Micro Finance Banks

SADC: Southern Africa Economic Community

UMA: Arab Maghreb Union

UK: United Kingdom

UN: United Nations

UNDP: United Nations Development Programme

UNESCO: United Nations Education Scientist, and Cultural Organization

USA: United States of America

WMO: World Meteorological Organization

DEDICATION

"This book is dedicated to my father, Elipokea Temba and to my mother, Nsianaeli Maswai who were taken from our lives in May 2016 and in August 2018 respectively. Baba & Mama- We loved you, but God loved you more. May God keep you happy in His eternal home till when He joins us together again."

Amen!

ACKNOWLEDGEMENT

Work on this book went on during the time COVID19 started to be seriously felt in Africa and the world at large. The widespread lock downs that were experienced from the end of the year 2019 to the beginning of 2022 had a lot of impact on the progress of the work. In view of the critical situation of the lockdowns and health measures that every one of us had to take and observe, things went extremely sluggishly, and at times the files had to stay on the shelves, collecting dust, while waiting for the pandemic to get less felt. But in spite of all that, members of the family and friends kept on taking deserving measures while encouraging some work to keep going, that being what happened though at a very slow and cautious pace.

All those situations notwithstanding I wish to take this opportunity first of all to thank God the Almighty for giving me the strength, courage, and guidance to cope with the difficult situation and environment that surrounded me throughout the time when the bits and pieces of this work were being put together. I am aware that God was with me throughout this exercise, because besides the COVID19 pandemic, the devil came our way, to tempt the family in various ways but with the grace of God we won in the battles. We thank you God for your mercy and for fighting on our side.

Special and specific comments are extended to my wife, Mary, for working very closely with me to ensure that things got properly organized and the health care was very well maintained to have things going. To you Mary I say thank you very much for the love and care extended to everybody involved directly or indirectly throughout the duration of this work.

Next, I wish to express my sincere thanks to Mrs. Aikande Emil Urassa, a highly visionary and experienced Scholarly Mistress, for the trouble she took to provide very useful advice and suggestions which assisted to sharpen ideas in the early draft of the manuscript, in a very tough environment of power-cut interruptions, COVID 19 pandemic lockdowns and many other challenges. To you Mama Urassa, I say once again "Thank you for the great contribution you made at a very critical moment".

Next, let me express heart felt thanks to Grace Temba, my younger sister, who has been operating rather remotely away in Moshi but has been doing wonderful job of ensuring our other family obligations in Kilimanjaro home are well taken care of. My peace of mind depended on the great effort she has kept putting on the home and gardens that needed close attention to allow life to keep going.

Last but not least, I say thank you to my Publishers, GOTHAM BOOKS INC: (not forgetting the exemplary work of my literary consultant, Brett Adams), for taking the responsibility to get involved in publishing this book and, for valuable expert suggestions and directions they provided to see this work completed according to international publishing regulations, and also for excellent impression of the book including matters of images that appear on the covers of the book to come up with this splendid job.

Finally, I am expressing my heart felt thanks to all friends including, the leaders of Kijitonyama Lutheran Parish, Dar es Salaam and those of Muroma/Ufishi, Hai District for taking care of me spiritually; without forgetting Mama Esther Kishimbo, a family friend of Kwaya Kuu ya Kijitonyama and Mama Mercy Msemembo, both of who always got in touch with me at all those times that I got faced with health challenges in the cause of drafting this book. To them heartedly wish them well, and God bless them. I also wish to thank all those who I have not been able to mention in these remarks; to them I say God bless them. I also wish to thank all those friends and neighbours who came and gave me moral support during the times of weak health. While my level of communication and cooperation was rather low, during the whole of 2021 period but I earned a lot of encouragement from many people from all over the world for their moral support. To all of them I say thank you very much for the tolerance and understanding that was shown to me. God Bless you all.

I
BACKGROUND AND INTRODUCTION

Africa has existed and has innocently been there, nursing humankind for thousands if not millions of years. Like a good mother, Africa has actually been nursing the human species since the first day of human existence in this world. Unlike any other continent, Africa's is the birth- place of mankind. It provided home for the first man on earth. Evidence of the good work of Africa has been found at Olduvai Gorge in northern Tanzania, where archaeologists have discovered enough information and evidence about the existence of the earliest human ancestors. Paleoanthropologists have found hundreds of fossilised bones, stone tools, and images in the area, dating back millions of years. The findings have led to the conclusion that humans first evolved in Africa. With time, Africa became the molder of human cultures including occupations such as hunting, fishing, tilling of land, animal husbandry, crafts, education, governments, defense, and moral organizations including religious groupings. Demographic movements led to the spread of people to various places inside Africa and gradually to the rest of the world. It logically follows that Africa was home for the earliest communities, villages, chiefdoms, kingdoms, and empires.

There exists a lot of evidence that the earliest movement from the said birthplace was towards the north mainly along the Rift valley regions and further on along the Nile Riverbank. As they moved, they settled, formed villages, chiefdoms, kingdoms, and even great empires. So, there were movements, stopovers, further group formations and splits as the population kept expanding. That prompted further movements and regroupings that led to the formation of new villages, chiefdoms or kingdoms and empires. Empires that were formed as various groups moved and regrouped, each in its own direction led to formation and development of great civilizations; but none of them lasted for too long before they collapsed due population growth and social conflicts thus making groups to seek for new breathing spaces. Group conflicts kept on creating misunderstandings, splits, and further demographic movements and further regroupings among and within their organizational setups.

Africa as it is, is itself a world wonder and heritage. The message that comes up in the next chapters will make us appreciate the fact that regardless of how a person looks at various theories or concepts of creation the work of archeologists provides a stimulating understanding of human being development. Their findings have shown that the first man: the **Homosapien** lived or rather, had his early development in Africa. Various religions have also shown that the first man was created and grew up in Africa, which also means that from there he developed and spread to the rest of the world. Whichever background used to describe the early home of mankind will lead to the conclusion that the first man's home was in the African land. The second Chapter of this book discusses how the human species developed from a place near the equator, in Africa, from where he spread. In that process many civilizations got developed before the population kept on spreading from Africa to the rest of the world.

God endowed Africa with many unique features unseen elsewhere in the world. We have also taken note of the fact that

Africa has itself been a world wonder. It is perhaps the only continent that, for reasons, had its good original name, the African name "***Alkebulan***" (or mother of mankind) got distorted or changed by foreigners, especially Europeans, as we know it today. What is unique about this African name is that it brought new emotional revelations. Africans have taken a lot of pride in the fact that, human life started in Africa. All the people of the world have now come to know that Africa is their earliest ancestral home. Not only that, for those who have read the Bible know about the Garden of Eden (which is said to be the birthplace of mankind). Logically then, the Garden of Eden was in Africa, which is consistent with the findings of archaeologists that the first human life first developed in Africa.

Very few people in the world have a proper idea of why Africa is what it is. What is commonly known is what has been provided by unreliable sources, presented in a way that keep perpetuating the negative impressions of those who have had very generalized and superficial or deliberately distorted information or knowledge of the continent. For instance, people in many parts of the world know Africa as a poor continent; mostly occupied by black people, most of who are illiterate, people that are at lowest level of civilization, and people in dare need for Western type of civilization. Many people also have conceived or understood Africa as a place mainly endowed with barren land, which has made agricultural production so inadequate that the continent has often been caught up in frequent famines that are causes of hunger and deaths of millions of people.

The fact that occurrences of famine have been witnessed in many parts of Sub-Saharan African countries like Ethiopia, Sudan, Somalia, Northern parts of Kenya, Burundi, Zimbabwe, and a several other places, has been used as a common phenomenon in the continent. Root causes of frequent occurrence of famines are usually never revealed or thoroughly analysed and discussed. The fact that those famines have often repeatedly hit specific parts of the African continent, has not found many persons who come forward to reveal the causatives of the mishaps. So, the rest of the world continues to believe that Africa is a place endowed with barren land that cannot sustain human life and so famine occurrences in Africa should be tolerated and accepted as a common and natural feature.

For over four centuries since 16th century, Africa fell prey of European domination. It started to be weak in all respects: economically, politically, socially, and even culturally. During the four centuries of foreign domination, Africa never got any breathing space because it lacked freedom of self-determination. From that time Africa has suffered under the heavy York of foreign domination, suppression, and humiliation; a process that made it to sustain the pains until 1950s and 1960s when most countries of Africa gained their political independence. Unfortunately, even after most nations of Africa had gained their political independence the road Africa kept walking remained thorny and slippery. As a rule, most points of the path Africa walked were thorny and pain ridden, so much that the movement forward to some destination of better hope proved to have many hindrances that were not easy to overcome.

As African countries kept on gaining their political independence, they got some reason to smile. But that was only for a while, until it was realized that those were only flag independences with nothing firm to lean on. The colonial nations kept on dictating policy, strategy and other conditions that made the young independent nation governments to believe that they were helpless without indirect presence and support of their colonial masters.

In the meanwhile, policies kept being formulated on the basis of directions dictated from the colonial nations. We could give the examples of the initial government compositions of the early independent nations. The composition was characterized by having most of the key Ministers drawn from the colonial countries, which to start with, was perhaps necessary because the new African leaders had no experience in the way to set up their governments. Logically, even the policy, plan frameworks and budget preparations depended largely on the thinking and ideas that were provided by the personnel from colonial countries.

All the aforementioned notwithstanding, the new African governments, which after a while were exclusively led by Africans, got submerged in very poor state of governance, doing a lot of fumbling in their managements. The administrative systems including policies, strategies, and actions remained with a lot that needed to be desired. Laws were enacted but were more or less replications of those of the colonial countries. As the fumbling continued some African leaders decided to take advantage of the ignorance of their citizens (who did not know that their leaders had to be accountable to them).[1]

Time came when the experts got from the colonial countries had to leave. That happened when the right personnel to replace them had not been trained. The African leaders cared least about the departure of foreign personnel. What followed was what got commonly known as Africanization process, which meant

---

[1] *At that early-stage citizens could not differentiate monarchy or colonial rule from democratic rule of la He was cw that their new rulers were supposed to observe that their new leader*

replacing any foreign senior position with an African, regardless of whether the appointed person had the ability to perform efficiently or not. So, the fumbling went on almost at all level of the administrative and development programmes. This gave rise to a period of stepped-up political propaganda. For anything that went wrong an accusing finger was pointed at colonialism or neocolonialism.

In the mean while African leaders resorted to extensive involvement in corruption. The accounting systems as well as lines of accountability remained almost non-existent. Such weaknesses made the African leaders to rule according to their own whims. They ruled with high level of impunity. The leaders felt it was their opportune time to accumulate wealth, and thus, most of them took the corruption path. They took pride in demonstrating that being in leadership amounted to being rich. To be rich one would have to temper with the public funds and resources. So, the first two or three decades of post-independence were highly marred with corrupt leaderships.

There were leaders who went further and decided to transform themselves to emperors or kings, a good example being that of Jean Bedel Bokassa of Central African Republic. He served about 11 years as president and three years as self-appointed Emperor of Central Africa. As he did so, the country still remained a de facto military dictatorship. His self-appointment as Imperial title never received international diplomatic recognition. He got overthrown by his predecessor, and then put on trial for treason and murder. He was cleared of charges of cannibalism, but still found guilty of murder of many school children and many other crimes. The death penalty that he had got earlier sentence got commuted to life in solitary confinement.

Unfortunately, leaders of Bokassa type were many. Many other African leaders also became great dictators, each with own style of authoritarian rule. A few examples of those dictators included Muammar Gaddafi of Libya who ruled his North African country continuously for 42 years. During his rule he quashed and eliminated anyone who attempted to oppose him. Next there was Mobutu Sese Seko of Congo (a country he named Zaire), who like others, never tolerated any idea that suggested opposition. He used Congo resources to lead luxurious life spending his holidays in luxury hotels in Europe. He bought many mansions and palaces in various cities of his choice around the world and terminated the life of anybody who opposed him in any way.

Other leaders of that caliber were Idi Amin Dada of Uganda who ruled Uganda for 8 years but proved to be a great terrorist and was rumored to be a cannibal and frightened human rights repression and involved in gross economic mismanagement. There were also dictators like Robert Mugabe who ruled Zimbabwe for a period of 30 years; proving to be one of the worst dictators of Africa and managing an economy that ended up to be completely ruined (characterized with massive inflation and very weak currency that was put under retirement immediately after his rule). On the list of great African dictators there was also Dr. Kamuzu Banda of Malawi, Idriss Deby of Chad, Obiang Mbasogo of Equatorial Guinea. Mbasogo hanged in power for 38 years, just like Paul Biya of Cameroon who ruled for 35 years; Eduardo Santos who hanged on in power for 38 years, and Albashir of Sudan who hanged in power for 28 years. The list is long and that the list that has been given is only of dictators whose level of atrocities went beyond human comprehension. Otherwise, it could be an understatement to say there are many African countries that at one time or another completely escaped authoritarian rule during the postcolonial times.

For decades many African governments went without any sense of rule of law and thus good governance lacked. A good number of the leaders remained excessively corrupt. There was the stealing of huge sums of money from public coffers as well as the plundering of their natural resources including minerals and others. They used their weak constitutions, illicit poor managerial styles, poor accounting systems, and corrupt security systems to further their own interests. The case of Houphouet Boigny of Ivory Coast who built a Basilica the size of that of Vatican in **Yamoussoukro** (his hometown he founded and wished it to be the headquarters of that country) could be cited as an example. He built the Basilica, named **"*The Lady of Peace*"** in his village hometown of **Yamoussoukro**. The Basilica has a finishing of Marble and Gold and was constructed with an estimated total cost of about US $115.9 billion (in 1990 prices). That amount could be compared with what it would cost to build Saint Peters Basilica in 2020, which would hardly be more than $6 billion. All the funds used were public funds of people of Ivory Coast, without the consent of people of that country. What makes it most painful is that that amount of money was being spent in the environment of poor rural community of Ivory Coast, which badly needed it to disentangle them from widespread poverty and vulnerability.

The African leaders did what they did with a high level of impunity. They did the plundering of their poor countries while the rest of the world just kept dumb founded. The resources kept being plundered without mercy while the people remained poor and undernourished. Actually, it is only now Africa is starting to rise up from its decades of total stagnation. But even with the change, like will be shown later, those people that are rising to power still retain a lot of dictatorial mentalities. They still hold on constitutions that deny citizens the rights to participate fully in their development efforts. Governance has a lot that needs to be desired in Africa.

Today, in 2020 many African governments and public services are still very corrupt. It would have been better if the money that has kept been stolen since independence in 1960s were invested in their respective countries; as economists say stealing from one place and investing in another place but in the same country has not as much harm to the overall economic growth as that which is completely taken and used or banked in foreign countries. If it gets invested inside the country it keeps stimulating the growth of the same economy, though the way it has been acquired will remain illegal and sinful. And that is what has happened in Africa, because the stolen money has often gone to be hidden in foreign banks; showing how bad the corruption that has kept taking place in Africa is. The plundering has been bad and detrimental to the growth of African economies. So, Africa has suffered not only due to foreign domination but also under corrupt and dictatorship administrations of local Africans. In the meanwhile, Africa keeps struggling under very stressed condition in the shackles of neo-colonialism and mismanagements of its leaders.

Africa's dream to get to a destination of economic emancipation, marked with high level of industrialization, high level of economic development and high standard of living, which the peers of the days just after independence described as **the Africa we want**, has kept far in the horizon. Getting to Africa we want vision there still continue to look like an imagination of a child raised in a poor family, who keeps wishing to go and live in a huge mansion located in the high –class suburbs of a tumultuous city. Economic emancipation has kept appearing like a far-fetched dream, which is explained by the fact that, the leaders have allowed themselves to harbour the thinking that there was no way Africa could excel itself without the support of their former political masters or international multilateral agencies. The question that is not asked is, if such support has been coming since independence in 1950s and 1960s but why has that failed to cause the desired transformation to the economies, and people of Africa?

Putting it bluntly, the multilateral agencies have also been party in misguiding African decision makers. In the initial four decades of Africa's independence, they prescribed structural adjustment measures that did not necessarily cope with the real needs of the countries that they supported. African leaders also took moves to introduce policies that in the end caused a lot of misguidances to their countries, such that their economies declined to a point of causing great miseries to their citizens. As though that was not enough the African leaders have kept beating about the bush, jumping from one policy framework to another with a view of finding easy solutions to their economies without much success.

Up to this point the major objective or the most pressing priorities and or ambitions have been to fight poverty, hunger, and diseases. In that effort African nations' policies have remained those, which were inclined to the directions and wishes of their former colonial masters, or to Western multilateral agencies. Things have kept being spelt in Europe and the so-called independent Africa has kept dancing to the tune. The situation has kept worsened not necessarily because the policies were so bad, but because they were not properly sharpened to fit the conditions obtaining in each of the African country. What is worse is the fact that the adjustment and reform measures including the resources have in many occasions fallen in porous hands of the African leaders and policy executives.

It is on the above grounds this book has been written with a view to make a sort of survey of where Africa has come from, the challenges it has had to encounter, the state it is in today and its ultimate ambitions and goals. Put very plainly, Africa has to keep on walking and wherever possible it should try to run. African leaders will have to transform, should do some cleansing of themselves and the people's attitudes too should change. People should be made to understand that they have only themselves to transform the continent. This is being said (cognizant of the fact that Africa, despite the plundering that has taken place for the last decades of African independence, but Africa is still endowed with natural resources which if prudently exploited, and if the income that is generated gets prudently used the continent will certainly leapfrog to great prosperity. Africa must leapfrog and must catch up with the rest of the world and the ultimate goal should be to get to the driver's seat of the global economy.

Towards the last chapters of this book extensive suggestions on how to move forward have been outlined. But those will only provide food for thought. Those are only suggestions that will help in opening up the eyes of African leaders and people.

Africa aims to get to a new destination of new hope. Truly, according to Africa's Vision 2063 the destination of new hope exists and everybody in the continent should aspire to get there. Just like the Israelites in the Biblical history, who walked the Sinai desert for forty years, making some of those in the expedition to die on the way before they got to what was popularly understood to be the promised- land. What the Israelites lacked was a road map that would give them a sense of how they could take a shortcut to their destination. The same delay or failure to get to Africa we want, **i.e to Vion 2063 and beyond,** could come our way if a good road map is not made available now rather than later. Lack of road map will make Africa keep moving directionlessly for a long time, maybe for a century before getting there.

2

DEFINING AFRICA AND ITS FEATURES

This chapter defines and provides a better view of Africa. It highlights what is there in Africa and provides some general understanding of the continent's people, features, culture, natural resources, interesting places, and sites and many more endowments. Those who have honest desire to know and appreciate the wonders of the African continent will benefit immensely from the exposure that is being made in this chapter.

We start by noting that Africa is a very easy, and yet a complex continent to define. Put in simple terms, Africa is a continent that comes at the middle of most continents of the world. It is sandwiched between America, Europe, and Asia. It is bordered in the west by the Atlantic Ocean, in the north by the Mediterranean Sea, in the northeast by the Red Sea, in the east by the Indian Ocean, and in the south by waters of Atlantic and Indian oceans and further South by Antarctica. Africa is the second largest continent in the world with a total area of around 11 million square miles that account for 5.7% of the earth's surface as well as 20% of the total surface of land on our planet.

There is the Equator, which divides the world into the northern and southern hemispheres. It also divides the African continent into two parts, i.e., the northern part which, is part of the northern hemisphere and the southern part which is part of the Southern hemisphere. The central location of Africa on Earth makes it lucky by having the Equator, which is the only line of latitude, which is a great circle. The lucky African countries that are crossed by the Equator include Gabon, DRC, Kenya, Uganda, Somalia, and Sao Tome.

Next is the Greenwich Meridian, also called prime meridian, which like the Equator, is an imaginary line. It was established in 1851 and has since been used to indicate Zero degrees longitude. The line passes through Greenwich, a borough of London, and terminates at the North and South Poles. Because it indicates Zero degrees longitude it also gets known as Prime Meridian. We can add that the line represents the historic Prime Meridian of the World- Longitude Zero degrees; and that since establishment every place on Earth was measured in terms of its distance east and west from this line. The line itself divides the eastern and western hemispheres of the earth just the same way the Equator divides the northern and southern hemispheres. The Zero degrees line of longitude (which as has been exposed) is called Greenwich Meridian because it starts at the Prime Meridian. It runs through Greenwich, in England. Then we can measure 180 degrees to the west or 180 degrees to the east.

The most notable is the fact that Africa is the most centrally located of all continents of the world. The Greenwich Meridian zero degrees line passes through the Atlas Mountains and cuts through the coast of West Africa close to Accra. The equator (latitude Zero degrees) also divides the continent into two equal parts North and South.

Looked at generally, Africa is a continent without very diverse extreme seasons, as is the case with Europe, North and South America where the year could be divided into summer, autumn, winter, and spring. Generally speaking, Africa is warm or hot and the year is usually divided only into two seasons i.e., dry, and rainy seasons. It is a generally warm or rather hot continent, of course with climates that change gradually latitudinally from equatorial, in or around the equator to tropical (within the tropics), to Mediterranean, temperate, arctic or antarctica climates in the extreme north and south of the globe respectively.

To start with the most noticeable physical feature in Africa is the Rift valley. There are two rift valleys; the Eastern and the Western rift valley. The Eastern rift valley also known as the Great Rift Valley is a series of contiguous trenches, approximately 7,000 kilometres in total length that runs from Lebanon in Southwest Asia to Southeast Africa in Mozambique. The East African Rift valley is one of the most famous rift valleys that are constantly forming. The valley's range is 6,400 kilometres long and is approximately 30 million years old. The East African Rift valley involves the Arabian and Somalian plate that is separating from Nubian plate. The East African Rift system also called Afro-Arabian Rift Valley is one of the most extensive rifts on Earth surface, extending from Jordan in Southwestern Asia, southward through eastern Africa to Mozambique. The system is long and averages 56 km wide.

The importance of the Great Rift Valley is that it represents a perfect environment to understand the evolution of mankind and also for the important paleoanthropological discoveries in Ethiopia, Kenya, Tanzania, Uganda, and Democratic Republic of Congo. African rift valleys are indeed considered the cradle of mankind. The Great Rift Valley is a long, deep depression, with deep wall-like cliffs, extending from Southwestern Asia southward through Africa to Mozambique, making it the longest rift on Earth Surface. However, the Western Rift valley branches from the Great Rift Valley and is one of the most biodiversity regions in Africa;

featuring a narrow corridor of highland, forests, snow capped mountains and also dotted with volcanic craters of the Pleistocene Epoch i.e., about 2 million to 11,700 years ago. While still at this juncture of African rifts let's have a look at new discoveries that scientists are making about Africa.

Recent scientific researches show that Africa is gradually becoming an Ocean2. The Horn of Africa region and especially the Gulf of Aden and the Red Sea will flood in over the Afar region and into the East African Rift Valley and will become a new Ocean. The remaining part will become its own separate small continent. What as been happening is that the map of Africa has been showing some of the historically active volcanoes (red triangles) and the Afar Triangle a triple action where three plates are pulling away from one another- i.e. the Arabian plate, the African plate and the Somali Plate. The African plate is comprised of both oceanic and continental crust representing the Atlantic Ocean and the continent of Africa. The African Plate boundary consists of both convergent and divergent boundaries. To the west, the African plate lies adjacent to the South American Plate.

The plate that is the African plate is such that the west side of the African plate straddles the South American plate and the North American plate. At this mid oceanic ridge, the two plate boundaries are pulling apart from each other. The diverging plate boundary will create some of the youngest oceanic crusts on the planet. The two plates that are involved in the East African Rift are that throughout the East African Rift the continent of Africa is splitting in two. The

---

[2] *Report by Ken Macdonald, Marine Geophysicist at University of California. The Scientists are saying that a new Ocean will form in Africa as the continent continues to split into two. The East African Rift Valley system made up of the Western and stretches from the Afar region of Ethiopia down to Mozambique. The process is said will take not less the 10 million years to come to its completion.*

African plate, sometimes called the Nubian plate carries most of the continent while the smaller Somali plate carries the Horn of Africa. The two major rift valley systems of East African Rift are the Gregory Rift and the Western Rift.

The three plates described above are separating at different speeds. The separation is not expected for about 50 million years. However, the newest ocean (the 6th Ocean) will be the newest Ocean. The US Board on Geographic names the new ocean as the body of water extending from the Coast of Antarctica to the line of latitude at 60 degrees South. Like we stated above the Scientists say new Satellite data supports the idea that, that split will give rise to a new ocean. The Horn of Africa region is identified to be the only place on Earth where you can study how continental rift will become an Ocean rift. In other words, the only place on Earth where a continent is splitting apart, and living in the newly formed gap land that will eventually be at the bottom of the new Ocean.

We will now have to move on to the specific mountains of Africa. In terms of breath-taking physical features that Africa has include its many attractive Mountains such as Kilimanjaro, Meru, Kenya, Mount Stanly in Uganda and DRC, and Mount Semien in Ethiopia. The Mountains are of two types, i.e. free standing mountains and the mountain ranges. Regarding the mountain ranges there is the Atlas Mountains in North Africa. The Atlas Mountain ranges stretch 2,500 km from Morocco through Algeria and Tunisia. Other Mountain ranges include Ethiopian highlands, Noba Mountains, Ruenzori Mountains, Virunga Mountains, Marrah Salartberg Mountains and Magaliesberg mountains. Of the Mountain ranges in Africa the longest of them is Mount Atlas. However, there are also mountains in West Africa, the highest being Bintumani Mountain

Peat on Loma Mountain, which is about 1947 metres high. This Mountain is on the west of Mount Cameroon.

Freestanding mountains include: Kilimanjaro, Kenya, and Meru and a few others. Of all the above listed freestanding mountains the highest is Kilimanjaro, which has three peaks namely Kibo, Mawenzi and Shira; of which Kibo is the tallest. Mount Kenya is the second highest mountain in Africa; which also has three main peaks, namely Batian, Nelion and Lenana point. Like can be noticed, most of the highest Mountains (Kilimanjaro, Kenya, and Meru) are free standing and are located in East Africa. What is more, Kilimanjaro is thus, the highest freestanding Mountain in the world. There are a couple of unique features in this mountain. It is far shorter than the highest mountain in the world, Mount Mauano-Keo found in Hawaii, USA (with a height of 10, 203 metres and Mount Everest, with a height of 8,849 metres (found in Nepal).

However, Kilimanjaro remains the highest free-standing Mountain be in the world. It is also a mountain just a short distance from the equator; and its top is covered with snow. The other thing regards the significance of Mount Kilimanjaro in Africa and the world as it is a very unique natural site in Africa. Besides its being located in very close proximity to the Equator, it is snow caped. Many people in Europe, especially during those early years of exploration of the interior of Africa, found it very difficult to understand, or to comprehend how a mountain right on close proximity to the equator could have snow covering its top. But that is a long story that for now should put at bay; meaning that in regard to how the Mountain was discovered by Europeans, will be brought up for discussion later.

All the odds aside, Kilimanjaro remains the highest Mountain in Africa. It has sometimes been nicknamed the roof of Africa. The Mountain has three volcanic cones, Mawenzi in the east, Shira in the West, and Kibo in the Centre. Mawenzi and Shira are extinct volcanos but Kibo, the highest peak is dormant, and is likely to erupt again. The mountain is a famous tourist destination. It is famous for trekkers that wish to climb it to the top. While only two out of three determined trekkers get to the summit, but one third of those who attempt, turn back some way before they get close to the top. That means good preparations, good health and a lot of determination is needed for those who attempt to achieve their objective of reaching the summit. Climbing Kilimanjaro needs people of strong characters. People of weak character have often thought that climbing Kilimanjaro is perhaps one of the most dangerous things a human being will ever attempt to do.

The higher you go on Kilimanjaro the less oxygen supply becomes. Every year approximately 1,000 people are evacuated from the mountain and approximately 10 deaths have been reported. At the summit, (Uhuru peak), the nighttime temperatures can drop to between -7 and -29 Celsius. Due to that, some climbers have been suffering illnesses caused by reduced oxygen levels at high elevations. An estimate of 35,000 people have been attempting to summit Kilimanjaro every year; but only two thirds become successful due to altitude sickness and other health challenges that cause climbers to turn back.

The other thing is in regard to the climatic diversity of Mount Kilimanjaro, which due to the mountain's great height, it creates its own weather. The ecological climatic condition keeps changing from below to the top. There are five major ecological climate zones, which are the cultivation zone (a combination of dry savannah and the slightly cooler but higher level with their density settlement zone). Here is where most people of Kilimanjaro are settled. Then follows the tropical savannah climatic zone, which is succeeded by the equatorial type of climate where you also find the equatorial type of forest reserve, which is also succeeded by the Heather-Moore land zone. Next are the Alpine desert zone and ultimately, the Arctic summit climate zone. The climatic changes occur as determined by the altitude level and temperatures that that is met as you trek some 5,000 meters from below to the summit.

Many people, especially during those early years of exploration of the interior of Africa, found it very difficult to understand, or to comprehend how a mountain right on close proximity to the equator could have snow covering its top. However, that is a long story for now. It is only enough to remark that temperature decreases as the altitude increases just the same way the temperatures decrease as you move from the equator to the higher latitudes. In regard to how the Mountain was discovered by Europeans, will be brought up for discussion later.

Rivers of Africa are the next area of interest and attraction. River Nile in particular has been know for many thousand years. Nile is the longest river in the world. It is 6,650 KM long and has been known since ancient Egyptian civilization, almost 5,000 years ago. What is strange is the fact that, despite the knowledge of its existence for many thousand years but its source and most of its watershed got known to the outside world only in the middle of the 19th century. It has often been known as the father of African rivers. The other thing about the Nile River is that it has for many centuries been the life giver of Egypt. What is of most interest is that while Egypt is basically part of the Sahara desert but its glory has basically been rooted on the existence of River Nile. Every aspect of life in ancient Egypt depended on the River Nile. It provided food and resources, land for agriculture, a means of travel and was critical in transportation of materials for building projects and other largescale project endeavours. The Nile is indeed part of the ancient world life giver. This river is known to have served as a critical lifeline that literally, brought life to the desert. The river brought fertile soils from the interior highlands and other River watersheds. For thousands of years it (the Nile) made Egypt a food basket for many lands in the Middle East.

Another famous river in Africa is the Congo River. It is not as long as the Nile, but it is the second longest river in Africa, spanning a length of about 4, 700 km. However, it is the world's deepest recorded river at 720 ft or 220 m. In parts of that river, it is too deep for light to penetrate. The Congo River in Central Africa is one of the world's great rivers Carrying 1.5 million cubic feet of water- (more than 13 Olympic sized swimming pools)- into the Atlantic Ocean every second. That is more flow than any other river in the world, the only exception being the Amazon. That makes River Congo a most powerful river in Africa. During the rainy season over 50,000cu.m, which is the same or equivalent to 1800000cu.ft of water per second, flows into the Atlantic Ocean. Opportunities for Congo River, and its distributaries to generate hydropower are therefore enormous.

It is very difficult to navigate river Congo. With its many distributaries, the river forms the African continent's largest network of navigable waterways; but whose navigability is limited by insurmountable obstacles, which include a series of 32 contracts over the river's lower course and the famous Inga Falls. At the bottom of the river there is the River Congo Canyon found at the end of the river. It is one of the largest submarine canyons in the world. Put in a different way the long Congo River system has a unique anatomy that divides it into three distinct regions: the upper, middle, and lower Congo. The upper is made up of tributaries and rapids, the middle is mostly steady stream and the lower consists of gorges and falls, which can make it very dangerous for navigators.

Other major rivers of Africa would include the Niger, Zambezi, Limpopo, Orange, Kasai, and Ubangi –Uele Rivers. Certainly, there are many smaller rivers in the east, south and west of Africa. Of all those rivers, Zambezi is 3,000 km. long, is considered to be among the world's most dangerous river to navigate because of reasons such as that it is peppered with an-exploded mines, killer rapids, and deadly animals, that include hippos, lions, crocodiles, baboons, and hyenas found around this river.

Now let's take a look at African lakes. These also have very unique features. We can start by noting that most of the central Africa region is doted by great lakes, which have made the region to be known as the Great Lakes Region (GLR). You have the Lake Victoria, Lake Tanganyika, Lake Nyasa/Malawi, Lake Rudolf (also called Lake Turkana), Lake Kivu, Lake Rukwa, Lakes Manyara, Lake Eyasi and Lake Natron. Each of these lakes has its unique features. We can start by looking at the greatest Lakes, i.e., Lake Victoria and Lake Tanganyika and Lake Nyasa also known as Lake Malawi on the Malawi side.

Lake Victoria is the 9th largest continental lake, occupying a shallow depression in Africa. In Kenya it is known as Nam Lowe (body of endless waters) and in Uganda as Nnalubaale (home of the gods). It covers a gigantic area of 26,000 square miles and has a coastline that runs for over 2000 miles around three countries (Tanzania, Kenya, and Uganda). Lake Victoria is an irregular quadrilateral in shape and its shores (saving the West) are deep ended. Its greatest length from north to south is 337km, and its greatest breadth is about 240 km, while the coastline exceeds 3,220 km. People wonder why Lake Victoria is not classified as a sea while there are other water bodies similar to Lake Victoria, some of them of even smaller size, but are called seas. The answer is that the great lake is considered a failed ocean. It is in a place where rifting started to create a new ocean system (and flooded) and that was eventually stopped. Those rifts were then later further excavated by glaciers.

The next lake is Lake Tanganyika. It is the longest freshwater lake in the world (660km) and the 2nd deepest after Lake Baikal in Russia. The lake is also the second largest in the world in terms of volume, and also the second oldest in the world. It is one of the world's natural wonders, holding about 17% of the globe's surface freshwater. It borders four countries namely Burundi, DRC, Tanzania and Zambia and it offers livelihood for over 10 million people. The major river flowing and feeding lake Tanganyika is the Ruzizi formed about 10, 000 years ago, and which enters the north of the lake from Lake Kivu. River Malagarasi is a second river that flows from the east in Tanzania and enters and feeds the lake from the east side. Lake Tanganyika is a unique habitat for biodiversity, conservation, and evolutionary studies. There are three fish species- which are Lake Tanganyika sardines, slack lates and Lake Tanganyika sprat. Those constitute the major commercial fisheries in that lake. Regarding navigability on Lake Tanganyika is a challenging issue with navigational charts being so far outdated, and with no enough navigational aids being installed, and safety being compromised.

Regarding Lake Nyasa, it is a very unique Lake in Africa. The lake has different names according to the countries that share the waters of the lake. In Malawi it is known as Lake Malawi, in Tanzania it is Lake Nyasa and in Mozambique it is Lago Niasa. It is the 9th largest, and third deepest freshwater Lake in the World. Lake Nyasa/ Mlawi/Niasa is distinguished by being home to great diversity of fish species than any other lake on Earth, the majority of the species endemic. Due to those qualities of the lake, i.e., its great size and biodiversity, the lake has been recognized as part of the global heritage. Lake Malawi/ Nyasa is noted for being the site of evolutionary radiations among several groups of animals, most notably cichlid fish. There is a conservative estimate of at least 700 cichlid species in Lake Malawi/Nyasa although some better estimates have it that the actual figure of cichlid varieties could be as high as more than 1,000 species. It is the largest fish water lake in the world by volume, 9th in the world by area and third largest and second deepest Lake in the continent of Africa.

Next is the Lake Rudolf, which is also known as Lake Turkana. It is the fourth largest of the Eastern African lakes. It lies mainly in northern Kenya with its northern end stretching into Ethiopia. The Lake Turkana covers an area of 2,473 sq. miles and lies at 1,230 feet above sea level. The lake is 144 miles long, only 10 to 20 miles wide and relatively shallow depth of just about 240 feet (73 metres). Lake Turkana is a unique feature of the East African landscape. Besides being a permanent desert lake, it is the only lake that retains the waters originating from two separate catchment areas of the Nile. The lake drainage basin draws its waters mainly from Kenya Highlands and Ethiopia highlands. This lake is the World's largest desert lake; it is part of Omo-Turkana basin, which stretches into four countries: Kenya, Uganda, Ethiopia, and South Sudan. Attractions survivors of an epoch long before mankind, lake Turkana's estimated 12,000 crocodiles are still the same in 130 million years.

There is also the Lake Chad whose basin covers parts of Nigeria, Niger, Chad, and Cameroon; those being the countries that surround the lake. What is most notable about this lake is that it is a drying up lake. So far it has shrunk by almost 90%, going from 25,000sq km in1963 to less than 1,500 sq. kms in 2001. The over 30 million people living in the Lake Chad region compete over water. The drying up of the lake could lead to migration and a lot more conflicts. The lake Chad has shrunk due to climate change, and an increase in population and unplanned irrigation using the lake water. The lake has been a water source for between 20 million and 35 million people that live in areas around the lake.

Looked at from historical perspectives it is found that Lake Chad was once the largest water body on the Planet, and due to climatic variability, climate change and human pressure on water source in the basin over recent decades things changed. Since 1963, the lake has shrunk by 90% from 25,000 sq. km in 1963 to less than1500sq.kms in 2001 and has moved further down to much less water by 2020. The Inter-Basin Water Transfer (IBWT)[3] plans to divert water from the Congo River watershed, more than 1,300 km away into the Chad River that feeds Lake Chad. It is estimated that the project could cost more than $14.5 billion, involving construction of a retention dam at Palambo, upstream of Central African Republic's capital, Bangui to serve as a catchment area.

Now we should now look, albeit briefly, at Lake Natron, which is fairly small in size but has features and characteristics that are more than worth revealing. In brief Lake Natron is ghastly lake in northern Tanzania. It is a Salt Lake; meaning that water flows in, but

---

[3] *IBWM here means inter – intra basin Water transfer. It can also refer to the Inter and intra basin water transfer (IBWT), which has been carried out throughout the world over centuries.*

does not flow out, so it can only escape by evaporation. Over time, as water evaporates it leaves behind high concentrations of salt and other minerals, like at the Dead Sea and Utah's Great Salt Lake. Lake Natron is the deadliest lake on earth. Scientist say that If by accident a person falls into the Lake, he will die immediately but will not be turned to stone instantly. But if the person will get drowned and stay submerged, the entire body will be hardened and could be preserved in that form for hundreds of years. In other words, if people found such person hundred years later, he might still have his hairs and organs intact-still looking spiffy after all those years.

Alkalinity of Lake Natron can reach a pH of greater than 12. The surrounding bedrock is composed of alkaline sodium-dominated trachyte lavas that were laid during the Pleistocene period. Flamingos have found paradise in environment like that of Lake Natron. Lake Natron shores have proved to be hot-spot beautiful life of flamingos.

Now it is time to look briefly at the mineral deposits in the African continent. Africa is endowed with many types of mineral resource deposits such as gold, diamond, iron ore, coal, copper, tin, graphite, crude-oil, natural gas, Tanzanite, and many hundreds more.

Gold is found in most countries in Africa but there are about five countries which are leaders in gold production. These include Ghana, which produces about 14,270 tons per year; followed by South Africa (118.2 tons). Other gold producers of that mineral include Sudan, Mali, and Burkina Faso.

Regarding diamonds, it is very exciting to note that Africa leads in the production of diamond. The continent produces as much as 50% of all world production. Today Africa has so far produced over

75% of the value of world's diamond worth more than 1.9 billion carats mined worth an estimated US$ 158 billion. Angola, Botswana, and South Africa are the leading producers of diamond in Africa.

Regarding oil and petroleum products in general Africa ranges low compared to the rest of the world, which is led by USA, Saudi Arabia, Russia, and China. USA produces 20.54 million barrels per day (mbpd) that is 20% of world total. More and more of petroleum deposits are being discovered but certainly it will take a long time for Africa to reach the levels of USA, Saudi Arabia, Russia, or China. We can for instance take the case of Nigeria which is today the leading producer of crude oil in Africa, which as of 2020 produced 1.36 million barrels per day, compared to USA which alone produced 20.54 million barrels per day. The other three leading world petroleum produces include China (14.1 million barrels per day), Saudi Arabia 12.3 (bpd) and Russia (11.3 million bpd)

Taking into account what has been shown above we get tempted to state that Africa is not a poor continent many reporters have portrayed it to be. Besides gold, diamond and of course oil and natural gas deposits, there are wealth's of other mineral deposits of various types and quantities such as copper, Uranium, cobalt, bauxite, iron ore, copper, and coal. The richest mineral deposits countries so far include South Africa, DRC, Namibia, Ghana, and Zimbabwe. Like was shown above Nigeria is the leading producer and exporter of crude oil. At $125billion per year, South Africa generates the most money from the minerals resources. Nigeria comes second place with $53 billion per year, followed by Algeria with $39 billion, Angola $32 billion, and Libya$ 27 billion. The five stated countries produce more than 66% of the continents mineral wealth.

Most if not all African countries have one type of mineral resource or another, though in some countries the money value of the minerals is negligeable. Southern Africa, West, East and North Africa are the wealthiest in terms of mineral deposit abundancy. West Africa region is very remarkable for its geological variety. Like in most of the rest of Africa, West African region is largely composed of ancient Precambrian rocks which have been folded and fractured over hundreds of millions of years. The oldest rocks of Africa consist of gneisses, granite, metasediments, and metavolcanic rocks which are estimated to be 3.6 to 2.5 billion years old. All are variably deformed and metamorphosed to some degree. Africa and especially North Africa formed in a variety of geologic setting at different time periods from the Archean to Quaternary. Mineral commodities include the gold, silver, cobalt, nickel, chromium, arsenic, copper, zinc, and iron. North Africa has vast oil and natural gas deposits; generally, the Sahara holds the most strategic nuclear ore and resources such as coltan, gold, and copper among others.

Being closest to Europe North Africa region has proved to be the leading tourist attraction and most visited tourists region in Africa.

People in the outside of Africa often think that Africa is one country, with one African language, universal culture, and a single government. Like it has been mentioned elsewhere, Africa is a place of great diversity in terms of culture, ways of living, languages, and even administrative systems. So far there are about 54 independent countries, some of which are very small while others are geographical very big, e.g., the Democratic Republic of Congo (DRC). The countries are at various levels of economic growth and development. These together comprise the African Union as known today. The other thing is that Africa has made quite a good progress in as far as organizing itself towards economic integration. The continent is now divided into 8 regional economic communities. The regional economic community regions are the Arab Maghreb Union (AMU), Economic Community of Sahel-Saharan States (CEN-SAD), Common Market of eastern and Southern Africa (COMESA), East African Community (EAC), Economic Community of Central African States (ECCAS), Economic Community of West African States (ECOWAS), Intergovernmental Authority for Development (IGAD) and Southern Africa Development Community (SADC). The functions of regional economic communities (RECs) are among others to mold various regions to economic communities, which in the end will assist in building up a single African Economic community or Union.

We have already said Africa is a continent of diverse ethnic, language and ancestry backgrounds. Some communities in Africa are basically peasants living in villages and depending on agriculture for sustaining their lives. The peasantry group forms the large majority of the African people, most of who live in the rural areas. The other group of people in the rural areas are the livestock keepers, the majority of them still living nomadic lives- shifting from place to another in quest for better pastures for their livestock. There are also the hunter groups. These form a minority group but spend all their lives roaming the forest areas in quest for suitable hunting grounds and for collection of fruit and tubers. It appears the future of these people is highly threatened by the ever-growing African population and urbanization, both of which are making encroachment to reserve lands and forests, and which nevertheless cause conflicts between themselves and the seminomadic groups due to the pressing demand for suitable land needed to support their lives.

This situation is calling for African governments to take measures that can preserve the lives of hunter and collector population. The threats posed by loss of reserve land that still exists are quite a critical issue. However, there are also the fishermen. These are commonly found in areas that are famous fishing villages in the coastal as well as river or lakeshore areas.

Next are the urban dwellers. Until the turning of the last Millennium people living in the urban areas in Africa were only about 35% of the total. Today, after only a span of two decades that proportion has increased substantially to almost 47%, partly because of the rural –urban migrations and also because of the high birth rates. During the period, some rural settlements have swiftly grown to small townships. There are also urban areas that were only small townships some two or three decades ago but have swelled to big towns and others to larger towns or cities.

Urban centres have recently kept on emerging in areas that were purely rural only a couple of decades ago; explaining why African urban population is increasing very swiftly. Not only that, some Small cities have swelled to Mega cites just within a relatively short while. A case could be given of the city of Dar es Salaam, Tanzania, which started only as fishing village about a century ago but today it boasts a population that is close to seven million people. It has proved to be one of the fastest growing cities in Africa. Certainly, there are many other, some of them larger and mega cities such as Cairo, Lagos, Kinshasa, Johannesburg, Nairobi, and Addis Ababa. A rapid increase of urban population has become an order of the day in Africa, especially in recent years.

However, as will be discussed in the later chapters urbanization has not always been something to be very proud of, because, often those places have been centres of vice and breeding grounds for crimes.

Like has been stated, Africa is not like a soccer field where people go to watch a match and go back home. It is a place with complicated landscape that varies from place to place. Like has been hinted you have high Mountains, valleys (e.g., the Rift Valleys), the plateaus, the grasslands, forests, rivers, lakes, deserts, and coastlines some of which could be classified as among the most attractive in the world; if well kept. Some mountains in Africa have active volcanoes. Generally, Africa is a place where you can find features that can demonstrate great diversity in climatic conditions – equatorial, tropical, temperate, tundra and artic climate in a single geographical area. Like we have just described some mountains such as Kilimanjaro could be our good case in point. As one starts to ascend that mountain, he will start with semi-arid savanna zone and soon he will get to the equatorial climate, better known as rain forest equatorial zone. The scenery here is wet and beautiful and breathtaking. As one moves on, he gets to the temperate type of climate, and gradually to the tundra and finally to the arctic type of climate. Otherwise, Africa remains the same hot place.

We now wish to take this opportunity to say that in spite of the interesting features that have been (listed) we are moving further to reveal even more unique features that at one time or the other a person from outside Africa should find a chance to see. Like we began to say, Africa is a place of wonders. Most of the features that are discussed below could perhaps be so unique that their significance cannot be matched elsewhere in the world.

The features or sites include the following:

2.1 OLDUVAI GORGE IN NORTHERN TANZANIA

We have started with Olduvai Gorge because it has so far been confirmed to be the home of first man in the world. Olduvai Gorge is in northern Tanzania in a place that is very close to the border with Kenya. Olduvai Gorge holds the earliest evidence of the existence of human ancestors. Paleoanthropologists have found hundreds of fossilized bones and stone tools in the area dating back millions of years, leading them to the conclusion that humans evolved in Africa. Substantial evidence of hunting and scavenging has been discovered in Olduvai Gorge and is believed by archaeologists that humans inhabiting the area between 1.9 and 1.7 million years ago spent the majority of their time gathering wild plant food, such as berries and roots. Those are believed to be the earliest human beings in the world.

2.2 SERENGETI NATIONAL PARK

There are sites such as the Serengeti National Park in Tanzania and the Masai Mara in Kenya, both of which are terminals for the famous animal (mainly wildebeests) migrations. For those who have been lucky to watch the Serengeti-Masai-Mara animal migration scenery will give witness that it is so unique and exciting that one will not see any such thing anywhere else in the world. The scenery qualifies, (and actually has been classified as the best tourist attraction site in Africa) and also as one of the seven natural wonders of the world.

Serengeti is one of the oldest and most scientifically significant ecosystems on the planet. Its weather patterns as well as fauna and flora, are believed to have changed very little over a million years, giving the area a pre-historic feel. The ecosystem includes Serengeti National Park proper, Ngorongoro Concervation Area, Maswa

Game Reserve, Loliondo Game Reserve, and Ikorongo Game Controlled Areas. It also includes Masai Mara National Reserve in Kenya. Ngorongoro has an area of 2,286 sq.km. It was established in 1930 as a game reserve in what is now southern and eastern Serengeti. Until 1937 sport hunting was allowed, after which all hunting activities were stopped. Serengeti is home to the world's largest movement of animals often called '**The Great Animal Migration.**' More than 1.7 million wildebeests, 500,000 zebras, 200,000 antelopes and gazelles make their way through the whole length of the 'endless plains to Kenya's Masai Mara.

Serengeti is a world heritage site teeming with wildlife over 3.5 million animals; which include over 4,000 lions, 1,000 leopards, 550 cheetahs over and 500 bird varieties. Serengeti is famous for animal migrations between it and Masai Mara. It is the oldest ecosystem in the world. It has a flat altitude of around 6,070 ft, making it most dry and warm throughout the year; hence contributing to the annual movement of animals from one sector to another as they look for new pasture and water.

Plenty of things make Serengeti very unique. While it is classified as one of the Natural wonders of the world, the Park is also a very popular destination among wildlife enthusiasts. It hosts most unique plants, birds, and animals. The Serengeti ecosystem is one of the largest and oldest across the earth and is a vast ecosystem in east and central Africa. It spans 30,000 square km giving rise to its name, which is derived from the Masai language and means "endless plains". The high diversity of Serengeti is a function of diverse habitats including riverine, forests, swamps, kopjes, grasslands and woodlands blue wildebeest, gazelles, zebras, and buffalos; all these being among the commonly found large animals in the region.

There are two very common features of the animals found in Serengeti. The features are that the animals are all prey to predators like cheetahs, leopards, and lions; and besides the predators they are all herbivores.

2.3 NGORONGORO CRATER

As the name suggests Ngorongoro Crater is a very breathtaking site to visit and see. Ngorongoro crater area is home for over 30,000 animals. The animals include wildebeests, rhinos, hyenas, zebras, gazelles, lions, hippos, jackals, antelopes, Kobs, and many more. The place has been declared one of the natural wonders of Africa. It is the largest inactive caldera in the world. The volcanic crater forms stunning backdrops to some of the most fertile and richest grazing grounds in Africa. The most famous such crater is without question Ngorongoro, the world's largest and intact volcanic caldera and home to the highest density of big game in Africa. The crater has the importance for biodiversity conservation in view of the presence of globally threatened species such as the black rhino, the density of wildlife inhabiting Ngorongoro crater and surrounding areas throughout the year, and the animal migrations of the wildebeest, zebras, Thompsons, and Grants. Ngorongoro has been named the "black- hole" by the Masai but it is often known as "the Eden of Africa".

The biggest problem that has been facing Ngorongoro especially in recent decades is the increasing human population co-existing with wild animals inside the crater that is eating away those landscapes. The loss of habitat is the main cause for the recent century's rapid decline in lions. While lions still co-exist with people, their main threat is persecutions resulting from human- lion conflicts. There is also the problem of climate change, which has impacts like droughts, habitat loss and spread of diseases. These problems have led to increased conflicts in wildlife areas. The lion is just one iconic species that continue to bear the brunt of retaliatory killing as a result of human-wild life conflict. Ngorongoro is a conservation area, which encompasses a great variety of ecosystems including montane forest, swamps, marshy, dry forest, as well as long and short grasslands as part of the extension of the Serengeti-Masai Mara ecosystems. The diverse ecosystem has attracted a large number of different wildlife species to reside within the conservation area within very close proximity. This variation also allows for a succession of feeding by grass-eating animals (herbivores) as the seasons change.

Masai livestock usually share the same grassing fields with wildlife. However, Masai livestock are made to avoid sharing the pastures with the wildebeest during the wet seasons, as those are the calving seasons for them. The wildebeest calves suffer from Malignant Catarrhal Fever (MCF), which is prevalent in gnu calves. Gnu calves accompany their mothers as soon as they can stand instead of hiding for days or weeks like is common with most other mammals; this being part of their adaptation to migrating.

2.4 GORILLA AND CHIMPANZEES WATCHING IN AFRICA:

The list of gorilla parks in Uganda is such that there are only two conservation that are home to a few remaining gorillas in the world. The Parks include Bwindi Impenetrable Forest National Park in Kanungu district, and Mgahinga national park in Kiroro district between the border of Uganda and Rwanda. It is easier to reach Rwanda's mountains' gorillas, but Uganda has more habituated mountain gorillas and so admits more trekking per day, than Rwanda. About 80 people a day are allowed to visit Uganda's gorillas. There are three national parks that offer some of the best gorilla viewing opportunities. These are the Volcano National Park in Uganda, Bwindi Impenetrable Forest National Park in Uganda, and Odzala-Kakowa Park in the Republic of Congo.

Regarding Chimpanzee watching the best countries to see these endangered creatures are Tanzania, Rwanda, and Uganda. Although all of the Chimpanzees in those places are wild, many groups have become fully habituated to humans. This means that along with your guide you can get much closer to them to study their behaviour and to take photographs.

In Africa, Chimpanzees can be found discontinuously from Southern Senegal across the forested belt north of the Congo River to Western Uganda and Western Tanzania. Gombe national park in Tanzania is the first Chimpanzee Park in Africa, especially created for Chimpanzees.

2.5 ZANZIBAR ARCHIPELAGO

Zanzibar has been a rapidly growing tourist destination in East Africa. It is an archipelago of islands, the most famous being Unguja, located 25 km from the mainland coast city of Dar es Salaam. The island is famous for its mix of exotic beaches, famous spice plantations, history, such as Stone Town, which was the capital and historical holding of slaves got from the African interior. It was also a famous slave- marketing centre for slaves that were brought from all over the Great Lakes, (that being before the abolition of slave trade on the Indian Ocean in the end of the 19th century). Zanzibar is also famous for its diverse cultures. The archipelago is unique as home of idyllic beaches, balmy weather, and warm water coral reefs. Zanzibar's rich marine diversity makes it a perfect underwater destination for snorkeling and diving.

The population of Zanzibar totals about 1.4 million mostly consisting of Africans and people of mixed Africa- Persian ancestry- (the Shirazi and Arabs). Zanzibar and Tanganyika united in 1962 to form the United Republic of Tanzania. It may not be very palatable to mention that the Stone Town that was a headquarters of Zanzibar during the slave trade era was also the key slave-auctioning centre. The details on the awful nature of that trade and the way the auctioning was done will be better exposed when we come to the Chapter on Zanzibar slave trade.

2.6 VICTORIA FALLS

Victoria falls is a waterfall on Zambezi River in Southern Africa. It provides habitat for several unique species of plants and animals. What is very special about the falls is that it is the world's greatest sheet of falling water and significant worldwide for its exceptional geological and geomorphological features and active land formation processes with outstanding beauty attributed to the falls i.e, the spray, mist, and rainbows. The fall is 108 meters tall and 1, 708 meters wide. It is one of the world's seven natural wonders.

2.7 UNDER WATERFALLS

Mauritius is a place where under waterfall is spectacularly found. The falls are found just off the coast of Le Morne on the islands Southwest. Sand and salt on the ocean floor run off in a way that makes it look like they were pouring down a waterfall or like the entire island was being sucked down a vast drain. The shelf is just 100 metres below sea level as is the largest of its kind in the whole world. However, the drop off of the shelf's edge plunges to depths of over 4000 metres into the abyss. Aplune pool is found at the bottom of a waterfall and is formed by erosion, which forms a pool.

2.8 TABLE MOUNTAINS

The Table Mountains are in South Africa. It is a flat top mountain that forms the prominent landmark overlooking the city of Cape Town, in South Africa. The mountain is the most iconic landmark of South Africa. It is also the most photographed attraction of that country and is famous for its top cable car that takes millions of people to the top of the mountain.

2.9 NAMAQUALAND

Namaqualand (Khoekoe: Nama-kwa, meaning Nama Khoe people's land is an arid region of Namibia and South Africa, extending along the west coast over 1,000 kilo metres, covering an area of 440,000 square kilometres. The Namib Desert spans part the Western of Angola and South Africa Coast of southern Africa; touching part of the countries of Angola and South Africa. It extends from near Wind Hoek (the capital of Namibia southwards into Northern Cape province of South Africa and from the Namib Desert to Kalahari. Namaqualand is in the Karoo and is famous for its proximity to the Atlantic Ocean, its wildflowers during spring, its wealth of minerals and cultural history.

2.10 MOUNT NYIRAGONGO IN DEMOCRATIC REPUBLIC OF CONGO (DRC)

Mount Nyiragongo is famous for its active volcano. It lies in the volcano region of Virunga Park (DRC). What makes Nyiragongo unique and famous is the peculiarity of its location on a highly active segment of the African rift favours quick ascent of magma (molten material) from about 100kilo metres beneath the earth's surface and extreme fluidity of lava. Nyiragongo is stratovolcano i.e., a steep sloped cone composed of alternating layers of hardened lava, solidified ash and rocks ejected by previous eruptions.

2.11 THE GREAT PYRAMID OF GIZA

The Great Pyramid of Giza is the oldest and largest of pyramids in the Giza Pyramid complex, bordering present day Giza in Greater Cairo, Egypt. The pyramid at Giza is very special. It is the largest in the World filling 13 acres at its base. At 481 ft tall it was the tallest structure in the world until the advent of modern skyscrapers. The pyramid builders used 23 million stone blocks, each weighing between 2.5 and 15 tons to construct the Great Pyramids. The pyramids of Giza are mostly solid masses of stone with very little to be found inside. Like many Egyptian Pyramids those of Khefre and Menkaure have pass ways at their base that lead to small subterranean burial chambers underneath each pyramid.

The pyramids were built by Egyptians, most of which people had earlier migrated from Southern Egypt or further South. The Great Pyramid of Khuffu is one of the 104 pyramids in Egypt with superstructure. For many who have knowledge of the pyramids but have not got to their sites wonder if you can go inside the pyramid; and the answer is yes. It is very possible to get inside the pyramid.

The Great Pyramid of Giza was built 4,500 years ago; and was built to endure eternity which is exactly what it has. The monumental tombs are replicas of Egypt's old Kingdom Era. One thing that is worth taking note of is that pyramids are manmade and were, built to last forever; and that is what has happened. Archaeological tombs are remnants of the old kingdom of Egypt and were built 4,500 plus years ago. Pharaohs that built the pyramids believed in the resurrection, that there is second life after death.

2.12 SAHARA DESERT

Sahara desert is a unique place; it is a desert in the African continent, with an area of about 9,200,000 sq. km. It is the largest hot desert in the world. Daily temperature ranges are considerable during both winter and summer months. Snowfall in a hot desert may seem a contradiction but certainly snow has been recorded several times in the Sahara Desert over the last decades, most recently in January 2022. Thus, the snowfall may be unusual but it is not unprecedented in the region. Although the precipitation is highly variable, it averages about 3 inches per year.

However, Sahara desert has attractive and very interesting features that include places like the Siwa oasis, Farafra Oasis and Wadi Oasis. Sahara is most famous for the sand-dune fields that are often depicted in the movies. The dunets can reach almost 600 ft or 183 metres high, and they can cover about 25% of the entire desert. Beneath the sands of Sahara scientists have discovered evidence of prehistoric mega lake formed some 250,000 years ago, when the Nile River pushed through a low channel near Wodi Tushka. The river flooded the Eastern Sahara, and its highest level covered more than 42,000 sq miles.

Sand dunes and sheets usually cover only around 25% of Sahara's actual surface. This desert also has numerous other land features including salt flats, gravel plains, plateaus, and even mountains where snow has been recorded. Among the most interesting features of Sahara desert are: the Sahara dunes which can reach the height of 180 metres; the many dinosaur fossils that have been found in several places in the Sahara; the Emi Kooussi Volcano which is the highest point in the Sahara at 3,415 metres and the

Monitor lizards, camels, foxes, and gazelles living in the Sahara. Other interesting factors or features include the following:

That, the Sahara desert receives less than 10 inches of rain a year;

That, most of animals that live in the desert are nocturnal;

That, the Sahara is the largest hot desert on earth (as contrasted with Antarctica and the Arctic in the north, which is the largest cold desert on earth). So overall the Sahara Desert holds the third position after the two cold deserts.

That, the Sahara is found on the Southern parts of North African countries such as Egypt, Libya Algeria, and Morocco.

That, the Sahara desert is estimated to be 4.6 million years old.

Like other deserts, Sahara desert has hardly any rains and is extremely dry and usually very hot; and

That, animals, and plants have adapted to the harsh environment, so they can survive the extreme conditions.

The region now holding the Sahara desert was once underwater, in striking contrast to the present-day environment. This dramatic difference in climate over time is recorded in the rock and fossil record of West Africa during a time range that extends through the Cretaceous–Paleogene boundary. Other records have shown that around 11,000 years ago, Sahara was not so much of a desert. It was covered in plant life and it also held bodies of water. There was even a mega- lake that covered an estimated area of 42,000 square miles.

2.13 NAMIB DESERT

The Namib Desert is a vast cold coastal desert in Southern Africa. The name has been derived from the World Nama- meaning **"there is nothing"** The desert is arid and uninhabited barring a few scattered towns. The desert is a local coastline desert extending for 1900 km along the Atlantic coast of Africa from Namibe in Angola, Southward. The Namib Desert is believed to be the World's oldest desert and it has been arid for at least 55 million years. The coverage of the Banguela upwelling and the hot interior have maintained, and perhaps increased the aridity in recent times, but they did not generate the aridity. Surprisingly Namib is a living place, home not just to the big cats such as lions, but to an impressive array of plants and animals.

2.14 CITY OF TIMBUKTU

Timbuktu is best known for its Djinguereber Mosque and prestigious Senkore University both of which were established in the early 1300s under the reign of the Mali Empire ruler, Mansa Musa. However, the city was founded by Tuareg nomads in the 12th century, and within 200 years had become an immensely wealthy city, at the centre of important trading routes for salt, gold, ivory, slaves, as well as major hub for Islam and education. In its peak during the 1400s and 1500s it had about 100,000 inhabitants a quarter of which were students. Timbuktu was home for the religious Koranic Sankore University and other madrassas. The city was an intellectual and spiritual capital and a centre for the propagation of Islam throughout Africa in the 15th and 16th centuries. Its three great mosques- Djingareyber, Sankore, and Sidi Yahia, recall Timbuktu's golden age. Timbuktu, French '*Tombonctou*' city in western Africa country of Mali, is historically very important as a trading post on the trans-Saharan caravan route and as a centre of Islamic culture.

Timbuktu started as a summer encampment for nomadic tribes of the region. During the First World War Timbuktu was used to house prisoners of war. Like the rest of the surrounding areas, Timbuktu is a city that is very poor and is constantly threatened by floods and droughts. The most popular means of transport is by camels. It is located on the southern edge of Sahara, about 13 km north of the Niger River. Timbuktu is today on the list of world heritage sites.

2.15 BASILICA OF OUR LADY OF PEACE

This is a Basilica similar to that in the Vatican but with more expensive finishing work built in recent years in Ivory Coast. The story behind this Basilica has been made elsewhere in this book; and so, the reader should bear with us until we get to that point.

2.16 THE BLYDE RIVER CANYON

The Canyon is in Mpumalanga, South Africa. It is a 26 km Canyon and one of the larger canyons on Earth, but is smaller than the Fish River, which is the world's second largest canyon, situated in in South Namibia and stretching for 180 km. (105.6miles) from Sesriem down to the Orange River. The Bylide Rive Canyon is thus smaller than Fish River Canyon and much smaller than those found in Asia. The Blyde River Canyon in Impumalanga, South Africa extends to 50km along the lip of the Great African escapement. From the Canyon you can look eastwards over the layered rocks of the walls and the three Roundvels to the lowveld plain, 1,600 metres below. Actually, the name means River Joy. Like has been said the biggest Canyon in Africa is the Fish River Canyon found in the Southern part of Namibia.

However, let's make a clarification on the difference between a river canyon and an entrenched river. The two are not the same. We are bringing this up because some readers sometimes find it difficult to understand what a river canyon and entrenched river means. By definition a canyon is a deep channel that is caused by river water pressure. Due to that pressure the river can cut deep into the riverbed. Sediments from the riverbed are carried downstream, creating a deep, narrow channel. Rivers that lie at the bottom of deep canyons are known as entrenched rivers.

2.17 THE AVENUE OF BAOBAB

The avenue is in Munabe, Madagascar. It is a stretch of giant baobab trees believed to be up to 800 years old. The Avenue of Baobabs is 853 foot long. The Avenue is situated roughly 405 miles away from Antananarivo, the capital city of Madagascar. It offers close proximity to Kindly Mitea National Park, which sits along Madagascar's west coast. Madagascar, being the fourth largest island in the world has been isolated for about 80 million years and many of the plants and animals are unique to the island. The prehistoric breakup of the Supercontinent Gondwana separated the Madagascar- Indian landmass from Africa around 150 million years ago. The baobabs on Munabe Avenue of Baobab be but are on a narrow rather dirty avenue and are so well-lined tup that it is easy to mistake that they are a result of human work; but they have been there naturally. The trees lining the avenue are just about a dozen, but it is a most exciting site worth seeing in that part of Africa. The baobabs are thousands of years old and thus they provide breath taking site deserving to be upgraded to Africa and world natural heritage.

2.18 OTHER UNIQUE SITES IN AFRICA:

Other very unique sites and features in Africa would include the Gorilla Parks in Rwanda and Uganda, Chimpanzees packs in Kigoma, Tanzania, East African Rift Valley, Atlas Mountains in North Africa, mud architecture in Mali and Niger, Sahara sand dunes, and Tibet Mountain ranges, to mention only a few.

Efforts to make a comprehensive definition and exciting issues on Africa will be an endless and perhaps unproductive. It is only enough to say again that till now features and exciting sites in the continent of Africa will satisfy or will cure the thirst of the reader in his pursuit to know the natural features of Africa. The features and sites have shown to include the wealth and abundancy of natural resources that manifest alongside widespread poverty. That revelation brings us to an anticlimax. Over 422 million people in Africa still live below the global poverty line; and that the poor Africans represent almost 70% of the world's poorest people, and that African poverty is largely a contribution that was created by Europe during the four or five centuries of slave trade, colonialism, and neocolonialism. Unfortunately, the coming of African led governments after independence of most African countries in 1960s the hopes for better economic management melted away. The introduction of policies and strategies that could not adequately address the needs of the people made progress highly constrained. That situation got worsened by unfavourable world economic order and also by the trade regime; which together worked in disfavour of the poor countries. These issues will be brought up again later.

3
THE HISTORICAL PERSPECTIVE OF AFRICA

We now know that Africa was home for the earliest human species, the Homosapien. That gives enough reason for the continent to be given deserving respect; it needs to be cherished. Africa nursed the human specie; she was the caregiver of the earliest man on earth; and continued to do so until human beings started to be self-caring, thus starting to move about, to settle into communities, to organize into tribes, chiefdoms, kingdoms and into empires. From Africa the human beings spread, developed population centres and empires.

It was hinted in the previous chapter that the earliest man, Homo Sapiens started to live in some place in East Africa, specifically in Northern Tanzania, according to the archaeological findings. He spread to various directions, mainly towards the North. As those early people spread, they also would settle in places as they kept multiplying and splitting as they moved on. As they moved, settled, spread, and regrouped, they kept pushing on along the Rift Valley and also along the Nile valley -from the upper River basin towards the River delta in the North. Evidence of that spread, grouping, and further movements can today be witnessed by observing the archaeological findings along the Great African Rift Valley and also along Nile River basins, from Kenya towards the North of Africa. Observation of the type of people who must have all along settled along the Rift Valley and in the Nile, basins can also assist to explain that process.

The leading groups of people that settled along the Nile included the Nilotics. These are the type of people that can even today be found in all countries that have close proximity to Nile River valley. They include the Masai in Kenya, Tanzania, and Uganda; the Dinkas in Sudan and South Sudan, and Luo in Kenya and Tanzania- just to mention a few. The history has it that at the beginning (especially during the ancient demographic movements and settlements they pushed to the north, drawing their livelihood along the banks of River Nile and its distributaries. Some settled in the Nile River delta and in Egypt. Today the Nilotic languages are spoken in countries like DRC, Ethiopia, Kenya, Tanzania, Sudan, and South Sudan.

As people groups kept on forming settlements, the process led to the formation of cities and empires. There emerged many great empires such as ancient Egypt, Karma and Cushi. Like has been hinted the early demographic movements were from East Africa (almost from the equatorial area) to the north along the Eastern side of the Nile, gradually keeping on the North and northeastern direction to places on both sides of the Nile and in most of southern Egypt. Another case is of the people that went northeasterly on the eastern banks of the Nile. These were what became the Cushietes. Today, you find people of Cushitic origin in countries such as Somalia, Sudan, Ethiopia, Djibouti, Eritrea, and most other parts of the Horn of Africa.

Like we will continue to show, as demographic movements and settlements continued tribes, chiefdoms, kingdoms, and empires kept on being formed each according to the extent and power of its organization and administrative set ups. As the people in settlements further organized themselves, forming new tribes, kingdoms, and empires such people organization kept growing but after some time they also disintegrated only to form others, perhaps more organized ones elsewhere. It will be enough to say here that there developed legendary kingdoms such as those of ancient Egypt, Cushi, and many others. Cushi in particular had its capital in an area in the present-day Northern Sudan. This helps to define the cultural and political landscape of Northeastern Africa for thousands of years. For over a thousand years Cushi stretched from Upper Nile to Red Sea. The Kingdom of Cushi housed the city of **Meroe**, which represented one of the earliest and most progressive and impressive states formed on the African continent, of course along with Egypt.

What is being said here is that in terms of its formation and existence ancient Cushi was much older state than ancient Egypt, also with people that had great technical knowledge, craft, and skills than others. For instance, in its towns of Karma and Napata (in present day Northern Sudan), Cushi produced the most fine ceramics ever known by 8,000 BCE. That was long before Egypt, which we know much more about, could produce similar products. Gradually, Cushi encountered problems with other equally developed states such as Axum, which emerged much later. There were conflicts between Cushi and Axum, each fighting for ivory. That was the time when Cushi began to have a decline in its military powers. Many years later Christianity also began to gain over the old pharaonic religion and by late mid-6th century CE the kingdom of Cushi completely collapsed after its many thousand years of existence.

The population of Egypt and neighbouring states such as Cushi were basically comprised of Africans that came from the South of those states. It has been shown that around 5000 BCE some Nilotics and Cushiests moved on to settle in Egypt. Those who got to Egypt organized and adapted to Egyptian life and became among the Egyptian Pharaohs.

It has been shown further that as the earliest man started to migrate to various places in Africa the major convergences which also led to formation of big communities, tribes, kingdoms, and Empires were mainly in northern Africa. In other words, the earliest major kingdoms and empires were in North Africa; that also explaining why the earliest famous empires of the world started in that part of Africa. Examples of the ancient North African empires that throughout history controlled North Africa were the Kingdom of Kerma, which existed between 2500 BCE-1500 BCE; ancient Egypt (3100 BCE-650 BCE); Kingdom of Cushi (1070 BCE-350 BCE); ancient Carthage (575 BCE-146 BCE); and the Kingdom of Numidia (202 BCE-40 BCE). Kerma in particular was a state in Nubia from around 2,500 BCE to 1,500 CE. It was based in the city of Kerma in Upper Nubia and was a major centre during the middle Kingdom period of Egypt. Kerma had a distinct civilization such as fine and original ceramics. Due to its military power, it constantly molested its neighbours including Egypt. In the end Egypt made several campaigns south, which ultimately led to destruction of Kerma. The fall led to Egyptian annexation of Nubia, which included Kerma and Kushi around 1,504 BCE, and the establishment of Southern frontier at Kurgus. In the meanwhile, and certainly thousands of years before the formation of the above listed empires human beings kept on spreading to places outside of Africa along the northeastern direction, crossing the Red sea, while settling and moving again to various places in Asia.

Later, there followed the medieval period empires that spread more evenly almost throughout Africa. The major ones could be cited to include the Land of Punt, Axum, ancient Ghana, Mali, Songhai, and Zimbabwe. There were a lot more of them such as those of Baganda, Kilwa, Sofala, Hausa states and Bornu. However, the period between 50 BCE and 1500 CE, trade between North Africa and Mediterranean region flourished. That is how and when the trade between the African Empires and Europe started and developed. The leading trading empires in the medieval time included Ghana, Mali, and Songhai. There were also Empires like Monomotapa in central Africa, as well as Kilwa and Sofala in Southeast Africa and also what remained of the Axum Empire after its fall around the 7th-centuy.

Once again, according to the work of archaeologists East Africa was the starting point for the spread of the human race to various parts of Africa and to the rest of the world. With the knowledge that is now available, especially on the basis of the archeological evidence in **Olduvai Gorge,** the first man started to move from there most probably towards the north. With passage of time and as the population kept growing people looked around to see life-supporting opportunities in their surroundings and further away. Those factors must have been the leading basis for determining the direction various family or community groups took. In other words, while the general direction is evidently towards the north, but the scattering to the south, west and east also took place. Those who kept on the northerly direction must have comprised the majority compared to those who split to other directions.

It is difficult to make precise clarifications about dates of various events that took place from the time when first man moved from Olduvai.

We have shown that in the north including the Sudan there flourished the ancient empire of Kerma, EGYPT, Kushi, Carthage and Numidia. Others were the, Empires of Axum under the Empress Makeda or Queen of Sheba, (which existed around the year 900 BCE). Surely there were many more empires that came after those that have just been listed. The empires emerged and collapsed in different places and times.

However, knowledge, skills and the structures that were produced by ancient and later day empires were monumental. The pyramids of Egypt are examples. The pyramids were so uniquely constructed that they have had nobody to even attempt to imitate their designs, leave alone reproducing them. It is important to remark here again that the recorded existence of African empires started just around 4,500 BCE. But the human race had been there for more than 200 million years before. That is to say the part of the human existence that is available in recorded history is very small compared to length of time human beings have lived in it.

It has been stated that from early times demographic migrations were a common thing throughout Africa. Africa had wars that were fought between chiefdoms, kingdoms, and/or empires. Actually, those became stimulants to further migrations and regroupings. Powerful nations built up military, economic and technological capabilities, which enabled them to be even more powerful. Those developments further enabled them to build internal tranquility, which served as a big anchor for innovation and social, economic, and cultural development. Those developments assisted to build innovative minds that were not threatened by the external forces or frequent famine and/or diseases. A case in point could be that of

Egypt whose civilization was built on a theocratic[4] monarchy. The king ruled by mandate from the Gods. The king had a role to respect and represented the god's will through the laws passed and approved policies. Due to the strict type of governance ancient Egypt grew politically powerful, administratively firm, nomically strong and technologically advanced.

Sound innovations in the continent were done before Africa was overwhelmed by threats from the outside. Some political scientists have put it, rather rightly that, most powerful innovative moves in Africa were almost exclusively done and taken by those societies or monarchies that had good administrative systems. Still using the example of Egypt, the Pharaohs were powerful leaders; they were respected by their subjects and by the whole world of the time. They had their own religion that solidified the Egyptian spiritual life. The economy was among the strongest of all others of the time. That country boasted to be self sufficient in food for its people. That sufficiency resulted from grain that was produced in surplus in the Nile valley. Due to its stability and good governance the Egyptian agricultural sector grew so strong that it served as a food basket for Egypt and neighbouring nations. Not only that, but those ancient Egyptians were also traditionally good craftsmen. Besides the fact that their pursuance of literacy path was a common tradition of citizens, but they (the citizens) naturally got committed to enhancing their skills for the enhancement of craftsmanship. These and many other factors made Egypt and other great Empires of the time very progressive and powerful.

---

[4] *By definition theocracy is a form of government in which one or more deities of some type are recognized as supreme ruling authorities, giving divine guidance to human intermediaries who manage the day today affairs of the government.*

Now is the time to go one step further, to find out more about this continent we call Africa. This brings us to the subject of the ancient name of Africa, the Alkebulan[5] which means **Mother of Mankind or Mother of Nations or the *Garden of Eden***. Alkebulan is the oldest and the only name of the African indigenous origin.[6] The term, Africa was first used by the Moors, and later by the 'Moorish' Muslims[7], Nubians, Catherginians, and Ethiopians. Alkebulan remained the only name for Africa until as late as 17th Century CE. The name got changed to Africa by European invaders, especially the Romans and Greeks. In other words, as late as early 16th century the famous medieval traveler and scholar, Leo- Africanus who had travelled across most of North Africa giving detailed account of all that he saw there, suggested that the name of the land he travelled on be "Africa"; which was derived from the Greek word "a-phrike", meaning without cold. The name Africa came to the Western use through the Romans who used the name Africa terra – land of the Afri- for the northern part of the continent, as a province of Africa with its capital in Carthage, corresponding to the modern-day Tunisia/Libya[8]

To further show that the word Africa was something just imposed by foreigners, even the Bible has never used the term

---

[5] *Dr Cheikh Anah Diop in Kemetic History of Afrika*

[6] ***Carthage*** *was the center or capital city of the ancient Carthginian civilization, on the eastern side of the Lake of Tunis in what is now the Tunis Governorate in Tunisia. Carthage was widely considered the most important trading hub of the Ancient Mediterranean and was arguably one of the most affluent cities of the ancient world.*

[7] *The Moors were the Muslim inhabitants of the Maghreb, the Iberian Peninsula, Sicily, and Malta during the Middle Ages. The Moors initially were the indigenous Maghrebine Berbers. Only in the later days the name also got applied to Arabs*

[8] *Afri (or Afer-singular) was a Latin for the inhabitants of Africa, referring in its widest sense to all the lands South of the Mediterranean especially the area today occupied by Tunisia (i.e. the ancient Libya)*

Africa, except in new texts, to make the modern reader understand that reference is being made to Africa. Otherwise, the Bible has always referred to Africa as the Land of Ham and his descendants. Ham, the second son of Noah settled in North Africa and his sons too, settled in places like Libya, Egypt, and Cushi. What this means is that the demographic movements that have been discussed led to the settlements such as those that took place after the Great Floods, as narrated in the Bible (Genesis 8:1-10).

However, the Empires that were built mainly in the north along the south coastline of the Mediterranean and in the North East specifically in the Horn of Africa stimulated further demographic movements. From the north and northeast the demographic movements proceeded swiftly due to increasing population and occasional droughts that forced people to move in quest for better supplies. People kept moving further using various means including on land and sea crafts to as far as the Asian Far East. In which years the populations got to various places in Africa and the rest of the world is a complicated topic, which has not been a subject in this book. However, the mobility must have been made possible or facilitated by walking, by using animals such as donkeys, and horses or by sea, floating on tree plunk crafts especially when they had to travel in water.

From Africa the demographic movements took various directions, to the Asia Minor and Asia and on to Indian sub-continent and further on to the Far East places such as, Indonesia, Papua New Guinea and Australia. The other groups that crossed the Africa continent borders did so through the North- east (along the Red Sea area) to various places in Asia Minor and further towards the northeast to as far places like China. Other groups, the smaller ones, branched and started moving to towards the west to Europe some to the north of Europe, others straight to the western direction and a few others taking the south European direction along the Mediterranean coast to places like the present day Spain and so on. The movement to Europe is believed to have taken place much later than that of other places, especially Asia. This in short is the way the whole world found itself getting populated from Africa. Here we are referring to many hundred thousand, if not close to millions of years ago.

It is at this juncture we have to state that some of the information that is usually provided by history scholars, especially on very far past historical accounts could sometimes be based on what they consider to be only logical guesswork, because the earliest chronologies date back only to the earliest civilizations of Early Dynastic Period Egypt, Mesopotamia and the Sumerians, which emerged independently of each other, from roughly 3500 BCE. This means the tradition of recording significant events in the history books started only with the Sumerians in Mesopotamia effectively from just around 2,900 BCE. It is good to be noted that history is written history. Before written history, everything is deemed to be prehistoric and there are no more than 4000, years of history so far. In short from time of the early man in Olduvai to the time of written history (just 4000 years), the gap (millions of years) is so much that the history is peanuts compared with what is unknown about our world.

However, Africa represented by the great ancient empires had many attributes that need to be taken note of. Good cases of those empires could include those of ancient Cushi, Egypt, Carthage and Numidia. Technological development in most of these empires was exemplary. Like we have mentioned Cushites were excellent producers of ceramics. The population was with no exception preoccupied with the tilling of the land and animal husbandry. The best example could still be found among Egyptians, who were not only good painters but also developed alphabet of their own type. In as far as painting was concerned the Egyptians became great experts in various skills including the two-dimensional paintings. They painted issues of everyday life, including those of important events and wars.

Egyptians were good worshipers, and their religion was basically pagan; and thus, they worshiped many gods, and sometimes believed that Pharaohs were chosen by gods or were gods themselves. They also worshiped the Nile River, which provided them with the means of survival. The Nile was even considered to be a major part of their after life. When pharaohs died, they were mummified to preserve their bodies for the after life. They developed good trade relations with communities that existed in the west of the River Nile including Cushi and other empires. The trade with foreign nations increased from the 5th century BCE onwards. This was specifically so with states such as Canaan, Lebanon, Nubia, and Punt. Just before the First Dynasty, Egypt had a colony in Southern Canaan.[9] The colony was a good producer of pottery which was highly demanded in Egypt and which was exported to all neighbouring states and areas surrounding the Nile River. In the Second Dynasty, Babylons provided quality timber that was in high demand in areas around the Nile River.

Many famous empires spread to areas in the north west of Africa and especially in areas close to the east and west of River Nile along the Mediterranean coastline to as far as the present day Morocco and further to as far places as part on present day Mauritania. In the

---

[9] *Canaan was a place in areas around Mesopotamia or in places that in the present day may include Israel Palestine, and Lebanon.*

neighbourhood there were two most notable Mediterranean civilizations of Greek city- states and Phoenicians. Both of them extensively colonized the coastline of the Mediterranean.

However, famous African kingdoms and empires that emerged both in the classic and the medieval times have been identified and would include Egypt, Carthage, Axum, Numidia, and Kingdom of Dogbon. Others would include empire of Ashanti, the Garamantes Empire of Ghana, empire of Mali, empire of Songhai, Kingdom of Zimbabwe, and the Bono State kingdom. These grew and became famous in the intervening period of the late 7th century, but especially in the 8th century-CE and continued so to the later medieval times.

The ancient Ghana Empire controlled the regional trade which was quite lucrative for the kings of Ghana, and which dominated the upper valley of the Niger River from the 6th or 7th century CE. The Empire traded in goods like gold, ivory, hides, ostrich feathers, and slaves to the Muslim merchants who sent camel caravans that crossed the Sahara from North Africa and which brought much-valued salt to the south. But the Ghana Kingdom had access to its own resources, notably iron and gold which the elite used to exchange for such luxury goods as fine textiles, beads, copper, and horses, which were all brought by Arab traders from the north. Another commodity-currency used in ancient Ghana, besides gold, was copper wiring.

The kings of Ghana were very keen with their gold trade business. They illustrated their supreme position by prohibiting anyone else but themselves from owning gold nuggets. Merchants had to be satisfied with gold dust. The Kingdom had a good regulation arrangement that ensured that the price of gold remained stable;

and this happened through a policy that enabled the king to control the gold market and ensure its value did not decrease by having too much of it in circulation at any one time.

However, towards the 13th century, after over seven centuries of its existence the Ghana Empire started to decline. The empire ultimately collapsed in the face of invasions from the Almoravids; and a series of brief kingdoms followed, notably that of Sosso (Susu).

The next, equally powerful African Empire was that of Mali. To start with let's say there has been confusing understanding between the Songhai and Mali empires. The names of the two Empires have often kept being used interchangeably, which has made it difficult for readers to differentiate the two. However, the two were both African Muslim empires. They ruled over a similar region. They were both native to **what** is currently Mali. The Songhai had a single state language, (Gao) unlike the Malinese. Songhai obtained greater power and wealth than the Malinese, but culturally there were a lot of similarities.

Ancient Mali Empire existed from around 300 to 1100 CE[10]. This Empire first formed when a number of tribes of the Soninke peoples had got united under their first king, Dinga Cisse. The various tribes each had its chief who got united under one feudal system. Each of the Chiefs ruled their lands as they saw fit but paid tribute to the high king.

Then there was the Songhai Empire. Like we have just hinted, the Mali and Songhai empires were related but were not one and the

---

[10] *English-abbreviation for Common Era or Christian era: used when referring to a year after the birth of Jesus Christ when the Christian calendar starts counting years: The Scandinavian countries became Christian between 900 and 1100 CE*

same kingdom. Songhai was a state that covered most of the Western Sahel in the 15th and 16th Century. During this period Songhai Empire was one of the greatest trading Empires of West Africa the exact point of the Empire being around River Niger in what is today, central Mali, and extending west to Atlantic Ocean coast and east to Niger and present day Nigeria. The Songhai people and state is known to have been established and its main city of GAO, established around 800 CE for reasons that are not clearly known, they failed to recognize it as their capital until the beginning of the 11th Century during the reign of King Kossoi, who happened to be a Songhai convert to Islam. From that time GAO prospered and expanded and in the next 300 years that followed especially from the first quarter of 1300 to the third quarter 1600 the rulers of Mali took it in their control and became part of the Mali Empire.

One common thing is that while the earliest African empires south of the Sahara region were in West Africa, they developed at the time when most of Europe was experiencing the Dark Age. That was particularly true after the fall of the Western half of the Roman Empire around 476 CE. The trade, especially with traders from across the Sahara in the North was significant and played an important role for development. In Mali, Songhai, and other smaller kingdoms the wealth, mostly made through trade, was used to build strength, and in order to protect their trade interests, these kingdoms built strong armies. Kingdoms that desired more control of the trade also developed strong armies to expand their kingdoms and protect them from competition.

In the meanwhile, long distance trade became popular. It helped the local economies and supported internal trade. Merchants travelling between towns in West Africa and across the Sahara needed places to rest and stock up with food especially for the long journeys across the Sahara desert. They readily got those supplies from the local African markets. The process contributed a lot to the promotion of the local agricultural production. This practice allowed merchants to plan long trips knowing that local markets would provide food and shelter along the way. This was particularly true for traders that originated the trips from/or to West African states.

The greatest achievement especially for Mali and Songhai Empires was in their schools. There were 180 schools just in Timbuktu. They became well known for their teachings on rhetorics, logic, Islamic law, grammar, astronomy, history and geography. However, in the period of the flourishment of the West African Empires Africa was seen by the rest of the World as a place of mature, wise and faithful people. During the time many parts of West Africa were growing in strength. That was the time when European businesses sought for business relations with Africa through the North African merchants. Business between the Africa and Europe continued for a long time until end of 15th century.

The next Empire worth a mention is the Kingdom of Monomopata. The Kingdom developed in Southern Africa in what is today Zimbabwe. The Empire was also known in various other names such as Matapa, Mwenemutapa, and Monomopata. It was a southern African kingdom located in the north of the modern Zimbabwe, along the Zambezi River and flourished relatively recently, compared to the West Africa Empires. Monomopata became powerful between 14th and mid-17th century CE

Mwene Matapa, is Shona meaning Ravager of the Lands also spelled Mwene Mutapa or Monomotapa, title borne by a line of kings ruling the Southeast African territory between the Zambezi and Limpopo rivers, in what is now Zimbabwe and Mozambique, for three centuries from the 14th century. Their domain was often called the empire of the Mwene Matapa, or simply Matapa. It is associated with the historical site known as Zimbabwe, which was, located in the southeastern part of modern Zimbabwe. According to oral tradition, the first Mwene was a warrior prince named Nyatsimba Mutota from the Kingdom of Zimbabwe sent to find new sources of salt in the north. A capital was established 350 km north of Great Zimbabwe at Zyongombe by the Zambezi.

Mutapa people made a living through their economy. The leaders mined gold from rivers streams and they traded it with other items like mined iron, salt, copper and tin, soapstone (a soft rock), and ivory. Gold was used as a trading item for luxuries like ceramics and beads that demonstrated a high status in the kingdom. They also traded other items for livestock, which included sorghum, millet, ground beans, cowpeas, and bananas from Indonesia[11]. Mutapa's people practiced taxation and forced labour of conquered people for gold mining. Mutapa also practiced agriculture because of their fertile soils. They also had Blacksmithing, Pottery, Weaving and basketry in the center of Mutapa's economy.

There were other famous but small empires in various other parts of the continent such as the Bennin in the South of the present day Nigeria, Baganda (in Uganda), Ethiopia (especially Axum), and Mossi Empire (which comprised of a series of small Kingdoms that were located in the present day Bukina Fasso).

---

[11] *Bananas had been indigenous in the Asian continent, especially Indonesia before it was introduced in various parts of Africa*

What we have done is to provide a brief exposure of the position held by Africa by 15th Century. Africa enjoyed a state of freedom and social economic development and management based on resources that abound in the continent, a situation that continued to provide strength until the early years of the 16th Century. Most of the famous African Empires and kingdoms were land developers, growing and exporting crops such as cotton, millet and sogham. They also had good manufacturing skills and actually, some e.g. Ghana and Mali exported textile products to many places in North Africa and across the Mediterranean Sea. Minerals such as gold and copper were common trading products in Mali, Ghana, Zimbabwe and almost the rest of African kingdoms that had been established by the 15th Century.

Most interesting and exciting was the way ancient Africa Kingdoms and/or empires such as Egypt, Ethiopia, Ghana, Mali, and Songhai had managements, religious and technological set ups that were so advanced that had they been left to prosper they would have possibly taken the modern development path much further than where the present nations have managed to reach.

Now we need to touch base on people who are known to have emerged from places north- central Africa. These are none other than the Bantus. As the human race kept growing and spreading from within Africa to the rest of the world, that did not deter demographic movements within Africa itself. People kept moving and regrouping and in the meantime tribes, kingdoms and Empires kept being formed and built and later they collapsed and life kept going. We could take the case of the Bantu expansions, which took place between the year 3, 000 BCE and 1,500 CE.

The Bantus were one of those groups, which started to form in places in the Southern neighbourhood of Egypt[12]. Their major early movement was from central Africa; from where they spread to West Africa, East Africa and to Southern Africa. There are also those who think the most ancient Bantu empire started in areas around Southern Sudan from where they spread southward to central Africa. In central Africa they split, some moved further on towards the South, while the rest further split, one group (the smaller one) moving to the west and the other (the major one) to the east. It is now commonly been agreed that the Bantu migration movement started around 3,000 BCE and finally ending around 1500 CE.

The migration of the Bantu people from their origins in Central Africa, spread a bit to the West, but mostly towards the east and south, saw a further gradual population movement sweeping through the central western and southern parts of the African continent. Though it is still debatable about the exact place of origin of the Bantus but it is now generally accepted that the Bantu speaking people originated from Western and Central Africa around 3,000 years ago. There is less agreement on the exact reasons for the course of their expansion. However, it is important to know a little more about these Bantu people.

Like has been outlined the history of the Bantu is long but the use of the term, Bantu, started only when Europeans were beginning to cultivate interest in invading and occupying some parts of Africa especially in 16th and 17th Century. Actually, Bantus remained better identified by Bantu language that has broken down to many dialects. For instance, today the Bantu dialects are many, estimated at between 440 and 700 distinct languages. Bantu speaking Africans,

---

[12] *Three Hundred Years on Kilimanjaro Mountain Are by Abisai Temba; Notion Press -India*

make up the majority of the South African black ethnic groups. What could be of interest is about where this naming, '**Bantu**' originated. The Zulu used the word **Abantu** to mean **people**; but the early Europeans in South Africa found it easy to shorten the word to "**Bantu**". Since then we have continued using the Word, Bantu meaning all those people who share the Bantu origin. The term is not only used in South Africa but in the whole world to refer to people who are of Bantu ancestry wherever they are in the world.

It has just been shown how the Bantus found their way to Southern Africa. The real cause of the Bantus migration from their places of origin in North/Central Africa to the South and also to the East was mostly engineered by drought. Those people were in search of new fertile land and water for farming and grazing of livestock, mainly caused by the fact that their places of origin.; especially the Sahara grasslands were further drying up. They pushed to the south and east to places that were better endowed with fertile land for agriculture and also with enough water for their livestock. That was in the period between 13th and 14th centuries CE. By end of 1300 CE the Bantus who comprise the overwhelming majority of the present day inhabitants of Southern Africa, had moved South of River Limpopo. Today, people of the Bantu origin especially the Nguni Bantus include the Zulu, Xhosa, Swazi, Sotho, and Ndebele, and partly the Ngoni..

In East Africa, the majority of Tanzanians, especially those of the three major tribes- Sukuma, Nyamwezi and Chagga, are of Bantu descent. The East African Bantus especially the Sukuma and Nyamwezi were part of that Bantu group that moved to the east from central Africa. The exception is that of the Chagga who are part of that group that moved from Central Africa to Sothern Africa where they became part of the Nguni people[13]. The Chagga can today trace their origins to Nguni-Bantus of Southern Africa, along with tribes such as Zulu, Xhosa, Swana, Swazi, Ndebele, Sotho and Ngoni. The question is on how the Chagga ended up to be the leading dwellers of Kilimanjaro in Tanzania, East Africa. In the early years of 16th century there was a lot of tumult in Sothern Africa caused by drought, which hit hard, leading to intensified fighting of people of that region, each of the antagonistic groups wishing to get part of the resources that remained and could be accessed. It was time of survival of the fittest. The tumult led to great wars commonly referred to as Nfecane ,which stimulated further migrations to different directions of the region- to the east as far as Drakensberg Mountains), to further south and to the north. The drought and the wars amongst the Nguni Bantu lead to collapse of the Nguni empires and in the meanwhile, people kept on the run to different direction for safety. The group that moved north got as far as Kilimanjaro Mountain area where it settled and became part of what today is known as the Chagga people of Kilimanjaro. The settlement of the Shaka people,[14] also known as Chagga on the slopes of Mount Kilimanjaro later made them indigenous in the area. This was in the closing years of 16th century or the early years of 17th century at the latest.

Overall, Africa did a lot of development in the period that preceded the take over of Imperialism and colonialism. Intervention into African way of life pulled back the forward strides that were being made by African Empires, Kingdoms, and chiefdoms. The major block that got imposed on Africa to hold it back to underdevelopment were the slave trade, Imperialism,

---

[13] *Abisai Temba: Three Hundred Years on Kilimanjaro Mountain Area" published by Notion Press —India;*
[14] *Abisai Temba: cited; "the Un-Walked Mile" published by Author House, UK.*

colonialism, and neo- colonialism. These issues will be brought up again later.

In concluding on this brief historical perspective of Africa it is necessary to state that a big chasm was created in the relationship that had existed between Europe and Africa. That was particularly so in the time after the 16th Century. Like it has often been stated, soon after the 15th century the good relationship that had existed between the two continents changed dramatically. That is the period Europe had begun to go through the industrial revolution, which made Europe to start cultivating undue superiority over other continents. European communities and entrepreneurs felt were super humans that could control others, especially Africa. With the industrial revolution Europe got more employment opportunities; they began to accumulate wealth; they used the wealth to control and exploit people in other continents along the lines of slave trading. Industrial revolution brought Europe to a new level of development. To make the industrial revolution going, more raw materials were demanded. Soon Europe realized that Africa was so well endowed with natural resources like land, water, and cheap labour. That made Europe to concentrate on Africa by way of first getting slaves from it for enhancing raw material production in the new World Americas (as demanded by the growing industrial revolution) and later colonializing the continent, thus making it a good source of the raw materials that European industries needed.

4

AFRICA'S TRADE PATTERN IN THE MEDIEVAL TIME

The Medieval Age, better known in Europe as the middle age era, is defined as the period between the 5th and late 15th century. It is also known to be the post-classical period of global history and also the period when the fall of Western Roman Empire begun. That also transitioned to Renaissance as well as the Age of discoveries. The early 900 years of the Medieval Age were also marked as the Dark Age. The Dark Age lasted from 5th century to 14th century. The period is marked as **"Dark Age"** because that is the time when civilization went through sharp decline. The many reasons that led to the downfall of European civilization during the Medieval Era included the decline of the feudal system in Europe, and also the decline of the Church power over the national controls. Swift developments that had been taking place in Europe faced a sharp decline, hence its reference as the dark- age.

However, even during the dark-age some trading went on, with 6th century Byzantine coins, pottery, silver dishes, glass beads and some type of textiles. During the period there was a lot of trade that was undertaken between the Arab world and Europe. The traded goods included slaves, spices, gold, perfumes, and jewels. African Empires also got involved in the trade with Europe during the Dark Age. There was a succession of African Empires that got involved, although the traded goods were few. Some of the goods included slaves, gold, salt, and ivory. West African Empires in particular traded in gold, ivory, and cloth. The goods that were bought by the

African Empires, most of which came from the North included, books, swords, and chain mail. The trade grew and became popularly known as trans Saharan trade because it crossed the Sahara desert.

The trade between West Africa and North Africa began due to surplus of such traded products per area. For instance, gold was plentiful in West Africa, so traders sent the items to North Africa, so they too, could have the valuable metal. In turn the North Africans gave salt to West Africa. However, before 1500 trade was operated in East and West Africa by making other places have an interest in the type of material that were traded, which included gold, ivory, and salt. We could remind again here that the three African empires that emerged during the medieval times and which proved to be the leading trading nations with North Africa were the ancient Ghana, Mali, and Songhai. The leaders of those empires dominated the West Africa region because they controlled access to West African gold.

In the period before the 16th Century the international slave trade was not yet very active. Trading in goods was most remarkable; the most famous African trading states being ancient Ghana, Songhai, and Mali. They traded mainly in gold, cotton, and salt. The gold mines of West Africa provided great wealth to West African empires. Other items that were commonly traded included ivory, cola nuts, cloth, slaves, metal goods and beads. The main trade route across Africa was the trans-Sahara route. They in particular traded salt and cloth from North Africa, and the Sahara for gold and the slaves. The trade led to the growth of cities in West Africa. Ultimately the rulers of these cities began to build a series of empires that attracted the attention of many traders of North Africa. By the end of the medieval period, Arab and Swahili had become heavily involved in the slave trade business because they needed slaves for working in the sugar-cane fields.

However, transatlantic slave trade began during the 15th century when Portugal and subsequently other European kingdoms were finally able to expand overseas and reach Africa. The Portuguese first began to kidnap people from the West coast of Africa and to take those they enslaved back to Europe.

European traders traded guns, rum, salt, and many other goods. Guns were in high demand in the interior villages and communities; they had the biggest impact on Africa because they gave African communities or villagers a sure way to protect themselves. The guns enabled villages to capture and enslave others because the weapons were superior to what the local African communities had or possessed. The African villages that had guns were sure to win in the battles they fought with others that had no guns. People who were captured in the raids or wars between African villages faced a terrible journey to wherever they were sent for sale, mainly to foreign traders and trade markets.

However, trade led to the growth and prosperity of the African chiefdoms /kingdoms; first from taxes charged to those who used the trade routes and then from the trade of domestically produced goods. It is noticeable that there were trading routes that went through the rain forest. The most famous cities that offered trade for goods from central Africa included Sofala, Kilwa, Mombasa and Malindi, among others. Those cities grew big and great, but collapsed soon after the 16th century.

To start with trade in East and Central Africa differed in some way from that of West Africa, mainly because in East Africa the main traded goods were cloth, pottery and manufactured goods which got exchanged for gold, ivory, and furs. We will come to this later.

Independent Portuguese merchants called *Lançados*[15] settled along the coasts and rivers of West Africa, a coastline which stretched from present-day Senegal in the Northwest to Angola in the Southwest. They also used those infrastructures and facilities to strengthen their positions and to defend their trading rights from foreign encroachments.[16] In exchange for what they bought from African traders, the European traders imported into African items such as cloth, iron, and copper in raw and worked form, cowry shells used by the local population as currency. The European traders, especially the Portuguese also worked under instructions from Catholic Church headquarters. The countries were, (in theory at least), forbidden by Papal injunction from selling items with potential military uses to non-Christians; but it is doubtful if that was seriously observed. In exchange for their wares, Europeans returned home with slaves, ivory, and gum.

It is also understood that, in the period before the beginning of slave trade, Africans were producing items of comparable, if not of superior quality to those of pre-industrial Europe. That was especially so in the period before the beginning of the end of 16th century when trade between Europe and powerful African nations flourished. The flourishing of the trade was owed to the advances in native forge technology, especially smiths in some regions of sub-Saharan Africa, who were producing steel of a better grade than

---

[15] Lançados: *literally meant the thrown-out ones. These were settlers and adventurers of Portuguese origin in Senegambia, the Cape Verde Islands, Guinea, Sierra Leone, and other areas on the coast of West Africa. Many were Jews, often New Christians, escaping persecution from the Portuguese Inquisition.*

those of their counterparts in Europe. Those products were relatively highly developed and valued; contrary to popular views about pre-colonial Africa local producers or manufacturers.

Actually, in the period just before industrial revolution, (ie i.e. the period before 16th century) the population of Europe had kept growing at a very high rate; so much that it began to be a problem to meet its utility needs. This is a problem that continued to exist all through to the middle of 18th Century. Due to the ever-growing population new methods of production became necessary. The greatest problem was in the rural population of Europe, which was basically agrarian. The agrarian nature of European population of that time made almost every type of agricultural production as well as non-agricultural production to be done manually, which explains why at times Africa was described to produce products which were of much higher quality than those of similar nature that were being produced in Europe. Consequently, till the advent of industrial revolution, production both in Africa and Europe were being done in home-based cottage industries. The advantage African producers had over European producers, especially in as far as agricultural products were concerned, was that Africa farm products were being raised in warm climatic conditions that made growth and maturity quicker than those grown in the temperate climates. This made even the quality of the African products to be higher, thus fetching better and higher prices than those grown in the higher latitudes.

A note has been made about the West African textile workshops. These workshops produced fine cloths for export long before the arrival of European traders. These found good markets in the nearby and even in regional and international markets. On arrival of European traders, they also bought some products from African sources and re-exported them to other African markets and abroad.

Products got from other African sources found many customers among other local people in the West African trade. Some of these types of products were also being produced in European cottage industries; some of which together, constituted a significant advantage over local products. Powerful African rulers readily adopted the imported clothes for use as the distinctive clothing worn and ornaments carried at formal occasions as an indication of status or as courtly regalia[17]. Trade for the products manufactured in the African regions also found good markets in many places in the Mediterranean world[18], western Asia, and the Indian Ocean regions.

Within the continent itself, local exchanges among adjacent peoples fit into a greater framework of long-range trade. All this was owed to the long African history, which is as old as the existence of the world itself. For instance, according to the modern scholars of African history[19], and also on the basis of what we learnt in the previous chapter, Africa has the longest and oldest social, economic, and cultural history than any other continent. The economic activities started to flourish as soon as human societies began to come together and trade some 200,000 years ago or much earlier.

It is true to observe at this juncture that the earliest humans were hunter- gatherers living in small, family groups. Even then there was considerable trade that covered relatively long distances. Archaeologists have found that evidence of trade in luxury items like metals and shells across the entirety of the African continent

---

[17] *Regalia is a Latin plurale tantum word that has different definitions. In one rare definition, it refers to the exclusive privileges of a sovereign. Here the term is used to mean the distinctive clothing worn and ornaments carried at formal occasions as an indication of status.*

[18] *Mediterranean World covered places including all European countries that surrounded the Mediterranean sea such as Sicily, Italy, France, Spain and others.*

[19] *Taylor Francis; Journal; "Economic History of developing Regions"*

had been going on, and at some stage the main traders were the Berber people that lived in dry areas especially in the Sahel. These were basically nomadic herders. In the savannah grasslands they cultivated crops and thus permanent settlements were possible. These were the Arab flock pastoralists[20](who among other business was to capture the black occupiers of the Sahara and Sahel region and sold the victims to Mediterranean region buyers) who went to sell the slaves to places across the Mediterranean Sea and especially the Southern Europe.

Agriculture started by supporting villages and then small towns and ultimately large towns. Eventually, large trade networks developed between two or more settlements, or between two or more towns, and so forth. The first agricultural undertaking in Africa is believed to have begun in the heart of the Sahara desert, which is estimated to be in the years before 5,200 BCE, that being long (4,000 years) before the Medieval Age period. During that time the Sahara desert areas were far more moist and densely populated than today. The indigenous people were black or rather dark- skinned people. Several native types of crops were grown, and some small animals were domesticated. The crops may have included pearl millet, sorghum, and cowpeas, which spread through West Africa and the Sahel. At that time, the Sahara desert area is believed to have been like what the Sahel looks like today. Its fields were open and wide, which made cultivation easy; but the soils were generally poor and thin, and the rains were limited, which made intensive farming close to impossible. The local crops were also not ideal and produced fewer calories than those of other

---

[20] *This explains why most of the Nort African region is today occupied by people of Arabic origin because most of the indigenous people that occupied the region were captured and sold to slavery.*

regions. These factors limited surpluses and kept populations sparse and scattered.

However, towards the Medieval ages the growth of trade led to the exchange of goods and ideas. The rulers of different tribes developed different forms of government and the culture of a tribe influenced traditional religions. Family was the foundation of African society and the slave trade tragically disrupted African society and changed their trajectory of development. However, the different types of occupation promoted the desire for exchange of goods produced in one place with those obtainable in another places.

Technological innovations, especially in agriculture, were exemplary. In those ancient times peasants in Kingdoms such Egypt used many advanced tools to work in the fields by the Nile. To till and soften the Earth they used ploughs pulled by cattle. As the ploughing went on a second person followed behind and scattered seeds, which was unique technological advancement in the world of the time. This made it possible to have expansive fields of crop, thus making that Kingdom a place of wealth and abundance of agricultural production. When harvesting season started, they would use sickles to cut down tall stalks of grain. These economic advancements were supported by solid social-economic structures, as exemplified by countries such as Egypt; a process which was emulated by a number of Kingdoms in the Northwest, in the West and partly in the west, east, and southeast.

The slaves from the east African region were bought by Muslim Arab slave traders for sale in Egypt to meet the demand for manual labour. However, slave trade in the great lakes also included slaves from Ethiopian chiefs and kings from the interior, which had for over the centuries been sold to customers in Egypt, Arabian peninsula the Persian Gulf, India, the Far East, the Indian Ocean Islands, Somalia and Ethiopia itself. The highland kingdoms of Ethiopia were good slave buyers and traders.

In Ethiopia slave markets were found in all major towns, but more commonly in the countryside, where fairs were usually held weekly at some distance from inhabited settlements. Such markets would be attended by local people coming to buy and sell their produce, as well as to exchange gossip, but also by travelling merchants, in many cases handling imported articles. Such traders would probably attend a different trade fair each day.

For reasons of security merchants often traveled together in large caravans. They made their way across the length and breadth of countries. Those seeking ivory, gold, civet musk, and slaves would journey to the rich lands of Ethiopia's southwest. If engaged in the import-export trade they would, make their way to the Red Sea port of Massawa, the Gulf of Aden ports of Tajurah, Zeila and Berbera, or to the Sudan frontier in the far west. As was the situation earlier Imports in this period, largely consisted of cotton and manufactured goods.

However, the drying of the Sahara created a big barrier between the northern and southern portions of the continent. Two important exceptions were Nubian Sudan, which was linked to Egypt by the Nile and Ethiopia, which could trade with the northern regions over the Red Sea. Powerful states grew up in these regions. Trade went hand in hand with demographic movements and settlements as the empires spread from North Africa to Southern Europe. Goods bought from the West African traders by the North African Muslim traders were taken into southern Europe. The merchandise that was traded together with other goods also included slaves.

African leaders in the interior kingdoms found the slaves business very lucrative, that being especially so in the West Africa and north east Africa. In the first place they monopolized the trade in all interior regions of West Africa. The slave trade agents became famous in all aspects of the trade, as they knew the various routes to the interior slave capturing or buying points and also the best coast selling points of the goods they brought from the interior. With the experience the African slave agents gathered over many years in such business they became very good in negotiating prices of the goods that they traded on.

Slaves were not a subject that had profound concern to the African leaders as most slaves had been got in form of loot during inter-tribal wars, which took place frequently and whose frequency increased as slave business became lucrative. African villages were based on clans and tribes that were different from each other. That means there were villages or settlements with population that had had no kinship or relationship with those of their neighbours. They were foreign to each other. In such situation a distant village could have most of its people as entirely foreigners to each other; making it possible for them to live in close proximity as complete foreigners. The leaders, chiefs, or kings of such villages, kingdoms or settlements found it possible or were at liberty to fight each other and the winner took the people of the losing village or settlement or kingdom as slaves. These were some of the slaves that got sold to slave traders.

However, during the middle age some African countries were lucky to produce products that were of comparable, or better quality than those offered by their trading partners elsewhere. The main items traded were gold, salt, and some textiles. Gold was abundant especially in ancient Ghana and Mali. The gold mines of West African kingdoms and/or Empires provided great wealth especially to Ghana and Mali. Other items that were offered for trade included ivory, cola nuts, metal goods, beads, and slaves. The tradable items could be divided into two groups namely, those for exports and those for local markets. Those for exports found markets in North Africa from where some of the goods crossed the Mediterranean Sea to the southern parts of Europe especially in countries like the modern day Spain and other neighbouring areas. The trade with Europe started before the middle age. It started when the major trade route across the Sahara desert started to develop between the South and the North African especially the southern side of the Mediterranean Sea. It was from there some of those goods were shipped across the Mediterranean Sea to markets in the Southern parts of Europe.

Regarding the goods offered for local markets included food, drinks, tobacco, sugar, and cattle. As hinted, Africa had been trading indirectly with Europe through traders that crossed the Mediterranean Sea. The south-north trade mainly involved the Sahel traders, led by the rulers of empires such as ancient Ghana, Mali, and Songhai. The trade also extended to kingdoms in the further south, especially the West African nations, such as Benin, which is today part of Southern part of Nigeria. The modus operandi was that Africa initiated direct relations both with the Mediterranean world of Islam with the European world of Christendom. In other words it was a North-South trade through the Sahara desert. From North Africa traders crossed the Mediterranean to Southern Europe. The leading traders were Arabs who mainly traded in gold, textiles, salt and carries most of which were got from the West African Empires.

It may be good to note here also that starting with the 5th century CE Arab sheep keeper nomads crossed from Persian Gulf and started conquering the black African occupiers of the region. The captured people of the area were sold as slaves to European slave traders in Southern Europe. North Africa today remains occupied by people that are mostly of Arabic ancestry.

In the next couple of centuries the trading arrangement changed to being more direct. This was the period when Europe had started to industrialize and trade. The impact of industrialization influenced by trade benefits realized from trading with Africa made European economies to keep prospering very rapidly. European traders brought into Africa enormous volumes of commerce. That included the whole range of European manufactured goods and hardware, notably firearms, textiles and luxury goods such as beads and alcohol. By this time Europe had also started to trade with Asia and thus there was a lot of trans-shipment of items such as textiles from Asia.

Let it be emphasised again that until the advent of the industrial revolution in Europe in the eve of 16th century, African goods were of comparatively admirable quality and had kept been traded in Europe for centuries especially by North African Muslim traders. That was the situation until the turning of the 16th century.

While in those early years the performance of Africa in the trade was quite satisfactory with the main goods that were offered for trade remaining to be gold, ivory, woods (to make dye), pepper, cotton, salt and some textiles. Unfortunately gradually Africa began to be complacent with the achievements it was making. As Europe kept on with their industrialization efforts, the African Kingdoms did not put up as much effort to survive in the trade (like they had been doing in the longer past). The complaisance made them forget about enhancing their production capacities and focused attention on cheap kicks. A lot of effort was directed to hunting for slaves by way of waging wars with their neighbours (the battles which they usually won, because they were being supplied with guns that were being imported by European traders). In those circumstances Africans became very instrumental in weakening their own social, economic and political systems. That made Europeans to move ahead to get more slaves, gold, ivory and other tradeable materials.. As the European economies kept strengthening, by way improving production technologies and getting raw materials that were increasingly being produced using cheap slave labour, the African economies kept being weakened, and ultimately African participation in the trade race wore out. Africa got pushed to a very weak position in trade terms. The trading relations between Europe and Africa completely changed because of the fact that Europe went further and included slaves captured from Africa on their list of goods they bought and exported from Africa. After a while slaves became the main commodity Europe wished to trade on. Portugal became the first European nation to take significant part in buying slaves from the west coast of Africa and in overall slave trading. They acquired slaves for labour on Atlantic Africa island plantations, and later for the plantations in Brazil and Caribbean. They also sent a small number of slaves for sale in Europe.

Portugal, being the pioneer European nation to take significant part in transatlantic slave trading, was soon later joined by other European nations. European slave trade business became so lucrative that within a short while most European traders were in full swing competition with each other. Britain, a small Island state in Western Europe made great advantage of the industrial revolution, which was well supported by transatlantic slave trade, enabling that nation to be economically the most powerful in Europe and the whole world until as late as the 20th century. The main slave market was the Caribbean and the Americas. As the transatlantic trade flourished it took a triangular form. The European traders would sail to West African coast, landing on the ports that had been established on the coastal areas, where they remained put, as they waited for the human merchandise to be brought from the interior by African slave traders. Like it will be shown subsequently the European traders never attempted to get into the interior to buy slaves or other goods.

Slave traders got organized in such a way that there emerged some African slave dealers who would move to various places in the interior of the continent, capture slaves and bring them to the coast for sale to European slavers who always kept waiting for the slaves to be brought for sale in the coastal ports. The African traders were not new to what they did; for a long time they had kept bringing merchandise such as gold, ivory, and many other products to the coast, for sale to any buyers who were easily found there. As the market for slaves began to flourish the African traders also added more slaves on the list of merchandise that were brought to the coast for sale.

The lack of unity among African leaders and the lust for money and for foreign goods especially firearms, liquor, and other fine products (especially now that Europe had started to industrialize) made the administrative systems in the interior of Africa to be very weak. The weak administrations paved the way for extensive slave trading. African leaders became full participants in the process to the enhancement of the slave trade. They handled fellow Africans as merchandise. They sold the merchandise to Europeans who kept waiting on the coastal points for slaves to be brought to them for exchange with goods that they imported from Europe. Like it has been explained elsewhere in this book over 30 million people were removed from Africa in form of slaves and got sold in the Americas.

There is one last but very important point that is worth pointing out at this point. Trade during the Medieval Era and even earlier, increased interaction between communities, kingdoms and also between regions and continents. In most times the trade was monopolized by rich merchants from the North of Africa who crossed the Sahara Desert and made trade contacts with Kings of the South such as those of ancient Ghana, Mali, and Songhai. The rulers sold their own people to slavery. The common people that had not been turned to slaves got some chance to get to local market places where they did barter trade with each other.

5
SLAVERY AND SLAVE TRADE AROUND AFRICA

Slavery' is defined as the practice of owning slaves. It is a condition of having or forcing a person to work very hard without proper remuneration or appreciation. In simple terms slavery creates a condition in which one human being is owned by another and is always under instructions and commands that ought to be obeyed, and action taken without question. Traditionally slaves were considered by law as a property or chattel and were deprived of most of the rights ordinarily held by free persons. Slavery was protected by law and was operated in the open like any other legal activity, because it was a legal activity anyway.

Then there is the 'servitude', which is slavery condition but can be more precisely defined as a state of being a slave or a person that is completely subject to someone more powerful. It is a condition in which one lacks liberty especially to determine one's course of action or way of life. Servitude also refers to something (such as piece of land) owed by one person but is subject to a specified use or enjoyment by another. A Servitude finds himself in a state of being completely submissive to and controlled by someone more powerful. When a person caters for every whim on need of another, such a person will be a good example of someone who would be described as servitude.

Slave trade on the other hand involves trading in slaves. It involves the capturing, the selling and buying of enslaved persons. While slavery practice has been there and has existed throughout the world since ancient times, trading in slaves has been equally universal. Slave trade was important in the development of the wider economy financial, commercial, and legal institutions, all of which emerged to support the activities of the slave trade.

The practice of slavery, servitude, and slave trade has not been exactly the same in all parts of the world. The practice has been different from one country or society to another, and the extent has also differed from one era to another. Like elsewhere in the world, in Africa slavery was practiced in almost all tribes, regions and cultural backgrounds. The differences in enslaving practice and even systems existed between one African community, tribe and another. Systems of slavery and servitude were common in most parts of Africa just the same way they were in most of the rest of the ancient and also in the medieval times.

Slavery in historical Africa included the domestic slavery, debt slavery, war captives' slavery, military slavery, pawnshop slavery, chattel slavery, prostitution slavery, criminal slavery and forced marriages slavery. All these forms of slavery were practiced in various ways in different parts of the continent. It could be added that domestic slavery, forced marriages, war captives and criminal slavery were the most common ones. While slavery has existed in Africa from the ancient times; but what was most unique was that Africans treated slaves, especially the domestic ones as family.

Slavery in Northern Africa started as far back to ancient Egypt. The New Kingdom (1558 BCE- 1080BCE) brought in large numbers of slaves as prisoners of war up the Nile valley and used them as domestic and supervised labour. Ptolemaic Egypt used both the land and the sea routes to bring slaves in.

Starting with the beginning of 1600 the Portuguese bought slaves from the West coast of Africa, transported, and sold them in Portugal for domestic use. Around 1619 the Portuguese slave-ship travelled across the Atlantic Ocean with a hull filled with human cargo; most of them captives from the coastal areas of the present-day Angola. Since then, most European nations joined in the trade of slaves from West Africa for sale in the Americas. The slave trade was highly facilitated by African slave dealers, who did the capturing, transportation of slaves on land to the coastal areas where they found ready market provided by European traders who kept on the wait for slaves to be brought there for sale. The largest proportion of the slaves got from West Africa, were sent to North America and South America, especially Brazil.

All colonial European nations enhanced slavery in their colonies. The practice went on smoothly as long as it was not extended to high seas or internationally. Plantation slavery got enhanced as part of the arrangement to go on in the colonies but under the pretext that the colonial governments at home were not aware of what was happening in the colonies. The situation made most colonial nations to enhance slavery without being accused of contravening international laws. Some colonial countries enacted laws that prohibited slavery in the colonies, but those laws were good only in their books of law; but were never seriously followed up or enforced because slave labour was needed in the farms or in the mines and products from those production points were badly needed for enhancing production in the factories in the colonial home countries in Europe; which made the colonial governments to behave as though they were not aware of the forced labour that was being practiced in the colonies.

The forced labour was commonly practiced in the Eastern coast of Africa and in parts of West Africa, especially in countries like Cameroon, which came under German colonial rule. It could be added that the importance of domestic plantation slavery increased during the 19th century due to the abolition of the Atlantic slave trade. Many European nations that depended on the international slave trade found themselves forced to reorient their colonial economies towards legitimate commerce and production worked by slave labour. The confinement of slave labour in the commercial undertakings established on the colonial land became true and necessary following the abolition of slave trade, especially on the Atlantic, during the early years of the 18th century.

Like it has been hinted, there were several types of slavery, namely the debt slavery, enslavement of war captives, military slavery, prostitution, and criminal slavery. All these were and some of them have continued to be practiced in one place or another in various parts of Africa, perhaps till this day. Slavery for domestic and court purposes was widespread in almost all colonies in Africa. Plantation slavery also occurred primarily on the eastern coast of Africa mainly practiced by Arab estate owners but later by the largescale European plantation farmers. The importance of this domestic plantation slavery (which actually increased during the 19th century and in the first half of 20th century), was that industrial revolution in Europe was exerting pressure for supply of more raw materials from Africa. That pressure became very evident in the colonial establishments following the abolition of the Atlantic slave trade. Many European businesses and/or governments had been dependent on the triangle slave trade and with its abolition the colonial governments and their business agencies had to transform to increase and/or focus their raw material production to the African colonies, where legitimate commerce was operated very successfully through use of the so-called local people labour, which was in any case entirely slavery.

Multiple forms of slavery and servitude have existed throughout African history and were shaped by indigenous practices of slavery, Roman and the later Christian views on slavery, the Islamic institutions of slavery via Arab slave trade and eventually the Atlantic slave trade. Colonialism apart, Slavery was a part of the economic structure of African societies for many centuries, although the extent varied. In the ancient kingdom of Mali for instance, the rich local inhabitants competed or rather vied with each other in the number of slaves and servants one could own. That was a common practice especially in the mid-14th century. The more the slaves the more esteemed a man was.

Generally, in Sub-Saharan Africa, the slave relationships were often complex, with rights and freedoms given to individuals held in slavery and restrictions on sale and treatment by their masters. Many communities had hierarchies between different types of slaves: for example, if differentiation was to be made between those who had been born into slavery and those who had been captured through war the two were different in terms of privileges that they could earn from their masters.

The proportion of slaves to free persons in Africa was generally big. Usually, some domestic slaves claimed no reward for their services except food and clothing, and were treated with kindness or severity, depending on the good or bad disposition of their masters. Depending on their traditions and customs certain rules got established with regard to the treatment of slaves, which it was considered dishonourable to violate. Thus, the domestic slaves, or others such as those born in a man's own house, had a chance of being treated with more lenity than those which were purchased with money or those who were captives of war. In other words, these restrictions on the power of the master did not extend to the care of prisoners taken in war, or to the slaves purchased with money. The two categories were different, as the former were closely related to the master and the later were considered to be strangers and or foreigners brought into the servants group; and thus, they had no right to the protection of the law). They could therefore be treated with severity, or sold to strangers, according to the pleasure of their owners.

As seen from what has been narrated, forms of slavery in Africa have in many cases been closely related to kinship structures. In many African communities, where land could not be owned, enslavement of individuals was used as a means to increase the influence that a person had and expand connections. This made slaves a permanent part of a master's lineage and the children of slaves could become closely connected with the larger family ties. Children of slaves born into families could be integrated into the master's kinship group and rise to prominent positions within society, even to the level of chief. However, stigma often remained attached and there could be strict separations between slave-members of a kinship group and those related to the master.

Then there was this issue about Chattel slavery that was a specific servitude relationship where the slave was treated as the property of the owner. As such, the owner became free to sell, trade, or treat the slave as he would do with cattle or other pieces of property and the children of the slave often were retained as the property of the master. There has been a long history of chattel slavery in places such as Uganda and Sudan as well as Northern Africa. What still lacks is the evidence of the extent and practices of chattel slavery throughout much of the rest of the continent. Like it was exposed, chattel was very possible for slaves that had no close relationship with the family of the owner.

Many slave relationships in Africa have kept revolving around domestic slavery, where slaves would work primarily in the house of the master but retain some freedoms. For European domestic slave owners, especially towards the turning of the 19th Century and in the course of the first quarter of the 20th Century, a domestic worker or slave had no special privileges. But those slaves in the house of African households, could often be considered as part of the master's household and would not be sold to others without extreme cause. The slaves could in special circumstances own the profits from their labour (whether on land or in products), and could marry and pass the land on to their children in quite many cases. Surely this was not a universal practice, but it was there in many African tribes in East, Central and West Africa.

Next was the military slavery. This type of slavery involved the acquisition and training of conscripted military units that would retain the identity of military slaves even after their service. Slave soldier groups would be run by a *Patron*, who could be the head of a government or an independent warlord, and who would send his troops out for money and his own political interests. This practice was most popular in the Nile basin, primarily in Sudan and Uganda with slave military units organized by various authorities, and with the war chiefs of Western Africa such as Dahomey. The military units in Sudan were formed in the 1800s through large-scale military raiding in of the area that is currently the countries of

Sudan and South Sudan. To a limited degree this was also practiced by the Chiefs of Chagga of Kilimanjaro who would raid neighbouring chiefdoms and young male captives forced to join into the army of the captors for further raids.

Besides military slaves there were the Human sacrifice slaves. It was most popular in specific areas of West Africa up to and during the 19th century. In Dahomey the human sacrifice type of slavery was most practiced. In Dahomey the practice was an annual event where hundreds of prisoners would be sacrificed. Such sacrifices were carried out all along the West African coast and further inland. Such sacrifices were also common in Benin Empire in what is now Ghana, and in the small independent states in what is now Southern Nigeria.

However, there is no country in Africa that can claim not to have practiced slavery of one kind or the other. Nations such as the Ashanti of present-day Ghana and the Yoruba (present-day Nigeria) have been extensively involved in various types of slavery. Groups such as the Imbangala of Angola and the Nyamwezi and Sukuma of Tanzania would serve as intermediaries or roving bands, waging war on African states to capture people for export as slaves. The local people would be captured and then sold to Europeans who shipped them in the Atlantic slave trade and other destinations.

However, the going was not as simple as explained above. Perhaps the international aspect of the trade practice would not have been as successful for the traders if it had not been facilitated through the complex business partnerships between African chiefs, African commercial agents, and foreign traders. All those groups benefited from that type of international trade that specialized mainly on human merchandise.

Looking briefly at what happened in North Africa, one finds that Chattel slavery was common and had been legal and widespread throughout that region from several years BCE. The Chattel slavery started and went on when the region was controlled by the Roman Empire between 145 BCE – 430 CE. It went on under the control of the Eastern Romans in 533 CE to 695 CE. A slave trade bringing Saharans through the desert to North Africa existed and continued in the Roman times. The trade was regulated in that region by treaties. Basically, the trade for all that period was chattel, and persisted so until after the fall of the Roman Empire in the largely Christian communities of the region. It could be added that while slavery and slave trade had been there long before the Roman occupation, it went on even to the days when Persian Gulf tribes had invaded and taken over the area.

There was the Islamic expansion into most of the North African region. The Islamic expansion displaced the indigenous people of that region with people from the Persian Gulf. Most of the indigenous people were included in those who were sold to slavery in the area around the Mediterranean and further north to Southern Europe. Due to the trade expansion across the Sahara the practices continued and eventually, the assimilative form of slavery spread to major societies on the Southern end of the Sahara (such as Mali, Songhai, and ancient Ghana). There are no good records of how many men, women and children were actually enslaved, but attempts which have been made to make the estimate, have been based on rough number of fresh captives that would have been needed to keep the slave populations steady and replace those slaves who died, escaped, ransomed, or converted to Islam; as the law had it that once a slave had been converted to Islam, he would have to be let free from slavery. On this basis, it is thought that around 9,000 new slaves were needed annually to replenish numbers.

Across the late 1500s and early 1600s the estimation is that around 35,000 European Christian slaves were held throughout this period on the Barbary Coast, across Tripoli, Tunis, but mostly in Algiers. The majority were sailors (particularly the English), taken with their ships, but others were fishermen and coastal villagers. However, most of these captives were people from lands close to Africa, particularly Spain.

There was a practice, which could be considered strange in places like Egypt. The ancient Egyptians were able to sell themselves and their children into slavery in a form of bonded labourers. Self-sale into servitude was not always a choice made by the individuals' free will, but rather a result of individuals who were unable to pay off their debts. The creditor would wipe the debt by acquiring the individual who was in debt as a slave, along with his children and wife. The debtor would also have to give up all that he owned. Peasants were also able to sell themselves into slavery for food or shelter. Some slaves were bought in slave markets near the Asiatic area and then bonded as war prisoners. Not all were from foreign areas outside of Egypt, but it was popular for slaves to be found and collected abroad. This act of slavery grew Egypt's military status and strength. Bonded laborers dreamed of emancipation but never knew if it was ever achievable. Slaves foreign to Egypt had possibilities of returning to their homeland but those brought from Nubia and Libya had to stay in the boundaries of Egypt.

One type of slavery in ancient Egypt was that which granted captives the ability of an afterlife. This brings us to the issue of

Shabtis who were funerary figures buried with deceased Egyptians. These figures represented an ideology of earthly persons' loyalty and bond to a master. Evidences of **shabtis** that exist show great relevance to that type of slavery system. Such slaves were promised to receive an afterlife in the *Beyond* if they stayed and obeyed their Master(s) and served as labourers. The origin of this type of slavery is difficult to pinpoint but some say the slaves were willing to be held captive in return for entrance into Egypt. Entrance into Egypt was also perceived as given "life". Willingness of enslavement of this type has remained known as *self-sale*.

There have also been suggestions that shabtis were held captive because they were foreigners. The full extent of the origins of Shabtis is unclear but historians do recognize that women were paid or compensated in some way for their labour, while men were not. However, payment could come in many forms. Although men did not receive monetary wages, shabtis were promised life in the netherworld and that promise could be perceived as payment for them. So Shabtis are associated with bonded labour, but historians speculate some sort of choice for the Shabtis.

In the slave market, bonded labourers were commonly sold with a 'slave yoke' or a 'taming stick' to show that the slave was troublesome. This specific type of weaponry to torture the slave had many names but the preferred term in Egyptian was *shebya*. Several departments in the Ancient Egyptian government were able to draft workers from the general population to work for the state with a corvee labour system, which was a form of unpaid, unfree labour, which was intermittent in nature, and which lasted limited periods of time, typically with only a certain number of days' work each year. For example, Statute labour was a corvée imposed by the state for purposes of public works. In real sense it represented a form of levy, which unlike other forms of levy, such as a tithe, a corvée did not require the population to have land, crops, or cash. It was thus favored in historical Egypt and of course other economies especially in situations where barter was more common than cash transactions.

The laborers were conscripted for projects such as military expeditions, mining and quarrying, and construction projects for the state. These slaves were paid a wage, depending on their skill level and social status for their work. Conscripted workers were not owned by individuals, like other slaves, but rather required to perform labour as a duty to the state. Conscripted labour was a form of taxation by government officials and usually happened at the local level when high officials called upon small village leaders.

The other thing was that the slave Masters were under obligations when owning slaves. They were allowed to utilize the abilities of their slaves by employing them in different manners including domestic services as cooks, maids, brewers, nannies,[21] and labour services like gardeners, stable hands, field hands, etc.. Masters also had the right to make the slave learn a trade or craft to make the slave more valuable. Masters were forbidden to force child slaves to harsh physical labour.

There were also many slaves who worked for temple estate. These lived under punitive conditions, but on average the Ancient

---

[21] *A nanny is a person who provides childcare. Typically, this care is given within the children's family setting. Throughout history, nannies were usually servants in large households and reported directly to the lady of the house. Today, modern nannies, like other domestic workers, may live in or out of the house, depending on their circumstances and those of their employers. There are many employment agencies that specialize in childcare. Nannies in many areas are a sought-after member of the workforce.*

Egyptian slave led a life similar to a serf. They were capable of negotiating transactions and owning personal property. Chattel and debt slaves were also there and these were given food but as usual, in most cases there were no wages.

In the Horn of Africa, the Christian Kings of the Ethiopian Empire often exported pagan Nilotic slaves from their western borderlands, or from newly conquered or re-conquered lowland territories. The Somali and Afar Muslim sultanates, such as the medieval Adal Sultanate, through their ports also traded for Bantu slaves that were captured from the hinterland.

In Ethiopia, slavery was legal and widespread; slave raiding was endemic in many areas, and slave trading was a fact of life. The largest slavery-driven polity in the Horn of Africa before the nineteenth century was the Empire of Ethiopia and the Ethiopian Highlands were the largest consumers of slaves in the region. This was so in spite of the fact that its intercontinental slave trade was also substantial.

The merchant villages adjacent to the major markets of southwestern Ethiopia were invariably full of slaves, which the upper classes exchanged for the imported goods they coveted. The slaves were walked to the large distribution markets like Basso in Gojjam, Aliyu Amba and Abdul Resul in Shewa. The primary source of slaves for the southern territories was the continuous wars and raids between various clans and tribes that went on for thousands of years. The wars resulted to widespread slavery very common during the battles of that era. Oromo and Sidamo rulers raided their neighbours, enslaved their own people for even minor crimes. These rulers were the ones that provided most Slaves. Famine was another source of slaves, and during times of recurrent drought and widespread cattle disease, slave markets throughout the country would be flooded with victims of famine.

Since religious law did not permit Christians to participate in the trade, Muslims dominated the slave trade, often going farther and farther afield to find slave supplies. In southern Ethiopia the Gibe and Kaffa kings exercised their right to enslave and sell the children of parents too impoverished to pay their taxes.

In the centralized Oromo states of Gibe valleys and Didesa, agriculture and Industry sector was done mainly by slave labour. In Gibe state's one-third of the general population was composed of slaves. Slaves were between half and two-thirds of the general population in the Kingdoms of Jimma, Kaffa, Walamo, Gera, Janjero and Kucha. Kaffa reduced the number of slaves by mid 19th century fearing its large, bonded population. Slave labour in the agriculture sector in southwest Ethiopia was done by slaves, which means that slaves constituted higher proportion of the general population when compared to the northern Ethiopia where agrarian producers were mainly free Gabbers. Gabbers[22] owned their own land as a risk measure, as their legal obligation was to pay part of their produce as land tax and as rat, another one-tenth, with a total of one of total production paid as tax to be shared between the guilt holder and the state. In addition to these taxes, peasants of north Ethiopia had other informal obligations; they were forced to undertake corvee (forced labour)" such as farming, grinding corn, and building houses and fences that claimed up to one-third of their time.

By the second half of the nineteenth century, Ethiopia provided an ever-increasing number of slaves for the slave trade. This became

---

[22] *People who got involved more in talk and /or idle chat*

even more real as the geographical focus of the trade had now shifted from the Atlantic basin to Ethiopia, the Nile Basin and Southeast Africa down to Mozambique. However, a large part of the increased slave trade in the first half of the nineteenth century consisted of captives being sold by other neighbouring clans and tribes in the south & in Oromo areas. The nineteenth century witnessed an unprecedented growth in slavery in Ethiopia, especially in Southern Oromo towns, which expanded as the influx of slaves grew. In the Christian highlands, especially in the province of Shoa, the number of slaves was also quite large by the middle of 19th Century. However, despite the widespread war raids, the Oromo were not considered by the highlander groups as being racially *barya*[23], owing to their common Afro-Asiatic ancestry.

However, slavery as practiced in Ethiopia, was essentially domestic and was geared more towards women, which anyhow was the trend for most of Africa as well. Women were transported across the Sahara, the Middle East, and the Mediterranean and the Indian Ocean trade more than men. Enslaved women, thus served in the houses of their masters or mistresses and were not employed to any significant extent for productive purpose. The enslaved were thus regarded as second-class members of their owners' family.

In the Kingdom of Congo, oral tradition recounts slavery existing in the Kingdom of Congo from the time of its formation with Lukeni Lua Nimi enslaving the Mwene Kabunga whom he conquered to establish the kingdom. The Kongo kingdom was

---

[23] *The name 'Barya' means slave in Amharic and is a reflection of an unfortunate theme in the Bronze Age contacts with Egypt. These slaves, known as 'Barya', constitute to this day a separate, well-defined group that stands in polar contrast to the category 'Choa', a term which signifies a free person, perceived as enlightened and cultured persons.*

located on the Western coastal Africa and South of the Kongo River (formally known as Zaire). The kingdom arose in the late 14th century following the alliance of several local Principalities, which had been in existence since the second half of the first Millennium, CE. While most slaves from the Congo were exported to Portugal, King Afonso of that country retained many slaves for himself. Both King Afonso and later Kings would keep slaves, particularly the enslaved criminals, but the slaves were freeborn Kongolese and therefore could not be sold to other parties. Nonetheless, mass suffering remained a way of life ever since the Belgium King Leopold enslaved millions in the 19th century. In the transatlantic slave trade over 5.7 million enslaved people were forcefully transported from present day Angola and Congo (DRC) into the Americas, and since then it has been found that people of African descent in Americas have the most genetic connections to Angola and DRC

However, Slavery was common along the Upper Congo River, and in the second half of the 18th century the region became a major source of slaves for the Atlantic slave trade, when high slave prices on the coast made long-distance slave trading profitable. When the Atlantic trade came to an end, the prices of slaves dropped dramatically, and the regional slave trade grew. A distinction was made between two different types of slaves in this region; slaves who had been sold by their kin group, typically as a result of undesirable behavior such as adultery were unlikely to attempt to flee. In addition to those considered socially undesirable, the sale of children was also common in times of famine.

The Congo has been a place in Africa where issues of slavery of one kind or the other became prevalent for many centuries, and that continued until as late as the end of the 20th century.. Fighting and capturing of innocent men and women who ended up to be used in various types of slavery such as working in the mines, illegal harvesting of natural resources for export, sexual enslavement and prostitution were wide spread. Towards the beginning of the first decade of the 21st Century there ere reports that painted an awesome picture of slavery in the Congo mines. The Democratic Republic of Congo (DRC) was until then been plagued by a history of widespread violence, often fueled by a deadly scramble for the state's natural resources. In eastern Congo, the mines had become a source of not only conflicts, but also a source of human slavery by many mineral business groups. Such groups strategically attacked and raped civilians. They used military forces in order to gain control. The armed groups were to a large extent financed by profits from the mineral resources, which were often extracted and transported using slave labour.

In most of the Great Lakes Region of Africa, linguistic evidence shows the existence of slavery through war capture, trade, and pawning going back hundreds of years; however, these forms, particularly pawning, appear to have increased significantly in the 18th and 19th centuries. These slaves were considered to be more trustworthy than those from the West Africa. They were regarded with more prestige because of the training they responded to. The language for slaves in the Great lakes region varied, which made it easy to capture slaves and transport them, because they could not communicate with each other. Captive, refugee, slave, peasant were all used in order to describe those in the trade. The distinction was made by where and for what purpose they would be utilized for. Methods like pillage, plunder, and capture were all semantics common in this region to depict the trade.

In the South and Southeast Africa there were a host of different categories of labour especially in Southeast Africa. The distinction between slave and free individuals was not particularly relevant in most societies of this region. However, with increasing international trade in the 18th and 19th century, Southeast Africa began to be involved significantly in the Atlantic slave trade; for example, with the king of Kilwa island signing a treaty with a French merchant in 1776 for the delivery of 1,000 slaves per year.

At about the same time, merchants from Oman, India, and Southeast Africa began establishing plantations along the coasts and on the islands. To provide workers on these plantations, slave raiding and slave holding became increasingly important in the region and slave traders (most notably Tippu Tip) became prominent in the political environment of the region. The Southeast African trade reached its peak in the early decades of the 1800s with up to 30,000 slaves sold per year.

However, slavery never became a significant part of the domestic economies except in Sultanate of Zanzibar where plantations and agricultural slavery were maintained. At various times, between 65% and 90% of Zanzibaries were enslaved. A case is known of one Sultan Barghsh of Zanzibar who had 99 slave concubines (mainly girls of between fifteen and twenty-two years). These were besides other slaves who worked on the land, which came to make Zanzibar what it is today as Spice Island. As has been stated, almost 90% of Zanzibar population comprised of slaves. The same was the case with the Kenya coast, whose over 80% of population, was comprised of slaves almost entirely owned by Arab slavers. The issue of Zanzibar and its slave trade will be brought up again in the later chapters of this book.

In South Africa the history of slavery and slave trade is rather complicated in that the enslavement of the local indigenous people is not as straight forward as in other parts of the continent. However, in 1652, the Dutch West Indies Company set up a refreshment station for ships bound to the Dutch East Indies in what is now Cape Town. With that establishment, they requested for supply of slaves to save in the area. The first slaves arrived in 1653 from Jarkata during the Dutch colonial period. Shortly afterward, a slaving voyage was undertaken from the Cape to Mauritius and Madagascar for more supplies of slaves. Eventually van Riebeeck forcibly enslaved locally found Africans for work in the Cape company.

However, in April 1657, there were ten slaves in the settlement, from a population of 144. That increased greatly the next year, when the Dutch captured a Portuguese slaver with 500 Angolan slaves, and 250 were taken to the Cape. Two months later, a further 228 slaves arrived from Guinea. The process was enhanced with the commencement of settler colonialism: when former Dutch East Indies company officials were granted land lots, which officially made it possible for the establishment of the agricultural settlements of the Boers. This move economically started to displace or rather to dislocate the Khoikhoi who were the local African pastoralists. The Khoikhoi were forced to serve as servants due to the loss of their grazing land. The colonial settlers continued to import additional slaves from Mozambique, Madagascar, and India. In the meanwhile, those who were put into slavery lived very miserable life due to various mistreatments including the poor and insufficient food that was provided to them, poor living conditions and whipping punishments done to them due to fleeing or disobeying orders.

Threats to Dutch control of the Cape Colony emerged in the 18th century, when the Dutch East India Company was weakened during the war between the Dutch and the British (popularly known as the Anglo-Dutch war). During the 1780s, troops of the French army got stationed in the Cape to prevent invasion by Great Britain. Nevertheless, the Cape was invaded by the British in 1795 during the so called war of First Coalition, which occupied the area until 1803.

Britain later formally annexed the Cape and later passed the Slave Trade Act in 1807 which started to be enforced in 1808, ending the external slave trade. However, slaves were permitted to be traded only within the colony. The British government passed an Act which relieved the conditions of the slaves in the colony allowing slaves to at least get married, purchase their own freedom, live with their families, and receive some basic education.

6

IMPACT OF EUROPEAN INDUSTRIAL REVOLUTION ON AFRICA

The Industrial Revolution in Europe started in the 1760s period. At its start it was largely confined to Britain. Aware of their head start, the British forbade the export of machinery, skilled workers, and manufacturing techniques. This stance was taken hopefully with a view to avoid competition with other countries. However, within a short while other European countries, joined in the race, which continued until 1830s.

The European industrial revolution transformed economies that had been based on agriculture and handcrafts and cottage industries to economies based on largescale industry, mechanized manufacturing, and the factory system. New machines, new power sources and new ways of organizing work made the new industries more productive and efficient. The process was very dynamic, which gradually kept changing in phases from the first phase of development to more advanced phases (i.e. from first, second, third and to the more recent 4th and 5th industrial revolution). The First Industrial Revolution marked a period of development in the latter half of 18th century that made a lot of transformation largely in the rural agrarian societies in Europe and America into industrialized urban ones. We can add that one of the major triggers of the unusually high growth was the population, which set in around the middle of the 18th century and produced a gigantic reservoir of workers. At the same time new, more efficient methods of production became necessary in order to supply the basic needs of the growing population.

Most of our discussion is focused on the First Industrial Revolution, which was, we believe, largely caused by emergence of capitalism, European Imperialism, efforts to mine gold and effects of agricultural revolution. While the industrial revolution started in Europe in the 18th century, it from there spread to other parts of the world. Basically, it was a process of change from agrarian and handcraft driven economy in Europe to one dominated or driven by industry and machines.

The Industrial Revolution in Europe became a milestone for Europe as it triggered economic development of European nations by marking the period of transition to new European and world economic order. The world started to see manufacturing taking a central role in national and global development. Europe and the United States in particular took the lead in the process, which within a short while was followed by a few other countries outside Europe, such as Japan, to import technology from Europe, enabling it to join the bandwagon of the industrial nations. The process to the first phase of the industrial revolution came to its height around 1760s to sometime in 1840s. Countries that were able to follow the example of the industrializing Europe (in terms of industrial and the technological developments) found themselves making swift strides to swift economic growth.

The industrial revolution made a lot of transformation not only in the ways of production but also in the behavior and ways of life of people in the industrializing countries. As Europe kept on industrializing, Sub Saharan Africa on the other hand also got transformed, but in the reverse way. While Europe increased the level of industrially produced goods using inputs that were being got through use of African land and labour, Africa kept losing its resources including the human resources. Through industrial revolution Europe kept on growing wealthy through industrial production and subsequent economic development. Simultaneously as Europe kept making positive economic growth strives African natural resources kept on being exploited, plundered, and diminished in various ways, leading to swift social and economic deterioration and underdevelopment.

What s being told above is that there was very close relationship between industrialization in Europe and African underdevelopment. To start with European industrial development could be sustained only with a steady supply of inputs i.e., labour, energy, and raw materials. Labour supply in Europe was plenty especially in the rural areas, which led to high rural urban migrations. Urban areas started to be overwhelmed by the influx of people from the rural areas that were in quest for new jobs. The growing level of industrialization absorbed more of the unemployed people who before the revolution experienced a lot of hard time caused by the worsening state of unemployment. With the growth of the industrial sector more people got jobs.

Energy, which was another basic industrial in-put, was sourced from coal. Fortunately, that source of energy was abundantly obtainable in various places in Europe. The thing that posed a lot of threat was the supply of raw materials, such as cotton, sisal, tobacco, oil seeds, sugar, ivory, hard wood and minerals of various types, which had to be imported. As the demand for raw materials kept increasing as industrial production capacity increased in the European factories, the industrial nations had to change their raw materials procurement strategies. Swift action to get and 5th new sources of raw materials was needed, failure of which could lead to the grinding of the operations.

Initially the above raw materials were being imported from the new World, but with passage of time production capacity in the European industries kept on growing which called for more supply. Production fields in the New World had to be expanded to meet the new levels of increasing demand; but for that to materialize more labour was needed to work in those fields. To meet the increasing labour demand more people in form of slaves were got from Africa. The increased demand for labour to work in the raw materials production fields triggered introduction and growth of slave trade on the Atlantic. Sustained supply of raw materials production enabled the industrial production in Europe to increase. The cost of supply of raw materials got substantially reduced because they were now being produced using slave labour, which was relatively very cheap.

The above linkage of Atlantic slave trade with the industrial revolution was a strange process but that is what it was. It can be better explained by stating that in order to enable production to keep sustained in the European industries production of raw materials in the New World using slave labour had to be stepped up. More fields were opened, and better methods of production had to be introduced to meet raw materials demand that was building up in the European industries. Expansion and opening of new fields would not be possible without increasing the scale of slave trade business. Land in the New World was there in plenty. That was why new fields were being opened up. But that opening of new fields would not make sense without greater supply of labour. The next input to industrial production was labour, which was not readily available. So, the demand for more African slaves got built up. The best reliable source of slaves was West Africa. So, as demand for raw materials increased; it boosted the slave trade business on the Atlantic. Slave trade grew up by way of capturing and transporting the human merchandise from West Africa to the Caribbean and also to other American markets for operating in the raw materials production fields.

The transatlantic trade involved not only African slaves but also minerals such as, gold, diamonds; such as ivory and all sorts of other natural resources that could be got from Africa. In short, the more Europe made advancements through industrial revolution the more Africa got exploited though slave trade and exploitation of other natural resources, and thus the more Africa became poor. The plundering and devastations that were being caused by both buying human merchandise and the plundering of resources moved the African continent to the brims of devastation and vulnerability. Europe kept growing rich and Africa kept sinking deeper into the ditch of poverty.

Transatlantic slave trade became a pillar for the sustainability of industrial production in Europe. The mass production that the industries were making led to higher demand for raw materials. The raw materials production needed cheap labour to make their supply cope with the ever-growing industrial demand. What it means is that the industrial revolution stimulated demand for more African slaves who were needed in the raw materials production fields in the Caribbean and the Americas. Industrial revolution further served as a stimulant for imperial expansion especially to Africa and Asia, where the potential for more raw materials as well as new markets, existed.

So, as the industrial growth increased, Europe became economically wealthier than any other place in the world. This does not mean that Europe would not have industrialized without the presence of Africa. To the contrary, Europe had a chance to make best use of other continents such as Asia and South America. But those sources proved to be rather expensive and less profitable because of distance and less chances of getting cheaper labour to exploit than Africans. For instance far-east Asia was long way away from Europe compared to Africa, which was relatively quite near. The other thing is that it is difficult to contemplate how it would have worked if Europe failed to access slave trade business from West Africa, from where slaves that were sent to work in the raw-materials fields in the Americas were found. It is necessary to remind again here that with the industrial revolution, Cottage industries were pushed to the brink of extinction. Mass- produced goods ended up to be cheaper, faster to produce and more affordable. Furthermore, industrialization transformed economies that had been based on agriculture and handicrafts to economies based on large-scale industry, mechanized manufacturing, labour specialization, technological innovations, and the factory system.

Working labour conditions during the revolution remained very poor and, in some cases, very horrific. The shift from cottage to big, automated industries brought about changes in culture as people moved from rural areas where job opportunities were becoming less and less to urban areas where more and more job opportunities were being created in the industries. Industrial sites, even those in the remote areas developed into urban centres as the population kept moving to those points seeking for jobs. As more and more people moved from the rural areas to the cities, increased workforce and the demand for efficiency and hence mass production led to important outcomes such as those related to the division of labour, which meant that a worker specialized in performing one task that was part of a larger series of tasks. At the end, a product got more efficiently produced. As labour got divided amongst workers, they were able to focus on a few or even one task. The more they focused on a task, the more efficient they became at that specific task, which meant that less time and less money was spent in producing a product.

However, this brings us to the issue of imperialism, colonialism and partitioning of Africa. In the early years of 19th century slave trade abolition campaign was gaining steam. The supply of raw material to European industries was getting threatened. Supply from America became threatened because of slave trade abolition campaigns, which intensified towards the closing years of 18th century, and which would certainly limit supply of slaves from Africa. Actually, the slave trade on the Atlantic was brought to an end with the British Enactment of Slave Trade Abolition Act in 1807. It was in that period Europe's attention started to be completely drawn to Africa for production and direct supply of raw materials to Europe. Clearly the New World had also begun to be too far way as source of raw materials for Europe. It was becoming obvious that if production of raw materials could be done a shorter distance from America chances of reducing costs of production and supply could be done more efficiently and more viably.

The above stated situation made the appetite for colonialization of Africa to be more real. That appetite led to the start of journeys of exploration, aimed to find out how it was in the interior of Africa. The reports of explorers quickly led to the scramble and ultimately to the partitioning of Africa. It is easy to see the close relationship that was being cultivated between industrial production in Europe and the scramble for Africa. Europe had the ambition of now getting raw materials in a more efficient and cost-effective way; both of which issues called for speed in colonization of Africa. Soon after the Berlin conference that took place in 1885-1886 colonial officers and businesses and institutions got encouraged to have their approval for full presence in their new African colonies.

The colonial agencies and businesses did not find it hard to get the amount of land and labour that they needed to facilitate production. Through enforcement of colonial rules and laws Africans were forced to let their fertile land taken away by the colonial investors. The Africans were also forced to work in those farms without deserving wages.

In the meanwhile, Africa kept on being devastated. The demand for more raw materials kept on increasing and production kept growing using African forced labour. Africans were pushed to the marginal land and in many cases to landlessness as they paved the way for colonial land users to come and operate. The laws kept being reviewed to enable the colonial enterprise to flourish. What became most surprising were the policies introduced by some colonial administrations, such as Germans, who prohibited Africans from involving in the growing of certain cash crops, such as coffee. So, coffee became an exclusive crop for white settlers. The explanation given for the prohibition to grow coffee was that Africans involvement could lead to lowering the grade of coffee in the world market. The implication was that even with the provision of extension services African had no brains and capacity that could enable them to get involved in the production of the desired high-quality coffee.

However, Africans secretly kept watching how Europeans cared for their coffee plantations and they also secretly started growing coffee trees inside their banana groves. The results of the attempt became exemplary; though illegal. That situation made the European farmers to illegally keep buying the coffee produced by Africans at very exploitative low price. That process made the European farmers very rich, because they were getting huge amounts of coffee from Africans who did not know the true price of coffee and who also were doing the production illegally.

In Europe the Industrial revolution brought about sweeping changes in economic and social organization. The changes included a wider distribution of wealth and increased international trade. Managerial hierarchies also developed to oversee the division of labour. Those were good results. But there were also bad results. While these results could have benefited Africa from where raw materials were being imported but at some point, of that chain Africans were cut off, hence perpetuating exploitation of African and Africa in particular.

In other words, the industrial revolution caused a lot of negative results on Europe- on Europeans, as well as outside Europe and globally. The problems included those of poor working conditions, poor living conditions, low wages, child labour, and pollution locally and across the borders of Europe. In as far as the poor working and living conditions were concerned workers were often housed in cramped, grossly inadequate quarters. Employers paid attention to increasing production and maximizing profits, not on the workers working conditions or the workers welfare. Working conditions were difficult and exposed employees to many risks and dangers, including cramped work areas with poor ventilation, trauma from machinery, toxic exposures to heavy metals, dust, and solvents. Resulting from those poor work and living conditions the workers got introduced to various types of diseases such as cholera, tuberculosis, lung cancer and many others. Many people died following those diseases attacks. As contact of Europeans with Africans in Africa increased some diseases and others such as tuberculosis (TB) the diseases got exported to Africa.

At the global level, industrial revolution caused a lot of harm to the environment. It put to risk the general safety of human beings, especially in as far as global health hazards were concerned. For Africa in particular the industrial revolution became the beginning of long lasting African developmental stagnation. Like it has been hinted the industrial revolution was done with a high level of impunity for Africa and Africans. Africa started to suffer the negative impact of the revolution the first day industrial revolution started in Europe. Take the example of the Triangle Slave Trade that was enhanced by there being high demand for raw materials in the ever-growing manufacturing in Europe.

During the transatlantic slave trade period family life in Africa got greatly impaired especially when members of a family got forcefully captured and sold to foreigners marking the end of family union. Africans in villagers kept away from working on the land for their own subsistence due to fear of being attacked and made victims of slave hunters. The trade made Africans to live a life of distrust to foreigners. The slave hunting and the trading that went with them were not confined to the capturing and trading on human beings for slaves, but also any other natural resources that the traders could spot. The heavy loads of other products that the slave traders found in the course of slave hunting or transportation to the coastal sale points were carried by the victims who walked the African jungles barefooted on paths that were full of poisonous thorns, snakes, and dangerous wild animals. The whole of West African interior became tumultuous and unsafe because the slave trade had triggered the spread of slave hunters in all parts of the region from the Northwest in the Senegambia down south to as far as Angola in the Southwest. The atrocities caused by slave hunters made foreigners on the African soil to be dreaded by the Africans.

The slave trade abolition and the scramble for Africa ironically became a booster to industrialization in Europe. As industrialization kept on promoting European economies, it at the same time served as a strong under developer of African economies and people. As colonization picked up momentum, more and more African land was taken away by European colonial investors to expand raw materials production. The major crops that were produced in such fields included, wheat, rice, cotton, sisal, oil seeds, sugar, coffee, and cocoa. More and more unpaid African labour was demanded to meet the requirement of the expanding fields for raw materials production..

Furthermore, the industrial revolution had many effects some of which caused long term negative impacts on Africa. The revolution impacted the environment. The world saw a major increase in population. Europe saw a great increase in living standards, but as far as Africa was concerned it led to the depletion of natural resources and stagnation of African development as a whole. The use of chemicals and fuel in European factories resulted in increased air and water pollution exacerbated by increased use of fossil fuels. The industries led to warming that spread to the rest of the world. In as far as the families were concerned the industrial revolution caused disturbance and pain.

To be fair we should say that while industrial revolution in Europe led to economic stagnation to African people, but Europeans too had their share of drawbacks. For instance, while before industrial revolution the cottage type of industrial units had been family based business (which brought the whole family together), but with rise of the industrial revolution the impact brought large scale production, which further led to specialization and to elimination of family ties; as members of the family had to work in different sections or units, or locations far away from each other; thus for the first time tearing the European families apart. Working hours became longer which made family life difficult to sustain. In factories, coal mines and other workplaces, people worked long hours in miserable conditions. Like has been hinted, the workers were paid low wages that barely allowed them to afford the cost of living associated with basic needs such as rent, food and others. What is being said here is that industrial revolution had negative impact to Europe as well. But the difference between the negative impact of Europe and Africa is that for Europe the revolution ended up boosting the European economies as well as the welfare of European people. In Africa it was the opposite. Africa was left devastated, people were left poorer, the environment got polluted and there was no improvement in people's welfare left behind.

7
THE HORRIFIC TRANSATLANTIC SLAVE TRADE

The Euro-American also known as Atlantic or Transatlantic slave trade was a slave trade that involved the transportation of enslaved Africans people from the West coast of Africa mainly to the Caribbean or Americas. The slave trade regularly used the triangular trade route and its middle passage. The trade started in a big way in the 16th century and went on until the 19th century. It led to a major economic development of both the Americas and Europe; but it marked the beginning of the great underdevelopment of Africa. The trade depended on the horrific treatment of enslaved humans whose violence and scale exceeded any other known instance of slavery in history. The early process of the slave trade will not be discussed in details here because the previous chapters have also delt with the subject in quite an extensive way.

However, following the colonialization of the New World, the Europeans took steps that would lead to fundamental changes in the political, social, economic, and cultural makeup of the New world. The consequences of some of these changes crossed oceans to impact the lives and livelihoods of people worldwide. The leading steps or change that came to serve as one of the most glaring example was the effect of the enslavement of humans from Africa; whose result has been described by some history scholars as an

African holocaust and a crime against humanity24. The trade marked an African historical landmark of its own kind.

The slave trade became unique within the universal history of slavery for four main reasons; first, the duration of the slave trade was long (lasting for a little more than three centuries); secondly, it coincided with the beginning of the first industrial revolution; thirdly, those victimized were mainly the black African men, women and children; fourthly, it led to great depopulation and devastation of African natural resources including human beings, wild life and minerals; fifthly, this European trade in slaves was unique and the use of slaves was also very unique.

It is commonly hypothesized that higher cognitive abilities promote racial tolerance and a greater commitment to racial equality, but an alternative theoretical framework contends that higher cognitive abilities merely enable members of a dominant racial group to articulate a more refined legitimizing ideology for racial inequality. According to this perspective, ideological refinement occurs in response to shifting patterns of racial conflict and is characterized by rejection of overt prejudice, superficial support for racial equality in principle, and opposition to policies that challenge the dominant group's status. This study estimates the impact of verbal ability on a comprehensive set of racial attitudes, including anti-black prejudice, views about black-white equality in principle, and racial policy support. It also investigates cohort differences in the effects of verbal ability on these attitudes. Results suggest that high-ability whites are less likely than low-ability whites to report prejudicial attitudes and more likely to support

---

[24] *Jake Thurman: The Transatlantic Slave Trade; Khan Academy*

racial equality in principle. Despite these liberalizing effects, high-ability whites are no more likely to support a variety of remedial policies for racial inequality. Results also suggest that the ostensibly liberalizing effects of verbal ability on anti-black prejudice and views about racial equality in principle emerged slowly over time, consistent with ideological refinement theory.

Keywords: racial attitudes, prejudice, affirmative action, group conflict, verbal ability

As a commercial and economic enterprise, the slave trade provided a good example of the consequences resulting from particular intersections of history and geography. It involved several regions and continents: Africa, America, the Caribbean, Europe, and the Middle East region. Entities directly involved in the trade included, governments, religious agencies (Christians and non-Christians), and individual entrepreneurs. The slave trade, which lasted from the 16th to the 19th century, constituted one of the greatest tragedies in the history of humanity in terms of scale, duration, and practice. Actually, the Europe- America slave trade has come to be rated the biggest deportation in history and a determining factor in the world economy of the 18th century. Millions of Africans were torn from their homes, deported to the American continent, and sold as slaves. The principles in the trade were European governments and businesses.

The Portuguese were pioneers in slave trading in the 16th Century. Local African slave hunters went to villages or community areas and either negotiated with chiefs of the area or just went to battles against local people with a view of capturing people who then got ferried to the coastal ports where they got auctioned to European traders, who in turn shipped the slaves to Europe. By the early 16th Century as much as 10% of the population of Lisbon was of African descent, which implies that the trade business with Africa had existed for quite a lot longer.

Earlier, i.e., in the period before 16th century many of those early African captives were transported on land across the Sahara and Mediterranean Sea to European countries especially those in close proximity to Mediterranean Sea, including Portugal and Spain. The trade across the Sahara was mainly done by Arab traders to North Africa and on across the Mediterranean to Europe. In those early times there were also slaves that were got from the East Africa especially the coastal areas and Indian Ocean coastal ports, from where they were shipped to the Persian Gulf where they got ready markets, while others were taken westward to European markets. Like the trans-Saharan slave trade, the slaves got from East Africa were a business of Arab slave traders. Clearly, for the whole period up to the 19th century Africa became a hunting ground for slaves that were sold to the Americas, Europe, and Middle East.

That brings us to what has come to be termed 'Triangular Trade' as opposed to the 'Middle Pass trade'. Triangle trade or Triangular trade meant the same thing. It was a historical term indicating trade among three ports or regions. In brief, the trade connected the economies of three continents, Africa, Europe, and America. It is estimated that over 40 million people, (men, women, and children), were deported from their homes and sold as slaves in the different slave trading systems. In the transatlantic slave trade alone the estimate of those deported is believed to be almost 35 million. This figure excludes those who died in the interior of Africa in the violence that led to slave capture, those that died when being transported to buying points on the coastal ports, and deaths of those on aboard the slave ships.

The triangle trade proceeded in such a way that the ships left Western Europe for Africa loaded with goods that were to be exchanged for slaves. The goods imported from Europe for exchange for slaves would include guns, gunpowder, cowries, textiles, pearls, beads, and other manufactured goods. These goods would be exchanged in the African ports for slaves, ivory, and minerals such as gold and diamonds. The African coastal ports were the key points of transactions.

There were quite a number of ports for that purpose along the West African coastline, which spread from Senegal in the North-West to as far south as Congo and Angola. In those ports the European buyers would keep on the wait for the slaves to be brought from the interior by African slavers. Initially most slave traders in the interior of Africa were Africans. The slaves that were taken to the sell points in the coastal points also served as the carriers of other goods like ivory that the slavers would sell to the Europeans that waited for the merchandise to be brought from the interior.

An important point to note is that on the slaves' arrival in the African coasts the captains would not necessarily be able to immediately get enough cargo especially slaves to fill their ships. In that case they would have to keep on the wait until more consignments arrived from the interior. The exchange process usually took a fairly long time ranging from one week to several months. During that period of waiting the slaves that had arrived and bought by European traders were kept in fortified places where mistreatments and various types of abuses started to be executed those who supervised the strongholds.

Next came the shipment process, which was a real heart-breaking moment as the slaves saw their fellow Africans moving freely in the close proximity to the anchored ships. After the shipment the process that involved the sailing across the Atlantic started. The voyage would cover a distance of up to almost 10,000 km. from the East to the West side of Atlantic. African slave commodity was taken to the Caribbean or to the Americas, where they found a ready market immediately the ship arrived in a port in America. Like has been hinted, the slaves were badly needed for use in farms in many parts of North and South America. The arrival in Americas made the end of the second leg of the triangle.

The third part of the triangle was the connection trips from America to Europe. In these connection trips the slave traders brought back to Europe mostly agricultural products, produced by slave labour. The main products brought to Europe included sugar, and also cotton, coffee, tobacco, oil seeds and rice. These were badly needed in the industries and also by other consumers in Europe. The circuit from Europe via Africa and America back to Europe could take up to 24 months.

However, the circuit could take the opposite direction. For instance, most of the British ships went to Africa where they bought slaves and other merchandise, transported them to Europe (thus finishing the first side of the triangle) where they off loaded the ships and sold the merchandise to other traders who loaded their ships ready for trips across the Atlantic to the Americas (finishing the second side of the triangle). After selling their human merchandise in America they in exchange got the goods that they felt were in high demand in the African coastal ports. Such goods included sugarcane liquors, molasses, guns, and cloth. The merchandise that was got from America would be brought to the African coastal ports where they got exchanged for slaves, (thus finishing the third side of the triangle) and then took the slaves to Europe, thus completing this circuit; and the process went on.

The movement was usually slow, especially for the Middle route or passage i.e., from Africa to America, because the transporters wished to see the ships carrying as many slaves as possible, which was made possible only by often removing the ship's steerage. Spain, Portugal, the Netherlands, Britain, and France, were the main triangular trading countries in this arrangement) while Spain, Portugal, the Netherlands, and France were the main users of the middle passage.

We said that the trade went on for three centuries, from 16th century to 19th Century. However, by the year 1480s, some European nations had been in that business for much longer. For instance, by the middle of 1470s Portuguese ships were already busy transporting African slaves for sale in the sugar plantations in the Cape Verde and Madeira Island in the Eastern Atlantic. Spanish conquistadors took African slaves to the Caribbean after 1500, but Portuguese merchants continued to dominate the transatlantic slave trade for another century and a half, operating from their bases in the Congo-Angola area along the west coast of Africa. The Dutch on the other hand became the foremost slave traders during parts of the 1600s, and in the following century. Then the English and French merchants started to control the slave business. They controlled about half of the transatlantic slave trade, taking a large percentage of their human cargo from the region of West Africa between the Senegal and Niger rivers.

As shown above no more than a few hundred thousand Africans were taken to the Americas before 1600. But by 1600 slave labour demand rose sharply with the growth of sugar plantations in the Caribbean and tobacco plantations in the Chesapeake region in North America. The largest number of slaves was taken to the Americas during the 18th century, in which case it is estimated that, nearly three-fifths of the total volume of the transatlantic slave trade took place.

The triangle slave trade had very devastating effects in Sub-Saharan Africa. Economic incentives for warlords and tribes to engage in the slave trade promoted an atmosphere of lawlessness and violence. Depopulation and a continuing fear of captivity made African economic and agricultural development almost impossible throughout much of western Africa. A large percentage of the people taken captive were women in their childbearing years and young men who normally would have been starting families. The European slave dealers usually were very selective, usually leaving behind persons who were elderly, disabled, or otherwise dependent—groups who were least able to contribute to the economic health of their societies. The demand was for healthy and enduring slaves who could survive the havocs of transportation on board ships on the Atlantic and also those who showed they were physically strong enough to endure the tough time that lay ahead of them. The slaves were always in chains; and the chains were so much of a burden that, most of them weighed up to 10kg.

The Spanish were the pioneers to make the first move of transporting African slaves to the Americas. They took the first African captives to the Americas from Europe as early as 1503. However, by 1518 the shipping of the captives from West African coast direct to America began. Many slaves on board the slave ships died because the long distance, nature of ships that were used to transports slaves, harshness of those who supervised shipments, almost absence of any medical services, inadequate nutrition, and absence of sanitary facilities. Those who died just got thrown into the sea to become food for the Atlantic Ocean fish.

Shipment of African slaves to the Americas is recorded with the arrival of the first captives to Jamestown in 1619. That marked the beginning of African black people slavery in America; though in reality enslaved Africans arrived in North America as early as 1500. The arrival of African slaves in Jamestown set the stage for slavery in North America. In August 1619, 20 Angolan captives, kidnapped by the Portuguese arrived in the British colony of Virginia and got bought by the British colonialists. By that year, i.e.1619 the Virginian colony had become home to about 700 Africans from West Africa. Like we have shown above and also basing on the studies made on the initial shipments across the Atlantic, it is clear that the journeys were very tough and disastrous. Most victims (almost 50%) on board the slave ships died before reaching the destinations in the Americas.

It is estimated that transatlantic slave trade reached its peak in the 1780s. On average close to 80,000 enslaved Africans were sent to the Americas each year of that decade. As would be expected, most of those slaves were got from West Africa. East Africa was a late participant in the transatlantic slave trade. It was only in the 1770s that a regular trade in slaves to the French islands of Mauritius and Réunion began from points on the East African coast. But, a small numbers of slaves from East coast of Africa had been carried around the Cape for more than a century, though very little is so far recorded about it.

While East Africa was a late participant in the transatlantic slave trade, but even the supply to places elsewhere was not as strong as was the case in West Africa. For instance it was only in the 1770s that a regular trade in slaves to the French islands of Mauritius and Reunion began from points on the South East African coast. But as planters on St Domingue cried out for labour, this trade became more profitable and systematic, particularly as the French government agreed to subsidised the shipment of slaves to the island.

West-Central Africa bore the brunt of this demand. But generally, the price of slaves from Eastern Africa kept on rising, and so traders looked further afield for their human merchandise. Although it took around 120 days to get from Mozambique to St Domingue, and almost 30% of slaves died on this long Middle Passage, with time it gradually became a profitable route. The practice was such that ships sailed from French ports such as Bordeaux and Nantes to buy slaves in Southeast Africa. The slaves were then taken to St Domingue and exchanged for tropical produce like sugar, coffee and indigo. The size and number of these vessels grew in the 1780s and some had the capacity to carry up to 1000 slaves.

By the closing of the 18th century, ship rebellions were frequent and slave ships carried large crews and the firearms needed to suppress any resistance. The Southeast Africa slave trade reached its peak around 1790 when about 46 ships, carrying more than 16,000 slaves, circumnavigated the Cape. Almost all were bound for the sugar and coffee plantations of northern St Domingue. Many French slavers stopped at the Cape during this time as the colony run by the Dutch East India Company provided them with a break in the long Middle Passage. Ship's captains often sold part of their human cargo at the Cape to rid them of slaves least able to survive the Atlantic crossing. It also made space for new stocks of fresh food and water.

However, in the early years of the transatlantic slave trade, the Portuguese generally purchased Africans who had been captured during intertribal wars, and then taken by African slave agents to the coastal points of sale, where they got sold to European slave traders. As the demand for slaves grew, the Portuguese began to enter the interior of Africa to forcibly take captives. But for most other European traders they generally remained on the coast and purchased captives from Africans who had got and transported them from the interior.

Generally, the Middle Passage was notorious for its brutality and for the overcrowded, unsanitary conditions on slave ships, in which hundreds of Africans were packed tightly into tiers below decks for a voyage of more than 8,000 km. They were typically chained together, and usually the low ceilings did not permit them to sit upright. The heat was intolerable, and the oxygen levels were so low that candles would not burn. However, crews feared insurrection. So, the black slaves were allowed to go outside on the upper decks for only a few hours each day.

As the slave trade business kept on growing large cargo ships got converted to slave ships. Even with those developments it is estimated that between 15% and 25% of the African slaves bound for the Americas died aboard slave ships.

Atrocities and sexual abuse of the enslaved people were widespread aboard the slave ships, although their money value as slaves was considered to be marginal. The abuses were not considered to be of much significance compared to what they were considered to be worth. Often the slaves were thrown overboard in situations where there was either urgency such as out-break of an epidemic that affected the slaves as well as the crew. In such situation the captives would have to carry the brunt of any such mishap or any matter of urgency on board. A number of the slaves would usually be thrown overboard. Despite the fact that such action was actually murder, it was a decision made singly by the captain. In many instances of epidemics captains allowed the slaves to be thrown overboard, although ultimately the captains went to file claims for compensation of the loss incurred.

In some occasions, the African captives successfully revolted and took over the ships. There were actually cases of slaves, who had some prior skills, revolted, and succeeded in the attempt. A case has been given of what happened of an incidence that occurred when in 1839 a slave named Joseph Cinque led a mutiny of some 50 illegally purchased slaves on the Spanish slave ship, killing the captain and two members of the crew. The accounts have it that the U.S. Supreme Court eventually ordered the Africans to be returned to their homes.

Slave ships were large cargo ships specially converted for the purpose of transporting slaves. Such ships were also known as "Guinea- men" because their trade involved trafficking to and from the Guinea coast in West Africa. The price of a slave at the other end would depend upon the physical appearance of each individual slave. The weaker, including the sick and the less enduring slaves were not spared, as they were a cost to the owners; these were shot and thrown into the sea to avoid further inconvenience and cost. The owners of slave ships held as many enslaved people as possible by cramming, chaining, and selectively grouping slaves to maximize space and make travel more profitable.

Slaves on board were in almost all cases highly underfed. The treatment was so brutal that it caused many slaves to die even before arriving at their destination. Dead or dying slaves were dumped overboard. In the absence of better words to express the scenes, it is only enough to say those victims were not treated as human beings; they were handled like worthless animals throughout their long voyage to the New World. While it took several months to complete the journey, the enslaved people stayed naked and shackled together with several different types of chains, stored on the floor beneath bunks with little or no room to move due to the cramped conditions.

Some captains would assign Slave Guardians to watch over and keep the other slaves in check. They spent a large portion of time pinned to floorboards that would wear skin on their elbows down to the bone. In some cases, especially in as far as the British Ships were concerned the government regulated the loading of the ships via a legislative instrument, but it is difficult to say how far the laws were enforced. In as far as the ships were concerned, the loading was regulated via an Act of Parliament known as Dolben's Act[25]. The Act placed limitations of the number of people that British slave ships could transport, related to tonnage.

The other dimension was with regard to the sailors. As a rule, the sailors were very cruel and very callous. However, they too suffered a lot in the hands of their bosses. In the 18th and early 19th centuries, the sailors on slave ships were often poorly paid and subjected to brutal discipline and treatment. Furthermore, crew mortality rate of around 20% became a usual thing during a voyage, with sailors dying as a result of diseases, flogging or slave uprisings, which were common features. For instance, there was a rebellion in 1764 when a slave ship-"Hope", with slaves in the hold, forced their way on deck twice, killing nine crew members before eventually

---

[25] *British Slave Trade Act of 1788,*

being seized by Spanish forces. The most famous revolt at sea took place on the Spanish slave ship "Amistad" in 1839. It involved black African slave victims that were being shipped out of Cuba.

While the crew too faced hard time on board the slave ships, but theirs had no comparison with the sufferance sustained by the slaves who were always crammed at any place that could hold them while always in chain, and without enough to eat. The hardships that the crew faced made them to remain harsher to the slaves on board. It made them to starve the slave victims and denied them any possibility for fresh air. Those hardships made more slaves to die. The conflicts on board the slave ships added to the high-rate deaths of slaves as well as the crew that often had to live and sleep without shelter on the open deck for the entirety of the Atlantic voyage due to the fact that the space below deck was packed with slaves.

Slave ships were designed and equipped to deal with African slaves resistance. From the earliest days of the trade, it was obvious that African captives, terrified though they were, would seize any opportunity to free themselves. Africans sought to escape even before they reached the coast, running away from their captors when possible. On board a ship, however, escape became more difficult. While the slave ship was anchored on the coast, European sailors loaded captives sporadically until the ship was filled, or it was time to sail.

The slave ship crew separated the men from the women and children when they were detained in the forts, castles, and coastal barracoons and this process of separating captives by gender continued on the slave ships.. It was then that the crew used chains, manacles, and padlocks to shackle mainly the adult males, who were placed in batches and locked below decks as the number of captive victims increased. In some way the women and children had more freedom of movement and were not shackled together unless they formed a threat to the crew.

The Middle [26]Passage served not only to erase a slave's sense of human dignity, but the journey also wiped away the collective knowledge and cultural history of those captured. Before boarding a slave ship, captives were stripped of any physical connections to their past lives, their heads were shaved, and their clothing and adornments removed. Denying captives these personal and cultural identifiers began the process by which slaves were systematically dehumanized. Once aboard the slave ship, this practice continued. Women in particular were subjected to brutal rapes and sexual abuse during their journey; many women arrived at the shores of the New World carrying the children of their abusers. Although women were frequent victims of sexual abuse, it is important to be careful not to view them solely through the lens of victimization. Women frequently resisted their sexual and reproductive oppression through the acts of abortion and infanticide. For instance, there were instances of women who used their sexual capital to improve their circumstances; this was particularly true in colonies with high Creole populations, such as Barbados.

Mutiny was not uncommon aboard slave ships and so to protect themselves against the threat of insurrection, ship captains typically kept male captives in chains and below deck at all times. Women, on the other hand, were commonly provided more liberties; typically left unchained, they were often allowed to remain above deck, sometimes even permitted to move about freely. This limited amount of freedom provided women opportunities to

---

26

communicate with the males and organize. It was actually women who planned, organized, and facilitated many of the slave uprisings that occurred during the transatlantic Passage.

Because of the demand for field labourers men constituted up to two-thirds of the captive victims taken from the African coast – although this ratio varied widely depending on geography. In the Senegambia region, this high demand for male slaves meant that men and boys were taken from all over the region, their ethnicities, languages, and cultures varying widely. Conversely, a large majority of female slaves from the Senegambia region were plucked from easily accessed coastal towns; they were primarily of Wolof[27] origins and would have been able to connect with each other through a shared language and culture. These women were in some way crucial in maintaining their community's cultural identity and history.

---

[27] The **Wolof** are the major ethnic **group** in Senegal. They are very influential culturally and politically. The earliest Portuguese explorers in the fifteenth century

8

ZANZIBAR: THE SLAVE TRADE HUB OF EASTERN AFRICA

There is no way one can talk about slave trade in East Africa or the Great Lakes region without some reference to Zanzibar and its slave trade business. Actually, Zanzibar was the centre point or hub for all slave trade business that took place in the Great Lakes region. Being an archipelago in the Indian Ocean Zanzibar became the safest place for keeping and auctioning slaves captured and brought from the interior of East and central Africa. Here is where the sorting out, (to get slaves that could fetch good prices in the foreign markets) was done. So most of foreign slave trade dealers went to Zanzibar to buy slaves. Following the auctioning that went on the lowest priced or those that did not get buyers were left behind for use in spices farms and in the construction works within the island of Zanzibar.

The history of Zanzibar has for many years remained complicated for many reasons. In the days before the arrival of the Omani Sultans-way back in the 16th century, Zanzibar was a place occupied by only black Africans. In those early times the whole East African coastline was occupied by Swahili[28] peasants and fishermen who did the fishing using simple canoes that could not get too far to high seas, meaning that the fishing was done only a short distance from the seashore and generally only for subsistence. From 16th century

---

[28] *The Wolof are the major ethnic group in Senegal. They are very influential culturally and politically. The earliest Portuguese explorers in the fifteenth century*

foreigners, mainly Arabs from Oman came to the Eastern coast of Africa. The trade that they carried out was basically barter trade. The local people offered gold and ivory. The Arabs, besides buying ivory, minerals, and other valuable items they also got slaves that they captured or were sold to them by the Swahili coastal dwellers. The slaves that the Africans sold to the Arabs were those that were got from intertribal wars or villagers that were found working in their gardens or young men that were ambushed when looking after their livestock's that were feeding in the surrounding forests or grasslands.

That is how slave trade started in this Eastern part of Africa. In the beginning the slaves were used to build garrisons and cities in the coastal cities that the Arabs started to build. The cities included Mafia, Kilwa, and Sofala. Some of those cities, Kilwa and Sofala for instance, grew to be big and very famous and became known in many parts of the medieval time world. However, the growth of those cities did not take long before they collapsed towards the beginning of the 18th century.

From the 16th Century and may be before that period, Zanzibar came under the foreign rulers. Like we have rushed to say, the rulers were Arabs from Oman. Before the Arab occupation Zanzibar was entirely occupied by black Africans. Arabs arrival on Zanzibar used the superior arms they had to hunt down and attack the Africans, and used them as their slaves, both within the island and in the other coastal cities that they started to build. Due to the Arab slave trade power on the Indian Ocean, the archipelago came under the rule of the Sultanate of Oman. The Omani rulers converted any black person found in the archipelago a slave. Gradually the whole coast of East Africa came under the monopoly of Arabs in terms of trading operations and ownership of the region. There were a few

Swahili people who succeeded to build trade relation with the Arabs. These were those Africans that involved in trading along the coast, but their role remained insignificant.

Traditionally the Swahili people that lived along the coastal areas were petty fishermen who did the fishing using tree logs made canoes, which allowed for fishing only close to the seashore, as the canoes were not strong enough to go further into the deeper sea. Occasionally the Swahili traders also went some distance to the interior, captured fellow Africans and brought them to the coast and sold the victims to Arab slave traders. The Swahilis also brought other merchandise like ivory, gold and other tradable items from the interior and sold them to the Arab traders. In that situation Slave trade became a preoccupation of both Swahili and Arab Slave traders. Time came when Arab slave traders joined hands with rich African traders who together moved into the interior of the Great Lakes, actually they brought them to Zanzibar for an auction.

Unfortunately, even the Swahili traders were at times victims of the Arab traders. The Arab slave hunters were lucky because they usually possessed guns, which they used in slave hunting battles. All the slaves that were got in the interior of East Africa were carried to Zanzibar where they got auctioned in the slave market. Zanzibar grew to be a major hub for collection, auctioning, and export of slaves from East and central Africa to Persian Gulf, Middle East, Ottoman Empire, Egypt, and Asia including India.

---

[1] *Swahili were an African people that came from various coastal areas and gradually developed a language that was a combination of the various tribes and Arabic.*

Following the sorting and auctioning of slaves, that was done in Zanzibar only those slaves that were considered the best in terms of their physical features were earmarked and bought for export. Those who failed to be bought in the Zanzibar slave market were retained and got used in the various sectors that formed the economy of Zanzibar. However, the selection or the sorting out to get the most suitable slaves was not an easy task. The sorting was done by way of whipping that was done using strong dry rhinoceros skin whips that once the lashing was executed on human flesh it cut deep into the flesh, causing a line of bleeding flesh that looked like a cutting or wound made by a butcher's knife. The whipping was meant to test the mettle of a slave. Those who did not cry while being whipped were considered to be strong enough to qualify for sale to slave buyers for export.

The slave market is another thing that may need further description or discretion. In short it was just an open-air market place. There was a big tree in the middle of that area; the tree was used as a whipping post and the slaves were brought to that point from their imprisonment chambers; which were another awful place. However, coming to the market before being auctioned was just a procedure to have their health tested, and that is what was done by whipping. Whether a slave was physically seen to be strong or weak he would have to pass the whipping test under the big tree. As the whipping went on anyone who showed the sign of crying, made the price to go down because that was an indicator that the person was weak. Those who did not cry were considered to be strong and that made their price to go up. The fit ones were sold and shipped to Arabia, India, the Ottoman Empire, Egypt and even to the Americas.

The permanent slave market started in Zanzibar from around 1500 and continued to operate till 1873 when it was closed. In 1879 the British Missionaries built the Christ Church Cathedral at the site of the slave market. Today the place where the Cathedral stands is the most impressive and significant marker of what occurred at this place.

It is estimated that between 1830 and 1873 around 600,000 people were sold as merchandise. In the 19th century as many as 45,000 slaves were passing through the slave markets of Zanzibar each year. Estimates made regarding the deaths that took place each year before ever reaching the island of Zanzibar was about 80,000. Putting into account those who were brought to Zanzibar and then exported to Persia and Asia, plus those who died during slave hunting wars and also those who died on the way from points of capture to Zanzibar and also those who were retained in Zanzibar to work in the farms and in the construction sites of slavers, the total could reach more than 130, 000 slaves, annually.

For many centuries Arabs had grown to be notorious slave traders on the Indian Ocean; actually, they monopolized trade and controlled most of the Eastern coast of Africa long before Vasco da Gama circumnavigated the Cape of Good Hope. Arabs had been trading in slaves albeit in smaller scales; the slaves were got from the Eastern coast of Africa perhaps even long before the triangle slave trade started. Till the time of occupation by kings/sultans of Oman the population of Zanzibar had remained scanty, and almost all of the occupants of the archipelago were basically of African origin.

However, it is easy for people to ask why Zanzibar grew to be such a strategic place that turned it to be a hub for slaves got from East and Central Africa. The answer is that it was very uniquely located in terms of safety and security due to factors such as its difficult position to be easily approached by enemies. An enemy could easily be seen from afar which made it relatively easy to get repulsed before he came too close to the Island. The other factor was that it was a good place for anchoring ships that came to the east coast to load slaves; thirdly it was a very short distance from the continental ports. The slaves were brought from the inland of the mainland places to the coastal ports of Bagamoyo, Mombasa and others on the East African coastline and once a slave got in, there was no easy way of escaping because being an archipelago each island was surrounded by sea water. Due to those factors, Zanzibar became a heaven for stay by the Omani rulers. It was a place of high security locational position.

The history of Zanzibar earnestly started when the archipelago became a base for traders voyaging between the African Great Lakes and the coast. From Zanzibar the slaves got shipped through the Somalian peninsula, the Arabian Peninsula, Iran, and the Indian subcontinent. Unguja, (the largest island) also popularly known as Zanzibar offered a protected and defensible harbour, so, although the archipelago had few products of value, Omanis and Yemenis settled in what became Zanzibar city (Stone Town) as a convenient point from which to trade with mainland coastal towns on the Swahili coast. They established garrisons on the coastal islands and built the first mosques in the region.

Now let's say something in regard to the beauty of the archipelago. Western visitors to some points near the Zanzibar Island during the period, described Stone Town as a fantastically beautiful place that was well equated with some Western urbanized developing centres. Adding to the beauty that were vviewed from some distance, the gleaming white minarets of mosques and the sultan's palaces in Stone Town, made the city appear to Westerners as an Orientalist fantasy brought to life. Ships that traversed the East Africa coast and had a long-distance view of Zanzibar always had a wish to visit the island and have a closer view of the capital of Stone Town. That fantasy or power or process of creating especially unrealistic or in probable mental image in response to psychology, needed an object of that fantasy. The images of fantasy lasted only for as long as the viewing was being done from a substantial distance.

Those who got a chance to get closer, described Stone Town as an extremely awful place. It was a foul-smelling city that reeked of human and animal excrement, garbage of various definitions, sewage, and bodies of animals and those of human beings, especially slaves that died every moment of the day. Stone town had no toilets, nor any running water and the population of the city eased themselves where they got space to do so. All the garbage including decomposing dead bodies of human beings, rats and mention it were all left out in the open to rot, each at its own pace. In other words, all those slaves that died daily in Zanzibar were not buried or disposed in any reasonable form such as by cremation, burial, or any other sensible way of disposing them, but were piled up in the rubbish heaps to decompose. That situation was not without horribly dangerous effects. Infectious diseases were a common thing that made death rates to be even higher especially among the slaves due to their weak health caused by gross under nutrition, dehydration, and complete absence of medical attention.

Zanzibar was a common transit point for foreigners especially the explorers and missionaries who wished to make expeditions to interior places of the Great Lakes. Here in Zanzibar is where the travelers or explorers got details of how to move into the interior from coastal towns such as Bagamoyo. Dr. David Livingstone who chanced to visit and live for a while in Stone Town in 1866 wrote in his diary: that "the stench arising from a mile and a half or two square miles of exposed sea beach, which was the general depository or damp of the filth of the town was most horrible". It was stinky and highly undwellable place. He thought Zanzibar could better be named "Stinkabar" rather than "Zanzibar". Being the place where the foreigners visited with a view to start their journeys to the interior regions, the explorers and missionaries got to Zanzibar with high hopes of finding an attractive place where they could stay and relax for a while before they took off to the main land ports and on to the interior. The rubbish in Stone Town turned out to be a demonstration of how the Arab rulers cared least about sanitation and hygiene in their surroundings. The human bodies of those who died after they had been brought to Zanzibar as slaves for auctioning were just left piled up and left rotting on open air heaps.

There were animal and human excrement found almost everywhere in stone Town, making the environment horribly bad. All these were sceneries beyond human description.

Besides for the pervasive foul odor of Stone Town, accounts by those who visited the place at that period described it as a city full of slaves on the brink of starvation and a place where cholera, malaria and venereal diseases all flourished. It was a place where one lived to see a real hell on earth. The place was full of slaves who came and got imprisoned in the slave holding chambers, which were horribly filthy and intolerably torturous. During the stay of slaves in these chambers they were always in chains, handcuffed and tethered on a pole of some sort. While the whole place in stone town was dirty and unhealthy, that did not cause any bother to the slavers, as they would keep moving about freely.

Of all the forms of economic activity in Zanzibar, slavery was the most profitable and was the mainstay of that Island economy. The vast majority of the blacks living on the island were either slaves taken from the interior parts of East and Central Africa or were descendants of the slaves got from various Islands of the archipelago in the Indian Ocean such as Zanzibar, Pemba, Mafia, and other coastal settlements or chieftains. The slaves were brought to Zanzibar in dhows. The dhows that brought slaves in and out of Zanzibar carried as many slaves as possible with no regard for comfort or safety. Many did not survive the journey to Zanzibar. However, for those who survived and got to Zanzibar, were immediately on arrival stripped completely naked, and then roughly cleaned and had their bodies smeared with coconut oil and forced to wear gold and silver bracelets bearing the name of the slave trader. This was not always the case but was necessary practice for those who were intended to fetch a good price. That temporary decoration was done especially for those who the slavers considered could fetch good price. As the time came for bringing them to the slave auction, the slaves were forced to march nude in a line down the streets of Stone Town guarded by loyal slaves of the slavers carrying swords or spears until someone showed interest in the procession.

Most astounding or astonishing was the way these marches were conducted and also how a buyer examined the slaves on display. The mouth and teeth were inspected, and afterwards every part of the body in succession, not even excepting the breasts, the other private parts of the girls, most of whom were handled in the most indecent manner in the public market by the purchasers. Then a slave would be required to walk or run a short distance on sharp and piercing stones, which were spread on the Stone town road to see if there was any defect on their feet. After the buyer had made his selections, and once the price was agreed upon, they got stripped of their finery (clothing and jewels) and then they got delivered over to their future master.

Women with newly born children hanging at their breasts and others that were old so much that they could hardly walk, were either dragged away or if the buyer still needed them the price was negotiated and got taken away. Those who were unworthy to the buyers were likely to be eliminated by shooting or left out of the parade with no food or water and after a while they died. Invariably all slaves wore a very dejected look; and as a rule, most of them got to a point they were so ill fed that their bones seemed as if ready to get out of the skin cover.

There were many other ways of testing the mettle of a slave, which involved whipping. But that was mainly for those who were considered to be strong enough to fetch good price. The selection parade was not as rigidly done as has been shown above. In addition to what has been described, the slaves could be led outside and lined up in order of size. Each would be tied to a tree and whipped with a stinging stick to test their mettle. Those who did not cry or faint fetched a higher price at the market. All these tortures were a measure or indeed a demonstration of how Africa was getting more than its share of cruelty and suffering. The British abolished the trade in Zanzibar in 1873. But black skin and poverty perpetuated that cruelty for a much longer time even after the abolition. Bearing black skin was a major reason why any such person deserved not any right of living a happy life.

Now let us look briefly at the Anglican Cathedral that stands on what was the site of slave market in Stone Town. The Church is a landmark historical church, as well as one of the most prominent examples of early Christian architecture in East Africa. Inside the cathedral, the altar marks the spot of the whipping tree where slaves were lashed with stinging branch or whips made of a thick, dry rhinoceros' skin. The Cathedral is a moving sight, remembered by a white marble circle surrounded by red to symbolise the blood of the slaves. The former whipping tree is marked at the altar by a white marble circle surrounded by red to symbolise the blood of the slaves.

There is more to be seen in the grounds outside the cathedral. Artists have prepared a pit and figure that depict the exact picture of what the slavery was like when the trade and operations in Stone Town were actually in operation. There in the pit is where there is the moving Slave Memorial that depicts five slaves standing in the pit. The poignant figures emerge from the rough-hewn rock. They appear hopelessly trapped shoulders slumped in despair. Around their necks the slaves wear metal collars from which a chain binds them. Unfortunately, today there is nothing much that remains of the slave market, but the slave memorial is a sobering reminder of the not-so-distant past.

During the time of construction of the Cathedral slaves that were employed in the church's construction are said to have made one big mistake. The supervisor of the works was, Bishop Edward Steere. He was called away on business and returned to find 12 pillars had been erected upside down. He decided to leave them, and so they remain.

Bishop Edward Steere eventually died of a heart attack in a nearby building in 1885 and got buried behind the altar of the Cathedral.

We mentioned earlier that the slaves that did not qualify for export were retained to work in the spices farms. Even here the conditions were so harsh that about 30% of the male slaves died every year, thus necessitating importation of other batches of slaves. Women too, had their own share of torture. Elderly women were given assignments in the farms or on construction sites. Women with lactating infants would have to carry their children as they worked in the construction sites or in the farms. Attractive young girls got crowded in a room where in a few times were allowed to have a bath and had to smear themselves with coconut oil to make themselves a little more attractive. These would serve as sex achiness for the sultan. For instance, Sultan Barghash had about 90 such girls who were always on the wait in a special chamber that looked like a crowded classroom, strictly monitored by guards. The girls would keep there until the sultan came and picked his choice for the specific moment. The selected girl or girls would be taken to Sultan's special sex performance place with slave girls.

When he finished, the woman would be hushed back to the waiting room; and soon thereafter he could call for another girl. It is said Sultan Barghash could sleep with almost ten women in a single day.. Barghash was so much of a sex maniac he died of heart attack. However, pregnancy became a qualification of a girl to be dismissed from being among those they kept in the waiting room for the Sultan.

Cruelty was inherent in almost all Omani Arabs. Judging from those who ruled Zanzibar they had a culture of violence where brute force was the preferred solution to problems and outlandish cruelty was a virtue. It was a common thing for a brother to murder his brother even for a trivial misunderstanding, and this was typical of the Arab aristocracy, where it was acceptable for family members to murder one another to gain land, wealth, titles and slaves. This explains their behaviour of treating other human beings cruelty including cold blood killings. The cruelty in Zanzibar was always a shocking hell, which was the way the Arab masters treated their African slaves, who were so cowed into submission that there was never a slave revolt attempted in Zanzibar. The cruelty that the Arab slavers treated their black slaves left behind a legacy of hatred which has for a long time kept breeding a sense of hatred between races in the archipelago.

The political systems in Zanzibar started to change towards the turning of 1890s. For instance, in August 1896, Britain and Zanzibar fought the so called 38-minute war considered to be, the shortest in recorded history after Khalid bin Barghash had taken power after Hamid bin Thuwani's death. The British had wanted Hamoud bin Mohamed to become Sultan, believing he would be much easier to work with. The British gave Khalid an hour to vacate the Sultan's palace in Stone Town. Khalid refused to do so, and instead he assembled an army of 2,800 men to fight the British. The British launched an attack on the palace and other locations around the city. Within less than forty minutes Khalid retreated and later escaped into exile. Hamoud was then installed as Sultan.

The government of Zanzibar continued as a protectorate of the British until the end of the first half of the 20th Century. For all this period the elite of Zanzibar continued to be suppressive to the black African majority while the rulers continued to be recognized as first class citizens of Zanzibar. In 1964 the Africans planned and made a successful revolution that was lead by John Gideon Okello, a

Ugandan revolutionary and the leader of such incursions. This revolution overthrew Sultan Jamshid bin Abdullah and led to the proclamation of Zanzibar as a republic. The Zanzibar Revolution led to the Sultan of Zanzibar and his mainly Arab government by the island's majority Black African population.

Reasons for the revolution had been simmering for many decades. Zanzibar, whose government until then had been under Omani Sultans, remained a British Protectorate from the turning of the 19th Century. Following the revolution in 1964 the Islands (comprising of the islands of Zanzibar and Pemba) united with Tanganyika on 26 April 1964 to form the United Republic of Tanganyika and Zanzibar, which then continued as a single Member, changing the name to the United Republic of Tanzania on 1 November 1964. The Zanzibar Revolution was basically the result of ethnic tension. For the whole time before the revolution in 1964 Zanzibar had throughout been ruled by an Arab Sultan and had a cruel Arab minority elite which was led by the Arab-led, Zanzibar Nationalist Party.

9

CONTEMPORARY SLAVE TRADE IN AFRICA

Each individual has the right to a life free from slavery. It was shown in the previous chapters that Africa has had more than its share of suffering from slavery. The end of past systems of slavery made people in the world to rejoice by celebrating the arrival of a new era that was free of elements of slavery. Countries of the world especially in Africa have kept coming up with laws that prohibit slavery in their countries. But right now, millions of children and adults are trapped in slavery. For readers who are not familiar with what modern or contemporary slavery means, we consider it better to start by defining what modern day slavery means. We will also try to show how wide spread it is and why.

Cotemporary or the new type of slavey is defined as the recruitment, movement, harbouring or receiving of children, women or men through the use of force, coercion, abuse of people in vulnerable state, deception or other means, for the purpose of exploitation. It is concerned with severe exploitation of other people for personal or commercial gain; and it is all around us, but often just out of sight. People can become entrapped in brick making, in manufacturing, in fishing, in domestic activities, in garage works, in mining, in prostitution, in farm work, in forced marriages and so on. Modern forms of slavery can include debt bondage, where a person is forced to work for free to pay off a debt, child slavery, forced marriage, domestic servitude and forced labour, or in places where victims are made to work through violence and intimidation. Unlike the traditional slavery that was legally instituted and operated, modern slavery is illegal and those in it are got illegally and the practice is punishable.

It is possible to spot modern slavery by observing certain characteristic. For instance the victim could appear to be under the control of someone else but remain reluctant to interact with others; or may not have personal identification on them; or may have only few personal belongings not because he/or she so wishes but that is what it is. The person could also be identified by wearing the same clothes every day or wearing unsuitable clothes for work; may not be able to move around freely and may be reluctant to talk to strangers or the authorities. According to the Global Slavery Index, statistically, modern slavery is most prevalent in Africa, followed by Asia and the Pacific. Unlike the traditional slavery, modern slavery is found in almost all countries of the world including the rich industrial countries of Europe, America, and Asia. But those who are found entrapped in the type of slavery are the poor people who have usually stowed away from their poor countries or communities, who in the course of seeking for the means to support their lives get in the hands of con people or agents of people who need cheap labour in the operation of their businesses..

Women and girls are disproportionately vulnerable to modern slavery, accounting for 71% of all such victims. The latest estimates show that over 4 million people are slaves in State labour at any given time. Like child labour modern slavery has complex root causes including poverty, conflict and crisis, cultural perspectives and lack of protective safeguards and legislation.

From the outside, modern slavery can look like a normal type of employment; but close observation will reveal that people are being controlled – they can face violence or threats; can be forced into inescapable debt, or have had their passport taken away and are being threatened with deportation. Many have fallen into this oppressive trap simply because they were trying to escape poverty or insecurity in their countries. They would escape with a goal to get to places that would enable them to live a more secure life, or where they could earn income that would in the end assist to improve their lives and support their families. Once they are in the trap it takes a lot of effort, resources, and luck to get out of it. Otherwise, it never works.

There are also many factors that have led to the development of modern slavery. On the part of industrialists the need to get such slaves arises following a state of shortage of labour. Such industrialists would seek for alternative sources of labour; the legal restrictions that lead to fixing minimum wages have often led employers to go against those legal procedures by employing and paying employees that are not on legal employment register and that are paid nominally (almost peanuts). Such employers seek for alternatives that will lead to maximizing profits. Other factors that lead to modern day slavery include racial attitudes. Desperate job seekers could accept to be paid extremely lowly due to nonavailability of any alternative. Others would include religious factors where believers are forced to work without any wage for years; all with promises that their payments would fall from heaven.. There are also the military factors, where people especially children have been forced to serve in insurgent military groups without legal support and meaningful wage..

Shortage of labour has forced employers to lure young people to go seeking for employment which they readily get after they have been promised they will get good pay. Usually the laborers get to such jobs without knowing the terms of the employment and without any contracts or reliable legal instruments or regulations. The employees end up working under controlled conditions and without permission to leave, as long as they are still needed in those places of work. At the initial stage the victims find themselves accepting such jobs before they know the employment terms; and that becomes possible because of lack of an alternative. They agree to start working with hope that with time things would improve or change, which never happens even after working for many years. In such case the employees find themselves working under very restrictive, secretive and without a chance to have access to people who can provide legal advice.

The fact that modern slavery is very different from the traditional or old type slavery, the major difference between them is that the state is no longer involved in the facilitation of slaves. In the traditional slavery, the government of the time would be heavily involved in trading and transporting slaves, like was the case in the triangle slave trade. The trade was backed up with laws and in certain situations matters could be tried in court of law. Like in any other business issues or conflicts could be resolved in the courts of law; which is very different from the way things go in regard to contemporary slavery. With the new or modern slavery, trafficking is by private traders or agents and always in very secretive ways. While the traditional type of slavery involved legal ownership asserted, high purchase cost, low profits, shortage of potential slaves, long-term relationships, slaves maintenance, and ethnic differences, modern slavery does not have any of those.

The new or modern type of slavery avoids any legal ownership/relationship, the purchase cost does not exist or it is relatively very low, realized profits are very high, and there is usually surplus of potential slaves, and also that the relationship of the master and slave are short term. In the modern type, the slaves are easily disposable and ethnic differences are not important. There are no official laws that defend it and transactions are done in a form that is informal, untransparent and illegal. There are about seven types or forms that have been identified in modern slavery. The forms include sex trafficking, child sex trafficking, forced labour, bonded labour or debt bondage, domestic servitude, forced child labour, and unlawful recruitment and use of child soldiers. The recruitment process depends on the type of job, the clients and agents involved, the place or country where the transaction takes place and many other attributes.

Contemporary or modern slavery is estimated to involve many people; in other words the number is big, so far estimated to be in the range of around 21 million to 46 million globally, depending on the method used to get the estimate and also depending on what falls in the definition that is being used. The status of modern slavery is such that it is growing to be a multibillion industry in the world with just the forced labour aspect generating about US $ 150 Billion each year. The global slavery index (2018) showed that, roughly US$ 40.3 million individuals were currently caught in modern slavery with 72% of them being females and one in every four persons beings children. While those figures are for the world at large, but Africa is one of the leading continents in that type slavery. Until the year 2020 countries in Africa with high proportion of population involved in modern slavery included Eritrea, Burundi, Central African Republic, Mauritania, and South Sudan.

Most other African countries were equally involved but at a much lower scale.

The estimated number of slaves has remained debatable, as there is no universally agreed method of getting the exact numbers. Those in slavery are often difficult to identify and adequate statistics are often not available. Some countries have claim that they do not have any such type of slavery but closely observed thousands of people are found involved in slavery in the many of the countries. The International Labour Organization (ILO) estimates that, by their definitions, over 40 million people are in some form of slavery today; out of who almost a million people are in forced labour, of which 16 million people are exploited in the private sector such as domestic work, construction or agriculture. About 4.8 million persons are in forced sexual exploitation, and 4 million persons in forced labour imposed by state authorities, whilst 15.4 million people are estimated to be in forced marriage.

While every individual has the rights to a life free from slavery but with the abolition of slave trade in the 19th Century gradually millions of children and adults got trapped in slavery in every single country especially in Asia and Africa.

The traditional type of slavery was easy to deal with because it was done in the open. For the modern day slavery it is opposite. From the outside, it can look like a normal job. But in the inside people are being controlled – they can face violence or threats, they can be forced into inescapable debt, or are sold from one owner or master to another, they can end up without the slavery type of transaction been noticed. There are many ways that are employed to make those conditions be enforced by the slavers. The slaves can have their passports or official identification documents taken away and are then threatened with deportation.

In 2016, an estimated 9.2 million men, women, and children were living in modern slavery in Africa. The region has the highest rate of prevalence, with 7.6 people living in modern slavery for every 1,000 people in the region. However, the situation that is seen in Africa is not unique considering the fact that this type of slavery is taking place in almost all parts of the world.

The conditions for good germination of this type of slavery are basically found in the dualities found in say Africa. The dualities could include the extensive state of capitalism against communism; rich against the poor, poor sanitation and squatters in the urban areas against poshy life in well planned and cared for areas of cities, poverty against richness, rural development against urban luxuries and supplies, illiteracy against accessibility to good education, industrialization that is starting to emerge against the traditional communal type of production, swift state of urbanization against rural life that has plenty of land for everyone to use but with no adequate infrastructure and utilities. Other factors have included aspirations of some governments to sustain themselves in power by way of maintaining and /or recruiting young people in military engagements, existence of huge armies of unemployed people, and many others. These factors have forced sections of the society to fall into vulnerability, giving room for those with economic, social or political muscle to take advantage of those without.

In Africa, suppressive conditions have not yet been sufficiently reduced. People are increasingly being denied the right to self - economic –sustainability. Poverty, which has kept pushing the poor further down to the ditch of destitution and vulnerability does not need to be overstated. Many people have no proper access to good medical services, education, capital, investment opportunities, land, and to employment. Some governments have shown willingness to provide partially free primary and secondary education; which is good in terms of minimizing illiteracy, but that has built up an amazingly huge army of educated but unemployed people. The education that has been provided at all levels has not been tailored to enabling young people to be innovative enough to use the education they have to be self- employed. That has made the young people to think of how to get short cuts, many have resorted to drug pushing or to prostitution, or to thoughtless borrowing which has plunged them to type of bonded slavery; and so on.

Corruption is another factor that has become fertile soil for germination of modern day slavery. For instance the handful formal jobs that are created by institutions and/or governments are sometimes awarded in a very untransparent way, largely in corrupt ways including the use of the jobs to trap young women into sexual slavery.

In Africa technical education that could tailor young people to innovative self-reliance is more talked than practically introduced. Absence of educational system that could lead young people to acquiring education that can make them self reliant, has lured young people to drug pushing, prostitution, robbery, and other illicit business. Those conditions have assisted to force young people to move to engagements that have landed them in imprisonment or debentured type of slavery inside their own countries and/or in foreign countries.

It has been noted that poverty and the tough life subjected to people in Africa has been the main cause for engagements that have been leading to modern day slavery. It is also clear that Africa and Africans especially those in the South of Sahara desert have been prone to all these traps. That has given the bad wishers or the misguided reporters the chance to argue that the problem is founded in what they describe as the crude untamable nature of people of black race, which is further claimed to be founded in their devilish nature, which has completely closed them from the serving light of Christianity and its civilization. What that means is that racial grounds continue to play a major part in explaining the causes of modern day slavery. The truth however is that getting into slavery trap is often exacerbated by the socio economic factors prevalent in Black African countries. In any case Africa will need to pay a lot of attention to racial factors, religions factors, cultural factors, social set ups, economic factors, legal and administrative conditions to reduce the number of those who are continually falling into slavery traps. These and many others factors are assisting to make our world a place of miseries because those with the power are using their muscles to lure the desperately poor people from poor countries to accepting their offers that end up to be big traps that ultimately lead to total enslavement.

The practice in any one country may not be exactly the same as that of another country and the figure may vary from year to another but generally speaking the number is steadily on the increase. This calls for the need to mention, albeit in passing how the practice in one country may differ from that of another country. But before we do so it is necessary to mention that, thousands of people are trafficked and forced to work in fishing boats, where they can be kept for years without ever seeing the shore. Young people are trapped in the mines, in the crops harvesting farms, in the brothels, in the coal mining grounds and many other places.

Wherever they are trapped they remain closely watched while ensuring that they keep working hard without deserving a wage and without enough food, clothing, housing, and other basics of life.

Let us now look more closely at what the actual situation is like in Africa. First of all Africa is recorded as a continent with the highest rate of modern-day enslavement in the world. Armed conflict, state-sponsored forced labour, forced marriages and wide spread poverty are the main causes of the estimated 9.2 million Africans who live in servitude without their choice to do so. Tough economic conditions, mainly caused by lack of enough employment are among the leading explanations for the growing prevalence of modern-day servitude. .

African economies are generally only beginning to take off. Most African economies are only on the first step of take off and thus it will take a long time to be strong enough to contain the fast-growing population. Actually, the economies have a long way to go to be of sufficient support to solve the problem of critical unemployment. The problem of unemployment has been like a dog that gets attracted to a motionless python which keeps its mouth open, thus attracting the hunting dog to its open mouth, the snake's motionless state makes the dog to keep creeping towards the open mouth of the python until it is easily caught and swallowed by the hungry snake.

We have often times seen cases of young men from various parts of Africa stowing away across the Sahara desert to North African or to South African states and whenever possible to places across the seas in quest for employment. They do so after receiving rumors that yonder there are plenty of employment opportunities. They organize themselves in groups to support themselves and then start to set out walking from their rural homes across jungles and dry lands, across rivers, mountains and lakes towards the direction of their chosen imaginary destinations. It takes many days of walking on unchartered routes before getting to any meaningful destination. They proceed without a map or a compass that can guide them to where they are going; and without enough money for their own up keep and without passports, visa, or any other important documents.

As they fumble in deciding which way to move on, they fall in the hands of hooligans that strip them of anything they have and if they are lucky the hooligans let them proceed with no proper knowledge of where they have come from, where they are or where they are going. Some keep walking until they are caught and arrested by police in the country that they are transiting. Here they are prosecuted for illegal entry and get imprisoned or deported after they have been interrogated and fined.

In many cases things do not go as smoothly as has been said. Many of them die on the way due to exhaustion, lack of food, dehydration, and diseases such as malaria. There are also those who get arrested by immigration authorities of the countries that they transit and get imprisoned for unlawful entry without visa. Those few who succeed to get to the planned destination after many days of interrupted travelling, they cross the border and if they chance to do so successfully through informal entrance points, they either get arrested immediately they enter the cities or if they escape any such arrest, they walk the streets directionlessly seeking for employment. In so doing they fall into the hands of drug dealers who engage them in drug business, which not only subjects them to great danger, including long term imprisonment if they are caught by Authorities or they secretly keep in the illegal business under conditions of slavery by those who employ them. Many thousands of young people in Africa, (a lot of them from the horn of Africa) have made attempts to get to South Africa but recently many of them have been arrested by police in countries like Kenya, Tanzania, Mawi and Zambia, after which they get prosecuted and imprisoned for illegal entries; or they get deported to their countries.

Similar or worst cases have been taking place in West Africa and in some Sahel countries. Young men and/or women plan to head northward, with a view to buy passage on smuggler's boats destined for Europe, where they have heard from friends that jobs were plentiful. The planned journey could take up to 2,500 miles or more across the trackless desert plains of Niger and through the lawless tribal lands of Southern Libya. Some of the lucky ones get deposited at the southern shore of the Mediterranean Sea, which is a very rare situation. Some end up being lured by some taxi men, who promise them to get to the city where they can get good employment. Instead, they get sold to dealers before they have gone veery far. Yet others get captured (by illegal dealers) the moment they arrived in Libya. They are then sold to armed men who keep a stable of black African migrants who get exploited for labour and ransom. They get both punished in various ways and are given a mark of identification.

Many such victims are captured annually. There are others that attempt to escape the fetid warehouses, where they may have been held as captive labourers in places such as Bani Walid, Libya, for several months and this is after they have been scarred for identification.

Some of the young men who have found themselves in these predicaments have been illiterate and have served without knowledge of where they were and also without knowledge of whether the marking done on their bodies were in form of numbers or letters or merely the twisted doodles of deranged men. Actually, the deranged men always see black Africans as nothing better than livestock that has a value to be bought and sold. What is worse some Arabs in North Africa see black Africans only as beasts of burden which need to be got and sold to buyers. Hardly the black Africans that get to that region are treated in a fair manner or with any sympathy or empathy.

It has roughly been estimated that over 650,000 men and women who have crossed the Sahara over the past ten years (between 2012 and 2022) dreaming of a better life in Europe have been put into this slavery victimization.

Looking at the victims critically one finds that some have been fleeing war and persecution at home. Others have been leaving villages where economic dysfunction and unreliable rainfall made it impossible to find work or even enough to eat. To make the harrowing journey, they enlist the services of trans-Saharan smugglers who profit by augmenting their truckloads of weapons, drugs, and other contraband goods with human cargo. From West Africa to North Africa tens of thousands escapees (from their villages) find themselves treated not just as cargo but as chattel slaves and get trapped in a terrifying cycle of extortion, imprisonment, forced labour and prostitution[29]. These victims don't only face inhuman treatment but are also sold from one trafficker to another.[30]" Essentially, they are free people who in their

---

[29] *According to estimates by the International Organization for Migration (IOM) and the U.N. Office on Drugs and Crime.*
[30] *Southern European regional spokesperson for UNHCR, the U.N. refugee agency*

efforts to find solutions to hard life in their villages and families end up being transformed to slaves.

Today there are more than three times as many people in forced servitude[31] as were captured and sold during the 350-year span of the transatlantic slave trade. What the ILO calls *the new slavery* takes in 25 million people in debt bondage and 15 million in forced marriage. As an illicit industry, it is one of the world's most lucrative, earning criminal networks $150 billion a year, just behind drug smuggling and weapons trafficking. The business is today most visible in Libya, where aid organizations and journalists have documented actual slave auctions; although the business is also now gradually seeping into southern Europe—in particular Italy, where vulnerable migrants are being forced to toil unpaid in the fields picking tomatoes, olives and citrus fruits and trafficked into prostitution rings.

Almost in all cases, many of the slaves are isolated by illiteracy, poverty, and geography, and do not know that life outside servitude is possible. Lack of proper knowledge could also explain difficulties faced by authorities to curb this type of slavery. In arid African countries the population is thingly spread and knowledge that people could be served from such malady has not reached the victims. The concerned governments do not know what happens in the remote parts of their countries even in situations the slavery is practiced in the open. Transport and Communication is difficult and thus it has proved difficult to swiftly get surveillance services there. In some countries the slavery is wrapped in culture wherein those who are enslaved believe that what is being done to them is

---

[31] *This is in accordance to International Labor Organization (ILO),*

part of life and anybody who convinces them otherwise has bad intentions for their eternal lives.

While modern slavery is often emerging as a by-product of poverty, countries that lack education, economic freedom, the rule of law, and have poor societal structure can create an environment that fosters the acceptance and propagation of slavery. Again, slavery is being reported to be most prevalent in impoverished countries and those with vulnerable minority communities, though it also exists in developed countries. Tens of thousands toil in slave-like conditions in industries such as mining, farming, and factories, producing goods for domestic consumption or export to more prosperous nations.

Government-forced labour, also known as state-sponsored labour, is defined by the International Labour Organization (ILO) as events which persons are coerced to work through the use of violence or intimidation or by more subtle means such as accumulated debt, retention of identity papers or threats of denunciation to immigration authorities. When the threats come from the government the threats can be much different. Many governments that participate in forced labour shut down their connections with the surrounding countries to prevent citizens from leaving.

It is also possible to make a brief overview of the growing impact of terrorist groups in Africa such as Bocco Haram, Al-Shabaab and others. Human trafficking constitutes one of the most serious human rights violations and one of the most profitable activities of organized crime. It attracts a broad range of criminal enterprises, from small local groups to international networks that deal in large numbers of trafficked victims through connections in source, transit and destination States. War and conflict enable human trafficking to thrive. People wishing to escape violence may turn to traffickers in the hope of finding a safe haven, but generally find them in an exploitative situation. Like other forms of illegal activities, human trafficking has become increasingly attractive to non-State armed groups, notably terrorist entities. Acts of violence associated with human trafficking have been central to the modus operandi of the religious highly influenced places in Africa such as, Boko Haram, Al-Shabaab, and the Lord's Resistance Army (LRA). Human trafficking is not a new phenomenon. However, it has been used in the context of war and conflict, it has attracted increased attention. Acknowledging terrorists' and other non-State armed groups' use of trafficking as a weapon of war, the Security Council has in recent years adopted a presidential statement and two resolutions on this phenomenon. Only in a few cases substantial military setbacks and territorial losses have been experienced by some terrorist entities. Acts of sexual abuse and enslavement against women and girls and acts of forced recruitment and indoctrination against men and boys have continued.

10

EUROPE SPONSORS EXPLORATION OF AFRICA

European exploration to various parts of the world is well known to historians. But world exploration goes many years before Europe began to have some interest in the continent of Africa. It began with the Age of Discovery in the 15th century, pioneered by Portugal under Henry the Navigator, who was a central figure in the early days of the Portuguese Empire and in the 15th-century European maritime discoveries and maritime expansions.

However, before we move very far, we need to put our discussion in perspectives. We need to differentiate those European explorers of the period before the 17TH Century and those who started their work specifically for Sub-Saharan Africa towards the turning of 19th Century. Those of the earlier period would include people such as Christopher Columbus, Vasco da Gama, Pedro Álvares Cabral, John Cabot, Juan Ponce de León, and Ferdinand Magellan. These went to explore various parts of the world. They were among the first and most famous explorers who decided to discover the world. They did so using very simple but strong vessels or ships but enabled the people of those days to gather a lot of knowledge about the world that lay around them. All these did not get directly to Africa except Vasco da Gama who went down along the West coast of Africa and succeeded to circumnavigate the Cape of Good Hope and on along the East coast to India and back to Lisbon.

In the earlier times of 16th century the European powers were content to establish trading posts along the coast of Africa while actively exploring and colonizing the New World. Little by little Europeans started to venture into the interior of the Africa. Most explorers that got a chance to go to various parts of Africa to rather explore what existed in the interior were young people still in their active youth life and always ready to involve in activities that were challenging. It is usually said they were the type of people who tended to be self-reliant and quick-thinking, ready to move to places that were dreaded by others, with personality minds that did not mind handling uncertain situations on the fly – in fact, they lived for those types of situations.

The reasons that gave rise to exploration work especially in Africa were mainly the satisfaction of Curiosity. Others and perhaps the most important reasons, were that most of the explorers especially those of the early 19th century were on mission, they were under sponsorship of those who needed certain specific information, which could be used for their future prospects. It could look harsh to say they were like spies or informers who wished to collect information without prior notice to the hosts. They moved to various places silently without making consultation with the local people, except in cases where they needed information on a specific issue. And even in those situations they worked more closely with Arab slave hunters (especially in the Great Lakes region).

From the early 19th century Slave trade on the Atlantic was getting abolished and alternative ways of supporting European economies were being sought. Gradually it started to be quite clear that solutions would be found in looking to the south, especially Asia and Africa. On those grounds European governments and big business firms began to feel that the South had to be explored thoroughly to discover opportunities that existed and could be exploited.

As the exploration proceeded European governments began to think more seriously about the need to know what lay in the interior of Africa. They wished to be sure what actions or strategies would have to be employed to especially get enough knowledge about the interior of Africa and if possible, grab any opportunities that could exist, for the sake of their economies, religion and glory. European economies needed a lot of support especially in matters of smooth supply of raw materials to enhance and sustain swift industrial growth that started from the 17th century.

The explorers did not move to African exploration without receiving terms of reference from those who sponsored their journeys of exploration. Improvement could be achieved through extension of imperialism as well as making alliances of various types. Europe needed raw materials and markets for products that were increasingly being produced by their industries. After all, America was far and any chances of getting alternative sources of raw materials for the growing industrial revolution in Europe would be a great achievement. For instance, they needed to acquire more species of plants, they needed gold, better and/or faster trading routes and also, they believed in the need to spread their religion, Christianity. Those who sponsored exploration work were also curious about different lands, animals, people, goods, and agricultural investments. In that case the explorers were mostly on missions to find new opportunities, markets for industrial goods as well as sources of raw materials and certainly land for occupation and if possible, for their national businesspeople. They further wished to find out where various facilities or physical features such as Mountains, rivers, Lakes, forests, wildlife for ivory and many other facilities and resources were located.

The physical feature's location information would be used in filling gaps in their maps, which would assist in planning their way forward. There was need to know better trading routes, and best places of European investments. They also needed to acquire knowledge on how best their religion (Christianity) could be reached to the local people, which was also a strategy to consolidate European presence in Africa as well as enhancement of wealth, foreign goods, and fame. Christianity was seen to be a useful instrument to civilize Africans, who would then be peaceful people as European entrepreneurs kept designing ways of forging further ahead. The whole thing was a strategy to European occupation and exploitation of Africa.

Unlike the medieval time explorers, the 19th Century explorers to the interior of Africa had some clue of where they were going before they started their journeys to Africa. They got to Africa with clues about what they were likely to see in the places they decided to visit. Imagine for instance that almost all of them had the same agendas to find the source of River Nile. In most cases all made their exploration when the industrial revolution was already at advanced stage, which made the explorations to be only part of the process to enhance the industrial revolution and also to speed up growth of European economies and businesses. They were on the watchout for new opportunities, which would minimize the gap that had started to be created following the abolition of slave trade on the Atlantic Ocean.

Of all explorers, the 19th century as well as the earlier ones had something in common; they had special motives, which put them under obligation to achieve for the sake of their societies, economies, religion, and glory. The primary objective was to improve their home economies. For instance, by acquiring more plant and animal species, various types of minerals, gold, better and faster trading routes. Also, they believed in the need to spread their religion, Christianity. That was also the case with non-European explorers. The Arabs for instance had travelled to as far as East African coast hundreds of years before the time of transatlantic slave trade. They sought for precious minerals such as gold, diamonds and ivory; and in the course of discovering places they realized that Africa was endowed with many types of resources that could satisfy the curiosity of exploiters and governments in Europe. African resources could find ready markets in many parts of the world including the Persian Gulf, Asia and even Europe. Africa, besides being endowed with gold and many other minerals, was also a good source of ivory, and special timber. As the explorers kept on with their information seeking assignments, some of them took that opportunity to spread religion.

However, for the first-time exploration of Africa South of the Sahara desert got great European attention. Not much attention was directed to the north of Africa. That was so not because of the fact it was a better-known region by the outside world, but also because from the earlier years of the medieval age Arabs had made their strong presence that led to been entirely Islamic. There was the abolition of slave trade, which shifted business interests of Europeans from the Americas. Then there was the start of the industrial revolution, which triggered the first phases of imperialism. The first phase of Imperialism saw the necessity for exploring new areas especially in the south (including Asia and Africa) for markets and sources of raw materials. Besides, Imperialism, the need for exploration of the Sub-Saharan Africa had its genesis in the so-called Enlightenment Age (1700-1790). That was the time when an intellectual and philosophical movement developed and dominated the world of ideas in Europe. The Enlightenment emerged out of a European intellectual and scholarly movement known as Renaissance Humanism. During that period European intellectuals developed new standards and tools for mapping, and since they weren't sure precisely where in Africa the lakes, the mountains, the rivers, the forests, the urbanized areas, the mineral sites and many other types of natural resources were, they began erasing them from popular maps.

Logically the erasing of those features from the popular maps made a lot of sense because there was no need to insert features that were known to exist but no one was sure where the features fitted in the maps. That was the main reason for removing most of the African features such as lakes, rivers, mountains, forests and even high population concentration areas from the popular maps. Actually the removal of the features meant that where the African continent was concerned, nothing was shown apart from the boundaries of the continent; but without any basic features reflected in them. So, besides other reasons, the popular maps needed to be accurately filled, as that would be the only way for governments and business communities in Europe to know how they could grab opportunities that existed in Africa. That situation remained so until when the so-called European explorers such as Burton, Livingstone, Speke, and Stanley, saw and identified some of those rivers, lakes, and mountains.

Then there was also the issue of Imperialism. By 19th Century imperialism was already global in the hearts of western businessmen. There were good differences between the hunger of imperialists to spread to Africa, and that of getting to other parts of the world. Under normal conditions most empire buildings began with the recognition of trading and commercial benefits that could be accrued. In the case of Africa, the continent as a whole was being annexed to fulfill the spirit of adventure, the desire to support the work of bringing civilization to the natives, including getting the Gospel to them, the hope of stamping out the slave trade, and possibilities of African occupation.

An explicit duality was thus set up for these adventurers- dark versus light and Africa versus Europe. The African climate was said to invite mental prostration and physical disability; the forests were seen as implacable and filled with beasts; rivers and ponds and lakes had crocodiles that lay in wait, floating in sinister silence in the great waters. There were dangers, diseases, and deaths that were considered to be part of the uncharted reality and the exotic fantasy created in the minds of European armchair scholars, intellectuals and bureaucrats. The idea of a hostile nature and a disease-ridden environment as tinged with evil was perpetrated by fictional accounts by quite a number of European authors. It was an unfortunate situation because any idea about Africa was conceived from negative angles. The North was white and attractive and the South, Africa in particular was dark, unattractive and above all dangerous and devilish.

It is easy to think that there was a problem or failure of Africa to expose itself to the external world, which was not so. Something else arises at this juncture. When talking about the external world, the Africans have till this day often implied or referred to any place outside the African continent; and outside the African continent the mind quickly shifts to Europe; which was in some way correct. For Europeans Africa was something that existed but was still enclosed in a type of cocoon of mysterious or undefined social settings. Time came when even Africans could not define themselves, they could not trust themselves so much that they started to rate themselves very low; and that was because of intimidation imposed on them by those with guns, slave trade, economic power, and self-imposed superiority.

However, Europe remained without much knowledge of Africa because the continent was, according to European people's minds, very remotely placed, which was in some way true, because the stories that were popularly told in Europe about Africa were very fiery. Africa, according to those stories was a place that could be ventured only by courageous people. Despite the fact that the continent was in very close proximity to Europe, but the mental conception of people in both continents was that they were millions of kilometers from each other. Until the middle of the 19th century Africa was dreaded because of the negative images that kept being painted in Europe about Africa and Africans.

From way back to 16th century, Africa got transformed to a major source of slaves that were needed in the new-world. But due to factors that have just been outlined even with the flourishment of the slave trade Europeans avoided venturing into the interior of the continent to obtain slaves from there. Later in the 18th century the slave trade abolition started which awakened business communities and governments to start to think about other avenues of governing and controlling Africa. To succeed in that endeavour there was the need to make a thorough survey of what was there in Africa. The new thinking prompted the idea of exploration of the African continent.

At this juncture we come to the work of Explorers. They were of various types and operated in various epochs, went to different geographical places, and went to various parts of Africa. We call it exploration simply because those were journeys which were aimed to find realities about places, resources and even cultures that would provide new knowledge that would be a foundation for the intended new Europe. For Europe it was exploration but for Africa it was a type of tourism. To Africans the journeys were nothing more than visits of European people to places that were well known. However, the information would enable Europe to invade Africa with a high level of success. The Europeans were well aware that information was power, and that was the power Europe was seeking.

Like we will come to see when we come to specific explorers, most of those of the period before 19th century were more of researchers who took note of whatever they saw to enable the world of their time more enlightened with knowledge. Those of the 19th century were just fact finders; they were surveyors who wished to be certain of what was to some degree known. We can give examples of those sent to find the source of River Nile were people who went to ascertain what was known to exist. They were largely agents of businesses or individuals from governments' or specific government organizations. Each of these in their own way, were curious and very eager to get any a report of anything that existed in Africa. Raw materials were needed to ensure continuous production in the industries that were rapidly growing in Europe. They also needed markets for products that were now being produced in massive quantities. But most of all, there developed anxiety to extend Imperial powers to these supposedly new regions. Africa was gradually being found to be a place where free or rather cheap labour could be found in plenty.

Taking into account that by the closing of 18th century slave trade on the Atlantic Ocean was finally losing its earlier significance mainly due to the abolition campaign that had been stepped up and also considering the increasing demand for raw materials and markets for the European industries; made the exploration of Africa more desirable during the 19th century than any other time before. By the end of 1880s, most key European nations were putting up the wish to be the first to get there-in Africa. The pressure was growing high due to reports that explorers were supplying to Europe, especially about the abundance of land and natural resources. The wish was now to control those resources without being seen to be contravening the spirit of abolition of slave trade.

There was need to know the physical features of Africa; such as the rivers and their whereabouts and watersheds, the mountains, the Lakes, mineral deposits, forests, climatic conditions, plants, people's settlements and many other features. Good understanding of these features and resources was necessary because they were going to provide a proper basis for European intervention, be it through trade or extension of Imperialism, or any other actions that would be of benefit for European involvement.

While European entrepreneurs, governments, scholars and missionaries had heard about Africa, but most of them knew more about slaves who were got from West Africa for sale in the Americas and other places. They knew those black people were got from Africa but there was no clue where exactly in the interior they came from. Given that the number that was being transported to the new world was very huge the assumption was that there was oversupply of such people in the interior. If chances allowed and had it not been constrained by the abolition of slave trade on the Atlantic, it would be only a matter of surrounding and capturing them to get the number that was needed.

The false knowledge about Africa persisted until as late as the 20th century. For instance, till as late as middle of 20th Century there were people outside the African continent who believed that Africans lived in trees like monkeys and those who went to hunt for them had to find forest areas where there were many trees to find, surround and catch them. This notion also made European investors believe that cheap labour would be readily available when time came and they started to take land in the continent, which explorers had been informing it was there in plenty. It was a matter of taking big tracts of land, which would be worked by slaves caught from the forest to produce the raw materials that were demanded by European industrials..

Despite the desired appetite for Europe to explore the continent of Africa but not many were ready to go into that adventure due to a number of other reasons. They could not navigate African rivers, which had many rapids, cataracts and changing flows. There were also problems of diseases that were deadly to foreigners. Some Africans were already immune to some of those diseases. Tropical regions were greatly infested with mosquitoes, which spread malaria. It was fortunate that as Europeans Empires stepped up their expansions in Africa in the 19th century, discovery of a drug to cure malaria was discovered in 1820. French Scientists, Pierre Pelletier and Joseph Caventou discovered the process to extract quinine from the Cinchona bark, which improved the potency of the medicine markedly. That discovery came as just in time for European Empires as they were expanding at dazzling paces into malaria -ridden parts of the world including tropical Africa.

Africa had many great rivers that flowed into the see from the interior. They knew River Nile, which for centuries had been emptying its water into the Mediterranean Sea. They had seen estuaries of River Congo and that of River Niger both of which emptied their water in the Atlantic Ocean. Some foreigners had also heard of or seen the river mouths of River Zambezi, Rufiji, Ruvuma and Pangani, and Limpopo, which emptied their waters into the Indian Ocean. Not only that, but there had also been stories about a high mountain which some ancient travelers had referred to as Mountain of the Moon in the heart of Africa. These and many similar features made enlightenment people in Europe to create curiosity to know more about the Dark Continent and its resources. They wished to find out more about what they had heard or read but could not relate that with what actually existed on the ground. Accessing those places would be a great challenge, especially when diseases such as malaria were known to be causing many deaths (that of course being before the discovery of quinine) to those who got exposed to mosquito bites.

Due to the above limitations, Europeans took time to get into the interior of Africa. There was also the unfounded fear that Africans were savages, they lacked any elements of civilization and thus it was dangerous to venture into the interior. Certainly in the deep interior parts of Africa village communities, chiefdoms, kingdoms (whichever that was concerned) had strong armies, which did not allow foreigners to filter in without knowledge of who they were. That explains why during the 18th century period quite many Europeans were reported killed by local people, as the local people were also under obligation to maintain safety and security.

Let us now make some account of the various explorers that got involved in Africa in one way or the other. The earliest we wish to mention was Joseph Banks who was a botanist who had sailed across the Pacific Ocean with Cook and in 1788 went to found an Association for exploration of African continent, which went with the name "The African Association". The founding of the African Association alone was a milestone. It formed a good basis for the exploration work that followed almost two centuries later. However before then Ibin Battuta had travelled over 100,000 Kilometers from Morocco to China. While he originated his trip from Morocco he remained ignorant of what existed in most of the rest of Africa and especially in the Sub Saharan part of Africa, because he never got there any way.

Other explorers that ventured to Africa before those who did so in the 19th Century included people like James Bruce, a Scottish explorer who set off from Cairo in 1768 to find the Source of River Nile. He is reported to have arrived at Lake Tana, confirming that the lake was source of the Blue -Nile, a tributary of River Nile.

The next explore on record was Mungo Park, who under the sponsorship of African Association went to explore the River Niger, in 1795. He was one of those unfortunate explorers of the time because on return to England he could not get public recognition as a great explorer. In 1805 he set out again to follow the Niger with a view of finding its source, but as the saying goes, misfortunes never come singly. In those efforts he was attacked by the local people as he reached the Bussa River falls. Following that attack he drowned.

Two other explorers were Rene Auguste Caillie and Henrich Barth. Rene Auguste Caillie was a French man, and was the first European to reach Timbuktu. His trip to Timbuktu had been aimed at seeing that city which the legends had it that it was made of Gold. When he got there he became very disappointed to find that the city was actually built of mud. In his caravan of almost 1,200 animals he returned by crossing the Sahara desert again to Tangiers and eventually back to France.

His disappointment could be said to be a result of unconfirmed reports he had got and read about. Judging from the way he prepared his journey with almost 1,200 animals in his caravan it means he was out to get the wealth that Timbuktu was said to possess. That can be further confirmed by the fact that he got to Timbuktu disguising himself as an Arab, which would make him to be more easily welcome than if he introduced himself a European. One could go further and presume that he was even prepared for war to grab the gold-wealth of Timbuktu if it could have really been in existence.

After Rene Auguste Caillie there was Henrich Bath who was a German working for British government. He got to Rabat, Morocco and then crossed to Alexandria in Egypt. Then he made a second trip, crossing the Sahara, and getting as far as Lake Chad, River Benue and Timbuktu before he went back again through the Sahara desert.

It is good to state here that quit a number of ancient as well as later day explorers had a lot of enthusiasm to get to Mali especially to Timbuktu not necessarily because they loved Africa and thus they went there just as tourists. They had heard great stories about the mineral richness of the African places and cities and had the ambition to grab some of those riches. We have shown that ancient Mali had grown to be one of the richest Kingdoms of the world of the time. The economic and trade mainstay of the state was gold and agricultural products such as rubber and cotton. Actually these ambitions to grab wealth from Africans started way back in 16th century, and continued until the 19th Century and first half of 20th century.. That state of grabbing or plundering resources from Africa has not ended until this day; but the process has been changing in form.

In other words, most explorers of 17th, 18th and early 19th Centuries did not only aim to know how Africa looked like but had their major interest in finding where the wealth of the continent could be found basing on legendary stories that they had read or heard about. For instance while they made a lot of effort to find the source of River Nile and also that of River Niger, but the most wealthy ones visited Mali, especially Timbuktu with a view of getting gold that was said to exist there in plenty. The case of Rene Galie who organized an entourage of 1,200 animals (horses, camels, donkeys and others) could assist to show how prepared this explorer was to ensure that he succeeded in getting what he needed even if that would necessitate going to war. He was well armed and had enough people to be engaged in any such war, which unfortunately did not work because the city he had been told was built of g gold had no gold to be easily seen.

The other explorers are those who made their journeys of exploration during the 19th Century. These included Samuel Baker, Richard Burton, John Hanning Speke, David Livingstone, Henry Morton Stanley, and Mary Kingsleys. It is not of much interest in this book to discuss each of these explorers in details except in the case of Dr. David Livingstone and Henry Morton Stanley. Samuel Baker, Richard Burton and John Hanning Speke who generally focused their attention mainly in finding the source of the Nile. Whatever else that they did were only coincidental to their main objective of finding the source of the Nile. As we have repeatedly said, the source of the Nile was an important issue because of many factors, most of them economic factors, which were swiftly becoming number one priority in the 19th Century economic development of Europe. The Nile River was assigned that high priority because it had proved to be the greatest natural resource for development of ancient Egypt. The river provided fish, transportation, and annual floods that fertilized the land for growing food and cash crops.

The most important thing the Nile provided to the ancient Egyptians was fertile land. Most of Egypt is desert, but along the Nile River the soil remained rich and good for growing crops due to alluvial soils that were brought from the source and deposited at the estuaries and delta. The Nile became so famous in the World of the time before the 20th Century besides the fact that it was the longest river in the world. Other factors were that the River flowed into the Mediterranean Sea. The Nile was not only the longest river in the World with a length of about 6,695 kilometers, discharging a lot of water coming from the interior of Africa, with average discharge of 3.1 million litres equivalent to 680,000 gallons per second. With the presence of River Nile Egyptians became rich through sale of a lot of their wheat throughout the Middle East. Egypt also had other items of natural resources in rocks and metals. Different types of rocks and minerals were quarried in Ancient Egypt.

During the 19th Century people in Europe also believed that knowing what lay in the places where the River Nile was sourced would provide a good hint of lands that could be taken for agricultural development, which would in the end feed well into the industrial development that was going on in Europe. We should also not lose sight of the fact that the European nations were already working on the Suez Canal which once completed would provide shorter shipping route that would connect the North and the South, and further assure the North to be in control of the South i.e. Africa and Asia. (This is a subject that will be delt with a little later). When we come to that we will be able to show that while Livingstone and

Stanley also had the agenda of finding the source of River Nile, but were also charged with other responsibilities.

Before we turn to Dr. David Livingstone and Stanley we consider it necessary to underline once again that all these explorers were not self-financed. They got support from governments, associations and rich individuals. So whatever emphasis they put to their work was expected to be in consonant with the requirements that were put before them by their sponsors. Livingstone for instance was under the sponsorship of government and the Missionary Society, whose major interest was to see where chances of spreading Christianity were. The other explorers too had their sponsors; that explaining why their reports about the places they visited and things they saw were highly applauded by authorities in Europe.

The other point worth underlining is that in spite of the fact that explorers' assignments were to be done in Africa but the focus was not on Africans but on those who sponsored them, namely the European governments, institutions and individuals. On those grounds obviously priority of their work would be expected to be on issues that were acceptable to their bosses. For instance there was Samuel Baker who was the first European to see the Murchison Falls and Lake Albert, in 1864. Actually that happened only by lack because that was not what he had been looking for or expecting to see; he had been hunting for the source of the Nile. But the finding gave him extra marks. The next explorer was Richard Burton who was not only one of those great explorers but also great scholar renowned for his production of the first unbridged translation of the ***Thousand Nights and a Night***[32]. Burton established himself

---

[32] ***The Book of the Thousand Nights and a Night*** (1885), subtitled *A Plain and Literal Translation of the Arabian Nights Entertainments,* is an English

as a formidable Shakespearean actor in the 1850s, and he gave a memorable performance of Hamlet in 1864. In 1857 he and Speke set off from Bagamoyo, the present day Tanzanian coast to find the source of the Nile. He took a straight route from Bagamoyo, following the popular central slave trade route to Lake Tanganyika where he began to fall seriously ill, leaving Speke to travel on alone. However, after he had parted with Richard Burton, Speke went on and got to Lake Victoria in 1858, which he initially believed to be the source of the Nile. Burton did not believe him but 1860 Speke set out again, this time with James Grant. In 1862 he found the source of the Nile, the Ripon Falls, which was just in the North of Lake Victoria.

Then there was Dr. David Livingstone that demonstrated to be a very special man to his European sponsors as well as the African allies. He had a firm interest and focus on Africa for Africans. He can be better understood by looking at his background since when he was a child to his school and college days to the time when he became an explorer in Africa. His long-term goal was to improve the lives of Africans through European knowledge and trade. He was a Scottish physician, Congregationalist, and pioneer Christian missionary with the London Missionary Society, an explorer in Africa, and one of the most popular British heroes of the late 19th-century Victorian era. Though it could sound immaterial but we should add here by summarizing that, he was a Protestant missionary martyr, working-class rags and riches inspirational story, scientific investigator and explorer, imperial

---

language translation of One thousand and One Night (the Arabian Nights) – a collection of Middle Eastern and South Asian stories and folk tales compiled in Arabic during the Islamic Golden Age (8th–13th centuries)

reformer, anti-slavery crusader, and advocate of British commercial and colonial expansion.

Livingstone became convinced of his mission to reach new peoples in the interior of Africa and introduce them to Christianity, as well as freeing them from slavery. These inspirations and aspirations influenced him to gear himself to matters of exploration through which he would be able to devote his life to transformation of African natives to Christianity. In 1841, he was posted to the edge of the Kalahari Desert in southern Africa. In 1845, he married Mary Moffat, daughter of a fellow missionary. In 1849 and 1851, he travelled across the Kalahari, on the second trip sighting the upper Zambezi River. In 1852, he began a four- year expedition to find a route from the upper Zambezi to the coast. These journeys of exploration assisted in filling many gaps in western knowledge of central and southern Africa. In 1855, Livingstone discovered a spectacular waterfall, which he named 'Victoria Falls'. He reached the mouth of the Zambezi on the Indian Ocean in May 1856, becoming the first European to cross the width of southern Africa.

Livingstone was deeply influenced by Moffat's judgement that he was the right person to go to the vast plains to the north of Bechuanaland, where he had glimpsed the smoke of a thousand villages, where no missionary had ever been. He visited Mabotsa, Botswana an area where there were many lions terrorizing the villagers. The local people expressed how the lions terrorized them and their livestock. According to the villagers' accounts made to him, the lions had become a menace because they attacked in the daytime and even in the night. He volunteered to go and kill at least one, which would make the others to get scared and keep their distance from the community people. He led the villagers on a lion hunt. Seeing a large lion, he fired his gun, but the animal was not sufficiently injured to prevent it from attacking him. While reloading the lion went on attacking him seriously wounding his left arm. The broken bone, even though inexpertly set by himself and his wife, bonded strongly, enabling him to shoot and lift the lions. However, that event remained a source of much suffering for the rest of his life. Since the time of sustaining that injury, Livingstone remained unable to lift the injured arm higher than his shoulder.

Livingstone advocated the establishment of trade and religious missions in central Africa, but abolition of the Afican slave trade as carried out by the Portuguese of Tete and the Arab Swahili of Kilwa, became his primary goal. He always remained disappointed by the way the slave traders treated their victims. He vowed to put that slave trade business to an end some day. His motto was Christianity, Commerce and Civilization; factors, which together, he hoped would form an alternative to the slave trade, and impart dignity to the Africans in the eyes of Europeans. He believed that the key to achieving these goals was the navigation of the Zambezi River as a Christian commercial highway into the interior. Those stood as some of his future commitment plans.

He returned to Britain to garner support for his ideas, and to publish a book on his travels, which brought him fame as one of the leading explorers of the age. In May 1857 Livingstone was appointed as Her Majesty's Consul with a roving commission, extending through Mozambique to the areas west of it. While in Britain, Livingstone was handled like a national hero. He did many speaking tours and published his bestselling 'Missionary Travels and Researches in South Africa' (1857).

Both him and his wife Mary left for Africa again in 1858, and for the next five years carried out official explorations of eastern and central Africa for the British government. They got to the East African coast to await the arrival of a steamboat, specially designed to sail on Lake Malawi (also known as Lake Nyasa in Tanzania). Mary Livingstone (his wife); died on 27 April 1862 from malaria- a bitter blow to her husband. Livingstone continued his explorations, with attempts to navigate the Ruvuma River. He failed because of the continual fouling of the paddle wheels from the bodies thrown in the river by slave traders. In the meanwhile Livingstone's assistants gradually died or left him due to disease infections and shortage of food supplies .It was in these conditions he uttered his most famous quotation, ***"I am prepared to go anywhere, provided it to be forward."*** He eventually returned home in 1864 after the government ordered the recall of the expedition because of its increasing costs and failure to find a navigable route to the interior.

Later and after a lot of effort to his sponsors, he made it to East Africa again. In January 1866, Livingstone set out from Zanzibar, the objective this time being that of finding the source of River Nile. Richard Francis Burton, John Hanning Speke and Samuel Baker had identified either Lake Albert or Lake Victoria as the source (which was partially correct, as the Nile bubbles from the ground high in the mountains of Burundi halfway between Lake Tanganyika and Lake Victoria, but there was still serious debate on the matter. Livingstone believed that the source was farther south and assembled a team to find it. The team consisted of freed slaves, Comoro Islanders, twelve Sepoys (better defined to be Indian soldiers serving under British orders), and two servants from his previous expedition, Chuma and Susi. His house in Mikindani in present day Southern Tanzania was the starting point for this Livingstone's last expedition. He stayed in Mikindani from 24 March to 7 April 1866.

Before Livingstone set out from Britain for this new and final expedition he made publications on the horrors of the slave trade, which is what enabled him to secure private support for another expedition to central Africa, searching for the Nile's source and reporting further on slavery.

The year 1869 began with Livingstone finding himself extremely ill while in the jungle. In March 1869, Livingstone suffered from pneumonia and arrived in Ujiji only to find all supplies that had been sent to him while he was away, stolen. He was coming down with cholera and had tropical ulcer on his feet, so he was again forced to rely on slave traders to get him as far as Bambara— where he was caught up by the wet season. With no supplies, Livingstone had to eat his meals in a roped-off enclosure for the entertainment of the locals in return for food.

On 15 July 1871, Livingstone stated in his diary that he witnessed around 400 Africans being massacred by men of the Arab ruler and slaver Dugumbe, an associate of his, while he was visiting Nyangwe on the banks of the Lualaba River. Actually he became the first European explorer to show serious concern for deaths that were being caused to Africans by slave traders.

This expedition lasted from 1866 until Livingstone's death in 1873. However, there was a long time that passed without being heard of. In Europe they took it that he had been lost in the African jangles and most probably he was dead. Nothing was heard from him for almost six years, which made Henry Stanley, an explorer and journalist, set out to find him. Stanley got to Zanzibar where he was told by slave traders that they had seen a European in Kigoma Ujiji and perhaps that was the person he was looking for. As he got to the mainland in Tanganyika he got a similar story from the local people who had travelled to as far as Kigoma that there were stories about a white man who had for a long time been seen living in Kigoma. Stanley recruited guards who lead the way, resulting in him and Livingstone meeting near Lake Tanganyika in October 1871; during which Stanley uttered the famous phrase: '**Dr Livingstone I presume?**' With new supplies from Stanley, Livingstone continued his efforts to find the source of the Nile. His health had been poor for many years and he died on 1 May 1873. His body was taken back to England and buried in Westminster Abbey.

Livingstone's fame as an explorer and his obsession with learning the sources of the Nile River as founded on the belief that if he could solve that age-old mystery, his fame would give him the influence to end the East African Slave trade. To him finding the source of the Nile had been one of his greatest goals and that was what would measure his achievement. He believed his contribution would be a valuable means speaking more loudly about issues that were a big problems to Africans especially the abolition of East African slave trade. To him slave trade was the evil that he always wished to fight. His subsequent exploration of the central African watershed was the culmination of the classic period of European geographical discovery and colonial penetration of Africa. His missionary travels, which led to his disappearance and eventual death in Africa— subsequently lead to glorification as a posthumous national hero thus leading to the founding of several major central African Christian missionary initiatives later carried forward by Europeans

Henry Morton Stanley unlike Dr. David Livingstone, did the exploration work motivated by fame and fortune. He traveled in large, well-armed expeditions. Despite his never having set foot in Africa before, he assembled a caravan of over 200 porters and struck out into the unknown. His first journey in East Africa aimed to find the whereabout of Dr David Livingstone who had remained unheard of for a long time. The type of reception he got in the East African coast was mainly from Arab slave traders who gave him a lot of confidence that he would find Dr. David Livingstone. This became the basis of his motto *"Wherever he is, be sure I shall not give up the chase."* On those grounds he later wrote to the New York Herald's editor33 stating *"If alive you shall hear what he has to say. If dead I will find him and bring his bones to you",* And indeed on 13th November 1871 Stanleys met Dr. Livingstone in Kigoma- Ujiji with the greeting: " Dr Livingstone I presume". But it s said Dr. Livingstone just

Livingstone I presume". But it s said Dr. Livingstone just responded, "**you have brought me new life."**

After meeting Dr Livingstone and following Livingstone's refusal to return to Europe with him Stanley stayed in Europe only briefly and then travelled back to East Africa only to make a second expedition setting off from Zanzibar towards Lake Victoria. He sailed around the Lake in his boat called *Lady Alice.* From Lake Victoria he headed to Central Africa towards Nyangwe and the Congo River, which he followed for some 3,220 kilometers from its tributaries to the sea, reaching Boma in August 1877. He then set off back into Central Africa to find Emin Pasha.

---

[33] *New York Herald was one of his sponsors for this journey of exploration.*

11

H.M. STANLEY AND KING LEOPOLD III ALLIANCE

The expedition Stanley made in 1874 became considered as one of the most audacious journeys in the history of African explorations. Over the course of 133 weeks, his party successfully trekked into the continent's central watershed and scoured its lakes in his 24-foot boat. Stanley became the first person to circumnavigate Lake Victoria, Africa's largest body of water. Afterwards Stanley sailed on Lake Tanganyika before venturing a 1,800 miles journey down the Congo River to the Atlantic Ocean. It was an ambitious and dangerous expedition, as approximately half of the members in the expedition of about 300 people died from diseases, drowning, and repeated confrontations with local African natives. He nevertheless gained from geography of the central African region, which enabled him to make his name as an adventurer.

Stanley was an explorer turned a business agent. In the Congo he got named Bula Matari which was a term that was coined by people of the Congo to refer to him.. Bula Matari partly referred to his honest hard work and also to his pointless aggression, which translated as Breaker of Rocks. Stanley earned the name witnessing how he acted and behaved as one of the most famous explorers and most economic development adventurers in central Africa. During his early years as an explorer in Africa, and after he had found Livingstone in his first trip to the great lakes region he navigated around Lake Victoria in only 50 days to find if it was a single water body. He went on to navigate Lake Tanganyika, the deepest Lake in the world, after which he explored the whole length of River Congo 1,800 kilometres from the beginning to the river mouth on the Atlantic Ocean. He used his boat, Lady Alice, as he did the exploration of the lakes and the river encountering the treacherous and rocky rapids of River Congo. As he moved down the river and as he got to the points which the rapids were too treacherous he ordered the boat to be lifted out of the water and carried by his African men for a long distance until he was past the dangerous rapids.

Stanley was adventurous and a man of many mysteries. He made his way as a waif out of a work-house to become the most famous explorer in Africa. In his early days he also had assignments in the Middle East and Asia under the guise of an American reporter. He also worked for the Belgium King Leopold III who in any case exploited him to the full. He was used by the Belgium King to approach African chiefs in the Congo, with who he signed fake treaties, which in the end made the chiefs to cede their land and property to king Leopold III. Following the completion of those treaties it became possible for the King to acquire the whole of the Congo River basin as his country, which got named Congo Free State (CFS). Following the conclusion of the treaties with the local African Chiefs King Leopold III directed to transfer the management of the land to William Mackinnon's company; the process that started to lay the foundation of the British East African Protectorate[34].

Besides those exploration assignments and undertakings, Stanley was specifically on mission for King Leopold II of Belgium who had

---

[34] *In 1990 British Protectorates were established over the Sultanate of Zanzibar and the Kingdom of Baganda (Uganda) respectively. N 1895 the company's territory in Kenya was transferred to the Crown as the East African Protectorate.*

directed him to establish treaties with local Chiefs in the Congo. Like it happened in other parts of the region, by other Europeans who vied to win territories in the continent of Africa (that of Carl Peters being a good case in point) the treaties concluded by Stanley with the local Chiefs of the Congo aimed to effectively give up their land to the Belgian crown35. When he had succeeded in convincing the Chiefs to sign the treaties Stanley was also required by King Leopold II to build a railway line and establish the groundwork for a colonial state, controlled by Leopold III.

From the going of things, King Leopold III was well versed with resources in the Congo Basin, which he planned to have exclusive rights and ownership. The result was the creation of the Congo, which came to be known as the Congo Free State (CFS). Following that success, Stanley's initial work was to enable King Leopold III to start the plundering of the natural resources of Congo Basin region. Congo was endowed with abundant resources such as minerals, ivory, and rubber. The area had hard wood and good fertile land. The local people of the Congo were also seen to be among the resources that could be used in form of slaves, which would provide free labour and enrich the King's coffers.

Stanley's trans-Africa expedition cemented his reputation as the heir to Livingstone. In 1878, the explorer signed on with King Leopold III for a project to bring trade to the African Congo. To realize international recognition King Leopold started by manifesting himself as one whose intention was to bring humanitarian services to the people of the Congo. In reality, King Leopold was only using charity as a screen or thick layer of icing on rotten cake. Through Henry Morton Stanley he created ***a Congo***

---

[35]Fake treaties were signed by Stanley, but a little later Carl Peters signed similar treaties with local Chiefs in the interior of Tanganyika which is today Tanzania.

Free State whose people and resources he would eventually exploit for his own enrichment. As has been hinted, the King's agent, Stanley, built roads, outposts and even a railway lines, earning the nickname *Bula Matari,* or *Breaker of Rocks*, for his tireless construction efforts. Historian scholars till this day have kept debating how much Stanley knew about Leopold's true plans. Certainly the infrastructure he built later helped to facilitate years of forced labour and violence that often led to the deaths of millions of people of Congo.

Stanley really proved to be "a Bula Matari". He worked so hard that he never allowed anything in his plans to fail. To do so his actions especially where African workers were concerned, he proved to be very forceful and cruel. A small mistake by an African could lead to losing his life. He built infrastructure, like for example the railway line that would support the work of evacuation of products that would be harvested in the CFS for King Leopold. He oversaw the harvest and collection of thousands of tons of ivory.[36] He oversaw the collection of other products such as rubber tapped from the Congo forest; he oversaw the harvesting of high value timber, and also involved in ensuring that land was cleared for construction of military camps, warehouses, and railway and ship terminals on the Atlantic coast.

Stanley and his European men were always well armed with guns, which made the defenseless Africans to behave and follow instructions as directed. Any chance of an uprising was put down by gunfire. In most cases African carriers or villagers that were in his company were armed only with machetes, spears. In various parts of the Congo the slave hunters and Staley's men ganged up and

---

[36] *The amount of ivory collected gave an indication of how many elephants and rhinos were being killed.*

invaded villages, and when such thing happened Stanley and his men claimed they were on self-defense against attacks by local people. In most cases the villagers lost in those battles, and consequently they got arrested, taken as slaves and others just got shot and died. The villagers would be rounded up, fire would be open on them making thousands of villagers that lived in close proximity to the route that Stanley and his men passed through got invaded and killed. To Stanley and his European men African villagers were worth nothing better than worthless creatures that did not deserve to be in this universe. Those villagers that could be apprehended alive got surrounded, arrested, chained up, and then taken away to serve as carriers or to be sold to Arab slave traders.

According to Stanley attacks on African villages was necessary because the Africans were cannibals (so they suspected) and also uncivilized. According to him it was good to arrest these people before they did any harm to his men. The Africans were cannibals and to teach them a lesson, they only had to be hunted down and punished. He also wished to clear areas where warehouses and military camps would be established, and African village areas would be easier to clean up to pave the way for construction of those warehouses and military camps. So, the village areas became the most targeted sites; meaning that the villagers would have to be forcefully cleared either by setting them on fire or by capturing the occupants, who would be enslaved or even killed to pave the way for the military camps, warehouses and, recreation grounds for the European men.

The case of the Congo is unique, as the villagers that survived sale to slave traders were recruited and ordered to go to the forest to collect rubber; an assignment that each villager would have to fulfill by observing the quarter of rubber that he would have to collect, failure of which very harsh punishments were executed. Cruel executions were exercised, as a condition to meet the interests of the governors of the CFS, which was under the overall control of Henry Morton Stanley on behalf of King Leopold III of Belgium. CFS grew to be a very horrific place for Africans.

King Leopold III never visited the Congo but controlled the country and its resources by remote means, through an agency company. His interest was not to be in the CFS but to plunder the natural resources of that African land. Following the treaties that had been completed for King Leopold III CFS sole property of the Belgium king, not the Government of Belgium. The CFS was operated as a corporate State privately controlled by the Monarchy. The CFS was a big chunk of African land, whose size was 2.4 million km2. Like has been stated, the state was managed by agents on his behalf. The central issue is in the way the CFS was mismanaged. Villages were recklessly put on fire to clear sites for the development of military centres and for construction of warehouses to store ivory, rubber, valuable hard wood, and minerals got from the Congo Forest.

CFS became a place that was eyed by many types of people with interest to take business opportunities of one type or the other. Arab slave traders were moving around to get slaves. Various types of agencies were around to buy ivory and rubber. In the meanwhile many agency spies were appointed to manage certain provinces. In the meanwhile King Leopold III wished to see all the revenues collected from the states including taxes, duties, and other incomes directed to him, but in essence each collection agency directed its collections to its personal accounts or coffers. The management of resources in the Congo Free State became so chaotic that every Agency or business tried the best it could to maximize its income from what it could collect. There was no system established to ensure that there was control and/or audit of the reports that were given by managers about the amount of revenue that was being collected. Furthermore, there was the problem of the African Arab slavers especially those of Zanzibar such as Tippu Tip who was a chief slaver in the whole Great Lakes region, and who under the influence of Stanley, and supported by King Leopold was nominated to be Liwali (or Governor of one of the Congo provinces). As an appointed governor Tippu Tip was logically and legally under obligation to submit all revenue collections to the King's accounts, but he never submitted the revenues he collected in his province to the accounts of King Leopold III.

The appointment of Tippu Tip to be governor of Stanleyville (or Stanley Province) was done under the assumption that Tippu Tip would make the coordination and management of that province easier. It was hoped that Tippu Tip would be a faithful governor given the fact that Stanley had recommended him highly to King Leopold III. However, Tippu Tip was a respectable man among Arab communities. His appointment as governor (or Liwali) of one of the Congo provinces he was a great privilege and it was hoped that he would assist in boosting revenue collection from the province. In the meanwhile, the appointment gave him greater liverage to have a wider ground for hunting for slaves which was his main preoccupation in the Great Lakes region). But Stanley's assumption and so much trust on him was too short sighted.

Tippu Tip was a renowned slave trader in East and central Africa. Appointing him governor of a province in CFS meant he now had the mandate to put all the people in his province, to slavery. No doubt the appointment took Stanley and King Leopold III too far in terms of their reputation; especially at this time when the whole of

Europe was in a campaign to abolish slave trade. The situation looked even more devastating considering that the new alliance was cementing relationship between Sultan Barghash of Zanzibar (whose economy was founded on slave trading), Stanley, King Leopold III, Tippu Tip to work together to enhance slave trade in CFS and in the Great lakes as a whole. The move made the external world, notably the West European countries increasingly concerned about the cooperation that was growing up between King Leopold (supported by Hery Morton Stanley) with the slavers of Zanzibar.

King Leopold had for a long time known Congo's wealth potential. He started by giving false reasons or objectives of the acquisition of the CFS; that, his intention was to uplift the social state of the local communities and also to do real development of the Congo area. Time proved King Leopold had been cheating to escape criticism from international community. Actually social life of Congolese people worsened soon as the CFS came under his control. Instead, he devastated the Congo to a level unprecedented anywhere in Central Africa. Under Leopold III the CFS experienced a lot of blood shedding. The local people got killed in various ways. CFS became so blood stained that it ended up to be one of greatest international scandals of the late 19th and early 20th Century. The CFS became depopulated and its resources got depleted so much that it went to history as one of the most plundered states of Black Africa.

Those who were involved in the harvesting of the natural resources especially rubber, were usually put to undue confrontation with each other. Supervisors served to be the leading conflict creators and harvesters were perpetually under harassment and torture. Conflicts sparked between one group of African rubber collectors and another. Conflicts were further exacerbated by the various governors of provinces. Each of the governors had come to realize that that was the time to make private wealth. The administrative system became even more chaotic when through Henry Morton Stanley who granted permission to use slavers of Zanzibar to be among the managers of some states of CFS.

The alliance between Stanley, King Leopold III, and the Sultan of Zanzibar made the slave traders in the region to rejoice. They became even happier when Tippu Tip was appointed manager in one of the provinces of CFS. The conflicts fueled further conflicts or wars that are estimated to have claimed over 50% of the population of the whole area of the Congo. Presence of foreigners in the Congo kept escalating the number of people who died due to lack of immunity to new diseases introduced by contact with foreigners in the area. Tuberculosis, syphilis, gonorrhea, and measles were among the new diseases that foreigners that visited the CFS introduced to the local population. The conflicts, the shameful mass-killing of local Africans, the reckless plundering of natural resources, the escalation of arrests of Congo people by slave traders, the killing of children and the endless arrests of women for sexual abuses and the ultimate killing of those women, painted a very bad image of King Leopold III.

The bad image that kept growing unabated led to the termination of the Monarchy's absolute rule in CFS. The great fall ultimately led to the take over of CFS by the Belgium government, in 1908.The account of what exactly happened was that in the Berlin Conference held in 1885/6 Leopold III made a lot of pledges to end slave trade but that was already too late for him. His humanitarian pledges to the Berlin Conference (to end slavery), meant war was now inevitable; and indeed open warfare broke out in late November 1892. Both sides fought by proxy, arming and leading the populations of the upper Congo forests in conflict. By early 1894 the Zanzibari/Swahili slavers were defeated in the Eastern Congo region and the Congo -Arab war came to an end. In other words King Leopold III stance turned confrontational against his once-allies. The war against the Swahili Arab economic and political power was presented as a Christian anti- slavery crusade.

It can be recollected -in February 5, 1885 King Leopold III with a lot of operational support from Henry Morton Stanley, his key agent in the Congo, established the CFS, brutally seizing the African landmass as his personal possession. Rather than controlling the Congo as a colony, as other European powers were doing throughout Africa, Leopold III privately owned the region. However, due to the gross mismanagement and brutality that was going on in the CFS the Belgium Parliament argued in the Berlin Conference and established that need to replace the previous, privately owned Congo Free State (CFS) after international outrage over abuses which brought pressure for supervision and accountability. The government argument assisted in providing the official Belgium attitude, which was to enhance sort of partnership. According to Belgium government Africans were to be cared for and trained.

There is another thing that needs to be said about the tapping and collection of rubber from the Congo Forest. Rubber was one of the major sources of revenue under the rule of King Leopold III. The African villagers were the ones who were forcefully required to do the tapping work; they were the ones who were ordered from their villages to go and participate in the collection of rubber. When they were out in the fields they were required to adhere to certain conditions. They would have to meet their rubber collection quarters or their hands would get chopped off as a punishment for failing to reach set targets. That sounded like a jock but in reality that is what happened. In most cases failure to meet the rubber collection quotas was punishable by death. Where lenience applied one of their hands would have to be chopped off.

Meanwhile, there was this serious issue of amputating people's hands, as a punishment to those villagers who failed to meet the conditions of collection of rubber. The public military forces, (i.e. militia) were required to provide the hands of their victims as proof that they had shot and killed someone, as it was believed that they would otherwise use the guns imported from Europe at considerable cost for hunting. However, the rubber quotas were in part paid off in chopped-off hands or legs. Sometimes, the villagers were required by the militia to collect the limbs and carry them in baskets to the camp where they got piled together.

Often, there were small wars where villages attacked and killed people of neighbouring villages with a view to gather hands. This to them was necessary because rubber quotas were too unrealistic to fulfill. From all the bodies killed in the field, you had to cut off the hands, which would be submitted to supervisors as proof or evidence of the number of hands cut off by each soldier, who had to bring them in baskets. The baskets of severed hands would be set down at the feet of the European post commanders. All these actions became the symbol of the Congo Free State atrocities. The collection of hands became an end in itself. *Force Publique* (the militia) soldiers brought them to the stations in place of rubber; they even went out to harvest the people's hands instead of rubber.

The depletion of Congo population from the beginning of King Leopold 111's era to the beginning of Belgian state rule in 1908 was remarkable. Estimates of the death toll varied considerably because no exact numbers could be estimated. Actually the number of those who died during the period could be a lot more than what has kept been stated. Estimates made by some contemporary observers suggest that the population of the whole area decreased by 50% or more during the period.

However, Controversy only continued to follow Stanley in 1887, when he led an African expedition to rescue Emin Pasha, who was a German territorial governor who was under attack from Muslim rebels in Southern Sudan. The journey proved to be a disaster on almost all fronts. The strategy that Stanley came up with was to split the expedition in two halves, the front or advance team that would be under his own leadership and the rear one which would comprise of most of his European young assistants. The front column eventually reached Pasha in 1888. However before they got to the point of rescue several hundred members of his party perished from disease and the alleged Pygmy attacks. Even more horrific were the atrocities committed by the expedition's unsupervised rear column, whose European members indiscriminately tortured and murdered countless Africans that they met on the way. The young Europeans men attacked the local villagers, they raped and killed hundreds of villagers using their guns. In some places the villagers responded in self-defense using their inferior weapons such as spears, arrows, and machetes. Actually, in that expedition along the way many villages were put on fire and hundreds of local people died and the lucky ones fled to hiding places deep into the equatorial forest.

The Pasha expedition would be Stanley's last. He returned to London in 1890, and later authored books and toured the lecture circuit before serving in the British parliament. He was widely hailed as a hero and even knighted by Queen Victoria; yet by the early 20th century revelations of his teams' brutality in the CFS permanently cast a shadow over his career. When the journalist-turned-explorer later died in 1904, his connection to the Congo atrocities saw him denied burial in Westminster Abbey alongside his old associate, David Livingston.

12

THE TIME OF IMPERIALISM IN AFRICA

Imperialism could be defined as a state policy, practice, or advocacy of extending power and dominion, especially by direct territorial acquisition or by gaining political and economic control of other territories and peoples. There is also what is referred to as the New Imperialism, which is characterized by a period of colonial expansion especially by European powers including USA and Japan during the late 19th and early 20th centuries.

During the 19th and 20th centuries, the Western powers individually conquered almost all of Africa and parts of Asia. The New imperialism became a necessary step for the development of new markets, new controls, and new authorities. Those were issues which were in turn necessary for the sustainment of social and economic development in Europe. As the Industrial revolution kept on growing, conditions got created where the process needed to be supported by smooth supply of raw materials and markets for products that were coming from those industries. The raw materials as well as markets would have to be found to ensure that the industrial operations continued smoothly, without worries of foreseeable impediments. The overall objective was to ensure there was a rapidly growing economy in the Western world.

There developed two types of imperialism namely the direct or formal and indirect or informal imperialism. The direct or formal imperialism could be defined as physical control or full-fledged colonial rule while informal imperialism was less direct but remained a powerful form of dominance by the use of indirect means, usually economic, but often with a lurking military threat, to control a nation or territory. Indirect imperialism was most common before the time of scramble for Africa; but a few countries continued to practice it, and that has been so till this day. Great Britain, France, Spain, Portugal, Belgium, Germany and most of the rest of European countries have been good examples of direct Imperialist countries, which went as far as taking colonies in various parts of the world, especially Africa and installed their direct control economically, socially, politically and of course militarily.

On the other hand, USA could be cited as a good example of a country which never got involved in direct Imperialism but has been a major indirect Imperialist country in the world, which until this day has indirect economic (including trade), political and even technological control of many countries or regions of the world.

What is common with the two types of Imperialism is the military and ideological control of the nations concerned. For instance, till this day USA has military installation in many parts of the world including Asia, Middle East, Far East Asia, some places in Africa and South America. Imperialism has commonly also taken the form of religious control or influence. Certain religions especially Christianity and Islam have had direct control in quite a number of countries in the World. An example could be taken of countries such as the Republic of Ireland, Argentina, Costa Rica, Denmark, England, Froe Islands, Georgia, Greenland, and others. Some of such countries have Christianity as their official religion, which is so stated in their constitutions. Similarly, most of the North African countries are more closely inclined to Islamism with no much room for flexibility. Indonesia too has all its policies completely aligned to those of the Islamic religion and what is most interesting is the number of people, almost the entire population of that country is Moslems.

What happened in the 19th century was that an imperial country tried to increase its wealth and extended its reach by controlling and taxing another or other countries, which happened in various ways in its grab, including through trading or other means. . To keep production costs down, imperial companies competed to find the cheapest workers, often settling on droid robots or slave labour. The empire directed its engineers to create the latest in military technology, such as Galaxy Guns, turbo lasers, and planetary shields. To dominate trade and high-tech innovation, an Empire made sure to control key natural resources, such as oil, gas and precious metals; thus, exploiting the wealth of the nation that was being subject to control but also involving in conquering and terrorizing the population. With time people who were suppressed under Imperialism sometimes rebelled; but most cases they got silenced owing to the superiority of the military technology that the imperial country or company possessed and employed when there was need to do so.

In those circumstances the core territory of an empire would usually consist of a dominant nation or kingdom with a shared language and religion. A case in point could be that of ancient Rome during the Roman Empire or the United Kingdom during the British Empire. The core territory of the empire would usually core conquer and then exploit weaker territories on the periphery of the empire by demanding unequal trade, taxes, tribute, or plunder. Most famous empires started when a dictator or emperor overthrew a democratic government. For example, Nazi Germany overthrew the Weimar Republic; the French Revolution led to Napoleon's

French Empire; and Imperial Rome overthrew the Roman Republic just the same way the Galactic Empire overthrew the Old Republic. These examples are those of the Old empires.

The implication here is that there was the old and new Imperialism. The New Imperialism characterized a period of colonial expansion by European powers, including the United States, and Japan during the late 19th and early 20th centuries. The period featured an unprecedented pursuit of overseas territorial acquisitions. In the age of new Imperialism, European states established vast empires mainly in Africa, but also in Asia and the Middle East. Due to imperialism, some aspects of life, such as education, transportation and medicine is alleged to have improved in quite a number of places in Africa. Those social services improved not with a focus to Africans but to ease supply of utilities for the Imperial government officers or personnel, which peripherally enabled the few lucky Africans to take some advantage of.

To begin with, some few privileged Africans strayed from their tribal beliefs and began adopting western beliefs (largely Christianity), and Western civilization norms, thus leading to internal cultural conflicts, which is what the colonial governments and its institutions wished to see happen.

Colonial administrations loved to have a state of divide- and-rule. Competition increased and conflict grew between imperial powers themselves. During the era of New Imperialism, the Western powers individually conquered almost all of Africa through what came to be known as the scramble for Africa. Some parts of Asia were also taken over almost along similar lines.

In Africa the age of new Imperialism started around 1870s but got better defined towards the end of scramble for Africa, which was towards the last two decades of the 19th Century. That was the time when European states established vast empires mainly in Africa, Asia and the Middle East. The Imperialism that was getting planted led to the assimilation and loss of unique indigenous cultures; it gave a few privileged native people some opportunities that enabled them to live a new improved lifestyle, it made changes in the legislative systems including laws that gave people a little more freedom and rights and a number of other changes that were geared to assimilating the local communities so that they could be aligned to those of Imperial countries. The effort of Imperial nations was to have a section of strong local community that was well brain washed to support the governance system of the colonial administration.

Between the early 1880s and 1914 the map of the world was redrawn, especially in Africa. Actually by this period African countries were under the social, economic and political influence of one or the other of the European Imperial nation.

Throughout world history, kingdoms and nations have competed to expand their territories and power at the expense of others. The largest empires such as Great Britain began small and expanded to rule over ethnically and religiously diverse groups of people, often with the aid of military and a technological advances.

In as far as Africa was concerned it became a big victim of both direct and indirect imperialism. The Western European countries established direct political control over African territories under what came to be known as the partitioning or the scramble for Africa. Each of the major European nations claimed and put up a strong struggle/demand to get a slice of African land. The slices got taken in form of colonies or protectorates. Some European countries had had experience in such processes of taking colonies. Britain for instance was a good example of European countries, which had been colonizers even before the 18th Century. There had been a British rule in America before 1776, in India in the years between 1858 and 1947, in Hong Kong in the years between 1842 – and 1997, in Nigeria from 1885 and in Kenya from 1880 to the time of political independence in 1963. In very few cases if any at all, Africans were involved in passing the laws that were made for the governance of their countries, the reason being that the Africans were just elements which were there to receive directions from the owners of the country, i.e. the colonial governments. This may also explain why it has often been said the Berlin Conference of 1885/86 only served to formally divorce or expel Africans from their countries. The local people got forced to live in the same country as colonialists as second grade citizens with no say in any of its resources. Colonialism became an evil introduction. It involved direct forceful occupation of a weaker state or country by a stronger and sometimes much more developed state. This imposition of foreign administrative governance on the weaker State led to economic exploration and exploitation, political dominance, cultural and linguistic domination, social oppression and suppression of local African people by the colonizers. It is these negative characteristic features of Colonialism that made it a repulsive political cum cultural phenomenon and made colonialism a target of severe criticism by politicians, religious leaders, journalists, enlightened academics, especially literary artists, and any other person who saw and kept watching on what was being done to the local people compared to foreigners in that same country.

In the meantime, informal rule was gradually proving to be the preferred option for the colonial nations. Formal or direct rule was proving to be too expensive; and thus administration of a country at a level below district level showed to be more viable if left to native authorities. So in those places where there was a tradition of Chiefs system, that got further encouraged. Where such system did not exist people who appeared to be influential, or headmen of some areas got appointed to be chiefs. Where such introductions were made the local governments became very chaotic, because of the fact that some chiefs had no experience to what it meant to be a chief.

History has shown that some empires survive for a relatively long time while others, actually the majority last for quite a short time; but in all cases they never last forever. The point is that in most cases empires often leave behind lasting legacy of changes in the forms of political, economic, and cultural influences. To understand this phenomenon better the following cases could be taken note of. The first case or example is that of Latin American countries where hundreds of millions of Latin Americans today speak Spanish and Portuguese, simply explained by the fact that, five hundred years ago, their ancestors were conquered by Spain and Portugal. In Africa since 19th century each European country left a lasting legacy to the country they ruled. First there were the British and the French, which respectively left legacies, which came to be as Anglophone and Francophone zones cultures, religions and even economic and educational systems. Similar legacies are found in other parts of Africa as left behind by European countries that ruled them. We for instance also have Portuguese legacies in Angola, and Mozambique, and Belgium legacies in the Democratic Republic of Congo (DRC).

Another example is that of the Islamic Empire which has spread its religion from Arabia to the whole of North Africa to as far as Morocco, Libya, Tunisia, EGYPT, and Mauritania, most of the Sahel countries and further to India and to the Far East Asia. This imperial expansion began from about 8th century CE and the Empire's religious influence lives on. This has been in spite of the fact that Islam originated from the Arabian Peninsula. Today, Indonesia in Southeast Asia has the world's largest Muslim population today. The influences should be seen as the outstanding legacies of Islamic Imperialism, which was put in place some 13 or 14 hundred of years ago but left behind far-reaching and long-lasting influences.

We could take another case of England, a small island nation on the periphery of Eurasia. This small country whose economic performance was not so remarkable by the end of 16th Century, but with tremendous transformations following the industrial revolution, which started only from early 18th Century led to quick expansion of Imperialism to Africa and Asia. Britain came to rule over many parts of the world and became the most impressive empire of all time. There was a time when they used to boast with a phrase " the sun never sets in the British Empire" which meant that they were there everywhere on the globe, and thus when the sun was setting in one area of the empire it was rising in another.

England became a dominant world power through its rule of the British Empire, the largest empire in the history of the world. Today we keep wondering how a small a small island country on the far edge of the Eurasian continent came to rule over one-quarter of the world's land mass and population. The explanation given for that success is certainly attributed to the wealth and technological advances that emerged from the Industrial Revolution, which in itself gained a lot from transatlantic slave trade. The crucial question is why powerful Asian countries such as China or India didn't conquer Europe instead of the other way around. Even when we come to the African context we find that before the 16th Centuries powerful nations such as Mali, ancient Ghana, Songhai and several others were quite advanced compared to some countries in Europe including Britain, but why didn't they have any chance to conquer Europe and instead the opposite happened less than a couple of centuries later?

A study of the modern empires enables us to understand about the origins of the uneven distribution of wealth and technology in the world today. Recently, it has been noted that the Western world (Europe and USA) had only 15 percent of the world's population but controlled 53 percent of the world's wealth. It is also not a coincidence these same countries have been on the lead in terms of technological revolutions that occurred in the last two centuries. The last interesting factor that we wish to bring up is that of the English language, which has stood up to be a dominant language of the world especially in matters of Information Communications (ICT). Despite the relatively small number of native English speakers in the world compared to Chinese or other languages, there are more English language websites than any other language. The answers to these questions could be found in a question "Why are Europe and the United States today so wealthy in contrast to the rest of the world?" In other words, a simple answer could be found in the fact that, factors such as innovation, competition, greed, and luck could have contributed to such success.

From the 19th Century European explorers were dispatched to investigate the Eastern and Central Africa, which were seen to be viable areas for the expanding level of European presence and Imperialism. It was not yet time for the new or formal imperialism through colonization, but paved way for the same. Until 1914, the time when the First World War broke almost all parts of the African continent had fallen to European control of one or the other of the European nations.

There have been questions about why Africa ended up to be so devastated, ignored, and improvised? At no point in recent history have calls for Africa to industrialize been stronger than they are now. Across the continent, industrialization is arguably the most talked about subject among policy-makers. So why has action on the ground failed to move the needle on this important development marker. For quite some time in the past Africa accounted for more than 3% of global manufacturing. That was particularly true in the 1970s, but that percentage had gone down by 50% by 2016; thus warning that Africa's manufacturing industry was likely to remain small throughout the foreseeable future, perhaps till beyond 2030. The state of African industrial sector today still accounts for a very low share of global manufacturing. The share of the region in global manufacturing value added fell from 1.2% in 2000 to 1.1% in 2008. In developing Asia, it rose from 13 per cent to 25 per cent. These are the type of issues that call for a lot more serious discussions not only in Africa but perhaps globally.

However, the scramble for Africa became the starting point of the new Imperialism, which involved the direct control and administration of nations in Africa. That new form of Imperialism kept consolidating itself from the year 1881 to 1914 when European control of the continent had reached almost 90% from only 10% of the previous type Imperial ownership. By the end of 1914 almost all countries of Africa were now under direct control of Europe; the only exception to the rule being Ethiopia, Liberia, and a portion of

Somalia. These were the only independent or one can say semi-independent states in the whole Sub-Saharan Africa that in some way escaped colonization by Europe.; but in any case, these countries never escaped control through indirect imperialism.

The rapid change from dark continent, (which Europeans had had least interest to have their involvement), to this state of direct involvement in the control of every piece of land in Africa was not without a reason. There were multiples of motivations for European colonizers. The motivations included the desire for valuable resources, the quest for national prestige, tensions between pairs of European powers, religious missionary zeal and internal African native politics. Actually, these developments led to the convening of the Berlin conference that took place in 1885/6. That meeting aimed to put in place regulations for European colonization and trade in Africa. That was the time when European nations got legal endorsement from among themselves to own slices of land on the African continent. Following the Berlin conference, it became certain that Africa was declared persona are non grata[37] The Africans automatically became losers of their continent. From that point they would only remain contributors of free labour to the new owners of the land.

We have already hinted that only countries that were until then not under the colonial control were Abyssinia (the present day Ethiopia), Some section of present day Somalia and Liberia; and this was so because of very special reasons. Ethiopia for instance managed to avoid falling under colonization because while much of Africa was falling to invasion, Ethiopia, managed to successfully resist colonization and maintain its independence. This great job

---

[37] *Personal non grata is a person who lives in his country without documents that legalized his presence.*

was a result of non other than its reforming emperor, Menelik II. On March 1, 1896, the Italians invaded Ethiopia from their neighboring colony of Eritrea but were repulsed by the strong army of Emperor Menelik II. At the time of European colonization of Africa, the nation of Ethiopia was divided into domains, each ruled by a prince one of who was Menelik II. Born in 1844, Menelik ruled the Shoa region in central Ethiopia for 24 years when he succeeded Emperor Yohannes in 1889.

What made Menelik to succeed to repulse Italy was in some way pure luck. What happened was that During Menelik's rise to power; the Italians allied with him and began supplying Ethiopia with weapons in hopes that Menelik would eventually surrender his power to them. Menelik built up an army of 100,000 and pushed back against the Italians after they declared Ethiopia was under their control. On March 1, 1896, the Italians invaded Ethiopia from their neighboring colony of Eritrea. Menelik and his army were prepared and decisively defeated the Italians at the Battle of Adwa. It was the first time in history that an African army had defeated a European army.

Along with being a brilliant strategist on the battlefield, Menelik modernized and reformed Ethiopia. He hired Europeans to plan modern roads and bridges to improve the country's infrastructure. He built a railway that linked the capital that he founded, Addis Ababa, to Djibouti. Menelik set up a western school system and introduced electricity as well as telephone service. He also founded Ethiopia's first modern bank and postal system. Menelik was Emperor of Ethiopia until his death in 1913. Because of him, Ethiopia was the only African nation, beside Liberia, to preserve its independence during this age of European invasion and imperialism. Ethiopia's current borders are a tribute to

Emperor Menelik's vision and his legacy of reform and modernization.

Regarding Liberia, which was another African country that never came under European rule, its story was completely different from that of Ethiopia. The sovereign nation of Liberia often never came under European rule because it was created so recently, in 1847 having got founded by the same imperial nations, in this case, Americans in 1821 and remained under their control for just over 17 years before partial independence was achieved through the declaration of a commonwealth on April 4, 1839. Considering that it was never colonized in the modern sense as it was being ruled from overseas by almost the same Imperialist countries. It does not deserve the credit that goes to Ethiopia.

However, looked at from another angle a different story emerges. Liberia was colonized in the sense of being settled from overseas. Freed American slaves settled there with the help of a Euro-American "back to Africa" movement. They ended out as the country's upper class. In 1847, ACS[38] encouraged those who were brought from America to proclaim independence, as it no longer wanted to support it, although some Northern state governments continued to provide money in the 1850s. The United States declined to act on requests from the ACS[39] to make Liberia an American colony, or to establish a formal protectorate over Liberia,

---

[38] *An* **independence** *referendum was held in* **Liberia** *on 27 October 1846. The result was 52% in favour, with* **independence** *being declared on 26 July 1847*

[39] *The* **ACS** *continued to operate during the American Civil War, and colonized 168 blacks while it was being waged. It sent 2,492 blacks to* **Liberia** *in the following*

but it did exercise a "moral protectorate" over Liberia, intervening when European powers threatened its territory or sovereignty.

Liberia retained its independence throughout the time of partition of Africa by European colonial powers during the late 19th century, while remaining in the American sphere of influence. From the 1920s, the America focused on exploitation of natural resources. Until 1980, Liberia was controlled politically by descendants of the liberated African Americans, known collectively as America-Liberians, who were a small minority of the population. Since 1980, the country has continued to be ruled by members of the indigenous peoples who constitute the majority of the population. However, years of civil war devastated Liberia and its economy.

Then there was Puntland, which was a province with a long and complicated history in an area curved from Somaliland. The term Puntland was derived from the Land of Punt mentioned by ancient Egyptian sources. The exact location of the fabled territory has remained a mystery. However, *Puntland,* officially the *Puntland* State of *Somalia* is a region in northeastern *Somalia*, centred on the town of Garoowe in the Nugal province. Puntland is an arid region of northeast Somalia. They declared the area an autonomous state in 1998, in part to avoid the clan warfare engulfing southern Somalia. Puntland is a destination for many Somalis displaced by violence in the south. Britain colonized the northwest of Somalia in order to produce food supplies for the British in the port of Aden. In 1887 Britain set up a Protectorate over Somaliland. France also colonized parts of the Somali AFRI coast. On the other hand, British Somaliland was officially a British protectorate in present-day Somaliland for which much of its existence, the territory was bordered by Italian Somaliland, French Somaliland, and Ethiopia.

In the Middle Ages the British Somaliland was a powerful Arab Sultanate, which got broken up in the 17th century. Its coast came under British influence in the early 19th century, but formal control was not acquired until it was taken from Egypt in 1884. Italy took control of British Somaliland in World War II in 1945. In 1960 it was united with the former Italian Somaliland to form Somalia. In 1991 a government opposition group declared the region comprising the former British Somaliland to be an independent state; but it was not internationally recognized. . In 1960 it was united with British Somaliland to form the independent Republic of Somalia. The one thing that Somalians were not affected was that while most countries in Africa during colonization period were, slavery. There are two main reasons for this. Firstly, going to Somalia for slaves was considered by slave traders as a waste in recourses for the western countries, because of the distance they would have to travel to collect the slaves.

The European nations that got direct rule or control of the continent following the scramble for Africa included Belgium, Britain, France, Germany, Italy, Portugal, and Spain. The scramble started in earnest after 1870s. Before then European nations preferred to concentrate on trading only on the coastal towns; and the most important holdings were Angola and Mozambique, which were holdings of Portugal. Others were, the Cape, which was the holding of United Kingdom and Algeria, which was the holding of France. Other European nations came in later as the need for involvement in the Imperialism picked up steam, which was towards the middle of 1880s.

European expansion of European interest to get involved in the imperial race was exacerbated by a number of factors. Number one was the technological advancement that facilitated European economic activity overseas. The second factor was the industrialization that was rapidly growing in Europe, such that markets for industrial products were needed and raw materials to feed the European factories were equally badly needed. The third factor was the rapid advancement of transport and communications mainly in forms of steam ships, railways, and telegraphs. The forth factor was the advancement in medical services, especially for tropical diseases which before then had proved to be a cause for many deaths. For instance the development of drugs such as quinine, which proved to be very effective for treatment of malaria, enabled a lot of accessibility of the Europeans to the tropical lands.

The above development opened new doors to the areas that had not been touched by informal Imperialism, namely Africa South of the Sahara. At that juncture Europe's leading elites started to be attracted for economic, political, and social reasons. Africa started to be a good destination point as it now provided an open market that would garner them a trade surplus, a market that bought more than it sold overall. This advantage became very vivid especially when Britain's balance of trade showed a growing deficit, with shrinking and increasingly protectionist continental markets due to the depression of 1873-96. Inevitably, surplus capital was often more profitably invested overseas, where cheap materials, limited competition, and abundant raw materials made a greater premium possible.

The curious question has always been why countries such as United Kingdom preferred the southern and eastern coasts of Africa. The answer was that that was a strategic point for stopover ports on the route to Asia and its empire in India. Yet, until 19th Century the amount of capital investment by Europeans remained very minimal compared to other continents. The only exception to this rule was the so called Union of South Africa where the British put a high priority in as far as the level of investment in the whole of African continent was concerned.

The companies involved in tropical African commerce were also relatively small. The only company that was big with substantial capital investment in the continent was the Cecil Rhodes DeBeers mining company. Rhodes himself had carved out Rhodesia (present day Zimbabwe and Zambia) for himself; while Leopold III of Belgium exploited the Congo Free State. Both Cecil Rhodes and Leopold III ruled their newly acquired states with high degree of brutality to the local people.

The fear that came to many, especially from the pro-imperialist arguments of colonial lobbyists who kept on arguing that sheltered overseas markets in Africa would solve the problems of low prices and overproduction caused by shrinking European continental markets. The shrinking of continental markets was seen in some quarters to be a key factor of the global new imperialism.

However, those arguments of relationship between capitalism and imperialism were at the same time somehow disagreed to have a link between capitalism and Imperialism, with argument that colonialism was being used mostly to promote state led development rather than corporate development. Further argument was that imperialism was not so clearly linked to capitalism and the free markets. On the basis of historical development, there was a very close linkage between colonialism, imperialism and state led approaches to development.

While Africa was considered to be a zone for only a small size of investment, other overseas regions were considered to be viable for higher levels of the investments that were made by the European countries. But slowly the vast interior of Africa between Egypt and the Gold and Diamond-rich Southern Africa started to be seen with a different eye. European nations started to see the strategic value in that vast area especially in securing the flow of overseas trade.

With that view, rivalry between powerful European nations started. In that rivalry there was Britain, France, Germany, and a few other West European powers. These accounted for most of the vast interior of Africa between Egypt and South Africa. They became leaders in the colonization of the large part of the African block. As we have indicated, while tropical Africa was not a large zone of investment, other overseas regions were. But the fact that Africa was lowly considered by the major colonial nations remained true only in the period before the 19th Century. With the new investment viability viewpoint the African block got assigned higher priority as the issue of shrinking markets and the need for raw materials for sustaining industrial development in Europe became more vivid. With that realization most attention got focused on Africa, hence triggering what became known or referred to as the scramble for the continent of Africa.

In that struggle European nations also found themselves under political pressure to secure lucrative markets against encroaching rivals in China and the eastern colonies, particularly India, Malaysia, Australia, and New Zealand. The idea of East-West trade became very fundamental. Britain for instance needed to get fully involved in the East West trade and in order to secure monopoly or at least a substantial stake in that area they became resistant to the idea of construction of Suez Canal. Initially the British government demonstrated to be strongly opposed to the construction of the canal.

However, the planning for the Suez Canal officially began in 1854, when a French former diplomat named Ferdinand de Lesseps negotiated an agreement with the Egyptian viceroy to form the Suez Canal Company. Since Lesseps' proposed canal had the support of the French Emperor Napoleon III, many British statesmen considered its construction a political scheme designed to undermine their dominance of global shipping. The British argued that supporting the canal would be a "suicidal act," and when Lesseps tried to sell shares in the canal company, British papers labeled the project "**a flagrant robbery gotten up to despoil the simple people**."[40] Lesseps went on to engage in a public war of words with Britain, and even challenged railway engineer Robert Stephenson to a duel after he condemned the project in Parliament. The British Empire continued to criticize the canal during its construction, but Britain later bought a 44% stake in the canal project after the Egyptian government auctioned off its shares in 1875.

However, the scramble for Africa could further have be found to have its roots in the need for acquisition of military and naval bases, for strategic purposes and the exercise of power. The growing navies, and new ships driven by steam power, required coaling stations and ports for maintenance. Defense bases were also needed for the protection of sea routes and communication lines. Most important was the fact that Colonies were also seen as assets that were crucial in the balance of power, negotiations, and were also very useful as items of exchange at times of international

---

[40] *Here they were referring to the poor Egyptians who initially were employed to work on the canal using very simple tools at very low wage. Certainly it was another project by implemented under the imperial muscles to exploit local Africans not for the benefit of the Africans but by the colonial nations and their people.*

bargaining. Colonies with large native populations were also seen to be a good source of military power.

Taking into account all those ambitions by the imperial nations we could now take a brief look at Africa and Africans. These had been subjected to miserable slave trade and all impacts that went with that trade. The Africans had been displaced and separated from their families forever. The various types of resources had been removed and more were going to be removed or plundered without involving the local people or rather the owners of those resources in any way. We could further imagine of the same imperialist guests who got to Africa masquerading as good people coming to bring civilization, as well as development with the message of transforming lives to the better as well as bringing salvation with a view of making the hosts as happy and rich as them.

One can figure what impression one would find in such persons? These issues and many others have needed to be critically looked at before going to the details about the impact of colonization of the continent of Africa. In short, it is not true that Africans gained a lot from presence of colonial administrations. The praises levelled on colonial administrations include the fact that they banned slave trade, taught people how to read and write, brought hospitals, built railways and developed large scale farms and so on. What is rarely asked is about who was the targeted beneficiaries of those actions. On the South there was Zimbabwe and in the East African highlands such as Kenya highlands, Kilimanjaro and Meru high land areas, land was removed from the people for opening up large scale farms for European farmers. On Kilimanjaro coffee, sisal, and wheat were the preferred crops. During the German colonial times i.e. from 1885 to 1918 Coffee was introduced as a crop exclusively for European farmers. The Africans were not allowed by law to get involved in coffee growing, for reasons that Africans had no capacity and/or competence to raise such crop. The obligation for Africans was only to go to the farms to contribute cheap or free labour.

Even in the health sector, dispensaries were established. The medical services were initially provided by European families mainly in form of first aid medications specifically to Europeans families that were operating in the nearby settler farms. Much later, dispensaries were established for Africans. The dispensaries were very poorly equipped with drugs and personnel. Only limited drugs to cure children and grown ups from round worms, tape worms and hook worms. A few better facilitated hospitals were gradually established under the ownership of missionaries who provided services to mainly colonial officers as well as Europeans in settler farms. At district levels hospitals that were established were exclusively for treating military personnel. Actually, it was illegal for Africans to seek utility services in places tat were earmarked for Europeans (which were the best facilitated with experts and facilities. What was worse, for almost eighty years of colonial rule in Africa, there was no single African doctor with a diploma or degree, and even with some certificate in any hospital catering for Africans. This was true in countries like Tanganyika. The handful medical assistants that were there were trained outside the country; and that was the status of all other sectors of the colonial economy.

Schools too were owned and operated by mission stations and as has been mentioned, only those Africans that had been converted to Christianity were admitted in them.

Before the times of Imperialism, Africans had their own routines in life. They had their personal schedules; they had their friends and family circles, and they had their way of doing things on everyday basis in their homes, in their communities and in their farms. Africans had their deeply held beliefs and ethics in terms of religion, politics, or social relations. On the arrival of colonialism things had to change. The Africans got robbed of their past ways of thinking or the style of doing things. The colonial officers as well as the missionaries suddenly, led to convincing the local people to forget those things that they were used to or the way they used to behave or else they would be declared misfits. All this got done in the name of civilizing the Africans with a view of ridding them of their savagery. Everything that the local person was used to doing got crushed and it was either to accept the new introductions or they got declared fools or people that had no discipline and the conflict between the two parties begun.

That was the type of social relationship that got built as the Europeans forcefully decided to take over various countries, regions and districts in Africa. Shock on the part of the indigenous people became the first effect of European imperialism in Africa in the late 19th century. The state of fear caused by threats on Africans became a normal thing that persisted until mid 20th century when most African nations started to win political independence. Imperialism meant that in various ways violences, (some formal and others informal), and some more hands-off than others.

Following the era of colonialism, i.e. from the 1880s onward, Africans had been living in a variety of ways. There were large kingdoms and sprawling urban centers, and there were smaller villages headed by elders and chiefs. As colonialism got entrenched some Africans kept on tending herds of animals while a few became educated elites of some sort. Others worshiped local gods and goddesses and their lives centered on the family and clan.[41] The European Imperialism/colonialism changed almost every social system that had been built by Africans for centuries; the Europeans disrupted the traditional ways and imposed their beliefs and social structures on colonized Africans. The colonialists went on to put in place laws and regulations that the owners of the land would have to follow, short of which they got imprisoned or hanged.

Colonialism became the number one hot nail in the African flesh, after the international slave trade. Colonialism disrupted traditional African ways of life. It introduced its own political organization, and social norms. Colonialism turned subsistence farming done by Africans into large-scale commodity exports done exclusively by European settler farmers. The patriarchal social structures were turned into European-dominated hierarchies and imposed Christianity and Western ideals. In other words, all this happened with the objective of enabling the imperial systems to work and achieve their objectives and goals. Africans remained dumbfounded because they were never allowed to be part of the new introductions. For an African to ask question or to query what was going on amounted to treason whose reward was capital punishment[42].

The above effects notwithstanding, the impact of new Imperialism and hence the colonialism was so great that the negative effects outweighed the gains got from it by far. We could start explaining this situation by stating once again that the main reason for colonization was to enable Europe to acquire raw

---

[41] *Abisai Temba: "Three Hundred Years on Kilimanjaro Mountain Area" Published by Notion Press (India) and "The Un-Walked Mile" Published by "Author House" UK.*

[42] *Abisai Temba; Three Hundred Years on Kilimanjaro Mountain Area; Published- Notion Press, India*

materials for their industries in Europe specifically during industrial revolution. This was so despite the fact that they were in a mission that has falsefully been reported to aim to civilize Africans. African colonization resulted to great negative impacts to the economy, social and political system of African States. The greatest negative impact was the exploitation of the natural resources by foreigners such that the local communities were not given a chance to benefit from them; instead the colonizers were given the upper hand. The impact of what happened in Congo Free State (CFS), tells it all. The foreign administrations used their administrative and military power to gain access to the natural resources, which led to major landscape destructions; they destroyed the otherwise peaceful lifestyle of the local people and made young men and women highly brainwashed.

Forests were cleared to get timber for shipbuilding, for furniture and for construction of houses in Europe. Trees were also cut down to provide firewood that was needed to power the steam engine trains and the forests were cleared odorlessly to provide woods that was used to construct rail tracks. These actions destroyed huge tracts of forests in the African colonies. The effects were almost catastrophic. The reckless cutting down of trees resulted to increased soil erosion since most forest cover was removed. Soil erosion led to siltation in rivers that greatly affected fishing activities. The communities that relied on fishing suffered the consequences of siltation because fish breeding grounds as well as fish habitats were greatly destroyed. The cutting down of trees contributed to negative impacts of the climate in the Africa continent. The cutting down of trees reduced the amount of rainfall received in various parts of Africa and also altered the climatic conditions including the wet and dry seasons, making it difficult for farmers to predict in exact terms the planting time as had been the case in the past.

During the colonization process communities had to be moved and relocated to pave the way to white settlements for largescale farming. The fertile land areas that were confiscated from the local people were not compensated for; which made life for Africans a lot worse than in the time before the arrival of colonialists. In some situations, the local people got resettled but that was done without consultations with the local communities. They got resettled in areas where it was less productive or less fertile or in areas with very harsh climatic conditions. Any resistance to move to resettlement resulted to prosecution, which in the case of German colonialists, could lead to death penalty by hanging. A lot of such hangings were witnessed especially on Kilimanjaro area in the period towards the turning of the 19th century or during the first two decades of the 20th century.

As can be recollected the devastation that was done in the Congo in what got known as the CFS will be remembered in Africa for many centuries to come. Congo got plundered, its local population got eliminated by fire-arms, its pygmy population was hunted down like one hunting monkeys which have eaten all crop in a farmer's garden; they got killed and others were exported to be put in museums.

Colonization also brought about different types of diseases. Some of the diseases were not common with the local communities. An example of diseases that got spread in the colonies by foreigners (especially the settlers) included the Rinderpest disease which affected the livestock of the Shona people of present day Zimbabwe and Botswana. The most interesting was the introduction to African communities of the jiggers which were brough by Indian labourers that were brought to Africa especially by the British to work in railway construction projects. The jiggers have remained a big problem; even today they are a big menace in many parts of East African region. The Indians also brought syphilis and other sexually transmitted diseases. In South Rhodesian, (present day Zimbabwe), the colonizers deliberately infected the local communities with different diseases to eliminate them and their livestock. Anthrax bacteria were used or put into the rivers so as to impoverish the locals by reducing their population and their animals.

During the scramble for Africa in 1885, the European powers divided the African continent into colonies for themselves that led to artificial creation of national boundaries. The boundaries were arbitrary and the locals were not consulted or taken into consideration. A boundary could run through the middle of one community and several communities with different cultural practices were brought under one colony. The boundary setting led to loss of sovereignty and the right to control their own destiny and to play a role in their own development or even conduct their own diplomacy and management of their resources. One could think of the situation in East Africa where some section of a tribe is found in Kenya, the other sections are in Tanzania and others in Uganda, and so on. Masai are a good case in point. These boundaries further led to the creation of present day independent states of Africa. Their effects are still felt today in the form of conflicts among communities in a country, some have even led coups and even genocides, as it was experienced in Rwanda in 1994.

Imposition of coercive and repression state rule by the colonialists completely destroyed the system of leadership that existed there before. The local societies were initially stable with their own system of governance and cultural norms and institutions.

The colonial rulers imposed their leadership on the people, by selecting their preferred individuals to rule over the rest of people. They introduced the subdivisions of land ownership, where everybody owned a piece of land for cultivation and other activities. The difference was in the type of ownership whereby Europeans were enabled to own the most fertile land while Africans were pushed to the marginal land. However, communities got used to communal land ownership. The land ownership was communal and everything was looked from a communal perspective.

A good case in point is again that of Kilimanjaro Mountain area, Meru, and some countries in West Africa the colonized countries such as Nigeria, Ghana, East Africa and southern Africa, assisted to introduce the indirect rule by introduction of Chief, and Paramount Chief (i.e. Chief of all other Chiefs). Such imposition was so artificial that the system chief Chiefs survived for hardly a decade. In the rest of the country chiefs were appointed even in places that had no experience in Chief system. Such imposition or appointments were intended to ease their work of tax collection. However, instead of achieving that goal the system ended up to be so corrupt that nothing of the type had ever been seen before in Africa.

Colonization introduced capitalism in Africa, which only assisted to divide people into classes of haves and have-nots. After independence in the 1960's, the same leaders who were imposed on the locals, and who were always viewed as collaborators with the White officials were the ones who took over leadership and acquired a lot of wealth of this of leadership allowed a concession to companies from former colonial masters to continue doing their business to date. These companies remained involved in several sectors of the economy varying from, mining to transport and farming. The concessions established tenures of up to 99 years or more. This has led to local communities feeling that the present leaders as perpetrating the same interest of the colonialists. The same have resulted in the formation of movement such as second liberation, by dissenting communities who feel they are disenfranchised and are wallowing in poverty and are unable to afford good education for their children like those who are in leadership.

Colonialism too, set a pace for urbanization in Africa. Since the turning of the 19th century urbanization spread throughout Africa, accompanied with emergence of many social evils. Some of the challenges associated with urbanization have included growth of slums and increased crime in most urban centers in Africa. Governments have tried to come up with solutions, but they have not been so successful. Poverty also remains rampant, both in urban and rural areas. The initiation of urbanization facilitated rural-urban migrations, which has resulted to many young people migrating from rural areas to urban areas in quest for white collar jobs (at least for those who have acquired some good education) and employments in industries as laborers for the rest. Unfortunately the jobs have been hard to find. Those people that are not successful in securing employment opportunities in the urban areas often find themselves engaged in criminal activities to earn their livelihood. Others engaged in prostitution. This has resulted to the wide spread of HIV/AIDs in African States.

The negative impacts that are associated with colonization have proved to be very numerous. It is not possible to point all of them, because they are more of a rule than exceptions. But once again they include degradation of natural resources, creation of capitalist tendencies, urbanization, introduction of foreign diseases to livestock, plants, and humans, and change of the social systems of living. Colonialism too brought bad impacts on Africa including the economies and social systems. Colonial Countries wanted land upon which they could harvest the natural resources, increase trade, produce inputs which were needed for the European industries, and gain power while at the same time introduced racism, civil unrest, and insatiable greed; all of which have had lasting impacts on Africa.

Africa road from colonization has been long and tumultuous. While the rush to colonize Africa started in the 17th century with the discovery of the vast amounts of gold, diamonds, and rubber, the colonization hit a fever pitch during the First World War .The repercussions of colonization have left deep wounds that still remain unhealed in the 21st century. Besides land upon which they would have exclusive right for natural resources, but the most negative effects of European colonization of Africa were those that brought racism, civil unrest, and insatiable greed; all of which have had lasting impacts on Africa.

The Land Acts that the colonial powers passed barred Africans from owning land in the same areas or in close proximity to the land that had been allocated to Europeans. The land for Europeans was fertile while the land that remained for Africans was very marginal. While in almost all African countries, Africans comprised of over 80% of the population, but were given only 8% percent of the land. Despite been the minority (approximately less than 20%), were given the most (over 90%) of the land to own43. That was the situation in

---

[43] *Mark Nyandoro: Senior lecturer in the department of Economic History, University of Zimbabwe.*

countries like South Africa, and Zimbabwe. Apartheid, which meant apartness or separateness, was officially declared in 1948 in South Africa even though separateness had been happening all along.

Besides all odds towards 1950s Africans in their respective countries began to cultivate a sense of nationalism. That mental transformation got highly prompted by sense of Pan- Africanism, which had started to germinate from the end of the Second World War. By the end of 1950s most African countries were exerting pressure on the colonial governments for self-governance. That pressure led many African countries to win their political independence towards the end of 1950s. Actually, by the end of the 20th Century the formal territorial ownership by colonial countries was wearing out; and that was due to the struggle by the local people to demand for political independence. Informal control by colonial countries kept sustained and kept on spreading more subtly. In the meanwhile, technological superiority, large loans (or debts) that were becoming governments' or private enterprises burden became impossible to pay; the self-governing governments sought for ownership of land or private industry, or got forced to agree to uneven trade agreements. Till the closing of 1990s most African countries had got faced with debt crisis, in which case they had to accept conditions set by Imperial countries that controlled financial institutions such as the World Bank and International Monetary Fund (IMF). The conditions emphasized on the necessity to restructure the African economies as conditions to get a debt relief.

13

SPECIAL PROJECTS FOR PROMOTION OF IMPERIALISM

As slave trade abolition campaign went on the European governments and businesses were sharpening their minds to tap resource potentials that existed in the Southern hemisphere especially in Sub-Saharan Africa. To start with explorers were dispatched to various places in Africa to find in details what was there to make those governments and /or businesses know how they could move in and harvest what ever resources that were there by whatever means that could be employed. Africa was understood by Europe to be a virgin place where most of the valuable resources such as minerals, forest products, land and many others had never been exploited and this was the time to do so. Explorers were dispatched to the interior of Africa to find out where features such as rivers, mountains, lakes, forests, and settlements were. That information would not only assist in improving the maps but also in designing strategies for occupation of Africa. King Leopold III of Belgium for instance was one of those imperial leaders who acted swiftly. He took the lead in the taking of what he referred to as Congo Free State (CFS) where he swiftly started to plunder the resources of the area. He used Henry Morton Stanley, the explorer, to go to the Congo, to make contacts with local chiefs with a view of making them cede their land and then, started plundering the resources of that part of the continent.

The authorities in the North were fighting tooth on nail to exploit opportunities to trade with the South not for the benefit of both sides but in a tricky way that would enable them to take as much as could possibly be taken from Africa. Until that time, Europe in general saw Africa as a no-man's-land, which was ready for taking and exploiting. What was most important was the fact that following the industrial revolution and considering that technological improvement was picking up very fast thus making production to grow very swiftly, need for enhancing the demand for more raw materials as well as markets for the products produced in those industries in Europe became a most pressing issue.

The major issue at this juncture was the speed and efficiency of delivery to the widening markets or from sources of raw materials. At that time the only route by sea to the southern markets especially Africa and Asia was along the West African coastline on the Atlantic to the Cape of Good Hope and up the East African coast. This was an extremely long route, which made great impact on cost of deliveries. That is how the idea of construction of the Suez Canal emerged. The idea was to find a possibility of opening the missing link between the Mediterranean and the Red Sea with the Indian Ocean, which would be possible by having a water route between the two water bodies.

The solution was found in the construction of a canal to connect Red Sea and Indian Ocean. The connection would allow ships to move straight South to the Indian Ocean. The Suez Canal's ability to stay open proved to be very important mainly because it was the shortest trade link between Europe and countries on the Indian and Pacific Oceans. Taking into account that the majority of the world's goods were and continued to be transported via sea, the Suez Canal would certainly reduce the time and cost of transporting goods from Europe to Indian Ocean and further on to Pacific countries. Due to imperialist forces the Canal originally started to be built by a French company, but British troops moved in to protect the canal from a civil war that was happening in Egypt. At that point, the Egyptian government sold shares to British government not only to enable Britain to own part of the canal but also because Egypt needed money to enhance the construction of the canal.

The Suez Canal stretches 120 miles from Port Said on the Mediterranean Sea in Egypt southward to the city of Suez (located on the northern shores of the Gulf of Suez). The canal separates the bulk of Egypt from the Sinai Peninsula. It took 10 years to build and was officially opened on November 17, 1869. Today the Suez Canal is Owned and operated by the Suez Canal Authority. It enables a more direct route for shipping between Europe and Asia, effectively allowing for passage from the North Atlantic to the Indian Ocean, without having to circumnavigate the African continent. The waterway has since its construction proved to be vital for international trade and, as a result, has been at the center of conflict since it opened in 1869.

However, the interest in a marine route connecting the Mediterranean Sea and the Red Sea dates back to ancient times. A series of small canals connecting the Nile River and, thus, by extension, the Mediterranean to the Red Sea, were in use as early as 2000 BCE; but, initially, a direct connection between the Mediterranean and the Red Sea was considered impossible over concerns that they sat at distinct levels of altitude. Therefore, various overland routes—using horse-drawn vehicles and, later, trains—were employed, most notably by Great Britain, which for quite a considerable period conducted significant trade with its colonies in present-day India and Pakistan.

The idea of a large canal providing a direct route between the two bodies of water was first discussed in the 1830s, thanks to the work of French explorer and engineer Linant de Bellefonds, who specialized in Egypt. Bellefonds performed a survey of the Isthmus of Suez and confirmed that the Mediterranean and Red seas were, contrary to popular belief, at the same level of altitude, implying that a canal without locks could be built, making feasibility and construction significantly viable.

By the 1850s, seeing an opportunity for Egypt, which governed the country at the time, Khedive Said Pasha (who oversaw Egypt and the Sudan for the Ottomans) granted French diplomat Ferdinand de Lesseps permission to create a company to construct a canal. That company eventually became known as the Suez Canal Company, and it was given a 99-year lease over the waterway and surrounding area. Lesseps' first action was to create the Commission known as "The International Commission for the Piercing of the Isthmus of Suez". The commission was made up of 13 experts from seven countries and it took a leading role in developing the architectural plans for the Suez Canal. The commission's final report was completed in 1856 and two years later, the Suez Canal Company was formally established.

The excavation work took 10 years, and an estimated 1.5 million people worked on the project. As was characteristic in projects that were undertaken in Africa in the 19th Century, the project implementation was planned to use labour intensive technology and most of the labour that would be used was slave labour. As we said in the earlier chapters, the European nations had been working very hard to abolish slave trade on the Atlantic Ocean but in the interior of Africa slave labour was increasingly significant and liked by European nations because it was cheap, and in most cases free and readily available. Of course the idea of intensive use of slave labour was greatly opposed to Britain, France and America, but nevertheless the process continued unabated; and it is believed that over 120,000 people died from cholera and other causes such as dysentery, and malaria while working on the Suez Canal.

Assessments show that Suez Canal has increasingly been considered the most important example of ship canals, though the number of vessels passing through it annually certainly does not equal that passing through other famous canals such as that which connects Lake Superior with the chain of great lakes at the south. In terms of its length it exceeds any of the other great ship canals, its total length being 90 miles, of which about two-thirds is through shallow lakes.

Original estimates indicated that a total of 2,613 million cubic feet of earth needed to be moved, including 600 million on land, and another 2,013 million dredged from water. The total original cost estimate was 200 million francs (1860 Prices). The material excavated was usually sand, though in some cases strata of solid rock, from two to three feet in thickness, were encountered. The total excavation was 2,160 million cubic feet under the original plan, which gave a depth of twenty-five feet.

As hinted above, Pasha Said was very much behind the project, and in most cases the project ran into great financial problems. Pasha Said purchased 44% of the company to keep it in operation especially when at first the company ran into financial problems. In any case the British government and Turks got to a point when they started to be concerned with the venture and managed to have work suspended for a short time, until the intervention of Napoleon III. Excavation of the canal actually began on April 25th, 1859, and between then and 1862, the first part of the canal was completed. By 1861 the Company that was contracted to do the work had been ostensibly at work for nearly ten years at a canal that was to be a hundred feet wide and thirty feet deep from sea to sea; and yet up to that moment, no work of any significance had been done in as far as the construction work was concerned, and this proceeded so despite the fact that a very large part of their nominal capital had been spent.

Factors that faced the constructions of the Suez Canal project included the type of technology that was initially chosen, which was basically slave labour. Slaves would be forced to dig the earth but being human beings their capacity was limited. Despite the force that was being used but for quite a long time during the initial years there was no much progress that was made. This situation was worsened by the fact that slaves were being poorly fed and thus they had no much energy to be exerted on the digging of the canal way. What was worse, there was a problem of keeping the slave labour in hygienic environment. The poor environment led to the outbreak of cholera, which wiped out a good proportion of the labour force. The labourers were also greatly infected by malaria, which was also another good explanation of the bad performance. All those situations were exacerbated by lack of proper tools for the type of work that needed to be done. As a result during the next couple of years there was no progress made on the physical construction of the canal, besides the Africans that kept dying on a daily basis. Actually, the initial five years of the project were a disaster in most fronts of the project. Financing became a problem and the death toll of the African slave labourers was so high that there were on the average more than 330 people who died daily, which, was equivalent to about 10,000 people monthly. These died of diseases, malnutrition, mistreatment, and many other malpractices in the project. Yet no progress was being made in the execution of the project all being due to poor planning.

It was only out of the above stated results, a decision was made for use of machines. The dredges used in the construction of the canal were of a new description. They were wonderful mechanical contrivances, without which the canal would not have been finished. The use of the dredging machines was prepared for by digging out a rough trough by spadework, and as soon as it had been dug to the depth of from six feet to twelve feet, the water was let in. After the water had been let in, the steam dredges were floated down the stream, moored along the bank, and set to work.

Political turmoil in the region negatively impacted the construction of the canal. At that time when the canal was under construction Egypt was under the control of Britain and France; but there were several rebellions against colonial rule. This, coupled with the limitations of construction technology at the time, caused the total costs of building the Suez Canal to balloon to $100 million, more than double the original estimate. Ismail Pasha, Khedive of Egypt and the Sudan, formally opened the Suez Canal on November 17, 1869.Officially, the first ship to navigate through the canal was the imperial yacht of French Empress Eugenie, the L'Aigle, followed by the British ocean liner Delta.

Mehmed Emin Pasha (born Isaak Eduard Schnitzer, baptized Eduard Carl Oscar Theodor Schnitzer; on March 28, 1840, was an Ottoman physician of German Jewish origin, naturalist, and governor of the Egyptian province of Equatoria on the upper Nile. He was appointed the Khedive of Egypt and Sudan from 1863 to 1879, when he was removed at the behest of the United Kingdom of Great Britain and Ireland. As Governor of Equatoria he was able to send and receive letters via Buganda and Zanzibar and had been informed in February 1886 that the Egyptian government would abandon Equatoria. In 1854-56 he granted many concessions to French diplomat Ferdinand de Lesseps to build the Suez Canal, a project which engaged a workforce estimated at 120,000 workers who died over the ten years of construction due to malnutrition, fatigue and disease- especially cholera.

Shortly before completion of the Canal in 1869, Khedive Ismail borrowed enormous sums of money from British and French banks at high rates of interest. By 1875, he was facing financial difficulties and was forced to sell his block of shares in the Suez Canal. The shares were snapped up by Britain, which sought to give his country practical control in the management of this strategic waterway. When Isma'il repudiated Egypt's foreign debt in 1879, Britain and France seized joint financial control over the country, forcing the Egyptian ruler to abdicate, and installing his eldest son in his place. The Egyptian and Sudanese ruling classes did not relish foreign intervention.

During the 1870s, European initiatives against the slave trade caused an economic crisis in northern Sudan, precipitating the rise of Mahdist[44] forces. In 1881, the Mahdist erupted in Sudan under **Muhammad Ahmad**, severing Tewfik's authority in Sudan. The same year, Tewfik suffered an even more perilous rebellion by his own Egyptian army in the form of the **Urabi Revolt**. In 1882, Tewfik appealed for direct British military assistance, commencing Britain's administration of Egypt. A joint British-Egyptian military force ultimately defeated the Mahdist forces in Sudan in

---

[44] *The* Mahdist *were a Muslim religious group of Muhamad Ahmad bin ABD aLLAH War was a war of the late 19th century between the* Mahdist *Sudanese of the religious leader Muhammad Ahmad bin Abd Allah, who had ...*

1898. Thereafter, Britain (rather than Egypt) seized effective control of Sudan.

Results of those financial, technical, and political problems made the Suez Canal to take ten years to build and to cost twice over budget by the time it opened in 1869. The Canal started without use of machinery using forced labour who, although they were paid a pittance (very small or peanut amount of money), were actually treated as slaves, and had no choice in the matter.

Cholera and other plague epidemics caused by the complete lack of sanitation facilities, presence of polluted drinking water and bad and certainly inadequate food were the main problems that faced the Canal company and from the moment the first spadesful was dug the workers began dying and the company was forced into making basic provision for the workforce.

The construction of the Suez Canal reduced the distance between India and Europe significantly. It is said that this distance was 7,000kms before the construction of the canal. Britain benefited the most from the construction of the Suez Canal. Distance from London to Bombay got substantially shortened; it was reduced by almost 5,150 miles. . The reduced distance led to faster transportation of Indian merchants. Since the British controlled Egypt, the Suez Canal came under their control. They were able to reach their territory in the Arabic Peninsula readily enforcing their rule and conducting trade.

The successful completion of the construction of Suez Canal became an incentive for the construction of other Canals in other parts of the world. For instance the story of the construction of the Panama Canal began almost immediately after construction of Suez Canal, in November 1869. The Suez Canal was already a moment of intense national pride and patriotic sentiment, a triumph felt by the entire nation of France. The motivation, pride, and passion to achieve success with the canal drove project leaders especially the French engineers who piloted the project to move beyond the past traditional barriers of doubt and finances and enabled them to surpass the expectations of the world. The engineers such as Ferdinand de Lesseps kept professing that he had "no interest in making money," His interest was solely in the completion of the Suez Canal, and the completion of the canal was what he achieved. The Engineer who became very famous had succeeded to manage and guide almost every detail of the construction of the Suez Canal, and, went about his great project of the canal by fearlessly overruling his technical advisors, defying the European bankers, and facing the scorn of the politicians such as those of Britain, who called him a swindler and a fool and who saw the canal as nothing more than a cheap French grab for power in the Mediterranean.

A couple of lessons can be got from the Suez Canal venture. First of all it was a historic project, which needed a lot of determination, foresight, experienced and committed engineers to accomplish their success. The start had a lot of fumbling which made them to lose a lot of resources. Then there was the role of politicians: in the Suez there were conflicts between French and British politicians who sandwiched the Egyptian politicians to a situation of lack of firm decisions. The Imperial nations always wished to have an upper hand in such plans because that is what they were there for. What is most notable however was in the way the project planners aimed to minimize construction cost by employing poor communities or workers who were given only hand tools for as complex project as the Suez Canal. The objective was to minimize costs through exploitation of poor communities. Things started to change when less human labour was used in favour of machines. But that happened when thousands of labourers had died and others were suffering from serious diseases caused by the poor environment in which they were subjected.

The Suez Canal project took many years at the initial stage to make much progress. The reasons were not only the workers were not well motivated but also because invariably the conditions at project sites were horribly bad. Many poor people, majority of who were of black African origin died, estimated at more than 50% of workers in the project. As we mentioned earlier the Suez Canal project claimed the lives of almost 120,000 people during the ten - year period of construction.

However, the next strategic projects for the enhancement of the colonial systems were those of construction of dams for generation of electricity and railways lines for transportation of goods produced in the hinterland to the ports. Railways were particularly important because they would support military domination of the imperialist countries. The lines were built to exercise effective control in the scramble for Africa and also for dispatching troops for better control of the native population. Other benefits included those related to enhancement of mining work. A line would be built to the interior to further European mining interests, this being in addition to railway line projects that wee constructed to enhance cash crop production, in which case the colonial power built the lines to connect agriculturally rich areas to the nearest ports to enhance export of those products, which were badly needed in the colonial home countries. With limited budgets, colonisers expected the railways to develop as profit making businesses hence they were designed to connect only areas of high economic potential.

Good cases of lines, which were built during the time of scramble, partitioning and colonization of Africa included that one in the CFS which was done under the supervision of Henry Morton Stanley. The railway, now known as "The Matadi-Kinshasa Railway" was built from 1890 to 1898 in order to circumvent the series of rapids and falls, which hindered access from the South Atlantic Ocean to the Congo Basin. Other railway lines were those built by the British in Kenya from the Port of Mombasa to Nairobi and onwards to Kisumu and Uganda and also in Ghana and Nigeria. Cases of the Ghana railway lines built during the period included that one which traverses from Cape Coast to Takoradi. Similar lines were built in Nigeria. The railways were important to support economic ventures that were being established in the areas that were in close proximity to the lines. For instance, while the Congo line was basically built to support mining projects those in Ghana were built to support the cocoa production which soon became a leading export crop in those parts of West Africa.

For the same purpose, Germany in German East Africa also made a lot of effort to promoted commerce and economic growth. They put a lot of attention on agricultural production. Over 100,000 acres were put under sisal cultivation, which was the largest cash crop in Tanganyika; two million coffee trees were planted, rubber trees grew on 200,000 acres, and there were large cotton plantations.

To bring these agricultural products to market, beginning in 1888, the Usambara railway was built from Tanga to Moshi. Then there was the Central railway, which covered 1,247 km and linked Dar es Salaam, Morogoro, Tabora and Kigoma. The final link to the eastern shore of Lake Tanganyika was completed in July 1914 and was cause for a huge and festive celebration in the capital of Dar es Salaam, with an agricultural fair and trade exhibition. Harbour facilities were built or improved with electrical cranes, with rail access and warehouses. Wharves were remodeled at Tanga, Bagamoyo, and Lindi. In 1912, Dar es Salaam and Tanga received 356 freighters and passenger steamers and over 1,000 coastal ships and local trading-vessels. Dar es Salaam became the showcase city of all of tropical Africa.

In the French territories railways were conceived to play greater role than just provide transport to production points and improved communication. The French put a lot of attention on the line called "Trans Saharan Railway". The Trans-Saharan was supposed to link the French West and North Africa and tie together the domains of the French empire. The preliminary studies for the construction of the Trans-Saharan began in the 1870s; it became popular in the interwar decades and was actively promoted in the Vichy period.

The official rhetoric highlighted the Trans-Saharan as not only an essential way to improve the integrity of the French empire, but also as a way to boost the spirit of the French nation. Railway blueprints powerfully redefined perceptions of the colonies in the imagination of the French. On blueprints, the long lines of railway crossing Africa justified the necessity to spend millions and millions of francs on these construction projects. It is ironic that such railway lines were almost never completed in Africa according to initial designs and target dates. While the blueprints and photographs of railways were essential to the prestige of the French empire, the railways themselves sometimes played an insignificant role in improving the colonial economy.

Very much unlike most other colonial nations, the French designed and constructed her railways with a view portraying French power and integrity. The railway between Saint-Louis and

Dakar, with a bridge spanning 511 meters across the Senegal River, catches the eye and powerfully redefines the local landscape. The bridge was many times reproduced on postcards, and could be said to be a symbol of the "French civilizing mission of French government officials, who claimed that unlike other colonial powers they had come to Africa to civilize the Africans and not otherwise. The name of the bridge encapsulates an important episode in the history of the French empire because Louis Leon Cesar Faidherbe, a French governor-general, played a central role in the colonization of the region.

In as far as the Portuguese spheres were concerned, the policy in the colonial home was to overcome their problem of connectivity between their own national boundaries, with the hope that with railways they would be able to turn the harbours of the Portuguese capitals into a cornerstone in global commerce. Simultaneously, they trusted that railways would overcome the geographical obstacles of the Portuguese territory and contribute to unity of the country. From the 1880s, this framework was applied in the Portuguese colonies of Africa, to legitimate the Portuguese presence in those areas, to assert Portugal as an imperial nation and to promote colonization and economic exploration of the colonial resources. Just before World War I, railways spread throughout 3000 km in the mainland and over 3500 km in Angola and Mozambique. Therefore, railways favoured the territorial appropriation of these regions, by encouraging a repetitive use of an area perceived as rightfully Portuguese. Railways also acted as portals of globalization, as places that promoted commerce, communication, and cultural transfers at a global level.

Overall a colonial railway line could start from nowhere and the endpoint of a line could also be at the centre of nowhere; but that was considered to have some advantages, because none of the localities in-between may have been considered worthwhile to connect. Railway placement was essentially an engineering problem – figuring out the cheapest (typically the shortest) route from a point A to a point B.

The Kenya-Uganda railroad could be a case in point. This railway was built between 1896 and 1901 to connect landlocked, and relatively prosperous Uganda to the coast (i.e. Mombasa). Kenya was merely transit territory. This line indeed followed the route that minimised construction costs. The best locomotives at that time could only overcome gradients below 5-10%. The contemporary critics called the Kenya-Uganda railway the 'Lunatic Express', 'going from nowhere to utterly nowhere'. In fact, the railway bypassed highly populated areas enroute to Kisumu (Lake Victoria) and Uganda. Hence, locations on or near the route were lucky to have received access to the railway, but others, with similar or better geography missed out.

The same was the case with the construction of the railway line from Dar es Salaam to Kigoma by the Germans who also built another line from Tanga to Moshi, and later on connected to Arusha. The Tanga Moshi line aimed to support investments that were being made by investors from the colonial country that specialized on sisal, coffee, and wheat. Like cocoa in Ghana exports of coffee and sisal as supported by the railway lines in Tanganyika, became among the mainstays of the colonial economies in the respective colonial countries.

In Ghana, the British proposed five railway routes, but, due to random events, the venture never materialised because: First, the Cape Coast–Kumasi line (1873) was proposed to link the capital of

Cape Coast to Kumasi, sending troops to fight the Ashante. This project was dropped because the war came to an abrupt end in 1874. Second, Governor Griffith wanted a central line from Salt pond to Kumasi (1893) in order to tap the palm oil areas and link the coast to Kumasi. Governor Griffith retired in 1886 and got replaced by Governor Maxwell, who gave in to the gold-mining lobbies. Maxwell instead built the Western Line, which connected European interests to the coast.

The important point to underline about these colonial development projects is that they were designed to support the colonial countries' interests. There was absolutely no interest put to what could be the accrued benefit to the local Africans. As we have said, the construction aimed to use the local labour that was forcefully employed with very low wages. An African was never consulted, incorporated, or considered in discussions that were related to enhancing skills, or providing living wages or in the provision of basic utilities. While we are still on this subject it could also be noted that wherever some skills were needed, Africans in the local areas were purposely avoided and importation was made from other far away colonies such as India. The colonial administration never liked to see Africans move a step to development because that would lessen the supply of labour that was needed in colonial investor enterprises.

Labour was needed in the production of the type of crops that foreign investors got involved in. A good example of how the colonial administrations hated to see Africans participating in investment activities, regardless of how small they might be was in the case of Kilimanjaro Mountain area where the colonial administration of the time, namely the Germans, refused Africans to participate in the production of coffee. The Germans refused or outlawed local people to engage in coffee production, a condition which was enforced until the end of the First World War, in 1918, which ended the German rule in Tanganyika (or Tanzania as is known today).

Regarding aspects of economic development, railways placement led to a curious situation, whereby lines traversed sparsely settled areas with no local Africa freight to transport. In the hope of creating an agricultural export industry, land was alienated and offered to European settlers, with plots near the railways the most sought after. Between 1901 and 1962, the railways in East Africa led to a concentration of both European and African populations. The cultivation of coffee and tea expanded along the railway lines. The effects would decrease when moving away from the railway line, and would reduce to zero after 30 km. In addition, is found that there is a strong effect of the railway road, within a distance band which will reach a zero point only less than 25 km.

14

PROCESS TO COLONIALIZATION OF AFRICA

We start by first defining three terms: scramble, partitioning, and colonialization. Wikipedia defines scramble for Africa, partitioning of Africa and Conquest of Africa, or the Rape of Africa, as though they were synonymous. However, there are some differences between them though the differentiating line may be very thin. The "scramble" was marked by high traffic or rush of European countries to get a share or portion or slice of the African land. It was an invasion for occupation of Africa, which resulted from the fact that most European powers had been slow to realise the benefits of claiming land in Africa. The sudden wish to obtain some piece of land created pressure leading to scrambling for the limited land that was available. The pressure was mostly exerted by the fact that the industrial revolution was beginning to give a headache to European countries, because procurement of raw materials from across the Atlantic Ocean was becoming very complicated following the abolition of slave trade on the Atlantic and the growing transportation costs.

That is about the scramble for Africa. The other term regards the "partitioning" of Africa, which has been referring to the actual slicing or division of African land to various European nations. This was quite a tough task because only those with strong muscles succeeded the most. It was a difficult task because European nations were behaving like hungry wild cats fighting to get a share of meat of a rabbit they had just killed. The strongest cat grabbed more and bigger pieces than the less powerful cats, which could have taken several pieces but lost most of them because the powerful cats were still around. In other words there were European countries, which ended up with only a couple of slices, some of them quite small in size and there were others which got away with many huge pieces. It was a matter of the survival of the fittest.

The next term that we mentioned above was "colonialization"; which could be defined to mean that a country acquired a full or partial control over another country, sent its people (to live there and benefit from it economically). Colonization definitely involved taking full control and sending people to live there. The indigenous people become part of those who were colonized. Consequentially, the major characteristic of colonization was that the actions of people who came to create the colony (i. e. the colonizers) usually created a lot of conflicts between cultures, including wars. That is exactly what happened as the scramble and partitioning of Africa went on.

Until sometime in 1870s the idea of acquisition of land in Africa was not yet popular. But soon later, the scramble started. Within a short while none of the major European powers wished to miss out. It is generally agreed that the Scramble, or rather the effort by Europeans to obtain land in Africa started to sprout when the exploration work was going on. Before exploration work started only a few Europeans had been in the interior of Africa and so they did not fully appreciate the richness of natural resources that could be found there. The imperial conquest of Africa by the major powers of Europe began with King Leopold III of Belgium who used the services of explorers, especially Henry Morton Stanley, to negotiate and sign fake agreements with local African chiefs of Congo, which would make the chiefs cede their rights of land for Him.

Colonization of Africa began in the Congo largely because Europeans felt that Africans did not know or were not well versed with the wealth of natural resources Africa possessed. And in cases where Africans could be aware of their natural wealth potential those who aspired to grip in (like in the case of King Leopold III) still believed that Africans could be suppressed using guns to cede their land. Europeans came ready for war with Africans. The approach used by the Europeans to get land from Africans was that of making fools of them. The consequences were with far reaching effects. For instance, while Democratic Republic of Congo was potentially one of the richest countries on earth, but colonialism, slavery and corruption gradually turned it into one of the poorest and has for a long time being among the world's bloodiest conflict places since World War II; a situation which has got perpetuated till this day.

In 1885–6, when a meeting was convened in Berlin by Otto von Bismarck the first Chancellor of Germany the Scramble for Africa was already at full swing. Its outcome was the formalisation of the scramble, partitioning and colonization process that was going on. That goal of convening the meeting aside, but it ran short of achieving its intended role of making the colonial nations to reach agreement on the methodology for the partitioning of Africa and the need for drawing of attention to bilateral agreements concluded before and after the conference. The conference contributed to ushering in a period of heightened colonial activity by European powers, which eliminated or overrode most existing forms of African autonomy.

In the Berlin Conference thirteen European countries and the United States met to agree on the rules of African colonisation. From 1884 to 1914 the continent was in frequent conflict as the colonial countries took territory and power from existing African states and peoples. In the period before the Berlin Conference European nations kept moving at high speed to obtain as much of the African land as they could, which actually meant the actual slicing of the continent. In this respect each European nation struggled to get as much as it could of the African land; a process, which led to determining which slice belonged to which European nation. Some countries ended up with many slices while others ended up with only a few or none at all. The slices were what ended up as colonies for the European nations. The Berlin conference was convened by German Chancellor Bismarck to settle how European countries would claim colonial land in Africa and to avoid wars among European nations over African territories. All the major European States were invited to the conference. The participants included Germany, France, Great Britain, Netherlands, Belgium, and Portugal. These were all considered to have a future role in the imperial partition of Africa.

The process further led to what came to be called the conquest of Africa. Africans ended up with no legal ownership of their land. Some scholars have gone even further to call it the Rape of Africa, which is true because everything was done without consent or notice of the original owners.

The United States was invited to participate in the Berlin Conference because of its interest in Liberia. However, US never participated for reasons that it had no desire to build a colonial empire in Africa. Also invited were Australia, Hungary, Sweden, Norway, Denmark, Italy, Turkey, and Russia due to the fact all were considered to be minor players in the quest for colonizing Africa. However, Italy would claim some colonial possessions in Northeast Africa. Most notably there were no Africans present in that conference, and also there were no Europeans that showed any concern about the absence of the native Africans who could have ensured that native Africans had any say in the proceedings.

The task of this conference was also to ensure that each European country that claimed possession over a part of Africa was obliged to bring civilization, in the form of Christianity, and trade to each region that it occupied. Also, a country's claim of a territory would be valid only if it informed the other European powers and if it established some occupying force on the ground. The occupying forces often comprised of a few military outposts on the coast and interior waterways with little or no actual settlement. Specific lands were obtained by having African indigenous rulers sign fake agreements for protection by a European power; but most unfortunately these rulers had no idea or proper understanding of what they signed, since most could not read, write, or understand European languages.

The conference only dealt with territories yet to be acquired in Africa. This meant that the interior of Africa, about which little was known, was the land area available. Most coastal land had already been claimed by various European countries, as had much of Southern Africa and Africa north of the Sahara. Besides the explorers, until now very few Europeans had set foot into the interior of sub-Saharan Africa prior to this conference. Following the Berlin Conference there was still little exploration into the interior of Africa beyond gaining initial treaties. Most Europeans continued to stay on the coastal regions while a few missionaries followed rivers inland to find Christian converts. By 1900, though, more Europeans moved into the African interior to extract raw materials such as rubber, palm oil, gold, copper, and also to get gold and diamonds. These natural resources made Africa a vital resource for the European economy.

The African colonies remained controlled by one or the other of colonial nations, and in the meanwhile the Berlin Conference allowed King Leopold III of Belgium to become the sole owner of the vast area of CFS, which is today the Democratic Republic of Congo (DRC). This area was given to King Leopold III by the other European powers with the intent that this be an area of Free Trade for all Europeans in Africa. Leopold agreed to this proposal as well as bringing Christian missionaries to the interior of this area. But in practice he kept out most other European traders while granting concessions to corporates to exploit the region's resources. In 1908, it was revealed that under King Leopold III's agencies, native people of the Congo were being forced to harvest wild rubber as a form of tax payment to the colonial government. Failure of the natives to reach their quotas of rubber collection, the hands or legs were chopped off, which was a high degree of human abuses. It was only when news of these abuses of power were brought to the public light, King Leopold was stripped of his colony and the vast Congo region was brought under Belgium government; which continued so until it became independent in 1960.

However, by 1914, 90% of Africa had been divided between seven European countries. Many of the boundaries drawn up by Europeans at the Berlin Conference still continued, with little regard to natural landmarks or historic ethnic or political boundaries established by the Africans themselves. The disregard of these boundaries, most of which were retained after independence, often continued to generate conflict in Africa.

To better understand the scramble, partitioning and colonization of Africa we also need to look at the genesis of those ideas and the practice. We could start with the understanding that Europeans called Africa the 'Dark Continent' because it was unknown to them. This got mixed up with the more sinister idea of 'Darkest Africa' a place where the inhabitants were considered to be savage and brutal. Europeans, after the industrial revolution, considered industrial towns and technology to be signs of civilisation. African peoples did not have these, so they were branded uncivilised. These attitudes allowed European colonists to ignore the established African tribes and kingdoms with their rich histories and cultures.

Europeans started to obtain land slices in form of colonies in Africa before exploration work completely ended. While the period of extensive exploration of the African continent ended in the last two decades of the 19th Century but informal imperialism had been there for a lot longer. Till then the imperial nations controlled other nations but only indirectly. In Africa they did not have control of land but did so through commerce, military influence and even spread of religion. The next stage was what got known as the scramble for Africa or the race of European nations to have direct control of the continent of Africa.

Let it be added also that the Race for Africa was the proliferation of conflicting European claims to African territory during the New Imperialism period. Britain, France, and Germany led in the struggle for power in Africa. Germany too, sought to send colonists to Africa in order to offset its population losses suffered as many Germans moved to the United States. Britain, anxious, to hold control in Asia as the Russian Empire sought to expand. For those reasons they geared themselves towards ensuring that the Suez Canal was completed. Many of these imperial powers also sought the prestige gained from acquiring colonies, as this was a major source of nationalistic pride. In many cases the boundaries were not clearly demarcated even after the Berlin Conference. Nevertheless, Industrial nations in Europe tried the best they could to ensure that the cheap labour and abundance of raw materials in Africa went as planned. However, it could be added that many of the colonial powers also sought the prestige gained from acquiring colonies, as this was a major source of nationalistic pride.

It was a period full of fuss because each participating European nation wished to get as much of the African continent's land as was possible. They behaved like hungry wild dogs fighting for a piece of meat. This was also the time when European business people made a rush to the African continent to make a fortune that largely came in form of doing investment ventures in areas that looked most profitable. Indeed they succeeded to acquire space in Africa which they did using various techniques and tricks. In the end the colonial nations took full control of the administration of the colonies that they had succeeded to grab, a process that got followed by the colonial country inviting its citizens to come and make business according to opportunities that existed in the particular country. In countries with fertile soil for agriculture, European citizens came and focused their attention on large-scale farming. Other colonies had the abundance of minerals as well as forest natural resources, which provided ample economic opportunities for the colonial country.

A good example of those who found a lot of resources such as gold, forest products such as rubber, and wild life resources for harvesting, ivory and hard wood were Belgium which occupied a vast area in the Congo Basin. Other colonies did not have much of any of the above -mentioned natural resources but had other features such as Rivers, Lakes, Mountains and coastlines or seas that had plenty of marine resources that once exploited contributed immensely to the enhancement of the colonial country. There were many other opportunities that the colonies provided including tourism and other trading opportunities. For example, from the very early-stage Europeans were invited to visit places such as Kilimanjaro Mountain with a view of inviting tourists from various parts of the world, to come and survey the local areas or to do the Mountain climbing with a view of seeking to be famous.

Gradually urban centres started to be developed in the colonies. The urban centres became centres for marketing industrially produced products from Europe. They also become the centres of collection of farm products especially the raw materials that were badly needed in the industries that were swiftly growing in various countries in Europe. In other places urban centres were focal points for military installations as well as administration centres. Like we have hastened to say, the later half of the nineteenth century saw the transition from the indirect or rather informal imperialism of control of military influence and economic dominance to direct ownership and management of colonial countries.

The way the scramble, partitioning and boundary markings went could arguably be said to be a type of an embarrassing situation. Ethnic groups were separated without regard to the social cohesion that existed among them. Europeans rushed to take space in Africa as though Africa had had no occupant, neither an owner. Realizing that, the situation was rather awkward, some scholars came up with self- designed explanation for what was taking place. The argument was that European nations saw Africa as ripe for the taking and that was by way of colonizing Africa. Europe was also claimed to be exporting civilization to a continent that was regarded as evolutionary backward and undeveloped. Those remained excuses by those who could not open their eyes, minds and memories to remember that just about two or little more centuries before the 19th Century, (that being the time before the Triangle Slave Trade), Africa and Europe were mutual trading partners and were almost at the same level of development. Actually Africa was then more admired and more advanced in some respects than Europe especially in terms of economic, social and technological developments that some kingdoms had succeeded to make45.

The truth is still that, till the 16th Century, Africa was better set for development than Europe. We may recollect about cases of empires such as those of Mali, Ancient Ghana, and Songhai which were good examples of relatively developed African countries compared to equivalent economies of that time in many other parts of the world including Europe. In the later years there also developed empires such as Monomotapa and even Baganda which without suppression done by European invasions they had a chance of getting ahead with substantial socio-economic development. Some people deliberately or ignorantly forgot or felt embarrassed to note that exciting features such as pyramids of Egypt were constructed by African kings that had emigrated from Southern of Egypt.

However, with the use of firearms Europeans succeeded to take Africans to slavery. Triangle slave trade became the pillar for the enhancement of European development. History changed in favour of Europe. With the growth of Triangle slave trade and the growth of industrial revolution in Europe opportunities to further suppress Africa and its people were created. Europe got ample opportunity to plunder African natural resources, and in order to continue with the

---

[45] *Walter Rodney: How Europe underdeveloped Africa*

plundering, Europe went further on with the colonization agenda. It was from that point real and intensified underdevelopment of the African continent[46] began to show all its colours. In the later years, some Scholars (influenced by pride and prejudice) felt that the presence of Europe in Africa was assisting to pave the way for African development, which has proved to be difficult to agree. It is like that story about which came first chicken or egg. Without African labour, which manifested in form of slave trade on the Atlantic and also without exploitation of labour in the colonies, Europe wouldn't have succeeded in its industrialization as much as it did.

Some scholars of African history have had it that Europeans took the initiative to act as trustees of Africa until Africans were mature enough to govern themselves. The question that has never got anybody to give answers to is about when the Africans were supposed to be mature. Time never came when the colonizers said they had stayed long enough, and time had come for them to quit and allow Africans to get on the driving seat. Colonizers never paid any attention to the development of Africans. In almost all cases the African elites, after new enlightenment, were the ones who demanded that it was time for the colonial rulers to quite. In many cases the colonialists showed clearly that they were not ready to leave and let Africans to take over. In some instances African had to use military means, or had to employ strategies that made the colonizers to surrender, hence deciding to quit their colonies. An example of Algeria which had been under French colonial rule for over 130 years got her independence in 1962. But that happened under great pressure of violence and guerila warfare as the only means by which independence could have been achieved.

---

[46] Ibid.

The above situation could explain why there were many guerilla wars against colonizers in in Africa; the wars forced colonizers to quit their colonies involuntarily. There is no single colonial administration that prepared good conditions for takeover of their administrations by Africans. This also provides an explanation for the legacy left behind by colonial administrations, which was characterized by the poor education, poor medical services, almost absence of technological knowhow all of which made it difficult to manage the projects that were established by the colonizers. Local people never got a chance to be part of the management of projects that colonizers established. That failure led to swift deterioration of projects that colonizers left behind. The Africans failed to manage or to fund the sustainability of the projects because they had never been part of them, as all the key personnel were got from the colonial country. The local people were lined up in the auxiliary positions. That may also explain why the Africans failed to cope with the management and sustainability, including good maintenance of projects that were left behind Africans got accused of being idiots, or people who were not hard working, incompetent to move with changing technology and the like. The quitting colonial administrations got room to despise the Africans, which gave the impression that the Africans demanded for independence when they were not ready for it. Those in this school of thought further argue that independence was given before Africans had grasped best ways of self-governance. Actually those in this category uphold the impression that colonizers came to Africa for Africans and during their stay Africans benefited more than what they deserved. Like the Swahili saying goes: "you are at liberty to hang the hungry one but he should be availed with what is deserving to him". In short Africans have not deserved to be blamed for mistakes it did not do.

Colonization process was in reality driven by commercial interests. Otherwise, there was no intimate relationship between the colonizer and the colonized. A case could once again be cited of what happened in the Democratic Republic of Congo, a country which until now is potentially one of the richest countries in Africa, but colonialism, slavery and corruption turned it into one of the poorest; with the world's bloodiest conflicts since World War II. Wars and corrupt practices, which started with colonialism, more than five million people have died since the end of the last two decades of the 19th century. Millions more have been driven to the brink of starvation and disease and several million women and girls have been raped. It started and continued to independence as a great war torn part of Africa, a conflagration that has sucked in soldiers and civilians from many nations and countless armed rebel groups, has been fought almost entirely inside the borders of the DRC.

With colonial rule mistreatment and lack of concern about the Africans was a common feature. Europeans were always the masters and the Africans remained to be the labourers. That also meant, for people in the same work place, same qualifications, spending same energics, in the same environment but, the Africans would have to keep in different locations or spaces and with lower pay, respect, and leadership status, which was the case in all aspects of life. We could take the case of schools that were established, they were few and the education that was provided was stratified for Africans (the lowest standard), Asians (middle standard) and Europeans (highest standard), which was part of colonial machination to deter development of the African. A doctor, an engineer, good management personnel and all people of skill had to be imported from the colonial country. A case could be taken of Tanzania, then Tanganyika which by independence in 1961, had been under colonial rule for almost 80 years) had hardly five University qualified graduates, most of those graduates being teachers that had received a push in Mission schools.

By independence there was no qualified medical doctor, engineer, skilled manager, and other African expert personnel; and the explanation given for that situation was that Africans could never be able to pursue such studies. Africans were considered to be not as bright as people of other races. It could be said once again that in the health sector it was even worse. Till independence in 196i in countries like Tanzania there was no qualified doctor and most of the personnel that served or assisted in dispensaries were the Rural Medical Aid (RMAs); meaning that any serious medical cases, at least for Africans had nobody qualified to handle them. Need for professionals in other sectors including engineers, agricultural experts, and all the rest till 1961 had to be imported from the colonial country. The implications were that the demand for such high-grade professional skills was not there. This gives a good picture of how colonization pulled Africa back to underdevelopment.

As though what has been said above was not enough, some European nations "hated" to see an African make a single step towards development. Here we could take the case of countries such as Mozambique and Angola, which came under the Portuguese, Congo under Belgium and Tanzania under Germany. In Tanzania besides the colonial country taking most of the fertile land from Africans for the development of estate agriculture (good cases being those of Kilimanjaro Mountain area) where they grabbed irrigation canals (popularly known as mifongo by the local Wachagga people

47. Mifongo were irrigation canals that had been develop by the Wachagga people before the colonial intrusion and control of the country. They forcefully took many of those canals for their exclusive use in their farms.

Also by the beginning of the first decade of 20th Century the German administration introduced coffee as a leading cash crop with excellent market in Europe. All European farmers were encouraged to grow coffee, but it was absolutely illegal for any African to grow such crop. Africans had the obligation to work in European estate farms where most of the labour contribution was with no wage. Even in the area of food and drink Africans were equally marginalized. For instance, Africans would not be allowed to take European drinks such as beer, whisky, brand and it was actually illegal to find an African drinking beer or other hard drinks. Africans could entertain themselves with their local brews, but not with European or other approved drinks. These policies were discriminative and racially based, but they somehow changed with the coming of the British, who took over from the Germans at the end of the First World War.

The above are only examples, but they applied in almost all colonial countries with variations existing here and there. However, now we should just try to compare the amount of resources that were extracted from the continent during the colonial period compared to the level of development that was made. This brings us once again to the brutality done by European colonizers when looking for ways to exploit the African continent. The brutality of King Leopold III of Belgium in his former colony of the Congo Free

---

[47] *Abisai Temba: Three Hundred Years on Kilimanjaro Mountain Area,-published by Notion Press- India and also "The Unwalked Mile" by the same Author- Published by Author House (UK)*

State, now the DRC, has been well documented. Up to 15 million of the estimated 30million48 native inhabitants died within a period of just twelve years of Leopold III's rule. It was a depopulation process done consciously because Africans were assigned importance only in as far as they were there to contribute free labour.

The truth remains that perhaps Africa with its abundance of resources including people could have today been at a much better level of development. Imagine going to a place and eliminating 50% of its population within a short period of just ten years as it happened in the Congo during the rule of King Leopold III. How would you make the people to settle down and start thinking of development? Also, imagine what would be the consequence if alongside the killing of the people all the key resources of the area got recklessly plundered by the killers. You can further imagine what it would mean if the remaining part of the population was subjected to meeting rubber collection quarters failure of which their hands and legs got amputated while others got subjected to inhuman arrests by slave trade captors under the support of the administration of the land.

On the eve of the scramble for Africa, only 10% of the continent was under the control of Western nations. For instance, by 1875, the most important European holdings were Algeria, whose conquest by France had started in the 1830s. There was also the Cape Colony, held by the United Kingdom, and Angola, held by Portugal

---

[48] *The figures of the population of Congo and the number of deaths during the 12 years of Congo Free State under King Leopold II are pure estimates as there has not been any reliable source to give something different. But certainly the number that is reflected could be highly underestimated*

implying that most of the seizing of Africa came after the Scramble for Africa period in the Berlin Conference held in 1885/6.

It may be recollected that Germany was one of those European nations that made a lot of swift advancements in its colonies. Most of their colonial projects were viably implemented. Other colonial nations as well as scholars in the subject praised Germany for being systematic and hardworking, and also for good achievements in their projects in the colonies. Their strict supervisions made their enterprises viable and profitable. But the crucial question is: what did strict supervision mean? While it is very true that Germans were strict and keen to see that their plans succeeded but if we go to the specifics, we see the ruthlessness of Germans against local people to be the central factor in their success.

Germans saw and took Africans as only tools not human beings. This is perhaps owed to the fact that Germany, had until the Berlin Conference and hence the New Imperialism, hardly been a colonial power. In that case, with the new developments it found itself eager to participate in the colonialization race more vigorously and more stingingly. Germany had not yet had the chance to control overseas territories, mainly due to its late unification, its fragmentation in various states, and its absence of experience in modern navigation. This could provide few of the reasons for convening the Berlin Conference of 1885/86, which as we have kept elaborating set the rules of effective control of a foreign territory. Their motive was to move fast and catch up with what they had lost.

The German colonial administration got praised for their successful implementation of their policies and programmes, very much unlike other colonial nations whose success was only marginal.. No African was targeted to benefit from those great plans, as his role was only that of carrying of the York. This would avail Alfred von Tirpitz to implement his aggressive naval policy49; thus, demonstrating that the main supports of the European nation states imperialism were the rising capitalist class50which according to Carl Max, lacked a human face.

Surely there have also been inherent problems among the new Africa administrations. Such administrators were trained in missionary and a few colonial government schools where the curriculum was well laid out to ensure that the graduates were well brain washed and well aligned with colonial policies and interests. The emerging African leaders wished to reach the level reached by Europeans as swiftly as possible. They had seen Europeans disregarding Africans who thought that was the way to do things. So they caused the deep-entrenched corruption in most African states. There also developed the selfish behaviour of some of the political leaders to sit tight in office even when they had obviously outlived their usefulness in the eyes of their people. That was also a result of orientation they got from colonial administrators, who applied no democracy in their administrations. For the same reasons some other African administrators had political parties that held tenaciously in power and efforts to eliminate oppositions were carried out to the extent that even options to take lives of those in opposition were there and have at times been on the increase.

The management and power mongering were passed on from colonial administrations and Africans failed to move swiftly

---

[49] *Alfred von Tirpitz original name Alfred Tirpitz was a German admiral, the chief builder of German Navy, in the 17 years preceding First World War and dominant personality of the emperor William II's reign. The essence of* **Tirpitz's naval policy** *was a great battle fleet, and he justified this by various strategic arguments. At times he spoke of a "risk theory"*

[50] *In Marxist context this was the capitalist class who owned most of society's wealth and means of production*

towards self-cleansing, thus becoming real representatives of the outgone colonial administrations. The evils were attributable to the effects of colonialism and imperialism for African states to overcome their present social, economic, political, health, education woes. There is thus need for urgent action for the people and the leadership to create their own indigenous clean identity, culture, technology, economy, education, religion, craft, etc. which would have to be interwoven in good governance.51

With the colonial rule urbanization started to take root but those were basically centres of business for the colonial administrations and businesses especially in plundering resources such as minerals, special trees' timber, ivory. Africans also sought to move to those urban areas with a view of taking advantage of the modern life that was emerging there. Their decisions were motivated by the fact that Africans had been expelled or dismissed from their fertile farming land which left them languishing in arid or other marginal lands or completely without land. But even there, in the urban areas, Africans were denied permission to settle, because of fear that they would only serve as polluting agents. However, the Africans resorted to settle in the periphery of the urban areas that were not officially designed and recognized and were not recognized by authorities and thus the areas were not supplied with any of the basic utilities such as water, electricity, roads and sewage systems. These areas became centres of filth, and the administration put a lot of their efforts in chasing the poor Africans away from those poorly provided areas which became popularly known as squatter settlements.

The colonial administrations enacted laws that aimed to restrict Africans in most key utility areas. Those laws and regulations only

---

[51] *Stephen Ocheni; and Basil C. Nwankwo:*

assisted to increase conflict and tension between European communities and African communities. The case of apartheid in South Africa can well be remembered. This situation triggered a new wave of antagonism between the Europeans and Africans, who in any case were losers in any such partitions.

Let's now cite a case of businesses such as mining or largescale farming where labour of indigenous people was desired. The establishment of such businesses aimed to employ local people with very low wages if any wage at all. Colonial countries enacted laws that demanded for the use of African labour. Yet there were many cases of Africans, who refused to work in those undertakings, a situation which led to being harassed and sometimes arrested and imprisoned for disobeying the directions of government authorities. Refusal of local people to work in European undertakings with peanut payment and at times with no payment at all made the colonial administrations to term Africans lazy, unruly, loiterers, disobedient and uncivilized people. The refusal made administrators to be infuriated and, in some situations, they invaded the villages and set people's houses on fire, which made the local people also to react violently, thus escalating the wars, which of course led to the death of many Africans. Case of what happened among the Wachagga people of Kilimanjaro under the German colonial rule can easily be remembered. All this happened after the new imperialism had started to deepen its roots followed by European businesspeople coming to the colonies to develop their investment undertakings.

There were situations where the colonial rule supported forced recruitment of villagers in remote places. A well-known case was that which made labour recruitment agents supported by the local chiefs conned the local people before they arrested villagers who ultimately went to work in distant settler farms. The villagers (mainly men) would be instructed to assemble in popular assembly point where a local administrator was going to address them. The local administrator, under the instructions of the local colonial officer, gave a long speech that made the meeting continue from the midafternoon hours to nightfall. That is when the African men started to suspect that something fishy was going to happen, though the chances of escaping was not there because the area was under surveillance of armed guards. Instead of allowing the village men to break and go back to their families, all of them, usually over a hundred of them, would be hushed to the waiting trucks to board on gun points. All the people who had been in the meeting would have to board and immediately after boarding the journey to the unknown destination started. They would have to travel the whole night.

Such journeys would be made without prior information to the men, and without allowing the village men to go to their families to at least say farewell. Neither the men nor their wives or children were made to know where they were being taken to. Ultimately, they got to remote farms; hundreds of kilometres away where they would from that day work in settler sisal plantation without wage, enough food, medicine, shelter, or sanitary facilities. Some stayed in the farm till they got old and died there because they did not know the geography of where they were, and never earned a wage that could afford them fare to their home villages; and of course, no permits were easily granted for those who requested to be given leave.52 This was typical scenery of the colonial administered slavery.

---

[52] *Abisai Temba: Three Hundred Years on Kilimanjaro Mountain Area. The book details on how recruitment for forced labour in settler farms was done for coffee and other settler farms in Kilimanjaro Mountain area.*

15

THE START OF MISSIONARY WORK IN AFRICA

Missionaries were people sent to Africa to deal with very specific assignments, to spread Christianity. But some missionaries were also explorers. Examples of missionaries cum explorers of central and Southern Africa were Dr. David Livingstone, Johannes Rebmann and Ludwig Krapf. Some, such as Dr. David Livingstone were among pioneer Europeans to get to the interior of Africa, to explore places and see how Christianity could be introduced to those interior parts of Africa. The London Missionary Society sent David Livingstone to South Africa in 1840, where he became one of the first Europeans to traverse the continent from east to west; but a lot has already been talked about him. Like we have shown above there were other missionaries (among them, Rebmann and Krapf) who also served as explorers.

However, Rebmann arrived in Mombasa, a town on the East Africa Indian Ocean coast in 1846 and began missionary work among the coastal tribes in the Mombasa area in the present-day Kenya. His work in Mombasa did not seem to attract promising audience, as that was a place of Muslim Swahili community who did not show much interest in what he preached. He planned to move to the interior places where he would meet people who could pay more attention to the Christian message he was bringing to people of East Africa. He began expeditions into the interior and in May 1848, he got to as far as Taveta. Actually, that is where he wished to restart missionary work; after his failed attempt in Mombasa. At Taveta he and a colleague of his, Ludwig Krapf, became the first Europeans to see Mount Kilimanjaro. Having sighted Kilimanjaro, the two men separated and decided to walk different directions. Krapf walked towards the north and ultimately in 1849 succeeded to sight Mount Kenya. Rebmann's wish was to walk further to the East to get a clear view and learn more about the snow caped mountain. That decision meant he would have to postpone his missionary work for a while.

However, even after postponing the establishment of a mission station, he decided to retreat back to Mombasa, from where he would make better preparations for an expedition that would take him to the slopes of Mount Kilimanjaro. The fact that, Rebmann changed to being an explorer after sighting Mount Kilimanjaro logically meant that he became only incidentally an explorer.

In the meanwhile, Mr. Rebmann wrote to people in Europe informing them about what he had succeeded in seeing, a mountain with a top covered with snow just in the equator. The report triggered a lot of criticism. People including intellectuals in Europe refused to accept the contents of his report, claiming that such reports could only be produced by someone that was lunatic. They queried how snow could exist on a mountain-existing just on the equator. The Equator was the hottest place in the universe, which for them meant that there was no chance for any mountain in such a place to carry snow on it. What those intellectuals failed to understand was that while temperatures became reduced as you move to higher latitudes, they also reduced as as you moved to higher altitudes. Kilimanjaro was the highest freestanding mountain in the world and therefore there was nothing strange about having snow that covered its top.

Rebmann made three trips to Kilimanjaro and in each of those trips he made detailed accounts of his findings including those of the people he met in the Kilimanjaro area, who were mainly, of the Chagga tribe and their rulers or chiefs who they called Mangi.

It is a pity that Rebmann faced a difficult time to convince colleagues including his Sponsors in Europe that he had seen a mountain that was covered with snow (in a place that was just close to the equator). In other words, while only a few people including famous geographers were willing to accept Rebmann's reports, others vehemently refused to accept such reports. Cooley, a famous intellectual geographer, was one among those who completely refused to accept Rebmann's report arguing that those were the "missionary's incomprehensible and vague stories" He also denied the existence of snow on Mount Kilimanjaro saying it was based solely on impressions of Mr. Rebmann. He continued to insist that Rebmann played with whims of his own imagination. Due to those arguments and counter arguments it took another 12 years to confirm that Rebmann's reports about Kilimanjaro and its snow caped top was correct.

However, as Europe kept on slicing Africa into territories and colonies, that became the time when, missionaries vigorously started to be dispatched to the continent to convert Africans or as they called it "to transform the uncivilized savages" into Christians. According to the Western world the arch objective was that of transforming the Africans from their state of savagery to people who had some sense of civilization and of course to create people who could be more usefully used to enhance the development motives that were driving Europeans to the continent.

Missionaries to Africa were constantly being dispatched to Africa to spread the Christian faith. Some missionary organizations used some of their Empire's resources and in return, the empire coerced them to use their teaching to subdue the Africans. The greatest incentive was the resources that Europe came to realize were available in plenty. The effort would now have to be to exploit the resources swiftly before the Africans opened their eyes. As the saying went "when the missionaries came to Africa, they had the Bible and Africa had the land. The missionaries said 'Let us pray. Africans closed their eyes and by the time they opened up their eyes the land had been taken away". That is only a type of euphemism, but what it seriously means is that some missionaries, actually most of them, came with a two faceted agenda or motive- converting Africans to Christianity and finding investment opportunities in the colonies. For some, the overriding factor was not to teach only what the Bible says but to lull the people into piety while fulfilling their other objective of taking away the land from the local people.

Cases have often been cited of the effects of missionaries in some parts of Africa, especially in the Sub-Saharan Africa. We will pick one example of how missionary work was introduced and initially operated in some places in East Africa. Immediately after the Berlin Conference in 1885/86 colonial administrators and missionaries started to move into their respective colonies. Missionaries took their positions according to their denominations. On Kilimanjaro Mountain area for instance, the District and Provincial administrations (or Commissioners) took the lead in providing guidance on how the missionaries were going to operate. Each Christian denominations was directed to go and occupy specific areas to avoid interference with each other. Under the directions of the district colonial administration the Roman Catholics were instructed to take the Eastern side of the Mountain area while the

Protestants (most of who were Lutherans) would have to take the Western side of the Mountain area. The eastern area would start from Kibosho and extended to Rombo. The western area would extend from Machame westward to Siha.

The allocation of areas of operation by colonial administrators had very good intention. It was aimed to ensure that there was harmony in missionary operations. The colonial administration feared that religious conflicts that had kept boiling and tearing Europe apart (where of Roman Catholics were always in conflict with the Protestants) the same could get repeated in the colonies, and to avoid that situation each of the two Christian branches were required to operate far away from each other.

There is no intention to give detailed account of how the separation of the denominations worked, but it is good to note that, in spite of the caution that was being taken by the colonial officers, the way things ultimately worked was very different from what they had seen in Europe. In this particular case the missionaries did not forget that they were in Africa and that they needed to cope and assimilate themselves to African conditions rather than forging towards the planting of Europe in Africa. In that particular regard efforts kept been made to create a new species of European missionaries in Africa. So initially the Catholic Missionaries started to operate in their area allocated to them, and the Protestants did the same. But as they started to spread none of them observed the confinement rules that had been given to them. In the end there was no specific area for specific denominations.

The British or the French including their Missionaries wished to see their European norms properly planted in Africa. In other words educating Africans meant making or grooming them to behaving or thinking like a Europeans. It meant talking in European intonation, eating European food, speaking European language, and where possible acquiring skin colour that was as light as that of Europeans.

Like we have already said, that type of education or orientation had great results. There emerged an African loss of cultural identity, a change in the unity of people in their respective regions, a spread of Christianity using the few trained black missionaries to support the colonial course, or the administration's norms, and the creation of classes within communities. While in certain cases or places majority of the local people remained in worse condition than before the arrival of the missionaries, but a few of them gradually started to enjoy the benefits that were brought by both the colonial administration and the missionaries. The few African beneficiaries of the colonial systems became the ones who held high the banner of the beauty of the colonial systems. For instance, while only a few Africans became Christians but those few that were converted were enabled to have their children joining mission schools, from which they earned some education which enabled them to get employed in government offices, or in missionary undertakings such as teachers in the handful primary schools, dispensaries and mission stations. These were the same ones that got employed in settler farms as clerks, storekeepers, and cooks. The rest of the citizens, actually the large majority, continued to struggle in highly suppressed conditions of vulnerability. The dual social system transformed the local communities into classes of pure African group that was illiterate, with a handful among them that formed the half cooked educated lot, who had been enabled to live European style type of life. It was until later especially towards the end of the 2nd World War the contradictions gradually began to enable Africans to see things with a better light, hence the increase of sense of nationalism.

The Missionaries like explorers came from all major colonial nations with support from rich individuals, companies or charity organizations, apparently with a view of bringing new Christian light to those who had been described as inferior and savages. When these missionaries encountered resistance, they blamed their failures on the inherent "darkness" of Africans. These missionaries believed that most Africans, especially those that had not been converted to Christianity were closed off from the saving light of Christianity.

Every indication showed that European missionaries especially from Portugal, Spain, France, Britain, Germany and even the other major colonial nations went to Africa under the premise of going to convert the locals, (all of whom were understood or conceived to be uncivilized savages) to Christian civilization. Some of the missionaries stuck to their missionary objectives, but others, actually the majority, paid most of their attention to aiding the colonization process. In many cases Christian conversion took the form of European process of self- transformation to Capitalists with power to freely plunder African resources.

Missionaries loved to see slave trading brought to an end, but the problem was in the definition they gave to slavery. Missionaries had workers in their farms or in other projects that they had investment in, but the payment was usually not there. Actually what is today named modern day slavery was introduced by missionaries supported by the colonial administrations, in the name of voluntary work that needed to be performed by the local converts. Some local people worked in the mission station farms or in their homes or in other commercial undertakings for many years without any pay. The workers only got consoled that their rewards would be provided by God in their eternal lives. In the meanwhile the Missionaries kept on living very posh life. Actually that legacy of missionaries has continued manifesting even among contemporary African clergy.

Missionaries went to Africa with the attitude that in all respects Europeans were superior to the rest of human beings; they had superior view of all things that happened in the universe and certainly did things in more sophisticated way than Africans. Missionaries like Dr. David Livingstone -the explorer of East and Central Africa and Fabri of the German Missionary Society in Namibia, was one of those Missionaries who believed that once Africans were colonized by Europeans, they would be more likely to seek after Western Education, Western Norms, Western standards and Christianity which the missionaries controlled. The mission of the missionaries was to do anything necessary to convert or rather to transform Africans from uncivilized, barbaric and very shortsighted nature to people whose culture and way of thinking would be at least close to that of Europeans. According to Dr. David Livingstone Europe was a standard measure of civilization. The thinking of Dr. David Livingstone was amplified by what he had seen done by Arab slave traders. The world was already aware of the cruel way Arab slave trade and the Arab inhuman treatment of black Africans was worse than that of devils. But what was it that was so strange about Arab slave traders; and why he thought Arabs were worse human beings than Europeans that had participated in the Transatlantic slave trade was not easy to comprehend.

To be fair, Dr David Livingstone's thinking went out of way. In this area his arguments and way of thinking were beginning to fail him. For the Europeans who had operated transatlantic slave trade, to be the new mentors for all Africans would be supported by a person who had transformed himself to a buffoon. He failed to remember that Europeans and specifically European clergy had been the same ones that were owners of transatlantic slave trade. They were the same people who managed Africans in a very inhuman way. Missionaries failed to remember that over 35 million Africans lost their lives in the hands of slavers in the transatlantic slave trade and that over 40 million more people were cruelly separated from their families and sold to slavery under the auspices of European traders and investors in the new world. All those were besides those who died of diseases and those who were drowned in the sea.

Most missionaries often failed to distinguish between Christian principles and those of the colonialists. They misused Biblical passages to further the causes of their colonial friends. The ideologies of most missionaries in Africa were not different from those of slave owners in America before the advent of slave trade abolition, which actually did not rid the slavery mentality in European entrepreneurs. Missionaries accepted slave trade abolition because the slave trade practice was increasingly becoming an embarrassment to Christianity and to all people who claimed to be civilized, which explains why Christian slave owners came up with many justifications that enslaving a black man was consistent with the provisions of Christianity. For the die hard, especially those slave owners in America who felt they could not live without owning slaves (even at that time when slave trade abolition campaign was at its final stage), argued that slavery was a very "necessary evil" and thus there was no reason to completely abolish it. Actually, this is the type of thinking the Missionaries carried with them to the colonies, as they tried to convert the Africans to European civilization.

The Missionaries encouraged Africans to rebel against everything that formed the foundation of African family and society. The missionaries went as far as underlining that salvation could only be realized through formal work, which meant one had to earn a paycheck. Most missionaries new to Africa believed Africans were lazy and were not using their land adequately, so it was in their best interest for Europeans to use it. Those impressions were enhanced by the their view that Africa had plenty of fertile land but Africans were not using it the way Europeans were, because they lacked competence, education, and to cape it all, they were lazy, not innovative and needed civilized people to think for them. The missionaries were among those who believed that Africans always needed to be pushed in order for them to do anything profitable for themselves. What made things worst was that Africans who by chance got educated in mission schools got highly brain-washed and shared the same European sentiments, that fellow Africans were lazy, lacked innovative minds and needed to be pushed to fulfill an assignment. That behavior by the handful educated Africans was in itself a strike of an ace by the missionaries because gradually the effort to build a class of Africans that saw things only from European viewpoint was beginning to bear fruits.

Some missionaries had developed friendships with local clans and used this to further European causes. Often African chiefs sought advice from missionaries on how to deal with other Europeans seeking treaties. However, the missionaries almost always betrayed their trust. That fact is known to have been a big problem in many parts of East, Central and Southern Africa where missionaries, instead of concentrating on the teaching of Christianity, spent a lot of time in getting huge tracts of land from the local people for their investments or to facilitate European investors to easily get the land which they would have otherwise found it difficult to get.

Missionaries of leading denominations got to Africa with clear instructions that they could establish a mission station at a place that met certain conditions. For instance, they would have to negotiate with local chiefs to get huge chunks of land, of the size of at least a 50 or more hectors. With those instructions from their home offices in Europe the Missionaries did the best they could; actually, with those guidelines it became possible for missionaries to acquire up to 1,000 hectors53 just for the establishment of a single mission station. The explanation given for that acquisition was that the missionaries would need a lot of land for the future needs of the stations.

As soon as they got the land the missionaries went back to Europe to mobilize funds for investment. The major explanation used to get the funds was that Africans were so uncivilized and most of them were in so vulnerable state that most of them lived in the caves, tree branches and in the middle of forests where they would have to be fetched and got back to civilization, which was a justification for huge sums of money, which in any case Africans benefited only in form of church building that was erected at one end of the 1,000 plus hectares of land. The rest of the money was invested in coffee, sisal, and cocoa plantations. Other missionaries invested in mineral exploitations and exports, or in forestry works and so on.

It was hinted above that the only a few missionaries showed strong commitment to the core business that brought them to

---

[53] *Abisai Temba: Three Hundred Years on Kilimanjaro Mountain Area. In this book the Author outlines at length the conditions Missionaries came with to enable them establish a Mission Station*

Africa. The missionaries demonstrated to be too lusty for African land and wealth. The Roman Catholic (RC) Church was most vigorous in taking such quick opportunities. As they acquired land, they swiftly went back to Europe to seek for funds from rich or big financial houses in Europe. Their efforts paid off because they succeeded to get many sympathizers who felt they had a role to get Africans out of the ditch of miseries they had been suffering in. Pictures of people wearing rugs were displayed to them; they saw pictures of dying hungry Africans, they saw mass graves of people that were claimed to have been killed because of immoral actions of Africans, they saw pictures of Africans in civil wars and so on. Such pictures were taken and used by missionaries not because they really portrayed what was happening, but were a strategy to win hearts of rich sympathizers. The approach taken by the missionaries was based on the experience the Church had acquired when it conquered Latin America, where for centuries the church had remained the greatest and most successful investor.

So, the process was not new to the missionaries. They knew what they were doing to make the church an economic power in Africa. The Missionaries were theoretically in Africa to spread Christianity but their minds centered more in obtaining land for investment. In most cases the land acquired by missionaries was aimed to take advantage of the colonial administration which could force Africans to forego their land in favour of Europeans, because once the colonial muscle was applied the only option available for the Africans was to succumb, they would have to do as directed. It is behind this scene it has always been said that Christianity was a secondary objective as the primary objective was to enhance the business courses.

It was natural that the missionaries would not be able to concentrate on church matters and at the same time enhance the investment path. One factor had to be given greater weight than the other. And that is what happened to most missionaries in Africa. They chose the investment path leaving the evangelization work to lay people. As has been mentioned elsewhere, the church established stations, but most initial evangelization work was left to the lay people most of them slaves that had been redeemed or bought from slave traders. The redeemed slaves, after receiving brief coaching and/or after they had been baptized they became the teachers for evangelizing the new converts.[54] That was what happened in Christian villages of the redeemed slaves in places such as Bagamoyo, in Tanzania and many other places. Even when the Missionaries went to establish new stations in the interior they established similar villages such as those in Bagamoyo and in all those cases, the converted persons who had at last been enabled to memorize the Lord's prayer as well as some elements of the Catechism, became the evangelizers while the Priests concentrated in matters of investments. Today, Kilimanjaro Mountain area is known to be one of those rural areas in Africa which have the highest rural population densities; the density is more than 1,000 people per square kilometre of land but with several mission stations each still owning thousands of hectors of land.

The missionaries, just like the colonial officers believed that what Africans needed were not the land but the "word of God". Africans needed to be awakened and wherever possible they needed to be supervised with the use of a whip or cane. This explains why the same missionaries have been considered to be no better than the colonialist or slave trader agents. A far-fetched example could still

---

[54] *Ibid*

be that of David Livingstone who is a renown explorer and missionary and whose history has been listed as one of the most committed missionary of all times. He had kind statements when he talked to Africans, but his mentality was that of making Africans cultivate a way of thinking that was at least close to that of Europeans which if emancipated could make Africans reason like Europeans. The achievement of mankind would be measured by the way an African got closer to the European way of thinking. To him Christianity would be the only means to transform the African towards that of a European.

That is where the African found himself in a trap. Due to suppression imposed on him, it provided enough room for the Europeans, through the missionaries to do the brain washing. Everything good was that which was Westernized. Western culture, which has so far been equated with Western civilization, Western lifestyle or European civilization, remained to be the terms which over centuries were used to refer to a heritage of social norms, ethical values, traditional customs, belief systems, political systems, and specific artifacts and technologies that had some origin or association with Europe. In situations where these terms continued to be used efforts continued to be deliberately made to bring in the fact that it was not the same culture that subjected the African in slavery for almost four centuries.

Missionaries endeavored to erase the fact that it was the same culture of civilization, which for reasons known to itself made a lot of effort to distorted contents of the Bible by claiming that the African was cursed; he had been cursed by God due to the fact that he was a descendant of Ham; and that by his nature he could not disentangle himself from the curse.. Unfortunately, this is also the mentality the missionaries carried with them when they came to transform the African to a civilized person, just as much as Europe had remained civilized throughout the centuries. As much as the Bible is concerned, there is nowhere God the creator of man has cursed people of dark skin. But this is what the Christian slave owners taught and that is what the missionaries in Africa continued to embrace for a long time. The Missionaries had pictures of Europeans painted white and bright and those of Africans painted black. That was fine in as far as it went; but they went further and painted the saints, angels and apostles and even Jesus white. All these provided images of holiness while the black colour represented evil. They produced black painted images, which represented the devil, which was a true reflection of what they thought, believed, and embraced.

However, the question remains; if the missionaries' views of Africans were so negative, how would they have been committed to the cause of Africans? In essence colonialism was partly a result of betrayal by missionaries. Even though we are grateful that they educated Africans and opened primary schools and clinics in remote villages we are not in position to use this as a demonstration of full commitment to the betterment of the African development. We can pose and think of a dispensary established by missionaries in one of those Central African colonies. Any of those dispensaries started only as a place where Missionaries and other colonial personnel went to get first aid treatments. Gradually the small dispensary in most cases owned and operated by a European family for European personnel in the locality, kept receiving European patients not only from the farm area where they were based but also from neighboring farms and mission centres. The colonial government saw the need to give more support to such dispensaries due to the good services they offered. For such dispensaries to provide services to the nearby Africans came later, only as a coincidence. In other words, as the dispensaries began to expand Chiefs also began to be accepted for simple diseases such as dressing of wounds, and treatment of malaria.

It was only a long time later when such dispensary had substantially developed, some Africans were admitted there, but they would have to stay or rather wait in the grass far from the hospital building while the missionaries and other European patients that kept waiting for treatment would be seated on a bench placed in the waiting space in the dispensary or hospital building.. What is being said here is that while services such as those of medicine or education were provided but their initial establishment did not target the Africans. Africans got in only by lack.

This may further explain why for almost 70 years of colonial rule in Africa a district or even a whole region in any country in Africa would be lucky to have one or two primary schools or dispensaries sponsored by the colonial government. Actually even these minimum services were available basically for Europeans in areas that had European communities or investments nearby. Otherwise, several provinces went without any such utilities for the whole period of colonial rule; which makes a mockery when some scholars or elites state that colonial rule left behind investments, which Africans failed to manage. The colonial administrations made no investments for Africans; any good thing you see today was established with a view of serving the colonial interests. The colonial administrations believed that they would be there in Africa forever. When Africans demanded for self-rule the owners of the facilities also decided to leave, leaving their investments to nobody to attend to them.

However, let's make a note again on explorers like Henry Morton Stanley. While Stanley used the term "Dark Continent" to build a mysterious allure around his travels in an effort to sell more books, the phrase on the other hand rightly entered European vernacular as a way to paint Africa as a wild, savage, untamed land. By dehumanizing the continent this way, colonizers and missionaries alike became unable to justify their, sometimes, brutal actions. They would have to do so because of the embarrassment caused to them. They justified their investments and their stay. However, that use assisted to be a lift in many people's minds; the idea of "darkness" certainly did not only become a reference to uncharted lands but more a descriptor for Africans that were considered wicked and unenlightened. It is understandable why some people may not be crossed and would object the use of the term wicked and would prefer the use of wild Africans to have been spoken only in colloquial language. Why would Stanley speak in colloquial language when his behavior and acts in Africa clearly reflected that his words meant what he said. It may be likely that the phrases could not be meant by Stanley to refer to skin color, but his acts and deeds were enough to make one believe that what he uttered was what he meant.

At the time when Christianity was being spread in some parts of the continent in the later years of the 19thCentury and of course in the 20th Century, black Africans who were said to be the target of missionaries portrayed Africans as representatives of the devils. The evidence to this was in Mission schools. A devil got painted black and any picture of a black African was drawn on the blackboard to show how ugly the devil was. Children felt very frustrated when they looked at their skin and saw it was black. That type of teaching went on until most African nations started to be politically independent in the 1950s and 1960s. A White man or anybody who did not resemble an Africa was conceived to represent the image of God. All angels were potrayed white and all agents of Satan were dark skinned.

The above also remains of a mission school -teacher, who was enrolling pupils for beginning Primary School in the later years of 1950s. The European teacher, in her effort of enrolling the children would keep asking questions whose answers would provide bio-data for each pupil. The questions and answers went as follows: "What is your Christian name" (meaning the first name) and the pupil answered "Ana-Maria" .The teacher went on "and what is the name of your father?" The father had been baptized because they never enrolled children of those who had not been converted, to Christianity. So, the pupil answered "Joseph" and finally the enrolling teacher finished by asking "and what is your Savage name?" the girl hesitated for a while because she was not sure what answer the teacher was expecting from her. But as she kept fumbling the teacher elaborated, "I mean what is your clan or grand father's name?" The girl quickly answered "Kirumbo". Clearly, to the missionaries and their agents Africans and their African names were savagery and Europeans including the missionaries were there to rid Africans of their savagery nature. Yes! That is the message the missionaries delivered to their converts. That is also what the missionaries wished colleagues in Europe to understand. In short anything that was African was savagery.

Missionaries sent to Europe a lot of useful information about the African continent. They reported about mountains and rivers, they reported about minerals and mineral sites, about the animals, the Lakes, the forests, and about the land, the good soils for agriculture, the various plants, birds, wild animals, and many others. The most distorted information was about Africans. Africans were portrayed as human beings that had not yet gone through the evolutionary process. That could explain why business people in America caught pygmies from their villages in the Congo forest and went to display them in wild animal zoos in America; which was a great humiliation of an African race. For those with good memories will remember that in in 1904, several Pygmies were brought to live in the anthropology exhibit at the St. Louis World's Fair. Two years later, a Congo Pygmy named "Ota Benga" together with four others were housed temporarily at the American Museum of Natural History in New York City—and then exhibited, briefly and controversially, at the Bronx Zoo. Actually, sometimes the information got very exaggerated; that Africans lived in caves like pythons or on tree branches like monkeys and wore only animal skins instead of clothes like the civilized people of Europe.

It will be remembered that Missionaries solicited and mobilized a lot of funds from Europe for enhancing investment on the land. For them to convince the donors they said they were going to use the funds for teaching the Africans how to wear clothes, how to build houses, how to read and write, how to cook food, how to stop cannibalism, how to behave like Europeans and so forth. The Protestants such as the Anglican, Baptists, and a few others employed those procedures to get support from rich organizations in Europe. However, the Roman Catholic Church, especially the Spiritans and others, worked even more vigorously to get the investment funds from sympathizers who included huge multinational companies.

All these missionaries would go to places where there were local people doing dirty jobs or those for one or other reasons were in rugs or were in a meeting under a huge tree (meaning that the tree was their dwelling place), took their photos and sent the pictures to the intended funders of their projects. But before they took the photos they would request the people in that meeting to strip, to show that they had not come across any dresses. That is how the missionaries succeeded to build huge church buildings (whose capacity would never be fully utilized for the next one hundred years or even more), or investment in big factories, or banks. It is not difficult to see in some mission stations some church buildings constructed in the 19th Century, whose capacity has not been fully utilized until this day. The reason was that there was a lot of money that was being collected in surplus so that even the planning on how to spend it was not easy. To be a pioneer in Africa for any purpose in those later years of the 19th century was a paying undertaking for Europeans.

It is along those same methods missionaries succeeded to make heavy investment in various sectors especially in largescale farms as well as in processing industries. Those who came from Europe to support the missionaries that were already in Africa were with the notion that they were going to meet people (i.e. the Africans) who were very strange human beings, who were very fierce and who had to be handled with maximum care because of their wild nature. They got amazed when they were not able to see any such people.

Reports written by missionaries about Africa were awesome. Missionaries were there to deliver the word of God to those who did not resemble them in terms of civilization, education and economic development. But they also intended to be rich and lead luxurious life. Any human being that was black or dark skinned, was made to represent the devil or was the real devil and anything white was either God or representation of God. Actually that was the type of message that got delivered as Christianity continued to be spread in the Dark Continent.

Black colour including the local language and intonation were not holly enough and could be the reason why till today some African church Ministers or Priests try to change their African intonation when they speak or when they make sermons so that they sound like European Ministers and Priests. That is enough to show how much Christianity and of course missionaries succeeded to brainwash the Africans. Through brain washing, black Africans who received and embraced Christianity also started to feel that fellow Africans who were not yet Christianized were second class, they were children of the devil and so they would have to pray more so that they could someday be upgraded to first class children of the Christian God. It is a sorry situation how the messengers of God tried to distort the Living Bible.

However, according to bad wishers of Africa and Africans, especially in Sub-Saharan region remained the most dangerous to venture into. There were many stories of various designs about this region. Of course, most such stories were true or false depending on what one wished to know or see. It could be true if one was looking at the wars that African communities fought against each other, or tropical diseases that were in most cases abhorred or witchcraft that some African communities performed.

However, the whole thing was over exaggerated because there is nothing new that happened in the continent that had not happened in other parts of the world. The interior of Africa was very unfortunate in the sense that it had too many negative images that had been imposed on it, that those who did the tarnishing were the very same people who used their energies to harvest much of the African wealth for their own benefits. The tarnishing was done not only by those who got to the Continent early, carrying the banner of liberators but also those who embraced ideas that would lead to take over of the continent for their own lavish goals. In the end all these came to be better revealed when it was too late to arrest the situation.

Missionaries began traveling to Africa with a view of planting Christianity, with a view of reaching the Gospel to those who had not been exposed to the serving light of Christianity. That was a job that at the initial stage caused a lot of frustrations to the missionaries because most of those who got directly or indirectly involved got very poor response from those who were to be converted. They expected to have their work cut out for them, but when decades later they still had few and sometimes no converts they began to say African people had hearts that were unreachable, and that their hearts were locked in darkness. Some missionaries went as far as saying those Africans were substantially different from Westerners. According to them the Africans were completely closed off from the saving light of Christianity.

16

CROSSING THE CHASIM TO POLITICAL INDEPENDENCE

It is to be stated again here that the end of the Second World War marked a period of vigorous pursuit for freedom and independence by Africa nations. That was the time when many African countries felt time had come for the colonialists to quit and allow the local people to pursue self-rule. On the part of European colonial countries, the two World Wars caused them a lot of fatigue, in various ways. For instance, those who lost in the First World War kept suffering from the defeat embarrassment because of loss of their pride as colonial countries, and also loss of economic and political benefits. For those colonial nations that won in the wars, especially Britain, French, and Belgium became contented that their prestige as colonizers was maintained.

However, the impact of the Second World War was high for almost all of colonial nations. They had spent a lot of resources in the war, so much that to continue pursuing colonial business did not make much sense. Consumed with post war debt, European powers found that they were now overburdened by the new post war needs, and for most of them it would be difficult to afford the resources needed to maintain colonial control in Africa. Nevertheless, they had to make hard decisions in regard to the colonies that were in their hands. So, the next twenty years from the end of the Second World War, I.e., in 1945 to 1965 saw over 37 colonies in Africa gaining autonomy or outright independence from their European colonial rulers.

Despite the decolonization impact, the 2nd World war in particular brought a new aspect to African nations. It helped to build a strong African nationalism, which resulted in a common goal for all Africans to fight for their freedom. The colonialist was thinking about how they could rid themselves of their colonial management burden while at the same time the Africans were beginning to think how they were going to put up the fight against colonial rule. Like we have just said the World War II led to the decolonization of Africa by affecting both Europe and Africa, militarily, psychologically, economically, and politically.

However, the African desire to fight for their independence germinated from another milestone, built by Pan-Africanism, which germinated from a Congress held in Manchester, England in 1945. The Congress marked a turning point for African nations. The meeting attempted to address the needs of all black people wherever they were in the world. From there the Pan-Africanism began to put pressure on participants about common experiences of blackness and sought the liberation of all black people around the World. That became the beginning of Pan-African movement, which would become more African based, after 1945. African leaders present in the meeting became more influential in the effort, as they used it to attack colonial rule. Furthermore, the Second World War impacted nationalistic movements in Africa by sharpening them. Ex- soldiers made easy recruits and workers who were working in cities for defense industries, became easy nationalist recruits. Britain and France adopted new policies towards their African colonies.

The decolonization process was not uniform for all colonies. Once again, for some colonies the process was very smooth and peaceful. For many other colonies the process was forceful, violent and independence was achieved only after a protracted bloody revolution. The colonial instability in Africa had started with the end of the First World War, in which, as has been stated some European nations lost their colonies. Germany, which miserably lost all its colonies after the First World War had its colonies divided between Britain and France to administer on behalf of the League of Nations.

The struggle to independence in Africa was not a dream that many African countries had or imagined of before the Second World War. But immediately after the Second World War, things changed drastically. The Second World War became a catalyst for stronger pursuit to African political freedom and independence. The War helped to build strong African nationalism, which resulted in a common goal i.e. all Africans started to see the need to fight for their freedom. In the end the Second World War led to decolonization of Africa by affecting both Europe and Africa militarily, psychologically, politically and economically.

The First and Second World wars taught Africa the importance of communication and the ability to work together. It in particular aroused the great need for unity among them. It is to be remembered, one of the many reasons that made Africa to be easily colonialized by European countries was lack of unity among African countries and/or their people. It could be noted for instance that at the beginning of European colonization of Africa, the African countries were often fighting with each other, while at the same time fending off European Imperialism.

During the wars, Europeans and Africans worked together to enable their colonial countries to win. The White soldiers were congratulated in all cases where their countries emerged victorious. The Africans that also fought in the same wars were immediately saved with a ticket home. The reason for that was that Africans lacked recognition and gratitude. Surely, that European attitude angered Africans. The attitude fueled fire that had been burning for many years in the hearts of Africans. It made them even more determined to become independent from European rule.

Nearly two million Africans were recruited as soldiers, allies and scouts during the Wars. When they returned home, they returned to the colonial states that still considered them inferior. Many war veterans expected that their dedication to colonial governments would be recognized, and they would be rewarded accordingly. That never happened. Worse still, they returned home to conditions that were getting worsened by a weak global economy. They had fought to protect the interest of the colonial powers only to return to the exploitation and indignities of colonial rule. Behind that scene these men became bitter and highly discontented.

What has been exposed above kept on paving the way to decolonization, though there were other factors as well. The first and most important factor was that European nations lacked the wealth and political support necessary to suppress revolts in remote places of Africa. They lacked the ability to oppose the new superpowers like the USA and Soviet Unions whose stand was strongly against colonialism. The third major problem was the existence and ever-growing independence movements in the colonies. The youth that had been timid to get involved in antagonistic resistances against the colonialists moved in the front line to resist the colonists.

The colonization inevitably ended at the time it did because the factors that led to its existence were decaying. It may be noted that decolonization was about cultural, psychological, and economic freedom for indigenous people with the goal of achieving indigenous sovereignty. It actually called for indigenous people to have the right and ability to pursue and practice self- determination over their land, cultures, politics, and economic systems. Yet, questions have kept been asked about why European powers resisted independence to their Africa colonies. The answer to that may be difficult to find, especially if we consider what was said earlier, that European colonial nations were beginning to feel the impact of the high costs of their involvement in the World wars, which in some way encouraged them to accept the decolonization process.

However, all that notwithstanding, European colonial nations still wished to use Africa's resources along with its people. In any case, they had to accept that the trend of issues was changing. The wind was starting to blow against their traditional wishes. Like the saying goes: "you cannot decide to eat the cake and still retain it". Decolonization was good and inevitable for both the colonizers and the colonized. The colonizers still saw Africa's resources as necessary for their social, and economic development, and that explained why they still reserved the idea of granting independence to Africans. The African nations similarly wished to be given their independence due to the fact it would return their integrity. With independence, colonial nations could value indigenous knowledge and scholarship; it would encourage African struggle against foreign domination and suppression and above all, it would enable Africans to preserve their cultures including languages and self - economic determinations. In summary, for the colonialists there was the sweet and the bitter sides in terms of the decision to grant independence to the Africans.

Now we come to the issue about what followed after the decolonization process. To put it in a straight language, decolonization meant the colonial governments had to quit. However, one of the most important effects of decolonization in Africa was the instability of the post-colonial political systems, which entailed other far-reaching consequences. The consequences included deep economic problems inhibiting growth and widening disparities between the northern and the Southern parts of the world-popularly known as the **North/South dichotomy**. All rich industrialized nations kept polarized in the north while the poor nations got polarized in the south. In spite of the abundance of natural resources in the South, but the poverty of the South remained and kept there as it had been exacerbated by the presence of colonial rule that used African resources to develop European economies.

Soon after decolonization, African countries found themselves highly dependent on European nations and their institutions for donations for revival of their economies whose development kept declining, swiftly. Reasons for the swift decline were many. They included the lack of articulate policies. The new governments tried to design and implement policies that they thought would change the economic and political set up of their nations and bring about more rapid development. The idea was good, but got constrained by the fact that they were preparing the policies without presence of experts that had experience in such functions. Even the few experts that were there were sidelined in favour of those who were got from the colonial countries. The local experts got frustrated by the behaviour of their leaders but surprisingly the good foreign experts also left because they were not paid for what they did as attractively as what they could earn in their home countries.

Colonial governments had never trained or involved Africans in technical jobs. So, Africans were getting involved in jobs they had never handled before. Due to lack of experience the political managers as well as the planners did a lot of fumbling in organizing, policy formulation, target setting and implementation. Governments just listed issues but failed to address the basic needs of their people. In other words their plan goals lacked prioritization and thus resources got scattered to projects that were not desirable at the material time. In the end many plans failed. Besides the shortcomings that have been listed in relation to planning, and management, strategisation, and accounting, there was also the lack of commitment by almost all stakeholders to achieve set goals. For instance, government bureaucrats would perpetually interfere in the planning process for their personal benefits or gains.

Furthermore, there were problems of corruption, which have remained a cancer in most countries of Africa. There is also the problem of poor and inconsistent laws on the part of political leadership at almost all levels. In many cases, once a person assumed power, he suddenly transforms himself to a semi-god. He found all the means possible so that he could remain in the office for as long as he/she wished. What is being said here is that in the early period of transition from colonial rule (i.e. the early days of independence) some political African leaders saw it to be their opportune time to transform themselves to rich tycoons and to succeed in doing so they became great dictators. Any idea of rule of law was put away. Constitutions were reviewed in favour of the ruler's interests. Such situation was witnessed in places like Zaire (present day DRC), Central African Republic, Uganda, Somalia, Malawi, Sudan, Libya, Nigeria, Zimbabwe and many other African countries. Most of those dictators had been leaders in their national armies during the transitional period, after which they overthrew the existing legitimate governments. Once they assumed power, they started to change the style of doing things. Their first move was that of eliminating opponents. Then they sought to change national constitutions and change multiparty states to Single political party states. Some went as far as pronouncing themselves Kings, as was the case in Central African Republic under Emperor Bokassa. The period saw families of elites becoming millionaires, resulting from embezzlement of public funds and many more types of mismanagement of African economies.

However, in the decolonization process, Ghana became pioneer to get self- rule or rather independence in 1957, just twelve years after the Second World War. The case of Ghana promoted the impetus for other African countries to press for their political independence. By 1962 twenty- four (24) African countries had succeeded to free themselves from the colonial rule. The decolonization went on fairly peacefully for those countries that were under British and French rule. But even in some of those countries that were under French and British the going was not so easy. Algeria, which was under French rule, went through a lot of struggles to be granted independence. For instance, Algeria had to put up a lot of struggle including involvement in guerrilla warfare to win its independence in 1962. The Algerian war, also known as the "Algerian war of independence" lasted from 1954 to 1962.

The Algerian war was not a surprise because it stemmed from the way things were being run during the French colonial rule. In short, until 1954 France had ruled Algeria for almost 130 years. So, the French citizens in France as well as in Algeria had adopted Algeria as only an extension of France in Algeria. Like it happened in many other similar colonies, there were what was called French Algerians, and other Algerians. The so-called French Algerian were actually French citizens that had decided to settle in Algeria. These were the most privileged thus assuming the 'first class citizenship' position while the rest of Algerians assumed 'second class citizenship'.

With the increasing heat for decolonization there were the supporters and opponents of the move. The local Algerians were all out for independence, but the French Algerians remained adamant to welcome the idea of independence or any other idea that would bring about change. The French Algerians wished to see French rule kept intact or even strengthened in Algeria. The other Algerians felt that time had come for Algerian colonizers to quit.

The other thing was that with the new wave of change for independence that was sweeping the whole continent of Africa following the end of the Second World War was growing too strong to oppose the pursuit for independence. These were the factors that made the Algerian war of independence to keep gaining momentum as time went by.

So, the French Algerians opposed to the idea of Algerian independence and also to an attempted coup in France by elements of French army, led to demonstrations (by French Algerians) in 1956. The demonstrations made the French government to stop making any further reforms. The combination of those unrests became the early triggers of the war, which were exacerbated by Jacques Soustelle's[55] repression. The chain of repressions made the Algerians population to rally behind the leaders of the Front de Liberation Nationale (FLN)[56]. After the Philippeville, Soustelle declared sterner measures, which triggered an all-out war.

---

[55] *Jacques Soustelle was an important and early figure of the Fee French Forces (FFF).*
[56] *National Liberation Front*

Ultimately things kept on weighing too heavily on the French government, and so it gave up and left Algeria. However, the departure was not so much due to economic reasons but to strategic and political reasons. Like it was common for almost all liberation movements in Africa, the FLN (translated in English to mean Nation Liberation Front -NLF) had its actions always termed by colonizers to be inhuman and brutal. But as the war escalated the French government increased its level of inhumanity and brutality on the Algerians. The French blamed FLN for their brutality against French Algerians but also the FLN blamed the French government for the same. That made the French government to lose popularity among the majority of Algerians and hence lost in the battle. On 18th March 1962 the French and the leaders of the FLN signed a peace agreement to end the seven- year Algerian war, signaling the end of 130 years of colonial rule in Algeria.

However, looking at Africa as a whole from the beginning of 1950s a wave of struggle for independence became very strong. Within that decade, many African countries crossed the chasm from colonial rule to independence. With the exception of isolated cases such as those of Algeria, the decolonization process (from French and British) was fairly peaceful.

Here is where we bring the issue of Southern Africa countries of Mozambique and Angola, both of which were Portuguese colonies. The decolonization in these colonies did not go without serious blood shedding. The crisis in Angola led to protracted bloody gorilla war- fares, which made many people to die and many more to flee their countries. For instance, such bloody wars made almost 500,000 Angolans to die and forced more than 200,000 to flee their country to the neighbouring countries of Congo (Democratic Republic of Congo or DRC) and others.

Mozambique, like Angola got involved in a protracted bloody War of independence between the gorilla forces of the Mozambique Liberation Front, popularly known as FRELIMO against Portugal. The war lasted for about 15 years from 1977 to 1992. It is estimated that over one million people were killed in that war. Like we have hinted Portugal was one of those colonial nations, which believed that there were no chances of quitting their colonies because they were the owners and demands for decolonization did not make sense to them. Portugal had turned the colonies legal extensions of the Portuguese nation, and thus the issue of independence was not there. After the 15 years of the bloody gorilla warfare, the Portuguese quitted Mozambique. But even after the Portuguese had left peace became a farfetched issue. There were a series of commanders of the war of further liberation that followed. The leaders, which have got known as commanders of the Mozambique War of independence were many; they included Edwardo Mondlane, Joaquim Chissano, Filipe Samuel Magaia, Samora Machel, Antonio Agusto dos Santos, and Kaulsa de Arringa. These came in succession from the first to the last respectively.

Most of what has been discussed relates to what happened immediately before or after decolonization. The conflicts that resulted were impacts of demand for independence. However, we should not lose sight of the fact colonial rule was imposed on Africa and rooting it out would not be expected to be an easy task.

In West Africa there were cases Nigeria Civil War immediately after the colonial rule. Nigeria went through the decolonization process early and fairly smoothly. But soon later that country started to be stressed by civil war fought between the government of Nigeria and Biafra, a secessionist state, which had declared itself as an independent state from Nigeria. It was an ethno- religious violence and anti- Ibo programmes in Northern Nigeria, a military coup, a counter coup and persecution of Ibos living in Northern Nigeria. There was also the issue of control of over the lucrative oil production in the Niger Delta.

The full story was that a political conflict caused by the attempted secession of the Southeastern provinces of Nigeria as the self - proclaimed Republic of Biafra. Nigeria was created as a colonial entity by the British and got divided between a mainly Muslim North and a mainly Christian and Animist South. From independence in 1960 three provinces were formed along tribal lines, the Hausa and Fulani in the North: the Yoruba in the Southwest and the Ibo in the South East. Following the military coup in 1966 in which an Ibo became president tribal tensions increased. This was followed by a northerner-led encounter coup a few months later. Iguiyi, the Ibo leader, was killed and widespread reprisals unleashed against the Ibo. Fearing marginalization within the State on 30th of May 1967 the Ibo (majority province) declared itself independence as a Republic of Biafra.

The actions that the Nigerian government did to make the Republic of Biafra surrender included blocking food supply to Biafra. The blocking led to humanitarian crisis of huge proportion. Under those conditions images of suffering people reached global community, and sympathisers stepped up humanitarian support. Nevertheless, Biafra surrendered in January 1970; making this Nigerian crisis to be one of the first most Second World War development of humanitarian responses to a very complex emergencies (either caused by natural calamity or by human hand).

The real cause of the conflict (that led to great disaster) was a combination of economic, ethnic, cultural, and religious tensions among different people of Nigeria. Very briefly we will explain some of those factors as follows:

Number one was the ethnic factor. Nigeria from the colonial times was divided into three distinctive ethnic regions namely the Northern part, which was predominantly an area for the Hausa and Fulani. These formed the majority of the population in the whole of the North of Nigeria. The Southwest part of the country was predominantly Yoruba, and the Southeast was Igbo. The second factor was religion. The north and south of Nigeria were two parts of the country, completely divided such that the north was Muslim, and the south was combination of Christianity and animism. The third factor was culture: Southeast had cultures that were more flexible permeating influences of people from the outside. The fourth factor was political.

The north was traditionally ruled under an autocratic Islamic hierarchy, consisting of some 30-odd Emirs, who in turn had allegiance to a Supreme Sultan. In other words, the system was semi-feudal. In that regard the Southwest, was basically a place for the Yoruba, who like the Hausa-Fulani in the north also consisted of a series of monarchies, which were however less autocratic than the Hausa-Fulani. The Yoruba political and social system allowed for more upward rise based on acquired rather than inherited wealth and titles. While Christianity in the north, was basically not allowable, but such restrictions were not so much in the south.

At the time of independence of Nigeria (in 1960) the North had the lowest literacy rate (2%) compared to the Southeast (19.5%). The southwest had even higher rate because it had been the entrance point of colonialist when they came for the first time to Nigeria. Regarding the administrative systems the Ibo in the southeast had petty monarchies only in the villages. The system allowed autonomous hereditary or elected leaders, who were just a little more than figureheads. Decisions among Ibo were made by a general assembly. Regarding the economic factors, the southeast was rich in natural resources, more schools were built and the level of people's wealth was generally high, the number of professionals was among the highest in Nigeria and the per capita income was also exemplary in the Southeast.

A combination of all these factors in Nigeria led to discontent, frustrations and disharmony, and above all lack of tolerance. Looking critically at all these problems, which in the end led to civil war and ultimately to the breaking of Biafra war, it becomes clear that the problems did not start at independence. That situation had been nursed since when the British started to rule Nigeria. Problems had therefore been there since when Nigeria gained her independence on First October 1960. Imperialism and colonialism started with the sowing of seeds of discord, which went on to germinate until the time when Nigeria got its independence in 1960.

The Nigerian issue was more critical than was generally expressed. The genesis was that, during the colonial period northern areas were renamed the Protectorate of Northern Nigeria and the land in Niger Delta and along the lower riches of the river was added to the Niger Coast Protectorate which was renamed the Protectorate of Southern Nigeria. With those changes Lagos still remained the capital of Southern Nigeria and Zunguru became the capital of the north. At the start of the First World War in 1914 the northern and Southern protectorates were united to form the colony and Protectorate of Nigeria, under a Governor General based in Lagos.

That was the state of things, but what cannot go without a mention are the following factors among others: That, the British ruled Nigeria but, like it was the case in other colonies in Africa, the colonizers did not have any clue of the local culture and customs. The introduction of colonial rule made the north to resist Western education and development policies because they were not in congruence with their ethnic or Islamic cultures. English language as well as Western education was introduced and spread rapidly in the South while it remained resisted in the Muslim North. The British chose to adopt the divide and rule policies, by introducing religious and development differences between the North and the South. These and many other factors led to a state of tension between the North and the South, which ultimately led to the Break of the Southeast state, which renamed itself, Biafra.

The immediate causes of the 1966 Biafran war included the ethno-religious violences, anti-Igbo pogroms in northern Nigeria and control over oil rich region and production in the Niger Delta. Other triggers of the war included military coups and counter coups, which were brought to the climax by persecution of Igbo living in Northern Nigeria, in which thousands of Igbos were massacred.

17

RACISM: PROMOTER OF SOCIAL DISINTEGRATION

There is often a problem of looking at racism, prejudice, xenophobia, social stratification, and poverty as though they were unrelated terms. Though those terms can be used in very different ways leading to completely different meanings what is achieved depends on the circumstances in which they manifest. While the terms may mean different things but have some close relationships. For instance, while racism could be defined as prejudice, discrimination, or antagonism by an individual, community or institution against a person or people on the basis of their membership of a particular racial, or ethnic group, typically one that is a minority or marginalized. Literally racism means an unfair relation or treatment of people of a particular race in a society especially, so as to distinguish them as inferior or superior to one another. On the other hand, social stratification refers to social categorization of its people into groups based on socioeconomic factors like wealth, income, race, education, ethnicity, gender, occupation, social status, or derived power.

For those people that have been under European colonialism would recollect that colonialists used to refer to black people as people of different caliber compared to themselves due to their social and biological and even economic constitution. The colonists to Africa were White Europeans and the colonized were black or coloured people. This became a serious dichotomy just on the onset. Being people from Europe all colonizers of 19th to middle of 20th century were Europeans and thus any colonizer got understood by others as White people as opposed to those of any other skin colour. White became a synonym for colonizer. Conversely, any black person got understood to be the colonized and suppressed. In places like South US people of mixed race especially the African Americans were referred to as coloured people, which was a descriptor used during the Jim Crow Era. In many other places people of colour it was considered a slur, though in Soth Africa during apartheid coloured was a legally defined racial clarification meaning anybody who was not white.

Being a non-white meant a shift from social classification to another. On the basis of that classification the black race was the lowest rated, above which there were the mixed or the Indian race group and above all were the white class. The African would have to bear the brunt of humiliation while any European deserved to be respected and obeyed. It happened further that the Europeans in Africa, who also were the colonizers, got the chance to accumulate wealth through exploitation of African resources, which provided an added advantage to Europeans. Since then, all Europeans got understood by Africans as naturally wealthy and esteemed race while black Africans got associated with poverty and vulnerability. Africans got recognized as humans that deserved to be ignored in most respects. Since the time of colonization, or we can move further back to the era of transatlantic slave trade down to colonial era, racism, prejudice, and poverty were brought together as inseparable terms.

Due to those reasons Africans were seen to be incapable of doing self-governance, which gives reason why some colonial authorities showed a lot of resistance to granting independence to Africans. The chaotic type of management that was done by Africans who took over from colonial governments have often been cited as factors to prove that African were people that had little power of thinking, people who had no competence of stretching their minds far enough to do things that were as good as those done by Europeans. Actually, such simplistic reasonings were seen to be enough reason to look at Africans as inferior specie and Europeans as superior and intelligent specie. The meaning of all this is that there is a relation of race and colonial enterprise.

Once again there is very close relationship between colonialism and racism but handled separately the two terms do not carry the same meaning. Racism takes many forms and can happen in many social setups and places. The term racism is derived from "***race***" which could further be defined on the basis of physical characteristics such as skin colour, hair type, facial form, eye shape and others. It may also be noted that race is based on biology; but analysts have gone further and noted that that definition was in fact created for social and political reasons; which forces us in this book to generalize by stating that in its application racism embraces all the negative factors that are associated with discrimination, prejudice, xenophobia, social stratification, slavery, poverty and underdevelopment. As we move on it looks like we are using some of those interchangeably, but only because of some relationships that exist between them.

The UN has often defined racism as "the social cancer of our time". The disease gnaws away slowly and insidiously until it invades the whole organism of society and erupts in violence and death. Racism has further and more importantly been defined as the marginalization and/or the oppression of people of skin colours that are different from yours, based on a socially constructed racial conceptions and hierarchies that privileges people of a specific race that is in power.

Courageous Combatants of racism have come out and spoken very plainly about the evils of racism. Once upon a time some institutions in many parts of the world including Western Europe became great combatants of racism. Some specific UK institutions, especially in the 1990s in many occasions came out and showed to be excellent combatants. A spokesman of one of city councils in the UK once said in their article on *"**Becoming an Ant-racist City**" **that racism was a state when a person was treated worse, excluded, disadvantaged, harassed, bullied, humiliated, or degraded because of their race and/or ethnicity*. The spokesman of the said city further stated that at an organisational level, racism could manifest in form of the collective failure to provide an inclusive and professional working environment to people because of their race or ethnicity. What could be added to that statement is that racism can be the deliberate or accidental outcome of an organization's policy or practice and could manifest in processes, attitudes, and behaviours, which amount to discrimination through unwitting prejudice, ignorance, and thoughtlessness.

Like slave trading or colonialism, exploitation, social stratification and prejudice, racism has caused a lot of devastating effects on societies in many parts of the world especially in Africa. In those devastations people of black race have often been the leading victims. While slave trade, slavery and colonialism pushed Africans to the brink or to an angle of state of absence of self-confidence for their self-determination and development it also brought about similar effects. Actually, racism has led to mass killings, forced migrations, terrorism, religious conflicts, poverty among people that are segregated, undue tension in societies and creation of uncalled for fear to integrate. Practice of racism where it manifests through national policies and laws has exacerbated lack of social or national cohesion.

Racism has great impact on human health. It is responsible for increasing disparities in physical and mental health. It has been causing stress, which usually leads to blood pressure. Discrimination in many societies has had a close link to higher rates of smoking, alcohol use, drug use, and unhealthy food eating habits. Racism has been found to be several times as likely to affect mental health than physical health. Depression stress, emotional distress, anxiety, post-traumatic stress disorders and suicidal thoughts have always been possible in persons that are over-possessed by racial or other types of discrimination. Depression caused by racism, social discrimination and prejudice have had impacts that put the affected organism in various other ways, or groups of factors such as feelings of sadness, anger, depression and being left out. A person who suffers the impact of racism or segregation could always find himself suffering from undue headaches, increased heart rates, sweating, trembling and muscle tension; and could also be in constant fear of being verbally or physically attacked; and such person suffer from little trust on anybody besides members of the family.

Racism has existed in many societies or communities in the world. In the early years of slavery in Europe the slaves were marginalized and highly mistreated. Like in many other places it has been usual to witness high level of racism in soccer fields. All these disheartening occurrences have often lead to a lot of disharmony, including verbal confrontations, wars, deaths, denial of social benefits or utilities and others.

In America the people of colour have systematically been marginalized and underprivileged by laws that were put in place by the group that was in power. In Asia the situation is worst especially in countries where the social set up assigns' importance to certain sections of the society, who also happen to be the decision makers. In India for instance, there are people that are considered to be of purity against the untouchables. The later live extremely unhappy lives.

Africa has not been an exception. Africans have been discriminating each other on the basis of social backgrounds, tribal differences, political, economic and cultural differences and so on. It has not been unusual in Africa to see people of one tribe discriminating against those of a different tribe. In many parts of Africa there are segregations between people of one race, tribal background, political party, religion and even the cultural background. In Olympic games discrimination used to be openly witnessed though today much effort is being made to combat it.

Racism was on the rise especially during the height of international slave trade. Actually the Magnitude of slave trade increased in the 17th and 18th centuries because people of one race, especially the Semists saw it to be right for them to enslave people of Hamit background. The prejudice and hence the racism made the Semists get convinced that they had the right to put the others into slavery. They even sought clauses in the Bible with a view to prove that what they did was fully supported by God; hence going ahead and handling other human beings as merchandise for export from Africa to the Americas. The triangle trade was operated in such a way that, black people got from Africa were cruelly captured, packed in crammed ships, mistreated when in the ships including going without meals, and many other types of torture when on board the slave ships on the way to the Americas.

In the period towards the turning of the 19th century racism kept on growing and spreading; but indications towards the end of the 2nd World War were that there would be a drastic decline. But the trend since 2nd World War showed that just the opposite. Since 1950s racism has been picking up steam. Racial hatred logically moved from discrimination to acts of indescribable horror and death camp massacres carried out on an industrial scale. The shock and repulsion that swept the world so discredited the doctrine of racism that it dared not show itself cynically and blatantly as it had done before.

At this juncture lets see again how racism can be a cancer that eats the tissues of the society, a nation and/or people of a certain ethnic background. The case of Nazi regime in Germany during 1930s and 1940s can easily serve as a good demonstration of how racism can fuel conflicts and genocide. The Nazi regime was built on racial hatred ideology and policies against people of all races that were not Semists. The Nazis viewed the world as being divided up into competing inferior and superior races, each struggling for survival and dominance. They believed the Jews were not a religious denomination, but it was a dangerous non-European "race" and that such dangerous people deserved to be destroyed; short of which the Jew racism against the Nazi regime would produce murder on an unprecedented scale.

Adolf Hitler, the leader of the Nazi regime, had grown to hating the Jews, although the hatred had been there among German Semists for centuries. The Jews in Europe had been victims of discrimination and persecution since the Middle Ages; often for religious reasons. Christians saw the Jewish faith as an aberration that had to be quashed. Jews were sometimes forced to convert or they were not allowed to practice certain professions. Hitler blamed them for everything that was wrong with the world. He believed that Germany was defeated in the First World War, and that nation continued to be weak because it was being sabotaged by the Jews influence. According to Hitler, the Jews were after world dominance.

Hitler divided the world population into high and low races. According to him the Germans belonged to the high race people and the Jews to the low ones. He also had specific notions about other peoples. According to him, Slavic people, for instance, were cast as inferior, pre-destined to domination especially by the high race people. He believed that Germany and its people could only be strong if that country was kept 'pure, and that once the Nazis had come to power, these ideas would be implemented by way of forced sterilisation and killing of other human beings, especially the Jews. For that matter, during the 1930s, he did everything he could to expel the Jews from German society. Once the Second World War started, the Nazis resorted to mass murder. Nearly six million Jews were murdered during the **Holocaust**.

Societies have become increasingly committed to the belief in freedom and equality. However, there has also been putative support for racial discrimination. Those who support this line of thinking have claimed that there are biological dangers involved in racial interbreeding. Because of that, countries like the US and South Africa held that there was need for statutory prohibitions against interracial intermarriages. The support for that line of thinking also came from the physicians of the time who claimed that, as a result of their mixed blood, half casts were considerably more susceptible to disease than either of their parents and thus exceptionally short-lived. Besides the physicians there were others, especially the anthropologists of the time who claimed that people of mixed race were progressively less fertile, eventually becoming completely sterile. However, genetic mismatches were once fairly widespread, especially in the 19th century and early times of 20th century. Today there is absolutely no evidence that racial interbreeding can produce a disharmony of any kind.

Referring to Nazism, in July 1943, the US Vice President Henry Wallace spoke to a crowd of union workers and civic groups, indicating that they would not encourage racism in America at the time when they were fighting racism abroad. However, the liberal American scholars have persistently been of the opinion that there was clear historical relationship between Nazism and white supremacy in the United States. That was in those days, but the same scholars remain harbouring the fact that the features are not entirely different even on this day.

In the contemporary African political arena, aspects of racism have often been surfacing in a rather different forms and under completely different themes. In those countries of Africa that are under dictatorships or autocratic regimes, all foreign, especially Western suggestions of democracy are termed bullish and imperialistic. Foreigners were avoided in policy making not because the advice they gave was always bad but because of some attitudes, which happened to have been preconceived against foreigners. Not only that, in countries with multiracial communities or differing ethnic backgrounds issues of discrimination against the less popular have often being surfacing. Looked at keenly, those who refuse to cooperate with those with good ideas do so because the advisors are foreigners or are people of different race. Those who are discriminated upon have been victims of prejudice, segregation or even racism. Colour of the skin is usually not an issue here. Statements such as "we are fighting against foreign policies or influences, because the foreigners are thieves or are the exploiters of our resources" are generalized statements, based rather on racism. A person cannot be bad only because he is a West European, East European, African or Asian. On the contrary a person cannot be said to be good and non- exploiter simply because he is black from an African country. Those attitudes of discrimination have usually been founded in racism. Similar racist tendencies are common in soccer fields in most of European countries against people of the black race. When a team with African players wins, every member of the team gets praised. But the opposing team that looses the game starts to call names to African players that made their opponents win.

Since 1960s racism has not shown any signs of rescinding. On those grounds the United Nations held a conference in Durban, South Africa in 2001[57] where a declaration against racism was strongly made. Another similar meeting was held in Genever in 2009 to review the performance of the 2001 meeting. However, the report of 2001 meeting has come to demonstrate that it was a comprehensive, action-oriented document that proposed concrete measures to combat racism, racial discrimination, xenophobia and related intolerance. The meeting was holistic in its vision; it addressed a wide range of issues, and contained far-reaching recommendations and practical measures. The Durban Conference Report embodied the firm commitment of the international community to tackle racism, racial discrimination, xenophobia and related intolerance at the national, regional and international level.

---

[57] *Report of the UNESCO, Durban meeting of year 2001.*

Today racism is an issue of global concern. Dealing with it needs a universal effort, and recognition of that situation deserves to mark an important achievement. In as far as Africa is concerned today the African youth is getting a lot of education against the hazards of racism. That education needs to get extended to other societies outside Africa due to the fact that the world has been growing to becoming a global village. If a sense of love and brotherhood is not properly cultivated today, the future of those who will deliberately decide to hold on in maters of discrimination and racism will certainly end up to be the losers in the game.

Twenty years since the adoption of the Durban Declaration and Programme of Action, racism and xenophobia were on the rise worldwide. The resurgence was visible in public discourse, the media and political rhetoric, and especially against migrants, refugees, people of African descent and others. The world and Africa in particular, still witnessed politicians and leaders using hateful and divisive rhetoric to divide instead of uniting societies; and this has sometimes been happening without reservations. Race-based police brutality and retaliatory killings, waves of hate crimes against minorities, and discrimination and violence towards migrants and refugees have emerged as signs of pervasive racism.

Some history scholars have described the transatlantic slave trade as African holocaust that eliminated almost 40 million people from the continent. UN exhibited the bill that said "US" and 'THEM": From Prejudice to Racism". The bill was on display in the United Nations Visitors Lobby in New York from 21 February until 4 May 2020. The display highlighted the International Day of Remembrance of the Victims of Slavery and the Transatlantic Slave Trade, which is observed annually on 25 March. The International Day's 2020 theme was: "Confronting Slavery's Legacy of Racism

Together". There is a lot that is intended to be learn from those displays. They depicted and continued to examine the science behind the concept of race; they showed how racism flourished during the transatlantic slave trade and have continued to divide societies; thus teaching human beings that racism is a social construct that is not inevitable and can be fought at multiple levels. International organizations as well as individuals in different fora have all along expressed that time had come for mankind to work together to eliminate social discrimination and racial prejudice, as it is one of the most pressing imperatives of our time. That is hopefully what is pushing the international community to take concrete steps to address global problem of racism.

The Sharpeville massacre that took place at Sharpeville in South Africa on 21 March 1960, is a good example of horrors of racism. The police opened fire on innocent children that were peacefully demonstrating against police disgrace. There were 249 casualties in total, most of them children. Evidently the opening as of fire on children was enough indication that the shooting was more than a result of just silencing mob demonstrations. Most of those injured and killed were people of the black race and the engineers of the shooting were the government sponsored white administration.

Besides the Sharpeville shooting, there emerged another shooting, based on what is popularly known as the Soweto (an area in the close proximity of Johannesburg) uprising, which was a series of demonstrations and protests led by black school children in South Africa. The demonstrations began on the morning of 16 June 1976. It is estimated that 20,000 students took part in the protests. They were met with fierce police brutality and many were shot and killed. Other equally bad events prompted by racism in the apartheid South Africa would include the Church Street Bombing of 20th May 1983 in which 19 people were killed and the Durban Car bomb of 3rd April of 1984 in which five people died. All these are consequences of racism especially in places where it has been allowed to grow strong and deep roots.

Apartheid meant apartness or rather separate utilities such as water fountains, schools, residential areas, shopping areas, restaurants, and even recreation areas. The utilities were restricted to people of specific races of South Africa. It was a political and social system in South Africa during the era of White minority rule. Under this system, the people of South Africa were strictly divided by their race and the different races were forced to live separately from each other. The utilities supplied to the different race areas differed in standard, quality, and adequacy according to the preference given to the different races. Certainly, the utilities supplied to black race communities were of the worst nature.

Another equally disturbing example of atrocities caused by prejudice, discrimination and racism are the killings that took place in Rwanda in 1994. The extensive coldblooded genocide provide another shocking example of how hatred between people of one race, society or tribe against another, can lead to horrific results. The story behind the Rwanda genocide is long but can be told in short as follows: That about 85% of Rwandans at that time were Hutus. At that time and even before the commencement of the genocide the Tutsi minority had long dominated the country. In 1959, the Hutus overthrew the Tutsi monarchy and tens of thousands of Tutsis fled to neighbouring countries, most of them to Uganda. While in exile a group of Tutsi formed a rebel group, named "Rwandan Patriotic Front (RPF)", which invaded Rwanda in 1990. The fighting continued until 1993, when peace was agreed under a peace deal.

On 6 April 1994 a plane carrying President Juvenal Habyarimana, and his counterpart Cyprien Ntaryamira of Burundi - both Hutus - was shot down, killing everyone on board. Hutu extremists blamed the RPF and immediately started a well-organised campaign of slaughter. The RPF said the plane had been shot down by Hutus to provide an excuse for the genocide. To make their motive most effective the Hutu extremists set up a radio station known as PTLM and News Papers, which were aimed to circulate hate propaganda. The propaganda urged people to "***Weed out cockroaches***" meaning to eliminate by killing the Tutsis wherever they were. Within a period of just about 100 days hundreds of people, estimated to about 800, 000 or more had been killed by the Hutu extremists. The killings targeted members of the minority Tutsi community, as well as their political opponents, irrespective of their ethnic origin. The case of Rwanda is another stunning example of horrors that can be caused to a community, society or country or even the world due to promotion or support of acts of prejudice and especially racism.

Generally, the Hutu-Tutsi strife had a long history. The strife stemmed from class warfare, with the Tutsis perceived to have greater wealth and social status (as well as favouring cattle ranching over what was seen as the lower-class farming of the Hutus). The universal underlying factors were that racial discrimination, or in this case tribal discrimination concerned the unequal treatment of races (or tribes), whereas racial inequality concerns, as well as unequal outcomes in income, education, health, etc. were underlining. Racism and tribalism in Africa is often implicated in both processes, while the contemporary racial as well as tribal inequalities and forms of discrimination are, (but not always) the immediate result of contemporary racism/tribalism.

Like has been shown above in the case of Rwanda, tribalism was a source of injustice and thus it led to chaos and instability. Injustice is always a threat to justice everywhere. Martin Luther King Junior once remarked that, "***human beings are caught in an inescapable network of mutuality, tied in a single garment of destiny. Those committed to fighting racism have had the idea that the malady must be fought by teaching respect and tolerance, by sharing the common history of all humanity, including the most tragic chapters***" The dynamics of exclusion and exploitation in our societies must be understood, due to their importance in combating discrimination around the world but most important for the benefit of supporting African development. It may be good to note that human rights extend to everyone, and we must work constantly to let everybody know that they have an obligation to work towards eliminating racism.

Racism is the answer to the question why outside Africa, people of African descent are often among the last in line for health care, education, justice, and opportunities of all kinds. Those are issues, which the world of today will need to raise voices against all expressions of racism and instances of racist behaviour. Africa urgently needs to dismantle racist structures and reform racist institutions. We can only move forward by confronting the racist legacy of slavery together.

It has often been argued that in as far as Africa is concerned, slave trade, colonialism and neo-colonialism provided the basis for racism that followed. Economies of colonizers prospered at a great human (African people's cost): The issue of the industrial revolution tells it all. Industries were developed upon the suffering of fellow human beings through slave trade. A very crude and cruel system of development impacted many lives and stole the future of successive generations. In some instances, the descendants of those who were enslaved continued to face enduring social and economic inequality, intolerance, prejudice, racism, and discrimination.

Even after political independence African leaders behaved not very differently from past colonial leaders. They behaved nothing less than photocopies of their colonial predecessors. That was a very bad method of making a fresh start. To show the way, Africa should now take the lead in committing to stamping out xenophobia, racism and racial discrimination. That could be done by way of each country coming up with a national policy that condemns all types of xenophobia, racism and discrimination. It needs an action plan that will make an important step towards addressing the wide spread human rights abuses arising from xenophobic and gender based violence and discrimination, both of which have continued to plague the African continent. The process will have to be inclusive specifically calling for the participation of the governments, civil societies, religious institutions, and all others.

Racism has remained a monster that pulled the integrity of Africa to the lowest possible level. Africa got dehumanized, humiliated and enslaved locally and abroad. A lot of false justifications were given to convince the world why that was inevitable. Those who were involved in human merchandise trading happened to be the most powerful in the world in terms of economic and military power, and thus they dictated the terms. The suppression went on for such a long time that Africa and Africans were given a very false image. Africa started to be seen as a cursed place with people that were portrayed to be incomplete spiritually and intellectually compared to those that considered themselves to be of superior race.

Instead of looking and seeing the Africans as true human beings of the black race, they started to be seen only as beings, notably mammals at an advance level of evolution to human beings. . Towards the end of the 19th century and in the first half of the 20th century the situation became so bad that some Africans got forcefully caught from their localities, transported abroad (especially to America) where they were put in zoos where they shared food and sleeping place with wild animals such as monkeys and wildebeests. They got forced to ease themselves in the same zoos as did the wild animals, not because they wished it so, but because they were always in chains. The case of **Ota Benga, a man of Pigmy ethnic background,** who was captured from his community settlement in the Congo forest and transported to United States where he was put in a zoo sharing facilities with monkeys could be a sad case to remember.

Modern variations of racism have often been based on social perceptions of biological differences between people groups. These views can take the form of social actions, practices or beliefs, or political systems in which different races are ranked as inherently superior or inferior to each other, based on presumed shared inheritable traits, abilities, or qualities. The problem has been there for hundreds of years.

Racism is an embarrassing subject to deal within a community of clean hearted people; it is a hot and sensitive subject, but it needs to be discussed because it, there in plenty in the world, I our societies and in our communities. The presence of racism is still growing while tearing societies apart. Racism is not a subject based on imagination, or exaggeration, negatively conceived emotional motives or bigoted ideas but has been there and can vividly be seen in operation in many parts of the world.

However, there is another important note to make. The racism scholars have had it that **it did not begin with race**. The roots of racism are thought to have stemmed from differing religions, the mission to Christianize, and the global acceptability of owning those of a different faith. It was acceptable for Christians to have non-Christian slaves, Muslims to have non-Muslim slaves, or African tribes to own others from enemy tribes. In the late Middle Ages, slave owners began to pivot toward making a profit, good cases in point being when the Portuguese began their exploration and triggered Western exploitation of African goods, services, and bodies. At first the justification was that African peoples were not vastly Christian, but after Christianization, slavers needed a new reason to justify their highly profitable industry.

The other line of argument takes us further back to the times of New Creation (that being the time immediately after the Great Floods[58]. In Genesis Chapter 9, Noah blessed his first and third son while putting a curse on the second son, Ham. That move puts the three sons at crossroads; it no doubt made Ham and his descendants to dislike their kins because of the undue favours that were piled on them. Such moves, even when applied to contemporary societies, tear social fabrics apart, and those who are favoured feel that they have the right to hate and mishandle those who are less privileged. Due to pride and prejudice that develops as a consequence, racism deepens its roots. The message is that in the beginning, the human society was made under conditions of love, but as time went by and people started to own property, those who had the power or ability to move ahead with the wealth accumulation started to think that they had the right to enslave those who lagged behind. The state of

---

[58] *Genesis: 6,7, 8 and 9*

pride and prejudice started to develop, of course in disfavour of the weaker or poorer group.

In as far as racism is concerned, the past could be explained in economic, social, cultural, and of course political terms. Like it was elaborated above, racial prejudice has been planted as a way of justifying racism. Unfortunately, racial prejudice has in one way or the other existed in all societies in all epochs. There is no race in the world that can claim to have been free from racist tendencies. Sometimes racism has been diluted to prejudice in order to make it more palatable to mention or to dilute the impact; but the fact remains that, whatever term used racism has remained racism, and has continued to tear the social fabric apart. The good thing is that racism is not written on a person's face though it may be well written in somebody's brain and heart and thus one cannot be judged to be racist just by looking him in the eyes, but only by his deeds, words, behavior, or reaction to people of different races.

From the time of human creation, the human beings were one, they were kins but pride and prejudice brought them to points of departure. The Whites started to think as whites and blacks as blacks, brown as brown and red as red. But all those were exacerbated by culture, economics, politics and social traits. Those factors assisted to neatly define racial aspects. As the society got divided according to the colour of their skin the issue of wealth distribution emerged and further teared the society into the haves and have-nots. The have nots got thrown into the ditch of slavery. Unfortunately, people started to forget that the skin colour was only a change caused by the environment and genetical transformations in human beings.

Preaching against racism may not necessarily remove it from a person but can only assist in glossing over it, which in the long term may further promote it. People can scorn racism, but the sickness keeps penetrating deeper in the social fabric. For instance, the African or the black people as a whole, wherever they are in the world, feel intimidated because of the fear that has been planted in them for ages. They move with those fears of racial intimidation, and to make it worse they still see people of their race being humiliated or being scorned and segregated or hated by other races, a situation which is promoted by many factors besides the colour of their skin. Their poverty and weak social status makes the people of black race to feel inferior and that state has the power of making them reactive against the mistreatments that are directed to them. Being reactive puts them to a state of being falsefully interpreted. They end up being seen not different from others. Reaction usually leads one to behaving unwisely, making us remember that English saying "never argue with a fool as people might not notice the difference."

The dangers that face people who get mistreated or scorned are that once they react, their molesters (or challengers) get immediate support, that they were being attacked. Those who were provoked to react are quickly judged to be guilty of attacking. The racist attackers get termed "innocent colleagues". The victims become not only victims of racism but also of the law that puts them in criminality. The end result becomes to perpetuate antagonism instead of peace. Like it has been stated, people are racists in nature because they love themselves and others of their race. But they react when others show prejudice against them. In other words people feel the pain of being discriminated or mishandled when others do what they wouldn't wish to see done to them. So in order not be a racist don't do what you would hate being done to you. In other words, love others as you love yourself.

In India the black skinned sections of the society (e.g. the Cidis) who are a small community of black Indians, living very poor life in isolated remote places of India, have for centuries been denied all means that would make that community get out of their cocoon of social isolation, enslavement and poverty. They remain poor with little hope for a self-determined brighter future. The reasons given for that state are that resources that are available for enhancement of the poor communities are said to be directed, consciously or perhaps unconsciously to people of lighter skin colour who are not on the list of those who are discriminated upon.

All the above notwithstanding, there are many questions to be asked. For instance, why have many human beings continued to embrace racism? Why are people racists especially if account is taken of the fact that we are all said to be part of the same human race? Why is racism growing despite the spread of religions that preach love? Why have religions, including Christianity got involved in preaching racism; and despite slave trade abolition why are racial tensions growing in many parts of the world? Why is this still happening if we take into account that there are no biological differences between people and if it is honestly agreed that there is no race that is superior or inferior to another? Why has the issue of love for each other a difficult thing to do especially when we are in interracial environment?

Surely, quick answers are not there. However, attempts to answer some of the questions, albeit not adequately, makes us to state that in many parts of the world no serious attempts have been made to deal with the subject matter. Those who have made attempts have kept dealing with symptoms rather than the underlying factors. Epithets, chants and derogatory language about African Americans, or African footballers in various teams in Europe, or African traders in China, or even black people in Asia and Australia are indicators of an underlying problem within the races, namely an antagonism based upon just very petty explanations. For instance, a White skinned person gets filled with the pride that his, is the best skin colour. The red skinned feels the same that his, is the best and that those of others are inferior; a proud black skinned does exactly the same. If in depth evaluation is made it will be realized that the pride on one's colour is good because it makes an individual to be happy with what he is. In other words, human beings ought to be sensitized to understand that individuals traits are only good for him, not for others and thus a culture of respecting the traits of others is fundamental for future harmony of the human specie.

National policies too, have often encouraged racism and this was there since the times of slave trade. In US as well as South Africa in the days before the end of apartheid, discrimination "separate but equal"; segregated pools, buses, trains, water fountains; workplace, housing, sports fields; and other forms of bias and animus. The segregation served as painful barometers of the nation's racial health. That situation created pain and those who came with the idea of redressing that situation, actually were never ready to deal with the fixing of the broken limb in order for the sick person to walk straight again when the opportune time came. The discrimination problem was handled or treated like the pain that accompanied the broken limb, while the effort was concentrated on reducing the agonizing symptoms of the break rather than fixing the limb. The consequences of failing to remedy serious problems of racism, xenophobia, discrimination, prejudice, and others was to prepare a time bomb similar to that which explored in Rwanda in the early 1990s.

Religion too, has for centuries reoriented the minds of Africans. People of one religion feel they are so important that those of other religions can be mistreated because they are not made of the same elements or spirits as those of their religion. Discrimination has been allowed to rotate around religious beliefs. The religious discriminations, and prejudices and whatever that goes with those have led to racism and slavery. An example could further be cited of Christianity which was considered to be a religion of Europeans, and which was considered to be a fundamental of civilization, and thus anybody who was not a Christian was considered to be a savage and did not deserve to live a free life of so called civilized people. Islamism on the other hand was a religion of Arabs and Asian people in general and that once one had been converted to that religion he became pure and free from suppression, he did not deserve to be enslaved, but any other person deserved to suffer under slavery. Sometimes countries have been shouting for democracy but when it comes to translating what democracy means, each country finds it has its own inputs or variables to it. The inputs, in most cases are those which make the elites achieve their interests, even if those interests are very divergent from democratic norms and are detrimental to the rest, especially to the general and vulnerable communities.

18

DARK SKIN: A SCAPEGOAT

The question that many contemporary slaves trade scholars ask is why was most of the wide- scale slaves business involve only people of black race and especially black Africans. We refer to Triangle slave trade. But also we take note of the fact that most slaves traded in the Indian and Atlantic Oceans were Africans who were forcefully caught from their homes in the interior of Africa, transported to the coastal points of sale and ultimately shipped for sale in foreign lands thousands of Kilometers away from their families .We have also been looking at what happened in other parts of the world such as ancient Europe, Asia, and even the Americas. Deep analysis leaves no doubt that while colour of the skin has been seen and considered to be the cause of most enslavement in some parts of the world (especially in Africa), but the truth goes further than that. To a large degree skin colour is only a scapegoat, as there is more to be taken into account.

What we have learnt from the previous chapters is that the trans-Atlantic slave trade started with there being agreements between local chiefs and traders who in the first place got the slaves from the interior of Africa to the coastal ports where they got exchanged for goods such as guns, liquor (rum), cloth, cowries, and beads. In as far as slave trafficking in the Indian Ocean was concerned the story was almost the same, the only marked difference being that the Arab slave hunters went deep into the interior where they made deals with local chiefs to obtain the slaves.

Guns were highly demanded by African leaders (chiefs/kings) for use in concurring neighbouring states or chiefdoms from where they got huge loots, some of which were in form of war captives. The captives served as slaves. Some of the captives served as slaves in the chiefs' compounds or estates and the rest got sold to slave traders. The motivating factor for this type of slavery was economic. Those African leaders aimed to get rich by way of getting more people who would work on their land as serfs or would be involved in domestic activities especially in the case of women and children, or would be recruited into the army, while those who remained got sold as slaves to foreigners who visited the areas; all with a view to enhance their economic status. For all those who were involved in capturing, in transporting or in the selling of slaves, it was a purely economic or rather, income generation motivated adventure.

However, we need to know if this type of slavery and trading was confined or was specifically done or practiced by Africans only. The answer is no, as almost all major nations of the world have been involved in slave business, in one way or the other. Investigation in other parts of the world shows that the slavery was extensively done in almost all nations of the world, the only difference between countries, or continents being in the nature and extent of the practice. Actually, the practice affected people of all races and all countries, in almost all epochs. While at some stage it was worse or harsher in some parts of the world or in some countries and places than in others; but it was there. As late as the 18th Century, slavery in Europe was normal thing. Slaves were got in various ways to work in the houses or in the undertakings of the wealthy members of their communities. Slavery in Great Britain too existed and was recognized from before the Roman Occupation until the 12th century when chattel slavery disappeared, at least for a time, this being after the Norman Conquest. Then former slaves merged into the larger body of serfs in Britain and no longer were recognized separately in law or custom. In Asia the slavery practice was even more pronounced in places like China, India, Indonesia, and all countries of the Asian far east.

From the 17th Century to the 19th century, Britain deported the people that were sentenced as habitual criminals/or offenders or indecent servants, to the colonies as a punishment for both genuine and petty crimes, or for simply being poor and viewed as undesirable' facilitated by the Transportation Act of 1718. For instance, More than 160,000 convicts — 80% men, 20% women — were transported to Australia from the British Isles between 1788 and 1868. Others were sent to the New World and other places for similar reasons. During the same period, household workers employed people whose poverty left them no other alternative than to work under forced labour conditions.

The chaos following the invasion of Rome by barbarians made the taking of slaves, habitual throughout Europe in the early Middle Ages. Roman practices continued in many areas –Welsh included provisions dealing with slaves – and Germanic laws provided for the enslavement of criminals, including those who could not pay the financial penalty for their crime and as a punishment for certain other crimes. Such criminals would become slaves to their victimisers often with their property. In Eastern Europe slavery took almost the same path, especially in the early period after the fall of the Visigothic kingdom in the 8th century. Slaves primarily came into Christian Iberia through trade with the Muslim kingdoms of the south. Most were Eastern European, captured in battles and raids, with the heavy majority being Slavs.

In Asia and other parts of the world slavery took place in various ways and scales, but it was there. For instance, in some Eastern countries including China slavery took many forms throughout history. Slavery was reportedly abolished in China as a legally recognized institution in as recent time as in 1909. The law that fully prohibited slave trade was enacted in 1910 although the practice continued until at least 1950s. The earliest evidence of slavery in China dates to the Shang dynasty when, by some estimates, approximately 5 percent of the population was enslaved. The Shang dynasty engaged in frequent raids of surrounding states, capturing slaves who would be killed in ritual sacrifices. Tang law forbade enslaving free people but allowed enslavement of criminals and foreigners. Free people could, however, willingly sell themselves. The primary source of the Chinese slaves was southern tribes and young slave girls were the most desired on the market. Although various officials later banned the practice, the trade continued. Other people were sold to Chinese including the Turks, Persians, and Korean women, who were sought after by the wealthy. The slave girls of Viet were eroticized especially in Tang dynasty poetry.

However, it is said that between 1368 and 1644 all forms of slave trade were prohibited in China but in practice slavery continued undisturbed throughout to the next dynasties. There is also this interesting case of Javans who sent 300 black slaves as tribute to the Ming dynasty in 1381, an administration which crushed the Miao Rebellions in 1460, which castrated 1,565 Miao boys, thus resulting in the deaths of 329 of them. They turned the survivors into eunuch slaves. The Governor who ordered the castration of the Miao was reprimanded and condemned by the new governor who came after him for doing so. Following the death of 329 boys, they had to castrate even more. In 1406, the Ming Emperor expressed horror when he heard of the castrated boys, some who were their own children, to become eunuchs in order to give them to Yongle[59]; who in any case did not accept the castrated boys because they were innocent and didn't deserve castration. For that reason, Yongle returned the boys to Ryukyu and instructed them not to send him eunuchs again.

The story goes on to say in 1644-1912 Qing Emperor initially oversaw an expansion in slavery and states of bondage. A law that forbade landowners from selling slaves with the land they farmed was passed in 1660 and 1681 and prohibited physical abuse of slaves by landowners. In 1685 all the Manchus' hereditary slaves were freed. Between 1723 and 1730 the Emperor sought to free all slaves to strengthen his authority through a kind of social leveling that created an undifferentiated class of free subjects under the throne, freeing the vast majority of slaves.

The Chinese case shows that till as late as 18th Century China was one of the leading enslavers of its subjects may be more than any other nation in the world. The message in these examples is that from time immemorial slavery has been there.

In the case of Triangle slave trading, we are told how the slave traders got bottles of Rum from West Indies. They brought the liquor to the Atlantic coast (West Africa) where they managed to exchange the liquor for black slaves. We are told a bottle of Rum could be exchanged for a number of black slaves. That was what trade was, the African slave traders valued a bottle of rum better than their fellow Africans thus making trading in African black

---

[59]The **Yongle** Emperor from 2 May 1360 – 12 August 1424— personal name Zhu Di; was the third Emperor of the Ming dynasty. He reigned from 1402 to 1424. Zhu Di was the fourth son of the Hongwu Emperor, the founder of the Ming dynasty.

slaves a lucrative business. Looked at from another viewpoint a black slave from the West coast of Africa was priced very low compared to what the slave trader was going to earn when he got to the market in the final destination. That is one of the major factors that explain why more European merchants chose to get more and more slaves from that region of Africa, thus enhancing the illicit trade. Like we have said a bottle of rum was enough to buy several human beings and that was done without sympathy or empathy. That also emphasizes that the trade was not entirely motivated by the fact that the slaves were black, but more so by terms reached to get those slaves.

The above conditions could lead us to another set of issues. For instance slavery in Africa was further promoted by the existence of other factors one of which was that of kinship-relationship. If someone was not one's kin it meant that he was not one of him. Such person was a foreigner and in case of conflict he could easily be sentenced to death penalty that was harsher action than selling such person to slavery. The local slave hunters usually avoided their villages and went to the neighbouring or far away villages where they were unknown to the victims that were captured for sale in the distant markets.

The other reason that made families to sell their children or other relatives was famine. Families made it rewarding to sell children to slavery than to let them die of hunger. In such cases they felt they were doing the right thing; they were serving the lives of the loved ones. It was on that understanding some sellers suffered no guilt in selling their relatives including their children because the alternative was to leave them to die a natural death, which was certainly more painful than selling them to those who could give them food for their survival.

There was also the war aspect. African tribes were always at war with each other. The winners in those wars took captives in the form of loot. These either got incorporated in the captors' armies (especially in the case of young men) or were used for ritual purposes or worked in the farms, and the additional ones usually got sold to slave traders. One of the explanations for frequent wars between Africa tribes was that the tribal settlements were results of frequent migration movements. One tribe moved from one place to another, often in quest for better pastures, as most of them were stock keeping nomads. That means, two groups or tribes could be living in very close proximity with one another but had no kinship relationship. The situation was worsened by the fact that the people of the two villages saw each other as competitors for the same grazing land, which led to antagonism and frequent fights.

We have noticed that in the ancient times slavery was acceptable practice by all nations, religions including Christianity, Islam, Jewish and Pagan. In the Mali Empire the most esteemed people were the rich ones who also had many slaves. The esteem of a man depended on the number of slaves he owned. As was shown in the earlier expositions, a visitor to such a rich man could be honoured by being rewarded with a young strong man- servant. Similarly in some European communities, especially in the medieval times a man who failed to pay debt could be required to forego his farm together with his farm servants, a situation that was not very different in African societies where a parent could pay his debtors by letting his daughter taken for slavery or as wife to his lenders.

One important point to note is that the black slaves in the Arab countries were considered to be most resistant against tropical diseases and despite the fact that they were the lowest priced, but they were preferred for tough field assignments. For the same reasons, black slaves who were first got from West Africa were sent to England where they served in chains but remained most preferred, but not the most priced, because they had greater stamina for hard work than the local white slaves. The same applied for those who were transported to America to work in the plantations. So yes, the reasons why the black Africans became most hunted and transported as slaves to foreign countries was due largely to easy availability, the low price, low cost of maintenance, the stamina for hard work, lawlessness in the whole interior of Africa from where they were captured (especially in the period until 18th Century), and existence of colonial laws which legalized slave trading.

Defenders of slavery have argued that the sudden end of slave economy would have had a profound and killing economic impact in those areas of the societies where reliance on slave labour was the foundation of their economy. The local mining economies would have collapsed without slavery. The cotton crop in ancient Mali and Ghana and Songhai would not be there in the fields without slave labour. Rice would cease to be profitable in many parts of the world, especially in Asia without slavery. Those facts notwithstanding, there is enough evidence that at some stage sustainability of economies in many parts of the world was entirely a function of slave labour.

However, subsequent factors show specifically that the black slave labour was useful only during the height of transatlantic era, but it is no longer true that even with the end of the First, Second, Third and Fourth Industrial Revolution phases demand for slave labour has persisted. As capitalism continues, technological revolution has taken over, leading to completely different ways of doing things. In other words, with the innovations and technological advancements the issue of slave labour has almost ceased to be a crucial input to development. With mass production resulting from New industrial revolutions, substantial reduction of demand for slave labour has not only been witnessed, but actually labour input has been substantially reduced, if not eliminated, leading to greater use of machines due to employment of advanced technology, thus, enhancing productivity, profitability, use of more chicy and specialized labour and increased human welfare.

It is asserted that slavery has been practiced in many parts of the world in spite of improved technology and improved level of production and productivity in the modern world. That is true when we consider aspects of modern slavery. There are the oil rich countries of the Persian Gulf, which have until now been most notorious in slave trading and slavery; they have income which can enable them to use properly hired labour and technology to develop their economies and social welfare, but there is a saying that "*those used to earning a living illegally will not find comfort in living on the basis of legal means*". So, slavery has never been a necessary input to human development, but humans derive pleasure in using slave labour. Habitual slavers are like drug users, they are addicted to enslaving others, and despite that they may be rich enough to hire paid labour but they derive more pleasure in seeing others suffer, which is equivalent to a type of **sadism**[60]. This situation further confirms that the slavers of the medieval times did not seek for black Africans simply because of their skin colour, but largely because Africans were easily available at cheaper cost/or price and because the laws (especially on the transatlantic) facilitated the procurement, transportation, and use.

---

[60] Sadist referrers to a person who derives pleasure, including sexual gratification, from inflicting pain or humiliation on others.

Defenders of slavery have argued that if all slaves everywhere in the world were to be set free there would be widespread unemployment, shortage of food and other needs which would lead to chaos. There were chances that if that happened the situation could lead to uprisings, bloodshed, and anarchy. Those who advocate this line of thinking, point fingers to the mob' rule of terror during the French Revolution. That, the continuation of the status quo, which was providing for affluence and stability for the slave holding class and for all free people who enjoyed the bounty of the slave society chaos could be eliminated. Unfortunately, such arguments have not gone far enough to tell whether that was also applicable to Africa and African slaves.

Defenders of slavery institution went further and used the Bible to defend their arguments. They alluded that Abraham had slaves. They point to the Ten Commandments, "Thou shalt not covet thy neighbor's house, *or his manservant, or his maid-servant*". In the New Testament, Paul returned a runaway slave, Philemon, to his master. Slavery was widespread throughout the Roman world and even Jesus never spoke out against it. But did that necessarily refer to Black African slaves. Of course, they continue to argue that the slavery **institution** was divine, and that it brought Christianity to the heathen from across the ocean. Slavery was, according to this argument, a good thing for the enslaved. Some scholars further argue that African slavery and slave trade in West Africa enhanced the welfare of the black race; it made Africans to attain a much higher state of civilization and sped up improvement of their lives, not only physically, but morally and intellectually. That we think is bullshit argument, for there has never been any genuine proof that the state of being a slave was enjoyed by the enslaved.

Looking at other parts of the world we see the existence, lack of recognition and suffering of dark-skinned people. In India black people exist although it has always become difficult to explain how they were related to the rest of the Indians, and why they lived the type of isolated life, engaged in labour level of activities. For instance, there are the "Siddis" who are actually known as the India's forgotten African tribe. The Siddis are an African origin ethnic tribe in India who are said to be living in near total obscurity in India for centuries. There are at least 20,000 of these African-origin ethnic in India. The Siddis are mostly confined to small pockets of villages in the Indian states of Karnataka, Maharashtra and Gujarat, and the city of Hyderabad; and there is also a sizable population in Pakistan. Being descendants of Bantu people of East Africa, Siddi ancestors, were largely brought to India as slaves by Arabs as early as the 7th Century, followed by the Portuguese and the British later on. Others were free people who got to India as merchants, sailors and mercenaries before the Portuguese slave trade went into overdrive. When slavery was abolished in the 18th and 19th Centuries, Siddis fled into the country's thick jungles, fearing recapture and torture. They have remained in almost the same state for 14 centuries and remain in the same state till this day.

It can be added that the Siddis who got to India as African slaves were originally known as Habshis, which is Persian for Abyssinian (the former name of Ethiopia). But those who rose through the ranks of royal retinue were honoured with the title Siddi, a possible etymon from the Arabic word for master[61]. It is not entirely clear when the use of the term Habshi declined and Siddi replaced it, but today, Siddis describes all people of African descent in India. Part of the cluster of Siddi settlements exist in the agricultural village of

---

[61] *In Arabic* sayed/sayyid *could stand for Master, or esteemed man*

Gadgera in the state of Karnataka. The hair of these Siddi people is curly and facial features are markedly different from the South Indian people, and although they still look African, Siddis have completely and wonderfully assimilated Indian culture, traditions, and language.

Siddis are Indian citizens but often the rest of India has a hard time believing they are so. They live isolated, lonely, and highly prejudiced, or racially discriminated life in India. The majority of Siddis in India are Sufi Muslims, possibly influenced by the Mughals who their ancestors' biggest employers were. But Siddis in Karnataka area are primarily Catholics, possibly influenced by their early Portuguese and Goan masters. Despite such glaring vestiges, Siddi history has been startlingly erased throughout India. Today, stymied by government indifference and ridicule at the hands of fellow citizens, Siddis lead marginalized lives, while aspiring for manual jobs such as boxing or serving workers in farms as those are the only job opportunities due to prejudice, Xenophobia, racism, and lack of education which make them to no longer have any chance for better prospects.

It cannot be denied that the colour of the skin is an issue in India especially among the Siddis. The hold of the caste system in India is deep, dark skin is the skin of the lowest castes, traditionally the subjugated people and, therefore, disagreeable. What gives a lot of pride to the light skinned people of India is that the country's past foreign rulers, whether Mughal or British, who were all light skinned. Indus religion recognizes various Gods, and there are some dark-skinned Gods, but a good majority of their thousands of Gods are light skinned. Colour prejudice against people with dark skin in India and such other countries of Asia defies common sense. According to Indian tradition including their religious beliefs, light skin is the image of God and dark skin is to the contrary, which could be interpreted to mean that, anything black or dark in the case of human beings, is evil.

However, we still continue to argue that, for those of us who believe in God, prejudice against dark colour was never there at the time of God's creation of the world. The other thing is that we are continuing to learn that people of African origin got to many parts of the world either as slaves of some traders or other undertakings only to end up as minorities in those countries they landed. The situation made them end up in enslavement because of their fewness, and lack of economic and military power for their defense. What is being underlined here is that basically the issue is not about skin colour but the economic status. If you take a person of any skin colour and for any reasons convert him to a very poor man, the whole society around him will start ignoring, humiliating, and segregating him. In other words, economic status is what made African to be ignored, humiliated, segregated, and enslaved.

Further it should not be forgotten that all black African administrations did not come after civilization, but came with early civilization, which ultimately got grabbed from them due to factors, notably economic and military powers. Economic power supported by militarism that most imperial nations managed to accumulate was supported by economic power.

19

ARICA'S FUTURE IN THE HANDS OF AFRICA

Colonialism, neo colonialism, and racism aside, Africa must start from a clean slate. It needs to paint a completely new image of itself. It is time for Africa to rid itself of the past, thinking that it has an uncle who is going to support her to future development. For a long time, the western mainstream media has been painting very negative impressions of Africa. For instance, through the Western mainstream[62] media Africa has been portrayed as a place of helpless poor people and also a breeding ground for terrorism, insecurity, civil wars, and lawlessness. Africa is rightly known to be the source of slaves that were traded during the transatlantic slave trade. Those memories still keep hanging on amongst Africans as well as non-Africans, which at times has made Africans intimidated about introducing their independent development strategies.

The widespread impressions about Africa indicate that Africa has a lot of natural resources, but Africans have failed to exploit those resources for their development. The explanation given is that Africa lacks capital and thus they have remained complacent or rather satisfied with their situations. Further to that, Africans are usually described as people that are not innovative and therefore, they don't see opportunities that exist in their environment. That school of thought goes further to explain the high level of

---

[62] *The media that is thought or popularly believed to be normal because what comes out of it is shared by most people. Western mainstream media is that which produces most popularly accepted news or information.*

unemployment for its young population. According to Western mainstream media, Africa needs the input of Western people and their institutions, which can assist in stimulating African socio-economic development. Africa needs a push; they need capital from Western governments and their monetary institutions. That has further created impression that Europeans or foreigners in general are needed to assist African governments in using their abundant natural resources for African development. At times this notion is held or shared even by Africa intellectuals who through Western education have been well brain washed to believe that African problems could find quick and easy solutions only in the Western world.

What can quickly be said at this juncture is that only Africans can find solutions to its problems. Reasons for that generalized answer can be found in asking further questions. Europe colonized Africa since the middle of the 19th century. During the period Africa became poorer than before colonial rule. Africa is poor today. But is it not the right time to say that Europe prospered industrially using African resources while at the same time Africa kept growing poorer to a level of being left destituted? Was all that not because its natural resources were being plundered? The other touching question Is, was it not true that transatlantic slave trade was perpetuated because Europe needed cheap labour to produce raw materials for sustaining their industrial production? How about what happened from 19th Century to the middle of 20th century, when colonizers of Africa engaged Africans to provide forced labour for production of raw materials inside the colonies, for exclusive use in European industries. What did Africa or Africans gain in those forced labour engagements?. Can anyone think of any possible project that Colonizers implemented with Africa or Africans in mind?

Let us go a little further and ask what the colonialists did during the whole period of stay in Africa, from middle of 19th century to the middle 20th century-approximately 100 years. How many schools, hospitals, bridges, and kilometres of roads were built. You could perhaps mention a few bush schools and primary schools. You could perhaps mention about isolated cases of secondary schools specifically for children of Chiefs, especially in British colonies. Otherwise, we commend missionaries for establishing secondary schools here and there.

Railways were built from European points of production (e.g., Crop farms or Mines). The railways were designed to connect the European undertakings to the nearest seaports. Why did that have to be so, if not with a goal to boost the European economies using African land and labour. Some scholars have dared say that when colonialist left the new African governments or enterprices failed to manage the enterprices that were left behind. We can ask if there were miracles that would make things to work in a different way. Africans were not made to be part of the enterprices that were left behind by Europeans. Some Africans got a chance to be employed in the enterprices but only at tertiary or low skill level, like messengers, cleaners, spanner boys, and the like. All the workers at the middle and high levels were imported from the colonial countries; because after all to train an African with a view of getting skilled labour was seen to be unnecessary because Europeans also needed the skills; after all those skills were available in Europe in a situation colonialists believed they would be there in Africa, forever.

In view of the above, Africa should know that it has only itself to solve its problems or challenges. It has a role to paint its own image that will make the world to change its opinion from what has been painted by the mainstream media, which has been sustained by

Western media; sometimes fully supported by African media; which is in any case sponsored by the western media.

But painting a new image without making those who are supposed to see it could be quite an unproductive job. But who are those that are supposed to see the new Africa's image? Put in a very simplistic way that audience is supposed to be anybody in the world that has shown interest, positive or negative, of Africa. In real life a person can popularize himself by doing a variety of things such as identifying his; seeking recognition for his expertise; showcasing what he knows by building a knowledge base; sharing his wisdom; building a community; trying as much as possible to be of service to others; being a social savvy; and always remembering who he is, which is in itself a new message a to the world.

Just like what we do in our expert life, Africa will have to promote itself. It must always show the world that Africa they know is not what it is today. It should as much as possible show the world that it is a place of knowledge seekers and has grown to become an embracer or friend of all those who wish to join in with it in African development process. Such knowledge should be in whatever headlines that can be used. Further, time has come when Africa should stop burying its head in the sand like an ostrich. It should carefully and strategically sprinkle the word "New Africa- a new place of Hope" throughout its profile. In whatever audience Africa should sell itself as the new place full of opportunities for mankind; and thus the rest of the world should gradually be used to hearing positive things about Africa; a process which will result in great positive results. Africa will become an investment destination for the rest of the world.

Just with that positive image painting Africa will quickly change to being an economic and also a political leader. However, economic and political leadership should be differentiated, as the two concepts are not the same. By definition economic leadership involves providing opportunities for growth and progressive development. It may involve establishment of growth and development related services such as educated population and robust infrastructure and natural resources exploitation. On the other hand, political leadership is often given after a certain party has won in an election. In Africa, such an electoral process has been demonstrated to be fairly fake following the rigging that usually takes place, due to the fact a sense of good governance is hardly there. That problem is still widespread despite the success stories that have been told; there has certainly been more talked than practiced. Undemocratic leadership still persists due to presence of irregularities in the African governments' processes.

Economic leadership is what is of much interest in this chapter, though both economic leadership and political leadership are desirable for faster development of a country. A country may be recognized by its strong economy characterized by things like a strong currency. When the economy is doing well, and at a boom period of the economic cycle implies higher interest rates to keep inflation low and many other stability measures. Growth is very necessary. It is usually influenced by four main factors, namely human resources, physical capital, natural resources, and technology. There are standard criteria that will commonly need to be employed to evaluate the level of a country's development. These will include but not limited to Gross Domestic Product (GDP), Gross National Product (GNP), per capita GDP, birth, and death rates; Human Development Index (HDI), infant mortality rates; literacy rate; and life expectance. Growth and development would usually be reflected in the level of industrialization, the general standard of living, and the amount of technological infrastructure.

However, with the industrial revolution Europe prospered swiftly at the expense of Africa. That is why it has always been stated that there is no any other continent of the world that has gone through economic and social mistreatment imposed by others, like Africa. As Africa got plundered left right and centre, Europe got resources with which to achieve economic emancipation. Besides slave trade, Africa suffered from imposed colonialism, racism, segregation, the resultant underdevelopment, and various other types of mistreatments.

At this juncture we should amazingly remind of the fact that Africa is estimated to have ruled the world for many centuries. Having been the birthplace of the human kind and considering that the rest of the world got populated from Africa it does not become a surprise that the first civilization of the world started in Africa and spread to the rest of the world. Like we have said, Europe led the world development only after the start of the industrial revolution, which commenced in the 18th century.

Owed to the success of the industrial revolution United Kingdom took over the world economic leadership and went on until the fourth decade of the 20th century, i.e. after the 2nd World War when USA took over from Great Britain. There is a saying "history always repeats itself" and that is what convinces Africa that by or soon after the 6th decade of the 21st century, Africa may resume its leadership role. The African economic performance during the last three decades shown that all things being equal, Africa will surprise the rest of the world by starting to flash the over take red lights. That certainly will happen if Africa will be sensible enough to follow principles that are fundamental for effecting swift growth as will be briefly reflected in the next chapters.

Africa, besides been sandwich in slavery and racism for many centuries, but that should now be viewed as a gone phenomenon; Africa should bank on what is ahead of it, as the future is bright, strong, and so convincing that all that needs to be done is to rise up and go. For instance, besides being home and raised the early world youth and population, it developed the earliest world civilizations, from as early as 5,000 years ago. Many great empires were built and monumental structures such as the pyramids and sphinxes are there to be seen until this day.

Harvard Business Review of 2019 had a long and elaborate discussion on how technology could accelerate growth in Africa. Such discussions in many academic and professional development institutions have come up with ideas that provide a lot of professional solutions to policy and planners for African development. Such analysis and/or evaluations have led to a lot of optimism. It is good to note that the African continent has the youngest population in the world, and it has major consumption market and is likely to remain so for the next three or for decades. Africa, if allowed to move uninterrupted by external forces will get to very high level of development by 2035. African people remain optimistic that tomorrow is different from that of yesterday. The optimism is based on the belief that with technological development, supported by the widespread adoption of digital technology will continue to support new ways of doing business. The use of mobile phones has been speeding up communications and information delivery. Other outcomes of use of technology include mobile payments that will help struggling African economies to 'leapfrog' from poverty to economic growth and stability. The use of mobile phones in Africa is among the highest in the world and that the emerging digital ecosystem is increasingly becoming crucial as a multiplier of growth. Access to smart phones and other devices has been enhancing consumer information, networking, job-creating resources, and even financial inclusion.

Africa is only at the starting point in terms of use of technology. In other words, the African continent is never really considered to be very active in technology. That state is most conspicuous in the informal sector as well as in the rural areas where the application of technology is at very infantry stage. That is the situation in spite of the fact that Africa is holding the world's earliest record of human technological advancement, dating as far back to ancient Egypt. Ancient Egyptian technology actively boasts of many inventions.

However technological progress is essential to economic growth and development. The more advanced technology available the more swiftly the local and global economy can improve. Technology role in economic development usually manifests in youth development, in African culture development, in improving our lives, in improved productivity, in easing up transport and communications, in processes and tasks, in allowing remote education, and in many other problem-solving solutions.

Despite the many developments drawbacks Africa has been facing the growth that has been realized from improved economic governance on the continent and the private sector involvement, has been quite remarkable. What is being emphasized here is that Africa's economic growth could not have come this far without major improvement in economic governance. It could be enough to say Africa is part of the global village. Basically, connectivity in Africa is provided mainly by ground stations by satellite especially those of satellite dishes of the Very Small Aperture Terminal (VSAT) type.

It is good to also mention that Africa's growth rate in 2021 was 3.4% after contracting by 2.1 in 2020. Africa is both the world's economically fastest growing continent and is also demographically the youngest. Contributions to growth can be credited to the robust economic dynamics of East African region. While in terms of economic growth, Africa is the fastest growing it is expected to maintain a stable positive percentage. In 1919 East Africa remained the continent's fastest growing region with an average growth of 5%. However, in 2022 Morocco, Kenya and Ghana emerged the fastest growing major economies in the continent. That should not be taken as a permanent feature as the competition among countries of the region is often quite stiff.

Projected recovery from the worst recession in more than half a century will be underpinned by resumption of tourism, a rebound in commodity prices, and in rollback of pandemic (COVID19) induced restrictions. The other impacting factors for the Africa development could include issues of Peace and security, conflict management, governance, democratization of economic transformation, globalization, **and** inter dependence. Things remaining equal growth rate projection could be estimated at about 5% year 2024/25

Africa is a vital world region. Despite the picture that has been painted above but as shown some of the fastest growing economies in the world are in Africa. Africa is a continent of thousands of languages and cultures, unparalleled eco-diversity, and over a billion vibrant and innovative Africans. Africa is known for Mount Kilimanjaro, Victoria Falls, Nile River, the Great Lakes, and game reserves such as the Maasai Mara and Serengeti and Ngorongoro. Africa is also famous for its diverse ethnic groups, unique historical sites such as the Egyptian Pyramids, the Sahara Desert, the Kalahari, and the Victoria Falls.

However, Africa must leapfrog, and to do so it needs to move to modernization, organized urbanization and industrialization. That may also entail what is called catch up theory of development. That translates into a sequence of investment in skills, production capacity, and developments that could make poor nations like those in Africa to move forward more swiftly. In any case **leapfrog** will enable Africa to bypass traditional stages of development to the latest technologies or explore alternative paths of technological development involving emerging technologies with new benefits and new opportunities.

Along similar lines sustained growth will have to be realised, knowing that it can spur development in various ways. It will raise per capita incomes and lift people out of extreme poverty. High income (which is the target) would also reduce wealth inequality. Faster economic growth will generate higher profits, which can then be reinvested promoting increased productivity and capacity.

20
AFRICA'S CHALLENGES

The type of destruction described above has been going on for decades if not centuries. Unfortunately, not enough mitigation measures have been taken to adequately deal with these situations; hence further contributing to the ever-worsening situations.

The African contribution to global warming is substantial but has only marginally contributed to the overall global warming. In other words, Africa is not the leading contributor to global warming, but it has had its fair contribution to it. There is now enough evidence that the main cause of climate change includes the burning of fossil fuels such as oil, gas, coal, gasoline, natural gas, and others related to those. When burnt fossil fuels release carbon dioxide into the air, it causes the planet to heat up. The phenomenon of increasing average air temperatures near the surface of the earth has now been going on for the past two to three centuries. The changing earth climate started to intensify especially since the time of industrial revolution in Europe. , The crisis started to become critical at that time, as the industries were getting established and operated without any deserving control of air pollution that was been caused by the burning of fuels in the industries. However, the current era of global warming is highly attributable to human activity.

The climate crisis is posing one of the biggest threats to both the planet and the health of the people who live in it. Agriculture and fisheries are highly dependent on the state of the climate. Increases in temperature and carbon dioxide (CO_2) can increase crop yields.

But to realize those benefits, nutrient levels, soil moisture, water availability, and other conditions must also be met. Changes in the frequency and severity of droughts and floods will pose challenges for farmers while uncontrolled livestock grazing will keep threatening food safety and security. Climate change in Africa has been affecting agriculture in various ways. Beyond a certain range of temperatures, warming will tend to reduce yields because crops speed through their development, producing less grain in the process. Higher temperatures have also interfered with the ability of plants to get and use moisture. Evaporation from the soil has been accelerating as temperatures keep rising while plants increase transpiration; thus, losing more moisture from their leaves.

Emissions have been estimated to be killing around 7 million people each year and are responsible for more than a quarter of deaths from diseases including heart attacks, stroke, and lung cancer. However, while opportunities may be very great in Africa, threats and risks have proved to be equally strong. Floods that terrorized many parts of East and Southern Africa between 2014 and 2019 greatly affected harvests and infrastructure. The poor harvests caused a shortage of food in many parts of the region. To counter the problem of food shortage importation of food became necessary. Due to effects of the flood's reconstruction, rehabilitation, and spot improvement of the infrastructure especially roads in various parts of the region could never be avoided. These interventions have kept eating deep into the national budgets, as they diverted budgetary funds from planned projects to emergencies that had not been envisaged. The budgetary problems have certainly been among those things that have pulled back efforts that are being made by African governments.

African governments have been doing commendable job to establish and enroll children in primary and secondary schools. That has resulted in the ever-growing army of school levers especially in Sub Saharan Africa, leading to critical shortage of employment, which has subsequently made the Africa youth to see no chances of bright future. Absence of new jobs among the African youth, will make the already pathetic situation of unemployment to get out of control, thus increasing illegal migrations of desperate young people, who will do so with the hope to get better opportunities in other African countries, or subregions or in other parts of the world.

The gap between the haves and have-nots is growing. The problem is most critical, especially in the areas of access to healthcare. Our view of current situation in the world shows that people in wealthy nations have been estimated to live 18 years longer than those from poorer countries. A very recent study found that rich people over 50 years can expect to live 8 to 9 years more healthy years than the poorest in their countries. At age 50, wealthy men could expect to live 31 more healthy years than poor men, while wealthy women could expect to live up to 35 more healthy years than poor women.

The health care insecurity gap between the haves and have-nots got widened by COVID 19 pandemic. The poorest communities in Africa had their adults that were several times as likely as the higher income adults to report food and health care insecurity and also for losing their employment during the time of the pandemic. In some African countries individuals without much experience in their places of work became the most likely to report work terminations and hence food insecurity, and absence of attention when visiting hospital and other medicare points. The pandemic had an extraordinary impact on communities or individuals that were already vulnerable and among the disadvantaged groups and that could explain why some international financial institutions, World Bank, IMF and African Development Bank each in its own way showed the need for providing strategically deployed relief efforts, and proposals for longer term policy reforms to challenge the perennial and unequal impact of disasters.[63]

Wealth provides great leverages because it can determine access to healthcare within a country as well as individual cities and communities. Rising global rates of diseases like cancer, diabetes and chronic respiratory conditions have had greater impact on low- and middle-income countries, especially in Africa where medical bills can quickly deplete the limited resources of poorer families. Although many people in the developed countries could take access to medication for granted, medicines and vaccines are not an option for almost 90% of African population. The growing malady and challenge of expanding access to medicines in Africa calls for immediate policy reviews and prioritization, before the situation gets completely out of hand. Here is where medical regulatory systems have been most required to control calamities which are likely to emerge from fake medical services and drugs. Besides the direct impacts as well as addition to putting lives at risk by failing to treat the patient's condition, these products could easily undermine confidence in medicines and healthcare providers.

Medical experts insist that infectious diseases have a chance to be eliminated and Africa should strive to achieve that. However, the infectious and noninfectious diseases continue to kill millions of

---

[63] *Parry Brian Aronson and Bernice A. Pascosolido: On Pandemic Precarity-(COVID-19). Derived from proceedings of the American National Academy of Sciences, 2021*

people, most of them, poor. In Africa, this situation looks unlikely to change in the near future. Preventing the spread of diseases like HIV, tuberculosis and malaria will depend on sufficient levels of funding and robust healthcare systems. In African countries where the services and drugs are most needed, these resources are in short supply. Greater funding and political goodwill could be even more desirable now to develop immunization programmes, share data on disease outbreaks and reduce the effects of drug resistance that goes in tandem with the need to build a sense of preparedness for epidemics.

The chronic problem in this area is that health workers are left to face the greatest risk of absence of appropriate self-protection measures. There is every indication that many people, especially in the rural areas of Africa, are not well versed with matters of protective gear. The issue of availing gear which may come in form of protective clothing, gloves, boots masks and disinfectants, especially when dealing with cases such as those of Ebola, COVID-19, cholera, TB, and other chronically communicable diseases, cannot be underestimated..

Furthermore, airborne viruses or diseases transferred by mosquito bites can spread quickly, with potentially devastating consequences. Currently, more time and resources are spent reacting to new strains of influenza or outbreaks of yellow fever, and more seriously on TB, and on various phases of COVID 19 rather than preparing for future outbreaks. The question is not whether or not dangerous viruses will come about – but when. In short, Africa needs stronger, unified responses to major health threats. Today, Africa has many highly qualified medical doctors but what still lacks behind is the coordination of their efforts through coordinated research and development to enable Africa to lead the way in this area of healthcare.

It has further been noticed that besides communicable diseases, the continent has often been faced with increasing problem of noncommunicable diseases such as cancer, blood pressure, diabetes, heart attacks, the kidney failures, and other killer diseases. This has not only posed a big threat to the lives of people, but it has been eating deep into government/public budgets, especially in complicated cases, some of which have to be referred to abroad. In some African countries, governments have constructed referral hospitals to reduce costs of treating people abroad, but requisite equipment and facilities are needed to enable those hospitals to be operational. Almost all referrals and even regional or district hospitals are located in urban areas. There are many cases where some rural people must travel 100 km to get to a district hospital, which could be very poorly provided with basic drugs. The distance could be much longer to Regional and Consultant hospitals. In some remote places of Africa even the basic hospital buildings, leave alone equipment, drugs and medical personnel are hardly there. A mention is also needed on outbreak of the Corona virus pandemic (COVID 2019), which (between 2018 to 2021) caused much havoc in Africa and the world. The disease did not only make the people of all ages in almost all parts of the world to lose their lives, but also disrupted people's working schedules due to the lockdowns that had to be imposed and observed by governments to limit the spread and impact of the disease.

The social and economic effect of COVID 19 has been great. For instance, by June 2020 more than 2.1 million people around the world had become infected with COVID-19, and more than 140,000 people had died from the disease, which happened in a span of just less than 18 months. Though Africa was the least hit continent in as far as COVID-19 death tolls were concerned, but the pandemic kept claiming more people's lives. Gradually the virus kept transforming itself, people failed to cope with the transformation, which led to more deaths. To appreciate the magnitude of the problem a few examples of the impact of COVID-19 in other places in the world can be provided. For instance, by 2020 the number of infected people in USA had risen to as many as 650,000 infections. By June 2020 cases that Americans had filed for unemployment benefits reached 22 million people, while the "Small Business Administration", which supports U.S. entrepreneurs with loans and funding, had run out of money for its paycheck Protection programme. Other economically powerful countries of the world, such as UK, Italy, Germany, France faced the same problem.

According to the World Bank, volatility in the global environment due to COVID-19 pandemic, by end of the year 2021 had kept taking a heavy toll on human life. The killer disease placed excessive pressure on health systems. The disease was like an enemy army that strikes with great force, leaving behind great devastation after a fairly short period of time. Having started to strike in 2019 but by 2020 the disease had claimed millions of lives. During the height of the disease no part of the world remained completely secure from its spared. The impact of COVID-19 was thus heavily felt throughout the world. By the year 2021 the spread of COVID-19 had reached an unprecedented extent geographically and demographically. The swift spread and the resultant death tolls caused a lot of panic to mankind. The impact of the strike was unprecedentedly great anywhere in the world. Just within three years about 528 million people were reported infected and about 6.3-milion people in the world had lost their lives, within that short span of less than three years. Besides deaths, economic and social impacts were immense, costing the African region between $37 and $79 billion in estimated output losses in 2020, and reducing agricultural productivity, weakening supply chains, increasing trade tensions, limiting job prospects, and exacerbating political and regulatory uncertainty.

Looking specifically at the East African region economic performance generally declined. It is to be noticed that from the year 2015 to 2019 Kenyan economy achieved broad based growth averaging 4.7 per year. In the year 2020 the GDP of that country decelerate to 1.4% from 5.7 in 2019. In Ethiopia, the country was expected to grapple with high unemployment, and GDP growth was revised to 3.2% from 6.2% in 2020. Similarly, the outlook in Tanzania and Uganda showed a similar decline trend with GDP growth being revised to 2% and 3.5% respectively (decline in 3.3% and 1.8% percentage points respectively). Tanzania kept showing waning demand for mineral exports considering global supply chain interruptions.

Looking at bigger economies of Nigeria and South Africa, the COVID-19 impact was perhaps most strong. Nigeria is Africa's biggest economy, with its GDP projected to grow by more than 3.4% after it had been contracting in the COVID 19 period. The Nigerian economic outlook in the height of COVID 19 was very dim. In 2020, Nigerian economy entered a recession, reversing three years of recovery due to spread of COVID-19. Overall real GDP shrunk by 3% in 2020. However, Nigeria acted swiftly to take mitigation measures to prevent further decline. The measures notwithstanding, the inflation rose to over 12.8% in 2020 from 11.4% in 2019. In the year 2022 the Federal government stated that it expected Nigeria's GDP per capita to rise to $,706.3 by year 2025, which would represent about 61% projected growth from the $2,300 GDP growth forecast for 2021.

Regarding the situation in South Africa, another major African economy, the impact of COVID 19 was very significant. The real GDP growth in 2020 was -6.45% with great improvement to 5% in 2021. Despite the marked improvement in 2021 but the economy remained very fragile.

We could finally take a look at [64]the impact of COVID -19 impact on North African states. North Africa is an African region that was the least hit by COVID 19 pandemic; induced by the lockdown measures which had the negative impact on the supply and demand sides, and the drastic reduction of world demand, fueling a drop in North Africa's exports. However, major economic recovery in North African countries was expected from 2021, subject to success of mitigation measures that have kept being implemented by the respective governments.

Generally, in Africa, a collapse in economic activity that resulted from the COVID-19 containment measures and macroeconomic instability was likely to increase poverty and endanger lives and livelihoods. Household welfare was expected to be equally dramatic with welfare losses in the optimistic scenario that had been projected in 2020, compared to a non-pandemic scenario. Africa was projected to recover in 2021 from its worst recession in half a century.[65] Overall the real GDP growth was estimated at 3.4% in 2020 and to 4.1% in 2021. Specifically, the ADB economic outlook for 2021 examined Africa's growth performance and outlook amidst the COVID-19 pandemic. It further explored causes and

---

[64] *UN Economic commission for Africa on impact of Covid 19 in North Africa.*
[65] *African Development Bank: Economic Outlook of 2021.*

consequences of Africa's debt dynamics and also took stock of challenges in the current global architecture for debt resolution and exploration of the link between governance and growth and hence suggesting growth and reforms to improve the process of debt resolution, governance, and sustainable growth.

Besides the problem of infectious diseases (including COVID-19) in Africa there has also been the problem of terrorism in some countries. By definition terrorism is anything that involves the threatened or actual use of illegal force and violence by a non-state actor to attain a political, economic, religious, or social goal through fear, coercion, or intimidation. The most prominent terrorist groups that have for quite a long time now been creating terror in Africa include Boko Haram of Nigeria and Al-Shabaab of Somalia. The presence of these terrorist groups, together with their allies across Africa, has led to property damage and huge numbers of people killed and many more sustaining injuries. In addition, terror activities on the continent have contributed to mass displacements of the civilian population.

On the one hand Boko Haram is as has been hinted a militant Islamic group working out of Nigeria, whose purpose is to institute Sharia, or Islamic law. In the local Hausa dialect, Boko Haram is described to mean, "Western education: forbidden". The terrorist group attacks consist of suicide bombers as well as conventional armed assaults on both civilian and military targets. The group is as of now one of the largest Islamist militant groups in Africa. So far it has conducted terrorist attacks on religious and political groups, local police, and the military, as well as indiscriminately and on attacking civilians in busy markets and villages and in social utility places such as hospitals, schools, open market points. Following the 2014 kidnapping of schoolgirls, majority of Boko Haram's suicide bombers are female; some are as young as seven years old. The kidnapping done in 2014 was probably meant to use the girls as negotiating pawns in exchange for some of their commanders in jail. There is no evidence that they have succeeded in achieving that goal. In May 2016, one of the missing girls, Amina Ali, was found after she had succeeded in escaping. She claimed that the remaining girls were still there, but six of them had died.

Next major terrorist group is Al-Shabaab; which in Arabic means "The Youth". It emerged as the radical youth wing of Somalia's now-defunct Union of Islamic Courts, which controlled Mogadishu in 2006. However, the terrorist group survived very briefly before it was forced out of Mogadishu. Al-Shabab advocates the Saudi-inspired Wahhabi version of Islam, while most Somalis are Sufis. For quite a long time Al-Shabab remained capable of carrying out massive attacks in Somalia and some neighbouring countries such as Kenya, a bit of Tanzania, Mozambique, and Yemen. It once held sway over the capital of Mogadishu and large portions of the Somali countryside. Like Boko Haram the group seeks to control territory within Somalia in order to establish a society based on its rigid interpretation of Sharia law. Today, Al-Shabaab has been reduced in power and size and that reduction in its power continues to be strongly felt in the neighbouring countries as well as in Somalia itself. As it gets weakened the group has maintained training camps in areas near Kismayu in the southern regions of Somalia. Like it is for any terrorist affected regions it has been unsafe to travel in Somalia due to crime, terrorism, civil unrest, health issues, kidnapping, and piracy. Violent crime, such as kidnapping and murder, is common in most parts of Somalia, including Puntland and Somaliland. Illegal roadblocks are also widespread.

However, terrorist attacks are not so significant or rather those, which could be in existence have not been publicized as much as Boko Haram and Al-Shabab. But there have been insurgence groups in other countries such as Mozambique and the Democratic Republic of the Congo (DRC). Actually, terrorists are very likely to try to carry on attacks in DRC. The attacks could be indiscriminate and thus you need to be vigilant especially in places often visited by foreigners. According to UN, unconfirmed reports have it that there are more than 120, armed groups operating in the DRC; yet, historically the DRC and the international community have generally not referred to these armed groups as terrorists. According to the UN Joint Human Rights Office (UNJHRO) in DRC during the year 2021, at least 2,024 civilians were killed by armed groups in North Kivu, in South Kivu, Tanganyika and in Ituri provinces. Most of the DRC violence is a result of long-lasting animosity between the Tutsis, the Hutus, and other ethnic groups. Other factors of the continued violence include control of land, control of minerals, and economic tensions.

We can now go back and ask, why has the DRC been so unstable? There are a number of reasons that could be given, but the major ones could be traced from the time of independence almost 60 years ago. In the first place Belgian wished to refuse the granting of independence. After an uprising by the Congolese people, Belgian surrendered. That led to independence in 1960. But the Congo continued to be unstable because Regional leaders proved to have more power than the Central government. Due to that power struggle Katanga attempted to gain independence but the attempt failed. For a long time that followed the DRC remained unstable, and that has been the situation until this day. The instability has not come without great consequences on the peace, economic performance, food production and supply in the DRC. In the recent years the DRC is reported to be the biggest food security crisis in the world with over 27 million people facing severe or acute food insecurity. Some areas like Tanganyika province are facing extreme food insecurity, bordering on a level where preventable deaths related to famine and starvation are likely to occur.

The growing trend of terrorist attacks in Africa, including in DRC has led to problem of refugees across borders. It is an issue that remains a major security challenge for policy makers in Africa. The impact of terrorism has kept on growing, despite the efforts being taken to put a check on it. Terrorism where it exists has been taking lives and has also been causing great havoc to communities, thus reducing people's attention to productive activities. Actually, terrorism has been serving as another hindrance to future efforts of Africa to emancipate itself. The DRC violence and its effects should serve as a lesson, especially in regard to how it can lead to starvation of the people.

This brings us to the need to look at the critical problem of food insecurity in the overall continent of Africa. So far food insecurity is a big challenge as it directly affects human survival. The question that keeps being asked is why many African countries have kept facing food security problems? Two of the many reasons why food insecurity keeps invading millions of people are the never- ending conflicts and incessant political instability on the continent. Often, in many Sub-Saharan countries foods are available and plentiful, but not accessible to everyone. A primary cause of food insecurity in the region is generally the decline in global supply and productivity.

The state of food security remains unsatisfactory. One in five people in Sub-Saharan Africa faced hunger in 2020[66] and in the meanwhile the number of hungry people continued to rise, due to conflicts, drought and economic woes triggered by COVID-19 pandemic. Not only that, an estimate of more than 33% of the continent's population was undernourished. The going has been such that about 282 million people have been experiencing hunger which is more than double the proportion of any other region in the world. Unfortunately, the conditions have kept deteriorating, especially in areas across East Africa, in countries like Ethiopia, Kenya, Uganda, South Sudan, and Sudan where 7.2 million people remain at risk of starvation and another 26.5 million have faced acute food instability[67].

Until the start of the year 2022 an estimated 13 million children in the Sub-Saharan region were acutely malnourished. It has been repeated that East Africa was the most critically affected region with countries such as Ethiopia, Kenya, Somalia South Sudan, Sudan, and Uganda being the most critically affected. The drought that struck Ethiopia, Northern parts of Kenya and Uganda together with the invasion of desert locusts in all those East African countries, were the major causes for the wide spread of food insecurity.

Besides social and political instability, the other causes of food-insecurity in Africa have mainly been floods and the recurring failed seasonal rains. The fact that agriculture in most parts of Africa depends largely on seasonal rainfalls, failure to have timely rainfalls means failure to have envisaged harvests. Sub-Saharan Africa, unlike other parts of the world that have developed irrigation agriculture (that can allow production in all seasons of the year), is

---

[66] *World Vision annual reports*
[67] *Ctd.*

likely to continue having recurring droughts or distorted seasonal rains due to the ongoing climate change. The recent years insecurity of food has also been prompted by swarms of desert locusts that invaded the region causing a lot of crop destruction and thus leaving people with barely enough to eat.

Conflicts, as a major cause of food insecurity, is a challenge that Africa can eliminate from the region if it so wishes. Conflicts can be uprooted if Africa as a continent stands up and say enough is enough with conflicts on the African soil. African governments should come up with policies and actions that will curb this situation.

The actions that could be taken to provide solutions to the recurring food crisis will besides conflict eradication, may include providing support to farmers and pastoralists especially in matters of maximizing output by providing drought resistant and fast maturing crops; enhancing market development; providing immunization for livestock; literacy training to enable farmers to recover from emergencies; and provision of education on the need to diversify rural people's agricultural production and other activities.

The violence that persisted for several decades in Sudan and later in South Sudan, and in DRC together with COVID 19 pandemic made people in some of those countries to run away from their homes. The violences, made people to abandon their farms, ending up with no enough harvests and no enough to eat.

There have been many other problems including those of poor infrastructure, especially in the rural areas of Africa. Most African rural areas are poorly supplied with roads, a situation, which makes many of those areas inaccessible by road. That shortcoming has limited transportation of food from farms, or food aid to the needy or to food that needs to be sent to market. A lot of effort and priority has also needed to be assigned to support road improvements in the rural areas to increase rural access.

Diseases, terrorism, instability of all kinds, and food insecurity are problems that inevitably ought to be squarely uprooted to give confidence to investors that Africa is a safe destination for investment. Those problems along with other issues related to enhancing development, need the support of the international community in all aspects of their manifestations.

Capital for investment is the next challenge that is facing Africa. While Africa keeps on struggling to get to a point of competitive economic performance, its reputation will get greatly impaired by elements such as those of limited capital. There is gross limitation of capital for investment, and there is evidence that not all African countries have put up enough efforts to have good policies and strategies that can lead to mobilization of capital resources to keep the pendulum going. The continent has no financial muscles nor policy and strategies that can prevent it from getting pulled back to the past mistakes that landed it in a state of an underdog. There is no short cut to getting Africa fully on the rails. But absence of short cuts does not provide reason for complacency, as every individual, every nation, and every continent is working hard to get ahead of others. That means, when Africa decides to step up the fight to get to the top, others will not be sleeping; they will equally keep striving to remain where they are or to move even further up, which will easily force the gap between Africa and others to keep widening. In short, all nations of the world are in economic development marathon race, and only competitors with enough economic stamina will get there as planned. So Africa will have to be sustainably steady or will have to keep increasing the pace relative to others, to get to the finishing line with or ahead of others.

In most times Africa has failed to take actions that can bring quick impact to its own development. Many such problems are seen in the rural setting. They include clear inadequaces in agricultural production, water scarcity, post-harvest losses, and limited market access. Population growth in the rural areas means an increased demand for homes and services. In the same way increase of farming population will often push up the price of land, and once the prices of land escalate it may mean that farmers won't afford to buy it. But sometimes farmers have failed to afford not to sell their land especially if the returns from it are low or if the opportunity costs are in favour of other preoccupations.

Generally farming in Africa is tough due to obstacles that limit the success of small-scale farming; which include climate, education and technology, financing, infrastructure and articulate policies. For instance, it has often been happening that an increase in temperature could mean reduced crop production and reduction of pastures for livestock. Variations in temperatures and rainfall will lead to food shortages, disruption of agricultural yields and productivity and to reduced income for farmers. Education and technology impacts on rural farmers in such a way that, advances in machinery will expand the scale and productivity of farm equipment leading to more efficient cultivation of more land. Good infrastructure, especially rural roads and bridges are highly desirable to increase accessibility to farms and facilitate delivery of inputs as well as evacuation of harvests to warehouses or to markets more efficiently and timely. All these are realized more easily where financing issues have been adequately addressed and also where policies including regulatory systems are articulate enough to motivate a village farmer. Seed, irrigation, and fertilizer also need to be vastly improved, to help farmers increase yields.

Small holder farmers in Africa are still among the poorest in the world. Production by smallholder farmers is largely for subsistence. That is so notwithstanding the fact that in Africa agriculture is by far the single most important economic activity. It provides employment for about two-thirds of the continent's working population and for individual countries agriculture contributes an average of 30% to 60% of gross domestic product and about 30 percent of the value of exports. Considering the great role of the agricultural sector the limiting factors that keep pulling it backwards demand to be addressed swiftly. For developing economies such as these in Africa, need strong rural agricultural sector, which will be there to provide desirable raw materials for the envisaged promotion of industrial sector.

Specifically, Africa faces many other specific and complex challenges. Less than 4% of farmland in sub-Saharan Africa is irrigated. Almost three-quarters of its soils are degraded due to years of planting crops without replacing nutrients; fertiliser use is by far the lowest in the world with most farmers unable to afford it. Other challenges include recurring incidences of famine in many parts of the continent, and also the chronic hunger that rural people often face due to recurring drought, conflicts, and instability. These and many others have led to severe food shortages and also to poverty and vulnerability.

People in many African countries keep battling with extreme poverty; which implies that more government and community support systems are needed. While a thought keeps being put in dealing with the various challenges of political, economic, social, military and peace instabilities, there is also great need to be mindful of the fact that climate change is hitting hard on the economies of the rural people. Increasing temperatures and sea levels, changing precipitation patterns and more extreme weather conditions have been threatening human health and safety, food and water security and socio-economic development. Climate change threats are also impacting heavily on human health, food and water security and socio-economic development. Climate change is having a growing impact on the African continent, hitting the most vulnerable hardest, and contributing to food insecurity, population displacement and stress on water resources. For a whole decade since 2011 many parts of Africa saw devastating floods, an invasion of desert locusts and looming spectre of droughts and increased demographic movements especially by livestock keepers in search of pastures and water.

Many parts of the continent are turning arid or something close to deserts because of impact of climate change. The range and intensity of desertification has increased in some dryland areas over the past several decades. Drylands currently cover about 46% of the global land area and home to 3 billion people. In Africa, desertification has reduced agricultural productivity and incomes and has also contributed to the loss of biodiversity in some dryland regions. Soils exposed to degradation as a result of poor land management are subject to becoming infertile as a result of climate change. The change could exacerbate desertification through alteration of spatial and temporal patterns in temperatures, rainfall, solar radiation and winds.

Climate change will affect land degradation. Land exhibited to degradation as a consequence of poor land management is likely to become infertile as a result of climate change. Land degradation hazards could include wind and water erosion, loss of soil carbon nutrients, decline mass movement, soil structure decline and surface soil and soil acidification. Clearly the major causes of land degradation may include land clearance, poor farming practices, over grassing, inappropriate irrigation, urban sprawl, land commercial development, land pollution including industrial waste and quarrying of stone, sand, and minerals.

Technology in the Sub-Saharan Africa is at very embryonic stage. This is true both in the rural areas and sub-urban areas. The most needed technological knowledge is in educational technology, which refers to the promotion, development and use of information and communication technologies (ICT), m- learning, media, and other technological tools to improve aspects of education in sub-Saharan Africa. Since the 1960s, various aspects of ICT have aroused strong interest in Sub-Saharan Africa as a way of increasing access to education and enhancing its quality and fairness. Technology in the rural areas of Africa has increased its application but there is a long way to go to cope with the desired technological development needs. Due to the lack of knowledge and low use of ICT in rural areas, development including productivity is still very low. There has been some improvement and advancement in the technologies provided by the government in some urban areas, but there is not enough that has been done for the development of rural areas.

Now let us take a brief look at the financing aspects. In the African rural areas, the financing aspect in all its manifestation has been assigned relatively low priority especially for low income people's development programmes. In spite of investment related policy reforms, Sub-Saharan African countries lag in supplying financial services for rural areas and worst for agriculture. A substantial amount of financing is needed for development of new products, delivery channels, and partnerships, along with greater attention to savings. The financing will provide fresh optimism for rural economic emancipation. Special attention is needed to develop savings groups and provision of financial innovations supported by making best use of mobile phones and information and communication technologies (ICT). The telecom revolution and other innovations suggest that their use may leapfrog some difficult transportation and communication problems that force up transaction costs and risks and restrict financial inclusion for the poor.

There is the issue of rural or village financing institutions in Africa. Such institutions have been established in quite a number of places and/or countries. They take different facets in different countries, or regions of Africa. Overall credit finance institutions or banks face regular changes in government policies. Some African countries don't even bother to provide requisite human capital. The rural financing agencies or institutions, where they exist, are faced with obvious infrastructural inadequacies and socio-cultural misconceptions. The financial units or banks' operations or performances have been further inhibited by a host of other problems such pro-corruption, frauds and forgeries and poor governance. Rural Micro finance Banks (RMFB) have kept facing the problem of inadequate finance, due partly to the fact rural people are not yet in position to save much to provide deposits that could sustain the operations of district finance; mainly due to poverty.

Related to the RMFB are the Cooperative Micro Finance Banks, which have been on the increase in most regions of Africa but the problem they face are the same. In other words, credit agency cooperatives and schemes have generally failed to meet the needs of the small and marginal farmers. The micro-financiers have often used the funds they claim to provide to rural communities as bait to get the borrowers to their hook and in the ends they confiscate their domestic assets such as furniture, radios, and farm implements like ploughs and even their oxen which have been used as collateral for the borrowed money. Thus, lesser attention has been given to the credit needs of the needy farmers/peasants whereas the comparatively well-to-do farmers have been getting more attention from the credit agencies for their better credit worthiness.

The financing challenges in Africa include the high costs and risks of financial transactions. With the existence of various types of poor communities seeking for credit to carry out their visions, credit to meet their needs is daunting. Such credits may involve short-term, long-term, and medium-term financing. The few existing institutions often fail to assess the type of credit that is suitable for various groups as well as the usefulness and ability of the borrowers to cope with the type of credit that is offered. There is also another problem of lack of transparency and accountability of financial institutions dealing with rural people. The micro financing agencies have mostly been all out to squeeze money from the rural supportless poor people in a state that they know the rural borrowers would be unlikely to be able to pay back the money they borrow. Governments have not been unaware of what is going on, but rarely react to the disadvantaged position rural borrowers are in.

The demographic characteristics of Sub-Saharan Africa are quite different from those of the other regions of the world, particularly with respect to swift population growth that will no doubt continue for a long time. The characteristics include all the cultural, social, political, economic, and environmental aspects of development.

What arises is the issue of the population dynamics and the social transformation mechanisms at work, that need to be linked to demographic behavioral changes. Related to that problem is the rural and urban growth and development. As has been emphasized rural areas are home for almost 55% to 65% of the 1.3 billion people of Africa. As the population keeps growing the absolute number of the rural population will keep on growing. For centuries rural population has been characterized or influenced by demographic movements which have further been caused by those in quest for pastures for their livestock, or those seeking for more fertile land for agriculture or those moving from place to another due to instabilities of wars or other social conflicts.

In recent years there have also been movements caused by conflicts between various users of land e.g. farmers against nomadic livestock owners. The climatic changes due to global warming has made land users of various types to remain uncertain about rainfall reliabilities. Droughts are also unpredictable because long seasonal rains can abruptly fall and last for only a short duration, thus perpetuating dry spells. Due to those unpredictable seasonal fluctuations discipline among land users has been very low. Farmers could prepare land and do the planting but rains could refuse to fall or could fall but come to an end sooner than expected. In some cases farmers have gone as far as drilling water to get supplies from underground for irrigation and others uses. That has been possible only for the well of farmers. But cases have been witnessed in several places where nomadic livestock keepers drove their animals to feed in the irrigated farms thus eating up the farmers' crops, especially during the night times and by dawn, they move away leaving the farmers with absolutely no crop. There are also cases where livestock keepers drove their animals to forest reserves also during the night and by dawn they are driven off; all those practices being due to unpredictable droughts and absence of pastures.

Since colonial times rural land has been divided to include areas that are for residential zones, for farmers or peasants, areas for pastoralists and for game reserves, forest reserves and for mineral reserve exploitation. The issue of rural land use planning has been highly desirable in Africa but the existence of various land users with their diverse interests and needs; and also the climatic changes have made rural life quite tough.

Now let us have a brief look at the urban setting. In recent years urbanization rate in Africa has been profoundly high. According to a recent report by the Organization for Economic Co-operation and Development (OECD),[68] the pace of urbanization and urban population growth in Africa has changed significantly across the continent generally as well as within its various regions. For example, there has been heightened inequality, less absolute poverty but poor housing manifested in the proliferation of slums, more traffic congestion and the absence of public transport, poorer environmental conditions, and run-down infrastructure.

Urban people change their environment through their consumption of food, energy, water, and land. In turn, the polluted urban environment has been affecting the health and quality of life of the urban population. For example, urban populations have been consuming relatively much more food, energy, and durable goods than rural populations. And in turn, the polluted urban

---

[68] *The Organisation for Economic Co-operation and Development (OECD) is an international organisation that works to build better policies for better lives. Our goal is to shape policies that foster prosperity, equality, opportunity and well-being for all.*

environment has affected the health and quality of life of the urban population. Migration too, has been influencing urban growth in various ways, as it is a demographic process that links rural to urban areas, generating or spurring the growth of cities.

Growing cities are beginning to be seen as the agents of environmental degradation, and thus urbanization is placing a lot of stress on the land through sprawl; and coincident industrial development. Growth of cities is beginning to threaten air and water quality and other environmental impacts. For city dwellers, relationships between cities and villages remain strong. The modalities of urbanization clearly have impact on rural areas. The rural areas are major sources of urban population. However, there are various other forms of migration and movements, which can be reversed as evidenced in return migrations from cities to villages, a phenomenon that has been found to be true in some few west African countries such as Ivory Coast and Cameroon.

Regarding urbanization per se the stress that it causes especially in Sub-Saharan Africa starts with the fact that more than half of the world's population lives in urban areas. It is estimated that, there will be about 2.5 billion more people added to the urban population by 2050, mainly in Africa. The world's urban areas are highly varied, but many cities and towns are facing terrible challenges such as those of lack of jobs, homelessness and expanding squatter settlements, inadequate services and infrastructure, poor health and educational services and high levels of pollution. Urbanisation is occurring mainly because people have kept moving from rural areas to urban areas, resulting in growth in the size of the urban population and in the expansion of occupied urban areas. These changes in urban population have been leading to other changes in land use, economic activity and culture. Historically, urbanisation has been associated with significant economic and social transformations.

Some of the challenges of urban growth include those, related to health. Health problems related with urbanization include poor nutrition, pollution-related health conditions and communicable diseases, poor sanitation and housing conditions, and other related health conditions. These have had direct impacts on individual quality of life, while straining public health systems and resources. Furthermore, environmental contamination has been contributing to undernutrition; street eating places especially in close proximity to industrial areas or in high density population areas are prone to great health hazards.. These areas are often characterized by unhygienic conditions, leading to outbreaks of food-borne illnesses. Urban dwellers also suffer from overnutrition and obesity, (which is now growing as a global public health problem). Obesity and other lifestyle conditions are now further contributing to chronic diseases such as cancers, diabetes, blood pressure and heart diseases. It is a challenge which has been facing especially the urban industrial workers or the various other lowly paid people who have to break from their working place to take plenty of junk foods including so called chicken –and- chips and other quick foods.

There is need to also bring up the issue of squatters in almost all urban areas in Africa. This also is to do with the issue of urban planning in the continent. It could be noted here that, before the time of partitioning of Africa and following the Berlin Conference that was held by European nations in 1885 (which formalized colonialism in the continent of Africa), indigenous African cities and villages had fairly well-ordered structures that varied in size and density according and along ethnic and religious lines and also according to geography. Land uses necessary for functioning-

markets, religious sites, farms, community assembly spaces- existed in ordered, rational ways as did land property practices and laws, most of which changed under colonial rule. Urban areas set-up changed significantly from the pre-colonial to colonial times. For instance, between 1500 and 1900s European influence and colonial rule created a number of major urban centres especially in Sub-Saharan Africa. Some of the cities arose from settlements founded by the local African people, which the Europeans changed and enlarged.

All along rural - urban migration and natural population growth rates in cities have become the major causes of the increasing rate of urban growth and slum proliferation in Africa. The problems include lack or inadequate supply of electricity supply, poor sanitation and insecure living. In other words there are many disadvantages of urbanization, which could include high level of air pollution, particle pollution, noise pollution, light pollution, littering, crowdedness, traffic jams, and high level of stress. Urbanization causes many other problems such as health problems that are related to poor nutrition, pollution related health hazards, communicable diseases due to high population concentrations, poor sanitation, poor access to good housing and other health conditions.

Surely urbanization has its good and bad or negative effects. The good or positive effects include economic development, which flourish there due to easy supply of raw material, power, skilled labour and infrastructure especially transport and communications. The negative effects are as we said earlier, include stress on existing social services and infrastructure, crime, prostitution, drug abuse, and street children.

Recent developments show that cities and the urban areas in general are going to grow faster than it has ever happened in the past. By 2020 the African urban population stood at almost 650 million or about 50% of the total of 1.3billion people. Until year 2000 the urban population was hardly 45% and by 2030 the population will have reached 55% of the total while by 2035 about 65% will be living in urban areas. Leading cities, Cairo, Lagos and Kinshasa will continue to grow swiftly. The secondary cities as well as smaller urban areas are also swelling very rapidly. Areas that were just villages by the turning of 1990s have recently grown to large townships, and those that were only townships have grown to big towns or to municipalities and others to cities.

As shown above by 2035, more, almost 65% of African population will be living in urban areas. This means an enormous amount of funds and management skills will be needed to plan and provide services in order to cope with the changing situations. The major challenges are going to be those of planning and proper management of the urbanized centres. Other challenges will include finance, and land to meet the need of expanding cities. As the cities expand the local people that own land in the close proximity to city areas will need to be compensated to allow their land to be acquired to meet the growing needs. In the past some autocratic African governments have forcefully kept acquiring land from rural people or from those who owned it, (some of who were very poor peasants) without any compensation. That was wrong and legally and even morally illegal. In those unfair practices the poor people were left without either the land or money to enhance their lives, all in the name of transferring land to public ownership. That callous practice made some citizens poorer and without land, just to benefit the richer public, especially the senior members of the government bureaucracy or the rich business people.

The other challenges that urban authorities will have to face are in relation to the influx of rural urban migrations. Sites and service provisions will have to grow ahead of the rate at which the population will be growing. The objective is to avoid squatter growth. To avoid squatter growth planning and supply of land to developers will have to move ahead of the expanding urban population. Urban authorities will also have to control flood risk zones and also deal with many other deficiencies in urban planning process. Surely, there is a lot of need to remove deficiencies of lack of information about a city and its inhabitants. There is also needed to address issues of inadequate managerial skills on urban land and provision of sites and services. The means to implement choices resulting from absence of good land registries and land use management deserves to be given a lot of attention if Africa really wishes to cope with future challenges of urbanization.

What all these amounts to is that urban development should be viewed as an opportunity not as an imposed enemy of Africa. As they are right now, some parts of the urban areas especially the slums and squatters spread in many parts of cities portray a bad picture to foreigners and to visionary local people alike. A lot of resources will be required to cope with the situation, especially if we consider the fact that Africa is in a marathon with the rest of the world; and aims to be among the good winners in the marathon; its poor state notwithstanding. This fact should be viewed with a very critical eye, especially if we are to take into account that financial resources that Africa so far allocates to urban planning and also for provision of utilities are roughly estimated to be hardly 1% of allocation done by developed countries for development of their urban infrastructure and services. Good urban planning will affect transportation system, infrastructure, layout, and prescribed densities of residents, commercial and industrial areas and more.

Without such planning the cities will fail to cope with those of the rest of the world; and thus, quickly become inefficient and uninviting for residents and business alike.

This brings us to the issue of urban designs, which addresses how people perceive and use their environment. People care about the look, feel and livability of their communities. Urban design tools are needed, as they are a planner's most effective tools to address this need. Urban planning will affect the densities of our residential, commercial, industrial, and social or community recreation areas and more. Without such planning, our cities could quickly become inefficient and uninviting for residents and businesses alike. This further brings us to the importance of having comprehensive urban masterplans. Put very briefly, a masterplan is a dynamic long term planning document that will provide a conceptual layout to guide further growth and development. Masterplans are about making the connection between buildings, social settings, and their surrounding environment.

21

SELECTING PRIORITIES OUT OF PRIORITIES

Selecting priorities out of priorities is a difficult thing to do. For a poor individual everything is a priority; he would prefer to have clothing, food, housing accommodation, transport, travel to places for various reasons, and so on. But in situations that only one or only a few of those things can be afforded or can be made available the poor man is most probably going to chose food as his top priority especially if he has been going hungry for a long time. He will chose food because that is what will enable him keep sustaining his life. Similarly for Africa, which has a long list of priorities, but with its limited financial capability, it will have to choose carefully to remain with what is most affordable. In other words, Africa has many priorities but there are no chances of implementing all that it considers to be on the list of its priorities. Efforts need to be made to select few things that can be done efficiently, but which could fit in the financial or budget limitations.

Priorities can be a lot, but there is no way all of them can be taken on board implantation plans all at once due to limitations in financial or other resources. Considering investment resources limitations selecting priorities out of priorities is important. The problem is how Africa can get to those few top priorities. It is a difficult question, but we must start somewhere. Let us start by recognizing that almost 65% of African people live in the rural areas, meaning that African nations individually and collectively must design development strategies and actions that can lead to fast rural transformation. People will have to eat to live and their food basket is in the rural land. Rural areas are where a high priority should be placed. Rural population needs food, health care, adequate physical and social infrastructure, education, safety and security, and technological development. Our development efforts should be people centred and rural people should be given the most immediate priority.

Africa is not expected to see pride in seeing the majority of its population in a ditch of poverty. The need to address poverty squarely has very often been mentioned but not with emphasis it deserves. The type of Africa that is being sought or is desired for tomorrow cannot be realised without first accepting that poverty has been Africa's enemy number one; and that it should be fought using all means available."

Application of the "family responsability system which has come to replace collective farming, and has the ability to maintain public ownership of land and some of the means of production, while making production the responsibility of households., could be very important for rural communities. Peasants need to acquire the right to exploit the land for and by themselves. Doing so will give them a certain leverage to choose their crops. The household should be the place where decisions on production can be taken independently, with the government only contributing in form of provision of the state-imposed regulations and extension services. Generally, the freedom to the type of crops to be grown should remain flexible and in congruence with the farmers' choice.

Along with these developments, the system for putting agricultural products onto the market should also be liberalised. The market system will need to undergo rapid reforms that lead to swift development and became a major outlet for agricultural products. The marketing aspect also needs agricultural products to be sold through the open market and the average peasant family product sold in this way. Within this liberalising context, the choice of which crops to cultivate should became determined by economic factors, and especially by the development of price differences for different products. The decisions on all these policies should be inclusive and the African farmer should be placed at the centre of all these decisions.

The farmer should be exclusive decision maker through the guidance provided by experts. Enough extention personnel will have to be made available ; and they should be equiped with modern scientific skills that will enable rural farmers to maximize their farm productivity. Extention services should be there on every stage of the way to improve technological advice, and hence increase output. With Africa's abundance of labour and the ever decreasing arable land due to the increasing population, people should be enabled to make decisions to reduce the production of products that do not maximize their earnings, or those that require a lot of land in favour of more labour-intensive commercial crops.

Power is another pressing and important input to rural production and development. Electricity in Africa today is about 700 terawatt- hours, with North African economies and South Africa accounting for 70% of the total. Power supply is needed for the rural areas where communities should be given a deserving priority. Rural areas need the power, which could be sourced from the regional or national grids. Between 2000 and 2014 low access countries received about 43.6 billion per year into the electricity sector from all sources. The bulk of the money went into extension of traditional universal grid. To achieve universal grid access in current low access countries by 2030 will require over $17 billion per year including about $12 billion per year for the new transmissions and distribution capacity and additional $20 billion per year will be needed to address current supply inadequacies and expand generation capacity to meet growing demand.[69]

Many governments have not made-up decisions to give rural areas the priority they deserve especially on matters of budgets for rural development. Alternative sources should be opted for rural areas. Renewable energy sources are often recommended as the most appropriate energy technology. Quantitatively fossil fuels and conventional energy sources such as electricity play a minor role in the rural energy supply, demonstrated by the low electrification levels. There are many, almost nine most commonly available alternative energy sources that could be opted for and which could be viably used in various places in rural Africa. The sources include wind energy, solar energy, hydro energy, geothermal energy, bio-energy, nuclear energy, hydrogen energy and tidal energy. All these energy alternative sources are in one way or the other good for rural areas, but that suitability will depend on cost and efficiency for specific rural area supply and application. Generally speaking, wind power is considered to be the leading renewable energy source. This renewable energy source is not as quiet as solar power but it does pack a solid efficiency rating and is generally environmentally friendly.

However, in spite of the fact that hydropower is not as easily accessible as other renewable energy power sources but it is currently the cheapest renewable energy source, costing just about

---

[69] *Michael Toman and Jorge Peters: World Bank on Rural Electrification; How much does Sub Saharan Africa needs the greed; Published on Let's Talk development.*

$0.05 per kilowatt hour on average. Hydroelectric power has been in place in Africa for a long time and it produces electricity consistently. Hydro sourced power is also considered to be one of the most widely used forms of eco-friendly energy. The ongoing global warming, which has been causing serious impact on climate change and which has also been leading to fall or drying up of river water sources, has scared those who depend on hydro- power as the only source power supply.

Appliances needed for production in the rural areas should necessarily be electricity powered to make them efficient and productive. This is with reference to grain milling machines, power tillers, grain millers, carpentry tools, iron grills, and many more. Affordable power supply will be very important because that is what will enable the powering of the milling machines, small industries for processing of agricultural products, and for rural social and cultural development and recreation. Good power supply in the rural areas has the impact of reducing migration from rural areas to urban areas. With power most activities that attract young people to urban areas can easily be provided in the rural areas whose effect is to reduce rural-urban migration.

With efficient infrastructure in the rural areas production of surplus for sale to urban communities will be a must, because farmers have surplus; in exchange for good supply of rural agricultural inputs such as fertilizers, ploughs, hand hoes, rickshaws, wheel burrows, cooking stoves and other rural community needs; all of which will certainly be needed. Market for industrially produced products in the urban areas will find ready market in the rural areas. Such products may include equipment and machinery needed for rural production. Rural communities need cheap but efficient machinery for tilling the land, for weeding and even for harvesting crop from the fields. Rural entrepreneurs also need grain milling machines, safe bags for packing and storing agricultural products and so on.

The rural people also need to be given basic education that will help to develop and lead to enhancement of the agricultural sector. Schools, agricultural research colleges, hospitals, electric power and warehouses, are some of the other components of infrastructure that is required for the development of agriculture. These are all the gifts of the industrial sector. Industrial manufacturing, largely located in the urban areas will have to necessarily be linked with agricultural production, power supply, and rural warehousing and food security in general. Infusing the literature on agricultural development with that of industrial organization and natural resource management will enable agriculture to be viewed as a set of small and large farms that need an enabling policy and institutional environment to increase productivity and shared economic growth.

The next thing is with regard to land ownership in Africa. Land ownership reform measures including the enactment of laws that will change the current situation of depriving poor or low income people of land ownership. These are issues that will have to be looked into as swiftly as possible. As of now, despite large amounts of arable land in Sub-Saharan Africa, small individual land holdings are rare. In many places the land is subject to tribal ownership and there is lack of a system of freehold land-owning; which in some places means the laws prevent people in disadvantaged groups from owning land at all. In certain countries in Africa the land is owned only by the state and ownership of land by citizens is at the mercy of government officials who are as a rule very corrupt.

Often land laws are ignored, and land sales to disadvantaged groups rarely occur. What is worst legal title to the land is not assured and so rural people rarely have clear title to their own land and have to survive as farm laborers. Unused land may be very plentiful and is often private property, but that should be enough reason to insist that changes or reforms that will address those shortcomings (such as those of lack of good land registration systems, absence of procedures to avoid squatter settlements and avoidance of land-theft occurrences) should be quickly addressed. The measures, if done well will hasten access and ease to get a mortgage or loan, as ownership of the property will often be established to the satisfaction of financiers.

To move fast in these transformational endeavours, African countries could borrow a leaf from successful countries like China and a few other Asian countries. China has today emerged as a major global power. It has lifted a good proportion of its rural population from widespread poverty to a much higher economic state and welfare. For instance, since early 1980s China began to open up and reform its economy, whose growth went on at an average of almost 10% or more annually. As a result, more than 800 million people got lifted up from poverty. Performance became even more exemplary as years went by. China's poverty rate fell from 88% in 1981 to 0.7% in 2015 as measured by the percentage of people living on the equivalent of $ 1.90 or less per day in 2011 purchasing price parity terms.[70] In the period between 2000 and 2015 more than 850 million Chinese people were lifted out of poverty.

Since the closing of 1990s emphasise on poverty elimination has been China's top priority. That emphasis on poverty eradication has

---

[70] *This is in accordance with most recent World Bank Reports.*

continued to be in China's policies, economic and social development strategies, and actions. Poverty elimination was one of Xi's most significant national policies. Since the time when Xi took power in 2012 China lifted over 100 million of rural population out of poverty.[71] That tremendous level of success made Xi call the poverty eradication campaign "**a complete victory**" a "**miracle for human kind**" and "**China's great contribution to the world**".

It will be appreciated that in early 1980s, China's GDP per capita was lower than that of India and almost equal to that of many of Sub- Saharan countries. But following the reforms, by 2000 it was already thrice that of India and since then the gap continued to widen. Over the past 30 years i.e. from early 1990s to 2020 China built up the world's second largest economy, tipped to overtake the US within the next decade or so.

China's amazing growth since 1990s, driven in large part by the government's focus on agricultural reform and productivity, is unprecedented in its scale and persistence. Today China can still boast growth that most other countries can only dream of. This is owed to China's well focused and articulate policies, and leadership which has been relying on research and development (R&D) which has assisted to play a significant part in putting China on transition to a service-based economy, placing innovation at the center of its plans. Chinese R&D spending currently accounts for an impressive 15% of the world's total and this is only likely to increase.

However, it is necessary at this juncture to also state that our emphasis is on borrowing a leaf from other countries; does not mean copying everything that has made those countries e.g.

---

[71] *Xi has been the leader of China, the most prominent political leader in the People's Republic of China (PRC) and Chairman the Central Military Commission (CMC) and President of PRC.*

succeed in their economic development endeavours. There are things worth borrowing or imitating and there are others that are not relevant to African situations. For instance China started by embracing their communist principles. They used those principles as a basis for their new development strategies. They blended their principles or needs with what they considered good Western approaches such as those related in parting private sector initiatives to rural transformation strategies. In order to make that blending a successful approach, China put a lot of emphasis on research and development (R&D) and also to Information Communication Technologies (ICT). These are the type of issues that Africa can evaluate and where possible adopt them to fit in African situation. That intelligent way of borrowing from others can enable Africa to leapfrog to economic development most productively. The objective is to make African policies and strategies home grown; yet remaining mindful of the fact that cooperation with successful partners or borrowing a leaf from those that have come from backgrounds similar to Africa's should be an important strategy.

For approximately one billion people of the world lifted out of extreme poverty since 1990s, China has correctly claimed an amazing 440 million (or about 40%) of them. For a period of 30 years from 1990 to 2015, China had contributed 76% of all global poverty reduction. China has also led the world in achieving other Millennium Development Goals (MDGs), with the world's fastest rate of decline in both maternal and child mortality. By 2013, China's maternal mortality rate was registered to be even lower than that of the US. China has waged a successful campaign against malaria, largely without any external assistance, reducing case numbers from 24 million in 1970s to just 57 cases of local transmission, in 2014. In the years towards 2020 China was vigorously on its way to total elimination of malaria. The message that is been delivered from this Chinese performance is that borrowing a leaf from that country could be hugely valuable to Africa.

There is no doubt that Africa has the potential and capability of moving to rural reforms with a view of swiftly achieving its goals the way China has done. In that process Africa must give sufficient emphasis on transformation, with special emphasis on agrarian reform and substantial improvement of rural life. In Africa, rural agriculture is dominated by grain production, low levels of productivity and income. Agricultural reforms similar to what was introduced in China in 1980s could be opted for. This means there is need for a considerable shift in the rural economy, from being based mainly on low yield agricultural production (like it is now), to high yield enabled by introduction of more scientific processes; and also becoming a diversified economy combining agricultural and non-agricultural activities.

From 1970s, i.e. approximately fifty years ago, China demonstrated that it hated poverty and from that point decided to take actions that would enable that country to completely disentangle from poverty. While efforts have been directed to poverty elimination, and also that for all those years poverty elimination has been among top China governments priority, China has nothing to regret about all that because today China is the most successful nation in the world in poverty eradication.

There are a few specific things that Africa can directly learn from China. Some of those things include the fact that:

- There is need for Africa to declare that poverty is an enemy that should be fought from all possible fronts, using as much of available resources as possible.

- African political leaders, may be through African Union, must seriously commit to transforming their economies in their countries, sub regions and regions by way of having specific action plans for elimination of poverty.

- Africa has been criticised for harbouring corruption, which is an ongoing malpractice and therefore that chronic disease must be strongly fought while instituting deterrent laws, and bringing the perpetrators to justice.

- Africa governments know the importance of Research and Development (R&D) but to a large degree only pay lip service to it. While China has recently been allocating almost 14% of its expenditure in R&D Africa has been spending an average of 0.3%. Notwithstanding the fact that African budgets are relatively small but for it to move forward swiftly must spend at lest 2% on R&D and gradually move to at least 5% in the next 5 to 10 years.

- Time has come for Africa to invest highly on high-tech industrial packs, as industrialization should be part of prime movers of Africa's development.

- Related to development of high-tech industrial packs the need for serious development of incubators, focusing on technologies such as artificial intelligence should start to be given a thought.

- Considering the importance FAST Internet high importance and priority should be given to its development in Africa as has been shown in the coming paragraphs.

- Then there is the Unicorns- privately held start up companies. These will have to be introduced sooner rather than later; and

- Last but not least, is the issue of branding to promote Africa. Introduction of a plan **"on made in Africa"** to accelerate the development of high tech industries with a view to make Africa one of the World top leaders in areas such as telecommunications, electrical power equipment, robotics, high end- automation, and electric powered vehicles will go a long way towards emancipation of Africa technologically and economically.

Like was promised above let us now touch base on the issue of ICT and connection of Internet in the Africa rural areas. ICT offers an opportunity to introduce new activities, new services and applications into rural areas to enhance existing services. ICT can play a significant role in combating rural poverty and fostering sustainable development. It does so by creating information rich societies and supporting livelihoods.

However, in the rural areas there are many challenges that always appear to slow down the progress and realization of the impact of ICTs. The challenges include poor infrastructure, technological illiteracy and the high cost of ICTs.

In the continent of Africa, several reasons have been given why Internet is necessarily needed. Some of those reasons will include the fact that:

- Internet can assist in closing the digital divide between urban and rural areas and can assist to accelerate development

- Internet will assist in improving health-care and in serving lives

- Connection will empower women and close the digital gender gap line and can respond to Africa Union (AU) call for a special focus on women's rights.

Other benefits of internet in Africa will include contribution to economic growth on local, national, regional, continental and global scales including creation of millions of jobs, the power to increase access to educational resources; and also can be a good tool to improve agricultural production and reduce poverty; It will connect people to access distances and enhance social wellbeing; has great impact in enhancing governance and in creating opportunities for citizens participation; and finally internet can assist in the improvement of public services delivery. Widespread access to FAST internet connection will encourage governments to move services online and will enable increased numbers of citizens to access public services that might not have previously being available to them. That will be a particularly critical development for those that live in rural areas or in areas lacking in government offices and services.

Earlier it was emphasise that Africa's high priorities should be in those actions that are people centred. Priorities should be those which provide answers to people's underdevelopment. This brings us to matters of urban development. Urban areas still accommodate an average of 45% of the 1.3 billion total population of Africa, have their homes in the urban areas. Put differently, so far, a little more than four out of ten people in Africa currently live in urban areas. That proportion will be a little higher if we take into account the newly emerging urban centres and the further growth of towns and cities. With urban growth rate of 3.4% the size of the population will rise to 5 out of every 10 by 2040 (i.e., in about 20 years from now). That means that by 2040 over 65% of the continent's population will be living in urban areas. Rural people are migrating especially to the rapidly growing cities, while the emerging urban areas are also receiving their fair share of the people migrating to them from the rural areas.

If deserving priority will be assigned to urban growth and development in general and to specific developments that the cities need, the results will be great. However, it is often said that people are not forced to migrate to cities; and that they do so at own will. But the truth is that their prime goal has been to seek for better economic opportunities. Most migrants from rural areas out of their own will but pushed from rural areas because of absence of basic amenities like passable roads in all seasons of the year, lack of utilities like electricity, clean water, healthcare facilities, employment opportunities, social welfare facilities and many other opportunities that are better provided for in the urban areas.

In almost all cases cities or urban areas in general have not been prepared to accommodate the ever-increasing immigrations. Unfortunately, also, there is a growing problem of managing migrations to urban areas. Urban areas are recipients of the migrants from the rural areas but do so without preparedness and willingness to do so. Urban managements have often failed to cope with the need to provide the residents with public amenities such as housing, water, electricity, healthcare, education, sanitation and jobs. That constraint has led to even greater problem of dividing the urban areas into two socio-economic territories, namely the well provided for territories and the poorly provided for territories. The well provided for territories provide home for happy and law-abiding citizens, who live in good formal housing, in areas well provided with reliable sanitary services, clean water, electricity, health care facilities, some recreational facilities, access to employment in formal or informal sectors and children have access to schools.

The poorly provided for territories or zones provide home for the unhappy poor citizens that are generally not law abiding and are always in confrontation with law enforcers. The housing is informally developed on informally acquired land, usually referred to as squatter areas. Residents in the squatter areas are always subjected to the wrath of the urban authority decision makers; who can do the clearing of the areas with short notice or no notice at all. The decision to clear those informally settled areas could include urban renewal programmes, development of industrial sites, infrastructure development, and many other programmes. Informal settlement urban zones or territories are home for those who are considered to be illegal urban dwellers or residents, so defined because of their state of vulnerability due to least attention paid to them by government authorities. All these miserable situations arise because of lack of preparedness of cities to receive migrants to cities.

Some African countries have responded to those pressures by building satellite cities, which are expected to shorten commuter services or to provide employments as near the residential zones as possible. Governments have also decided to build new cities and/or rehabilitate and upgrade the existing old cities. But even with those interventions, very marginal results have been realised, especially in situations where the overall supply of services and utilities remain static, again due to either very limited resources or lack of ability to set urban development priorities right. Whatever the approach that is used to develop equitable development, only two options are available. Authorities should try as much as possible to provide services and facilities that will make rural people love the idea of living there in the rural areas. In the meanwhile strategies to prepare better for immigrants to the urban areas should be found.

It may be unfair to desist from remarking that most urban renewal programmes have never had those sections of urban dwellers that live in informal settlements on board. The claim is that they are where they are illegally, and thus they deserve no compensation for what they lose when their areas are cleared for planned developments. Moreover, authorities have been there and have kept looking at those who came to occupy what later comes to be defined as illegal settlements, long after the occupiers have made their settlements. In some cities squatter settlers are more in terms of numbers than those who live in formally planned areas. We could start imagining of disturbance, commotion, loss of property, and miseries that result from irresponsibility of urban authorities that thoughtlessly rush to destroy informal urban residences and their properties. We can imagine of the costs, which could have been served if the authorities had given stop or quit orders immediately before the spread of the squatter settlements.

Now we should discuss briefly on what has emerged in the name of sustainable cities. By definition those are cities that are designed and managed with environmental sustainability in mind. The underlying factor is that it is not possible to solve the climate crisis without getting cities right. There is a very strong link between the quality of life in urban areas and how those centres draw on and manage the natural resources available to them.

To date the trend has been that is accompanied by increased pressure on environment. Accelerated demand for basic services, infrastructure, jobs, land, and affordable housing particularly for the nearby urban poor who live in informal settlements has been exerting even greater pressure on resources availability. Due to the high concentration of people, as well as the provision of infrastructure, housing and economic activities, cities have become particularly vulnerable to climate change and natural disaster impacts. In these circumstances building urban resilience has proved to be very necessary to avoid human, social and economic losses, while improving the sustainability of urbanization process to protect the environment and mitigate disaster risk and climate change. Cities with their concentration of people, economic activity and infrastructure are among the most powerful levers we have, to drive decarbonization and build resilience fast enough.

Building sustainable communities, whether they are villages, cities or countries and societies at large will be critical to eliminating poverty and boosting shared prosperity. Here is also the issue of sustainable community, which can be described as a place where the needs of everyone in the community are met and people feel safe, healthy and ultimately happy. It is a place where our environment is appreciated, protected, enhanced and damage to environment is minimized. A sustainable community is desirable in a sustainable city, which is therefore an urban centre engineered to improve its environmental impact management. In an eco-city one should expect to see parks and green spaces, solar powered buildings, roof top gardens and more pedestrians and cyclists than cars.

Benefits of sustainable cities are basically those related to better health. In addition to their positive action on air pollution, green urbanism will also improve physical health, say by installation of sports grounds, mental health by the relaxing of plants, and social health by creation of spaces designed to promote human contact. What all this will amount to is that sustainable cities will be seen, charecterised by saved lines, reduced damage to property, reduced economic loses, minimized social disruption, ability of local government or city authorities to resume operations quickly and shorter recovery period for the community. It is necessary to have a sustainable community due to the fact that, it can manage its human, natural and financial capital to meet current needs, while ensuring that adequate resources are available for future generations.

To recognize sustainable cities or societies is not a difficult task. Such society will be easily seen and/or recognized because it will not allow damage to the environment; it will be resistant to overuse of resources; it will be insistent on keeping and living beautiful; and it will have peaceful and bountiful earth that future generations can continue to inhibit. Sustainable communities must necessarily protect the environment it is in, in order to thrive in the long term. Basic human needs must be met, including access to clean air, clean water, and uncontaminated food sources. Biological diversity needs to be supported and fostered and natural resources must be conserved for future generations. Sustainability is important to the society for many reasons that include environmental quality. To have quality communities, we need clean air, natural resources and a non-toxic environment. A sustainable urban community will be able to survive if certain factors are given deserving considerations. The factors include cultivating simple traditions or practices such as:

Always trying to think twice before shopping and building a tradition of making sure big or bulky shopping have big environmental benefits;

- Trying to ensure freedom against plastic materials;

- Avoiding products that endanger wild life;

- Paying attention to labels;

- Being water wise by for instance avoiding wastage, pollution, or misuse

- Driving less and driving green; and

- Taking measures to green our homes or compounds by say flower gardens, grass lawns, shrubs, or other useful green set-ups.

22

CRITICAL DRAWBACKS

Africa has reasons to be hopeful; that the Sub-Saharan Africa's turnaround over the past couple of decades has been fairly dramatic. Many years of economic decline in Africa, caused a lot of drawback to African economic development. The drawbacks were founded on Africa's history especially that part that starts from the transatlantic slave trade, to colonialism, neocolonialism, and subsequently to the world economic order. Those drawbacks have had their negative impacts that have been exacerbated by poor economic policies adopted during the post-independence period.

In most parts of Africa there is lack of strategic environmental assessment, which is basically caused by limited resources and technical knowledge. The problem is exacerbated by the fact that the volume of work required to conduct Environmental Impact Assessment (EIA) more often than not exceeds the number of qualified personnel. The challenges can be categorized according to various aspects such as absence or shortcomings in policy planning, finances, and complexities in environmental issues. The process is often weakened by prioritization of infrastructure development over protection of ecosystem, an inadequate comparison of alternatives, poor timing of environmental and social studies, a focus on mitigation measures rather than prevention of harm, and lack of accountability of all players involved. The challenges have made implementation of land use plans quite difficult.

Besides insufficient funding the difficulties are perpetuated by, lack of political will, political interference, and corruption. All these have brought about challenges facing land use planning strategies for environmental sustainability. For instance, in Nigeria, inadequate information or data has been identified as the major problem facing land-use planning and management. There is lack of data on land use and also there are no comprehensive and up to date plans or maps showing land use patterns and structures of ownership in most areas.

In East Africa, especially in Tanzania the challenges facing land use planning include conflicts on land use in rural areas. That is especially between farmers, rural forest or park reserves authorities, and livestock keepers. There are also persistent land disputes resulting from rapid expansion of towns encroaching farmers areas; tenure conflicts between customary and granted land rights, and other social problems. Currently, Tanzania faces numerous challenges related to land ownership, especially in rural areas. The challenges include farmers and pastoralist conflicts, tenure disputes and alienation of peasants.

Currently, land use challenges include urban sprawl, infrastructure congestion, accessibility to services, urban density, urban regeneration, and negative externalities such as pollution and the displacement of population due to excessive house prices and land hording. Land use planning is often carried out in a highly polarized public context in which decisions on land allocation and use are a source of conflict and tension. Only with clear policies and actions on land use planning can help to manage such conflicts, ease tensions, and bring about the more effective and efficient use of land and its natural resources.

Issues of land use planning policies in Tanzania are fairly widespread. For years there have been conflicts in Loliondo[72] surrounding land and natural resources users. The conflict has been fairly complex with many stakeholders involved', but the root of the problem has been land. The drought of 2009 brought conflict, tensions to a head resulting in burned homesteads, reported human rights abuses, over 50,000 cattle displaced and considerable economic losses to local communities. Until as late as year 2020 the conflicts were far from resolved. At the core of these conflicts are the community land rights, which must be upheld. This in brief means, communities must maintain control over their land in Loliondo.

However, we still need to know the root cause of the long land conflicts in Loliondo area. Put in different perspectives it is noticeable that the conflict is complex and at some stage government has been using its muscles to remove the pastoralists from their indigenous lands in the name of attracting foreign investors. The conflict has been going on between the pastoralists on the one side and the government and tourism industry on the other. The reason is the 150, 000 hector corridor of land in Loliondo, in Ngorongoro district bordering the Serengeti National Park (SNP).

However, the going dispute goes back over two decades, but the Tanzania government has kept on to contend that the pastoralist have often been urged to keep away from the area because the area is being over grassed and that it has planned to split the disputed land, which is classified as the Loliondo Game Controlled Area (LGCA)) into two parts; with one area that will be owned by the

---

[72] *Loliondo is situated n the northern Ngorongoro District in Arusha region in Northern Tanzania.*

local community and the other will remain in government hands. It is not easy to say how that move will assist in avoiding overgrazing in the whole of Loliondo land area. Local civil leaders are not in agreement with the government plans, and so they have at times threatened to resign if the government plan goes ahead.

The reason for the dispute is claimed to emanate from the granting of hunting License to a foreign company called Otterlo Business Corporation (OBC) registered in the United Arab Emirates in July 2009. That deal has a long history, which traces itself far back to 1992 when it was first granted. The history goes on to show that in 2009 the government of Tanzania evicted Loliondo residents from the area used for hunting by OBC. Following that government move, about 200 local Masai pastoralist homesteads were put on fire, resulting in the loss of property, houses, including their cattle and other livestock. It has been further alleged that up to 20,000 residents of Loliondo, were impacted and over 50,000 head of livestock were displaced from grazing and water sources.

There are many questions that keep been asked about the absence of inclusiveness in this process. That weakness together with the way this issue of granting long term lease to OBC has made people to cast doubt about the transparency of the hunting license between the two parties i.e. government and OBC. The Loliondo communities have always remained disfavoured by government actions on this issue while they are the ones that have natural rights of the land in that disputed area. The government has kept holding that the local people have no rights, as the conflict keeps on simmering and attracting the attention of local and international observers.

However, what is happening in Loliondo and other places in Tanzania is not unique; it common in many countries in Africa. What lacks in most Sub-Saharan African countries are issues of unclear and overlapping duplication of terms of reference of those that deal with land use planning in the urban as well as in the rural areas. In most cases those involved in planning work prefer to follow clearly defined planning procedures but none of those procedures exist.

Generally, the African population is growing. The increasing population, income growth, and urbanization have begun to drive up the demand for food of animal origin (e.g. meat and milk). Meat and milk demand in Sub-Saharan Africa has kept growing for the whole of the last four to five decades till 2020s. However, African countries have not taken full advantage of the poverty reduction opportunities of the increased demand for food and of food of animal origin. Livestock production has not kept pace with meat and milk demand trends and a number of countries have become net importers of meat, and dairy products. Livestock development methods in Sub Saharan Africa have remained extensive with unimproved breeds with minimum productivity for the farmers. Land tenure issues are mostly regulated by African policy makers. And the land policies are ineffective, and the land tenure is insecure; both of which cases make it difficult for livestock keepers to take advantage of the growing demand for animal based food; which can also be considered as a endogenous determinant of rural conflicts.

Policies do not sufficiently and consistently address land tenure issues for farmers and pastoralists. This is what is often explained by the weakness and also strengths of the current land tenure system. However, inadequate and insecure access to land not only could contribute to inefficient resource allocation but might provide farmers and pastoralists with incentive to increase livestock numbers beyond the land carrying capacity, thus enhancing competition to secure resources and contributing to violent conflicts in rural areas.

Now let us look briefly at issues related to livestock mobility in Sub Saharan Africa. There is strong relationship and similarity (but also wide variations) in the seasonal travel movement between base locations of daily grazing movements of herds around base locations (e.g. village areas). That means mobility only responds to the nutritional needs of livestock. The UN Food and Agriculture Organization (FAO) report of 2020 tells a lot about the need for land use policies and planning among pastoralists. According to FAO report, cross border coordination of livestock movement and sharing of natural resources among pastoralists communities in the Greater Karamoja cluster for instance, have shown that the frequent and persistent droughts are a recurrent feature of the area[73] which encompass the Southern parts of Ethiopia, Northwestern Kenya, the Southern parts of South Sudan and Northern Uganda.

The impacts of these droughts have often been exacerbated by climate change; advancing desertification to the area; and the environmental degradation of rangelands. The result of those changes has been persistent food insecurity of the pastoralist communities. The situation is often worsened by the occurrence of transboundary animal diseases and the eruption of conflicts over natural resources within countries and across country borders.

Intervention is often necessary and should focus on livestock mobility and natural resource management, which can play an

---

[73] *UN Food and Agriculture Organization (FAO) Report, 2020; also Planetary Security Initiative*

important role to strengthen livelihoods, sustainability of peace and indirectly preventing conflict. Cooperation and coordination between communities and countries can maximize the benefits and minimize conflicts. The situation in the Greater Karamoja Cluster is such that sharing of pastoral resources cannot only promote the resilience of resource poor communities but can also create new opportunities for cross border trade and will open up new markets.

The question that is often asked is whether the present nature of pastoralism can be sustained for a long time in places such as Great Karamoja cluster. This is the right time for authorities to think of positive reform policies that should be implemented before things go completely out of hand for the pastoralists as well as the land, which is becoming less per capita due to encroachment of desertification. The pastoralists believe in keeping in their traditional land while still keeping large numbers of animals, which has a direct impact of overgrazing. What has been worsening the situation is the extensive pastoralism, which makes animals to eat all the vegetation to the roots. Long periods of drought also leave animals without enough grass and water. The fact that most of the pastoralists in the Karamoja Cluster have opted for extensive pastoralism, which demands for extensive grazing land, and is prone to loss of other land resources such as grass and water, has made them live nomadic life always in search of new grazing areas. What is being said here is that despite the capital and skilled labour outlays that are needed, but the output, productivity and profits earned will always be much more than from extensive pastoralism. Their high earnings are realized, both in the short and long term. In the short term the pastoralist benefits by earning much more from a few animals because the prices of the animals raised in that way are of higher quality and the demand in the market is much higher. In the long run the land sustainability is maintained because the grass is allowed to continue growing and that bad effects such as aridity are prevented.

Let's end up by stating that pastoralism is good and places no burden on ground water resources. It requires no irrigation, and during the rainy season animals can often obtain their water needs from the plants that they eat or ingest.

In discussions in the previous Chapter we stated very emphatically that our priorities should to a high degree be based on human centeredness and also on environmental sustainability. We further underlined the fact that the land area in the world and of course in Africa is fixed and surely is becoming less due to population growth and the global changes that are taking place. With the changing situations all these natural resources must be planned well and their utilization should take cognizance of the increasing population in a diminishing land area as well as environmental sustainability factors.

What we are insinuating is that time has come when policy reforms should look more critically at what is coming up the lane in the not very far future. Land use planning should be given high priority. The land use plans should look at the long-term situations and mitigation measures should be designed and implemented soon rather than later. For instance, the time has come when pastoralists should be given education about the need to give high importance to the maximum and intensive utilization of available pastoral land.

The land that we see today will soon be very inadequate because of the growing population. In not very far future pastoral land will keep diminishing and become very scarce due to population growth. With the increasing African population, the per capita land supply will be very small. What that implies is that pastoralists must be given education to start appreciating the importance of destocking, as a move towards intensive pastoralism as opposed to the ongoing extensive pastoralism. Extensive pastoralism should start to be discouraged because it requires large areas or a widespread grazing area, which also entails demand and consumption of a lot of land resources such as grass and water, thus leading to diminution of the other land and land- resources such as fertility and water. Too extensive pastoralism has the impact of encroachment of aridity and hence to desertification. The benefits that are being realized from extensive pastoralism are also very low and in cases of drought many animals die like it happened in many areas of East Africa in recent years. Intensive pastoralism will demand for very little land though the capital outlay to make it successful is high, but the income realized from it is also a lot higher. Here is where government intervention in terms of viable credit policies are needed.

Transformation of pastoralists from extensive pastoralism to intensive pastoralism will be the only way land can effectively be made available for the present and future generations. There are pastoralists in a few places in East Africa, that have opted to move to intensive pastoralism and the benefits they have realized are exemplary. A good case in point is that of Masai people in areas adjacent to Kilimanjaro International Airport (KIA) in Hai and Siha districts of Kilimanjaro region in Tanzania. Those people have been extensive pastoralists, but due to shortage of grazing land and also following constant conflicts with farmers in the area authorities urged them to prune their large herds and remain with a few that they can handle within the small pieces of land they own. They also decided to invest the money they earned from the large stock sales and invested the money to other commercial businesses; a move that has enabled many of them to be relatively rich compared with the state in which they were before they decided to transform. Today the pastoralists as well as the farmers in the area live in harmony with each other.

The basic thing is that government authorities should at the initial stage be supportive to those transformation moves by way of extending desired extension services so that the current extensive pastoralism can be reformed to minimize the imminent land crisis in Africa. There is also the problem of the tropical climate, which has been a cause of droughts, exacerbated by the going global warming, which together have led to crop failures, death of livestock, loss of feeding grounds for wildlife and hence famine. These together have caused vulnerability to societies especially in Sub Saharan region.

Having dealt at length with the problem of land use planning and also the need to transform the lives of pastoralists and other livestock – keepers, let us now move to problems or issues related to international market access in Africa. For quite a long time now there has been a lack of openness to participation in international markets. Some of the reasons for the inaccessibility are geographical such as lack of access to the sea. Land locked countries have especially suffered from lack of access to the sea which has meant excessive costs of transporting goods over land to the sea, which has in turn depended on transiting through countries that have seaports. The costs involved have highly contributed to poor access to international markets.

The continent's economies picked up in the mid-1990s to 2015 and the macroeconomic growth was also noticeable. During the period people became healthier, many more children attended schools, and the rate of extreme poverty declined from 54% in 1990 to 41% in 2015. Furthermore, political and social freedoms expanded, and gender equality advanced; conflict in the region also subsided, although the conflicts are still claiming thousands of people's lives in some countries such as DRC, and still drives pressing numbers of displaced persons. Despite those widespread economic and social performance accomplishments, the African continent challenges remain daunting. The overall economic growth has slowed in most recent years, notably from 2018 to 2022, largely due to the impact of COVID 19. That COVID 19 terrorism notwithstanding, recovery appears to be on sight; though that state of peace could be further disrupted by the Ukraine/ Russia war, which has already caused some impact on Africa. The conflict has been feared could cause a lot of impact on food security in some African countries both through availability and pricing in some food crops, and particularly wheat and oil seeds especially sunflower. It is also going to impact on social economic recovery and growth triggered by rising uncertainties in global financial markets and supply chain systems.

It is very unfortunate that any harmony destabilization in countries outside Africa causes some shaking in Africa because of the continent's state of vulnerability. A good case in point is that of the war between Russia and Ukraine. However, from Africa's perspective Russia and Ukraine's agricultural imports from the continent have been marginal; averaging only $1.6 billion in the whole period of 2018 to 2021. The dominant import products have been fruits, tobacco, coffee and beverages in both countries. However, most serious impacts of Ukraine and Russia war on Africa is poised to be the pain caused by rising fuel and wheat prices. For instance Russia is a major producer of commodities such as oil, gas, aluminium, nickel, palladium, wheat and corn. Sanctions and market concerns about the war's disruption on supply chains will continue to cause commodity prices to rise.

On the continent of Africa, the countries that could be most vulnerable to the conflict are those that import a large amount of share of the wheat they consume, such as Egypt. Africa oil importers such as Kenya will also feel the greatest pinch of the surging oil prices. Russia, which is one of the largest exporters of unrefined oil is poised to be hit by sanctions, disruptions to the fuel exports and potential embargo.

However, commodity exporters like Nigeria, Angola and others in Africa are most likely to be the biggest beneficiaries of the war as the supply constraint induced commodity price boom that started in 2021 will most probably be prolonged. From Africa's perspectives Russia and Ukraine's agricultural imports from the continent have been marginal.

From a global perspective, the biggest concentration of poverty has shifted from South Asia to Africa; and thus poverty reduction in Africa explores critical policy entry points to address the demographic, societal, and political drivers of poverty; improve income-earning opportunities both on and off the farm; and better mobilize resources for the poor. There is urgent need to address issues of macroeconomic stability and growth; there is even more pressing need to ask what more could be done and where policy makers should focus their attention to speed up poverty reduction.

The pro-poor policy agenda should serve as the centre point not only for economic growth where the poor work and live, but also mitigation of the many risks to which African households are exposed. There is urgent need to focus squarely on the productivity and livelihoods of the poor and vulnerable sections of African society, which may definitely call for what it will take to increase people's earnings. As soon as possible Africa must come up with a roadmap for financing the poverty and development agenda.

The other issue that is worth looking at is, in regard to frustrations in industrialization development efforts during the early years of post-independence. Although Sub-Saharan Africa began its post-independence economic development with a strong commitment to industrial development, but the progress could not be sustained. The terms of trade shocks and economic crises of the 1980s made sustained development difficult. That called for two decades of macroeconomic stabilization, trade liberalization, and privatization programmes, resulting to slow growth partly due to uncertain and very little private investment in industry. Africa re-emerged around the turn of the 21st century, with its industry no longer competing with the high-wage industrialized countries. Slow growth and fiscal austerity also meant that there was a growing gap in the basics—infrastructure, human capital, and institutions—between Africa and the rest of the world. Since then, a huge variety of studies have been undertaken, suggesting which way out. But African leaders have not assigned much importance to the suggestions or recommendations that come from the studies. The studies and reports have largely only been good for the shelves. In the meanwhile decisions keep on being made on the basis of individual Africa leaders' whims or emotional decisions.

It could be said here that, historically industrialization anywhere in the world is associated with increase of polluting industries heavily dependent on fossil fuels. That situation was most noticeable in the industrialized countries in the past. But gradually Africa is joining in the race. The rate of pollution is increasing and the impact is also taking its toll. With the increasing focus on sustainable development and green industry policy practices industrialization has increasingly included technological leapfrogging with direct investment type of financing.

However, for now Africa wishes to make swift strides to industrial development. The new phase of industrial development will have to be competitive and will have to be very supportive to agricultural development. That is what Europe did during industrial revolution. That is also what China, India and Malaysia did to leapfrog to where they are today.

Africa goal is to industrialise swiftly, but for it to do so the process will have to be blended well with technology in the right and timely way. Industrial development strategies will have to be properly designed to take into account the local environment. Generally industrial development strategies will have to consider one or a combination of the three conditions:

a) Industrial development strategy that will have to depend entirely on external capital inflow,

b) Industrial development strategy that will depend on utilizing local resource and/or

c) The industrial development that will use a combination of both external and local resources in certain agreed proportions.

All the above three strategies can be opted for depending on the policy of the country concerned. For Africa external capital is highly desirable for infrastructure development such as roads, railways, ports, and dams and mostly necessarily for assets such as refineries, power plants, heavy industrial production plants such as fertilizer, cement, iron and steel, sheet glass and others. These are heavy industries, needing a lot of capital investment as well as high level of technological input. The Investments of this nature may call for a lot of foreign capital inflow.

However, the option of strategizing to use a combination of foreign and locally sourced capital could be a very good one for industries that are considered strategic and which a country may show the desire to have involvement in their development. Where foreign capital can be procured it will be very desirable to use it in combination or partnership with local business or capital that can be directed to the project. This does not preclude the importance of having foreign capital for the entire investment in privately owned and run companies because the country will still benefit hugely from such investment. The advantages of FDI over licensing agreement with a foreign partner is that it will provide protection against possible interlopers.

But there are also disadvantages of FDI, which include the fact that it is costly and time consuming to establish a foreign presence in this manner. Further, FDI could also be more vulnerable to political risk. FDI can also affect local business in various ways including the fact that investment of a foreign company with its new technologies and products can force local business to lower their prices and recognize their operations in terms of costs. It should be recognized that FDI is a company's physical investment into building a plant in another country, acquisition of a foreign firm or investment in a joint venture or strategic alliance with a foreign company in its local market. Small businesses often experience the effect of FDI by hosting foreign companies in their local markets by investing internationally. Like we have mentioned above, investment of a foreign company can provide new technologies, capital, products, organization techniques, management skills and potential cooperation and business opportunities for local business.

However, the local capital use strategy could be the best for small and medium size or light industries development. The advantage of doing so does not only manifest in optimization of the use of the available capital but also similar purpose industries could be spread to many economic development points using a relatively low capital outlay. Light industries do not call for a high doze of investment, and thus could be spread to many population points in consonance with its limited availability, while causing development impact faster.

The other relevant factor is that of poor or absence of basic infrastructure such as electricity, roads, ports, poor state of water supply. These need a lot of consideration because they drive up the cost of production and of movement of raw materials and industrial outputs as well as shipping out finished goods. For fast development, two acceptable dimensions of industrialization must be observed: a change in the types of predominant labour activity (farming to manufacturing) and the productive level of economic output. This process includes a general tendency for populations to urbanize and for new industries to develop.

The period of transformation from an agricultural economy to an urban, mass-producing industrial economy—has accompanied every period of sustained per capita gross domestic product GDP growth in recorded history. Less than 20% of the world's population lives in industrialized world, yet they account for more than 70% of the world's industrial output. The transition from agrarian to industrial society has not always been smooth, but it is a necessary step to escape the abject poverty found in less developed countries (LDCs) and Africa in particular. The other thing is that with industrialization, economic and historical research has overwhelmingly shown that industrialization is linked to rising education, longer life spans, growing individual and national income, and improved overall quality of life. These are some of those important issues that will have to be carried on board African nations action plans and programmes implementation work schedules.

Integration of Africa into the world economy through trade will have to be given a chance. It will be a powerful means for African countries to promote economic growth, development, and poverty eradication. Over the past 20 years (i.e. between year 2000 and 2020), the growth of world trade averaged 6% per year, twice as fast as world output. While the resulting integration of the world economy has raised living standards around the world, developing countries including Africa have had a small share in this prosperity. In some instances, incomes have risen dramatically. Unfortunately, progress has been less rapid for some countries especially the least developed ones many of which are in Sub-Sahara. Those have seen their share of world trade decline, and they risk further decline because they have taken the option of going without lowering their own barriers to trade.

The next measure that Africa should take to speed up development is in relation to assigning high priority to human capital. **With a big population of about 1.3 billion people, Africa has a huge asset and a strong competitive advantage.** Human capital is perceived to increase production and thus profitability. So the more the investment is done on employees (i.e., in their education and training), the more productive and profitable it can be. Elements of human capital, which include skills, qualifications, and education, work experience, social and communication skills, habits, personality traits, individual fame and brand image, are among actions which businesses and governments in Africa should assign high priority.

Equipped with education, skills and jobs, African youth stand to be the most important **driver of economic growth**. By 2063, Africa is envisioned to be a continent with seamless borders, and management of cross-border resources through dialogue; and a continent where free movement of people, capital, goods and services will result in significant increases in trade and investments among African countries and strengthening Africa's place in global trade. **Inclusive economic growth will ensure Africans can reach their full potential and are on a path to unprecedented prosperity.** Harnessing individual potentials of Africa's human capital will be the most sustainable key to economic transformation and social progress.

The next line of action will be found in asking why Africa is poor and why Africa should move swiftly out of poverty trap. The lack of transparency, accountability, safety, and the rule of law; the bloated public sectors and the squeezed small businesses should be necessarily dealt with. In Africa patriarchy, which embrace factors such as hiring practices that discriminate against women, exclusion of women from decision-making, institutional discrimination against women, and the relegation of women to the domestic sphere could be a major cause of vice and crime including terrorist tendencies, which should necessarily also be eradicated. Poverty in Africa is partly founded in the lack of provision to satisfy the basic human needs of certain people, women being the leading victims.

African nations typically fall to the bottom of any list of fighters against poverty as well as the causes of poverty. The way out is for African nations to pronounce in one strong voice that they hate poverty in their nations and communities. Once that pronouncement is made and once policies and actions leading to removal of poverty are taken, things will certainly start to change for the better.

Africa is poor, but that is accelerated by lack of provision to satisfy the human needs to sections of its people. So, African nations will have to strive to move away from any further fall to the bottom of any list measuring small size economic activity, such as income per capita or GDP per capita and this is possible taking into account a wealth of natural resources Africa possesses. There is nothing to be proud of when we learn that in 2006, 34 of the 50 nations on the UN list of least developed countries were in Africa. That list has somehow marginally reduced since then, but the route out is still long. Average per capita incomes in Sub Saharan Africa have barely changed over the last decade, moving from $762 per year (2005 measurements). On the other hand Europeans have kept on changing their incomes from a model of producing foods for need to mainly the production of cash crops and capital goods.. All crops produced by Africans have been exported and prices have been set on criteria designed by Europeans. Actually, in recent years there has been a decline of income especially in Sub Saharan Africa from $608 to $556, which makes Sub Saharan Africa to be among the poorest regions in the world.

The relationship of Africa and Europe remains both unequal and inequitable. Such is the widening gap between the two continents, implying that the concept of partnership is quite illusory. There has been little transformation of the tenets underpinning the ties between the two continents since colonial times.[74]

Rapid changes in Africa are very possible if we consider that countries like China, the most populated country in the world, which only less than 30 years ago was among the poorest countries of the world, but by the closing of 2015 had succeeded to raise almost 400million of its population from absolute poverty levels to above average levels. That is the achievement realized in a span of just about 30 years.

The sad thing is that Africa's share of income has been consistently dropping over the past 50 years by any measure. For instance, by the beginning of 1960s the average European worker earned about three times what the average African did; but by the closing 2020, the average European earned more than twenty times what the average African did. These statistics should be used to open the eyes of African governments and businesses with a view to change the trend through transformational policies and strategies. Although GDP per capita incomes in Africa have marginally been steadily growing, measures are still far better in other parts of the world.

Further, there is the issue of democracy. Political scientists emphasise that while the concepts of democracy have it that incomes will rise if production also rises. The question is why Africa has decided to lack behind in all issues related to production and productivity. Why are governance issues not given the attention they deserve and why do some African leaders avoid issues of inclusiveness, democracy and good governance? . We have learnt that good governance entails the efficient and effective reciprocity

---

[74] *Blogs.csae.0x.ac.uk.; on Purchasing power parity- adjusted USD.*

between rulers and the ruled, with it incumbent upon governments to be responsive. One of the central empirical findings of the political economy literature is that, high income per capita causes democracy. In other words there is strong cross-country correlation between income and democracy, but do not typically control for factors that simultaneously affect both variables. Lipset's Law posts an appositive and significant relationship between income and democracy. Based on dynamics and heterogeneous panel data estimation techniques, it gets found that there is a significant and negative relationship between incomes and democracy: higher/lower income per capita-hinder/trigger democratization. In short it is found that democracy is associated with high human capital accumulation, lower inflation, lower political instability, and higher economic freedom. Democracy is closely tied with economic sources of growth- like education levels and life span through improvement of educational institutions as well as health care.

The explanation given notwithstanding no relationship has been found to exist between democracy or civil liberties and aggregate measures of economic inequality. However, governments can intervene to promote equality and reduce inequality and poverty through tax and benefits systems. Employing progressive tax and benefits systems takes proportionally more tax from those on higher income levels and redistributes welfare benefits to those on lower incomes levels.

Now let us look more closely at the democratic process in Africa. This brings about the issue of majoritarian democracy, which entails a broad consensus on values and procedures, the participation in the selection of ruling elites, and the accountability of leadership to the electorate. Democracy and accountability are related to processes in society within the context of reciprocity. Democratization could even more elaborately be defined to embrace a state in which the people have the authority to choose their governing legislators. The decisions on who is considered part of the people and how authority is shared among or delegated by the people have changed over time and at different speeds in different countries, but they have always included more and more of the inhabitants of all countries.

Cornerstones that should be used by all African countries to build meaningful democracy should include freedom of assembly and speech, inclusiveness, equality, membership, consent, voting, right to life and minority rights. In a democratic system one expects the establishment of free and fair elections, and democratization would then embrace the process by which the civil liberties and political rights, necessary to achieve this goal are put in place.

In any case, for African governing elites to assist in getting the continent to the envisaged destination, they have to bring drastic changes to enable the mass of the population to keep on board the sailing ship of democracy and peace of mind. Africa has a goal to achieve, and that will not be realized by the thinking that a few individuals know where Africa should go and the majority do not. Democratization process should be inclusive. The move that is suggested here can lead into faster transformation of Africa if handled honestly and with maximum care.

The above issues, once again make it inevitable to bring up a recommendation on issues of harmony to African societies and also in working harmoniously with everybody in the world, especially now that the world is changing to a global village. For Africa and the rest of the world to move in the right path, especially with regard to the issue of democracy, racism, racial discrimination, xenophobia, and related intolerances, there is need to emphasise the great need of addressing these issues squarely.

23

THE NEED TO BE STRONG AND SAIL ON

Today Africa has a big population now estimated at around 1.3 Billion people[75]; but it is not one of the most densely populated continents. Had it not been due to the impact of slave trade that removed tens of millions of people from it annually, the population would have been much higher, probably higher than that of the continent of Asia. This point is being emphasised against the Malthusian theories of population, which brings up the issue of exponential population growth and arithmetic food supply growth. Malthus believed that through preventative checks and positive checks the population would have to be controlled to balance the food supply with the population level. According to Malthus, the population control was necessary so that a nation would not plunge into poverty due to population pressure and ultimate explosion. But a modern day economist would look at it in a completely different way.

Malthusian theory does not hold much for Africa that we are thinking about today. Africa has recently shown to be swiftly growing. Rapid rural transformation is being witnessed although there is much more to be desired. Rural agricultural dependence is still very high (over 60%) there is a lot of light at the end of the tunnel. Certainly agricultural transformation that is going on is demanding the supply of enough and well oriented people who will

---

[75] *These are estimates made by the UN for the year 2019*

serve as a means to achieving the transformation and hence, the needed growth and development. Technologically well-orientated labour lacks. Industrial development strategies, which could result into higher level of marketable products also lacks. In short the population in Africa only needs to be made more productive through education and technology. The population needs to be seen as an opportunity rather than a problem.

The quantity, quality, structure, distribution, and demographic movement are still low and more may be needed to help in speeding up the rate of economic growth and development. The implication here is that low population density in a continent that has a high percentage of technologically oriented people will need an increase in population in order to cope with envisaged surge in production. In other words it is still too early for Africa to start crying foul about its big population, which in terms of its density is only about 104 people per square mile compared to Europe with 188 people per square mile,[76] and Asia with 258 people per square mile. Africa's population density is just about 50% of Asia.

There is need to make further impressions on common features in Africa. To do so it is important to revisit a few things. Among them are the damaging marks of man's activities, easily seen in form of devastations in most parts of the continent. For instance, many ecological zones are now very fragile. Going around the continent one sees large-scale soil erosion, resultant cycles of drought and floods, and downgraded ecosystems. Such sites are only signals of

---

[76] *Population densities in different continent of the world are as follows: North America - 60.7 people per square mile; South America - 61.3 people per square mile, Europe - 187.7 people per square mile, Asia - 257.8 people per square mile; Africa - 103.7 people per square mile, Australia - 7.8 people per square mile*

dangers that Africa is likely to face in the future if the right actions are not taken in good time to address the situation.

There are big population points in Africa, especially in the many cities some of which have grown to mega cities. But accessing some of those points still remains highly challenging because of bad roads or the absence of the right type of bridges or other transport infrastructure. Connectivity between one region or country of Africa and another be it by road, railway, air, or sea transport remains a highly challenging issue. . For instance, it is easier to connect by air through Brussels to Kinshasa in DRC than from Dar es Salaam in Tanzania to Kinshasa. DRC and Tanzania share a border on Lake Tanganyika. Both of them are today members of the East African community. Yet, it is quite challenging to connect the two neighbouring states by road or railway. In Africa it can also prove to be very problematic to connect between two points in the same country. In DRC for instance, it could be quite a challenge to move by road from Lubumbashi in the East to Kinshasa in the West. Similarly, it could be quite challenging to get to Maputo in Mozambique from southern part of Tanzania (while the two countries share a border, Tanzania being in the north and Mozambique in the south of the border). Even inside Mozambique, it is a big challenge to move from the capital, Maputo, to Cape Delgado in north due to absence of good infrastructure and elements of terrorist threat. Like we have just hinted communication problems are not critical only between two African nations but also between two specific points of the same country.

Most rural dwellers in Africa are peasants who depend on subsistence agriculture for their living. But, the ongoing global warming has had impacts that have far reaching effects. For instance, seasonal rains have lost their patterns and peasants who used to depend on those seasonal rains cannot predict when the next rains will fall. They also cannot predict the right type of crops to plant to assure them of good harvests. Similarly, when the rains fall, they could be too small or too much for the crops in the fields. Due to global warming, snow on Mount Kilimanjaro has kept melting, which has had bad effect on ecosystems. Also, sea and lakes water levels have been rising, thus flooding the beaches or settlements that are in close proximity to the water bodies, a process that has often led to great disturbance to people.

Conflicts between countries of Africa have not been entirely removed, as wars and/or killings of innocent people remain witnessed in several countries. Issues of governance within countries have continued to have a lot to be desired. African leaders continue speaking democracy but many of them remain dictators, autocrats, and embezzlers of public resources. It is said some, even order the opposition leaders to be arrested for fear of facing challenges.

The level of peace has been further disturbed by pandemic diseases such as cholera, Ebola, COVID19, TB, malaria, and several others. Lately the non-communicable diseases such as diabetes, blood pressure, heart attack, asthma, kidney problems and other related ones have been on the increase.

It is surprising that despite all these odds, Africa is still there, struggling through horribly devastated situations. What can be said for sure is that in spite of those challenges, Africa has started to show signs of recovery; that it will have its economic growth continuing to grow despite drawbacks such as those of COVID19. The signs are showing that, Africa will make a lot more progress by 2030 and most of them will have got to the higher levels of economic growth and development (with GDP of US $1,500 or more by 2030 and beyond).

Africa has been nursing the idea of speeding up its growth and development, to enable it to get out of where it is today. The African leaders who saw African states receiving their political independence in the 1950s and 1960s are remembered to have put it very clearly that Africa needed to free itself by pulling off the shackles of imperialist domination. As the saying goes, "Rome was not built in a day"; and Africans generally know that Africa will not grow and become a world power in a day. The other saying has it that "those who endure will eat the fruits of the land". Africa has endured for a long time and slowly it is building up energy to carry its economies to the next levels.

Slave trade is gone, colonialism is gone, neocolonialism is still being fought and racism is a way of life for a wide spectrum of human beings. Africa will have to cope while fighting to remove huddles on its development path. There is the issue of the war against governance, unemployment, poverty, contemporary slave trade, pockets of terrorist tendencies, and diseases. These are wars that continue to be fought, and in some situations, they may prove very difficult and costly to eliminate, but the war must be won.

As of 2013 Africa was the world's fastest-growing continent at 5.6% a year, and GDP was expected to rise by an average of over 6% a year between 2013 and 2023. This situation continued to 2017, when the African Development Bank reported Africa to be the world's second-fastest growing economy. Until the end of 2018 growth throughout the continent, was exemplary with over one-third of African countries posting 6% or higher growth rates, and the other 40% of the country's growing at about 5% per year in the years before COVID-19 pandemic. Of course, a slump was experienced for the period between 2019 and 2022 and gradually some recovery started to be noticed towards the end of that period. It was expected that things would start to stabilize at an average of 3.6% during the next three years from 2022 and could continue to remain for some time below historical highs. But the outlook remains promising. Growth fundamentals have also been shown to be improving, with a gradual shift from private consumption toward investment and exports. Several International business observers have recently named Africa as the future economic growth engine of the world, explained by the bounty of its resources, improving performance of human resources and application of ICT.

24

AFRICA YESTERDAY, TODAY AND TOMORROW:

We are being asked to answer the questions: where has Africa come from; where is it right now, and what is the tomorrow going to be? Those are questions that need answers. Unfortunately, some of the answers have been provided in the previous Chapters. At the very beginning the early history of Africa was outlined. Topics that followed included those related to slave trade, imperialism, colonialism, and impacts of racism, while for many other cases the answers still need to be found. Slave trade, imperialism, and colonialism discussions revealed that the continent got crippled, and since then it has kept limping. Devastating factors such as colonialism, discrimination, exploitation, racism, and others, have also been discussed extensively. In short, the going has never been easy for Africa, but Africa is still here, limping after many casualties of slave trade, imperialism, and colonialism as well as mismanagements including the lack of good governance that followed after colonialism. All those still abound almost throughout the continent. This situation may explain why Africa has been nick named a place of many challenges.

The challenges notwithstanding, people have been contemplating where Africa plans to go after here, when, and how soon? The answers to the questions will start providing some clue of how to shape Africa's tomorrow. One thing that is undisputable is that Africa must move forward swiftly to some defined destination, which African peers have defined under the African Vision 2063.

That vision defines the destination of Africa for at least the next 4 decades from 2020. From the Vision there is absolutely no doubt Africa wishes to catch up with the rest of the world. So, the Africa Vision 2063 must be attained without fail. What that means is that wherever they are, Africans must be versed with the African Vision 2063. For reasons of inclusiveness all citizens of this continent must be enabled to be part of the Vision. The economic growth and development process should be made to gain more speed at least to regain some of what has been lost over centuries.

The African vision 2063 seeks to deliver on a set of Seven Aspirations each with its own set of goals which, if achieved will get Africa to its vision for the year 2063. The seven aspirations reflect the African desire for shared prosperity and well-being, for unity and integration, for a continent of free citizens and expanded horizons, where the full potential of women and youth are realised, and with freedom from fear, disease and want. The seven aspirations are as follows:

ASPIRATION NUMBER 1:

"To have a prosperous Africa based on inclusive growth and sustainable development." The goals are to achieve a high standard of living, quality of life and wellbeing for all. Regarding the standard of living the goal is to move the majority of the African people from the level of vulnerability in which they are to a much higher level of happy living with enough food, medicine, housing, clothing, transport safety and security. The other goals for this aspiration are to have well educated citizens and skills revolution underpinned by science, technology, and innovation; healthy and well-nourished citizens; transformed economies and jobs; Modern agriculture for increased proactivity production; Blue/Ocean Economy for accelerated economic growth; and environmentally sustainable climate and resilient economies and communities.

ASPIRATION NUMBER 2:

"To have an integrated continent, politically united and based on the ideals of Pan-Africanism and the vision of Africa's Renaissance since 1963". The goals for that aspiration are to have a United Africa, which could be in form of Federation, or at least a Confederation ; infrastructure crisscrossing Africa; and decolonization of the territories that may still be remaining unlawfully occupied. To achieve this objective African leadership should show readiness to change/transform. Managements and planning to achieve future goals must be inclusive, and leaders should rid themselves of selfishness and must have clear understanding of why the peers that came up with these aspirations, put a lot of emphasis on the need for African integration and unity..

ASPIRATION NUMBER 3:

"To see an Africa of good governance, democracy, respect for human rights, justice, and the rule of law. This is a goal that most African leaders have failed to observe. However, to achieve the goals of this aspiration Africa will have to be a continent that has good governance, democracy, respect for human rights, justice, and the rule of law; entrenched institutions and transformed leadership in place at all levels.

ASPIRATION NUMBER 4:

"To have a peaceful and secure Africa, which will lead to achieving: mechanisms for peaceful prevention and resolution of conflicts, which should be functional at all levels. The aspiration goes further to require that as a first step, dialogue-centred conflict prevention and resolution will be actively promoted in such a way that by 2020 all guns would be silent. A culture of peace and tolerance would by that date be nurtured in Africa's children and youth through peace education." The goals are to achieve this aspiration by way of making Africa to achieve an African continent of peace, security, and stability; a stable and peaceful Africa; a fully functional and operational African Peace and Security Architecture (APSA); and the eminent Africa cultural renaissance.

ASPIRATION NUMBER 5:

"To have a Great Africa, whose development is people-driven, relying on the potential of African people, especially its women and youth, and caring for children." This aspiration aims to see all the citizens of Africa to be actively involved in decision-making in all aspects of society.

ASPIRATION NUMBER 6:

"To have Africa which shall be an inclusive continent where no child, woman or man will be left behind or excluded, on the basis of gender, political affiliation, religion, ethnic affiliation, locality, age or other factors". The goals to be achieved by this aspiration will include full gender equality in all spheres of life and engaged and empowered youth and children.

ASPIRATION NUMBER 7:

"To have Africa that is a strong, united, resilient, peaceful, and influential global player and partner with a significant role in world affairs. Affirming the importance of African unity and solidarity in the face of continued external interference including, attempts to divide the continent and undue pressures and sanctions on some countries". The aspiration has two major goals namely: having Africa that will be a major partner in global affairs and peaceful co-existence, and also Africa that is able to take full responsibility for financing her development.

The above seven aspirations can be better understood by first trying to know what the word aspiration means. By definition the word could mean hope, a wish or ambition. So African Aspirations portray the ambitions, hopes or wishes of pioneer African leaders. Nobody is supposed to temper with the seven aspirations because they are complete in every aspect of them. But like we have started to say these are ambitions or hopes or wishes. For them to be realized we in Africa of today need to come up with policies, plans, strategies, and time bound action plans that will enable each one of the aspirations to be realized. One such plan is what has been outlined in the next chapter regarding issues of governance. But governance is only one of the many key lines of action that need to be implemented to enable the seven aspirations to be realized within the time frame that has been given in the Africa's vision 6063.

In this book we have tried to come up with some ten priority areas that if implemented will get us somewhere in implementing the Seven Aspirations of Africa. The next paragraphs in this chapter provide the ten priority areas.

The ten areas need to be given attention and should be actioned to realize the Vision 2063. The 10 priority lines of action if successfully implemented in their completeness will have tackled all the needs of the seven Africa's aspirations. Each of the 10 areas or lines of action will have to be put in a comprehensive way to leave no stone unturned as we work towards achieving Vision 2063. The plans should show Africa's responsiveness to the Aspirations of our predecessors as outlined above, which if seriously implemented, will bring Africa to a new level of development. That will get Africa to its "New Dawn or to a New Canaan". It will bring back deserving respect that the continent and its people lost during the last four centuries of slavery, colonialism, and neo-colonialism.

Not only that, the attainment of the tenets of the African Aspirations will certainly bring back Africa we want. Being the continent's strategic framework that aims to deliver on its goal for inclusive and sustainable development and also being a concrete manifestation of Pan-African drive for unity, self-determination, freedom, progress, and collective prosperity pursued under Pan-Africanism and African Renaissance, Africa will have achieved and regained the long-lost glory.

Once the 10 priority areas that are proposed below have been adopted and implemented for Africa's development, what will need to be done further is the implementation work. Basically the 10 priority areas will bring quick and meaningful impact, and thus they will have to be given deserving priority. The areas include need for industrialization, agriculture and rural development, tourism, population and human resources development, natural resources exploitation, governance, safety, and security. The priority areas have each been discussed, albeit briefly as follows:

1. INDUSTRIALISATION:

Africa has an urgent need to industrialize, especially now, that it has a duty to attain its aspirations with a view of reaching its Vision 2063. African countries should see industrialization as a number one area of high priority especially in this early stage of its economic development. The case of industrial revolution that took place in

Europe from 16th century, that transformed European cottage industries, became a turning point for Europe. With industrialization Europe did not only cease to be what it had been before, but more employment opportunities were created, more exports were made possible, other sectors such as agriculture were enhanced, people's standard of living increased, more schools and hospitals were established, governments were enabled to earn more revenues in form of taxes and levies, and better utilities started to be provided, transport infrastructure networks were expanded and improved and so on. Industrialization enabled Europe to make a U-turn from agrarian based production to mass industrial production. The U-turn enabled governments to earn enough revenue to revolutionize their entire economies, thus making Europe to be the most developed region in the world...

The situation in Africa today is such that, while a lot of natural resources were exploited and plundered during the colonial days, but they still remain highly unexploited. The little that is being exploited is sold to external markets in raw form, thus making African countries to earn relatively very little. Establishment of industries that will do at least some semi processing will give these countries the ability to export and earn more from what they export in raw form. Semi-processed products will serve as inputs for more specialized production that are of high benefit to the individual countries, regions, and the continent at large. The semi processing is certainly not the ultimate goal as full processing still stands to be Africa's objective to achieve vision 2063 and more. In other words, the stage of semi-processing industrial development will only serve as a step to full processing.

The type of steps to full industrialization that is being proposed will not only benefit Africa alone because even industrialized countries and other importers of raw materials will benefit from semi processing that will be done in Africa. However, industrialization should be planned in such a way that it will have a link with agricultural and other sectors that produce primary products, such as livestock, fishery, and forest and forest products, minerals and water.

No country has industrialized and failed to make strides to higher levels of development. African states need to move to sustained and inclusive economic development. Industrializing Africa must have a strong linkage to domestic economies. Doing so will enable African economies to achieve high growth rates, diversity of their economies, and will also reduce the exposure to external shock. Like has been hinted from the time of industrial revolution in Europe to the present time, industrialization has been instrumental. The linkage of the local industries with other productive and even service sectors will promote a strong local economy and will also give deserving impetus to improve productivity for Africa; it will allow for mass production and raise the standard of living.

Without structural changes, Africa will not be able to cope to sustain recent growth. Surely, the economies with more diverse and sophisticated industrial sectors will tend to grow faster. If Africa will expand internal consumption by trading among member states, if it moves decoupling from old colonial trade routes; that will lead to industrialization as it will have developed a sizeable market to support its industrial companies.

However, we need to further underline that there are quite a number of factors that could deter the efforts to industrialization in Africa. Technology is one of them. Technology is feared it could reduce the demand for the low skilled workers. The other factor is to do with poor infrastructure, which drives up the cost of moving raw materials to the industrial points and shipping out finished products to external markets. Africa will need to restructure to enable it to have private sector led economies. In so doing the public sector should be expected to focus more on those issues that are most suited to it, such as governance, infrastructure development and regulation.

2.TRADE:

Trade has very close relationship with industrial and other productive and service sectors development. There is no doubt that quite often some African countries underestimate the importance of having a strong trade regime. Trade allows countries to expand their markets and access goods and services that otherwise may not have been available domestically. Ultimately trade results in more competitive pricing and brings a cheaper product home to the consumer. Actually, trade means more jobs and higher wages. It also means lower prices and more choices.

Africa is chronic for many trade barriers. The barriers take many forms, such as tariffs, non-tariff barriers to trade, subsidies, voluntary export constraints, currency devaluation, trade restrictions and embargo. All these, when applied either by the country concerned or by some external forces, can serve as trade barriers whose results are to deter other sectors and overall economic development.. Of the above the most common barrier to trade is a tariff, which is a tax imposed on imports. Tariffs on imported goods raise the price of imported goods, which subsequently leads to spending more thus raising the cost of living of the people in the importing country. This also brings in the reality that the government could serve as a big agent of trade barriers, especially through government subsidies or other import restriction measures.

The leading trade barriers in Africa are those that are related to non-tariff barriers (NTB). They include port congestion, technical standards, customs valuation above invoice prices, theft of goods during transportation or in the port yards, import permits, antidumping measures, violation of intellectual property rights, inefficient bureaucracy, and or excessive regulations. Depending on how these trade barriers are imposed on trade, they always serve as great limiting factors especially to international trade.

However, there exist a lot more barriers to international trade. The most common of such barriers include natural barriers such distance, language, tariff barriers, tax on imported goods and non-tariff barriers. We could also add other hidden physical trade barriers such as difficult terrains, unpassable roads in the remote parts of Africa, and expansive deserts the Sahara Desert being a case in point. With a wish to promote trade there could be a lot of need to encourage voluntary trade that will help the African economies to grow. Such trade will encourage specialization, which can bring in more profit for the enterprices. There are also the informal or indirect trade barriers to trade. These include license requirements, environmental regulations and health and safety measures. If the imposition of these measures is done without sufficient sectoral and professional coordination the result can be very detrimental to trade and ultimately to national economic growth and development.

We also ought to look at intra- African trade, which is hereby defined as trade that is done within Africa among African countries and within individual African countries.. Actually, trade among Africa countries is relatively very small. Intra African trade for 2019 was valued at only US$ 69 billion, which was almost 5% less than in 2018. These estimates have been based on the data collected from 35 out 55 African countries. However, intra Africa trade accounted for only 5 % of Africa's total trade in 2019; the same as in 2018. Over a period of 10 years (i.e. from 2009 to 2019) intra-Africa trade remained low, the highest having been recorded in 2015 and 2016 with a low margin of 19% and 20% of the total trade in the two years respectively.

Most of the intra-trade has been among countries which are members of the same regional economic community (REC); where the countries are members of the Free Trade Agreement (FTA) or Custom Union (CU) of the REC. Clearly what this implies is that Africa has a lot that needs to be done to enhance trade amongst African countries. The intra trade between countries of the same economic community ought to be further boosted, because even at that level it is too low to be proud of it. What makes things even more discouraging is when we look at the overall continental context where the intra trade is highly insignificant. Today African countries are trading more with China and other Asia countries than with each other, a situation which will have to be addressed to remedy the situation.

For now, the common goods that are traded under the intra trade umbrella consist mainly of consumables such as food, drinks, tobacco, sugar cattle and meat. In recent years the consumables have also included paints, limestone, roofing iron sheets and some petroleum products, especially from countries with well performing oil refinery plants. The growth of industrialization in some countries has been accompanied by an increase in the trade of durable and non- durable manufactured goods such as motorcycles, cement, and electrical parts.

Intra-African trade can certainly strengthen product value chains and facilitate the development of technology and knowledge. Trade is an instrument that can and will incentivize and spur infrastructure development and attract foreign direct investment; thus further expanding the intra- African trade. All these are key to accelerating economic growth on the continent of Africa.

Like has been hinted the non- tariff barriers notwithstanding the problems of lack of financing of infrastructure is major thing that is hampering intra-trade. To build quality infrastructure the continent needed at least $300 billion by the year 2020. Further, Africa's competitiveness has continued to be limited by both domestic factors- such as low agricultural productivity and investment, poor transport and communications infrastructure, and the cumbersome and inefficient custom procedures. Despite the opportunities, challenges facing free trade areas may also include fear of significant tariff revenue losses and uneven distribution of costs and benefits. All these drawbacks need to be looked into with a view to removing them as soon as possible to pave the way to achieving Africa's vision 2063.

3.AGRICULTURE:

The next very high priority sector should logically be the agricultural sector. Agriculture is a very important sector for development in Africa. The sector plays a crucial role in the economies of African countries as it provides the main source of food, as well as land use income and employment to the rural areas. Improvements in agriculture are fundamental to achieving food security, poverty alleviation and overall sustainable development. African governments will have to accord very high priority to agriculture taking into account that the lives of people can be sustained and further developed only with good performance and enhancement of efficient agricultural sector. Achievement of the aspirations of Africa will remain a farfetched dream if the agricultural sector does not receive the high priority it deserves.

To enhance the agricultural sector, rural oriented companies will need to be encouraged to move in and make production move on smoothly. The companies should include those for production of rural activity demanded instruments and supply inputs such as fertilizers, seeds, farm equipment, and for processing. The issue here is that the processing could be weakened if agricultural sector failed to perform as well as other sectors. Let it be said again that rural agricultural sector development should never be taken for granted; it involves the process of creating circumstances for overall agricultural potential to be realized. Agriculture development will create the right circumstances for farming, so that crops may be planted, harvested, and processed efficiently thus reducing poverty and serving lives.

The implication is that agriculture should be modernized. Modernization is an important foundation of national modernization; it can also serve as power source for sustainability and the healthy development of the country. Agriculture is a fundamental input to further processing. As modernization progresses it will have to be ensured that there is a long period of stability, which is fundamental way to change the backwardness in rural areas and improve the farmers' and overall rural peoples' lives.

African agricultural development will not be sound without bringing in the issue of rural development, which tempts to bring up the issue of Green Revolution (GR). Green revolution is defined generally as a great transformational process leading to increase in production of food grains- such as rice, wheat, and maize due to the introduction of high yielding varieties, to use of proper pesticides and to better management techniques. The Green revolution has benefited most regions of the world, particularly East Asia and the Pacific, where cereal yields quadrupled between 1960s and 1990s. Africa missed out on this and thus, the continent has lacked progress in agricultural productivity, a situation, which has been blamed for holding back the continent's overall economic growth. In recent years the African Development Bank (ADB) under what it has called 'Transforming Africa's Agriculture to Improve Competitiveness' has came up with a number of recommendations or suggestions. The suggestions if seriously taken on board Africa's plans and strategies could take African agriculture to the type of revolution that has been witnessed in Southeast Asia. Some of the solutions prescribed by ADB together with other agricultural experts worldwide include but not limited to the following:

i) The urgent need to develop high-yield crops by way of increased research into plant breeding that will take into account the unique soil types of Africa. There is also the immediate need for increased use of fertilizers. The explanation is that soil fertility in most parts of Africa has kept deteriorating. Fertilizer use must increase, and governments should ensure the right types of fertilizer are made available to the farmers at the right price, and at the right time.

ii) Boosting Irrigation systems by way of taking into account the growing effects of climate change on weather patterns; and the need for putting more land in irrigation because average yields in irrigated farms are high- (almost 90% higher than those of nearby rain-fed farms). Related to this is the need to ensure that farmers are given the right incentives, including reductions in food subsidies, which could raise agricultural output by nearly 5%.

iii) Improving market access, regulations, and governance by taking into account that in improving rural infrastructure such as roads is crucial to raising productivity through reductions in shipping costs and the loss of perishable produce.

iv) Better use of information technology. This is seen as highly desirable because it will support better crops, fertilizer and pesticide selection. Through improved technology, improved land and water management, accessibility to weather information, and connection of farmers to sources of credit will become easy and possible.

v) Adopting genetically modified (GM) crops; which remains limited in Africa and whose resistance from overseas customers, particularly in Europe, has been a hindrance; but with Africa's rapid population growth, high-yield GM crops that are resistant to weather shocks provide an opportunity for Africa to address food insecurity.

vi) Taking urgent action on land ownership reform. The process should lead to productivity and inclusiveness taking into account that Africa has the highest area of arable uncultivated land in the world (202 million hectares) yet most farms occupy less than 2 hectares; which results from poor land governance and ownership.

vii) Stepping up the move to integration into Agricultural Value Chains (AVCs) taking into account the issues driven partly by the growth of international supermarket chains, the progressively diversified African economies from traditional cash crops into fruits, vegetables, fish, and flowers. Account will have to be taken of lack of access to finance and poor infrastructure, which have slowed progress and the call for government support to coordinate the integration of smallholder farmers into larger cooperatives and groups.

Agriculture in Africa cannot be taken for granted. Over 70% of the continent's population depends on agriculture. Rural development and agriculture are inseparable. Food production and food security is necessarily dependent on agriculture. So any development of African population will depend on how well agriculture is managed. No nation can boast to be safe and healthy if there is food insecurity, and if food supply for its population is not satisfactory. People may produce enough but proper storage will remain important. Issues related to off-season and occurrences of bad weather requirements, efficient storage, and hence food safety and security need to be given high priority; failure of which Africa will start losing its sense of direction.

4.TOURISM

Today, a lot of emphasis has been put on development and promotion of tourism in Africa. In the global economy tourism is one of the most noticeable and growing sectors. The sector has been playing an important role in boosting nations' economies. International tourist arrivals have almost quadrupled over the last three decades and domestic tourism has also intensified in industrialised countries. Africa has at its own slow-paced been following the footsteps of others in the world. In the meanwhile, tourism has become an important economic sector in terms of income generation, foreign exchange earnings and employment creation. In African countries tourism has the potential to bring positive economic outcomes especially in boosting Gross Domestic

Product (GDP) and employment opportunities. The main benefits of tourism are income creation and generation of jobs. The ability of national economies to benefit from tourism depends on the availability of investment to develop the necessary infrastructure, and its ability to supply the needs of tourists.

Tourism will bring much needed foreign money into African countries' economies. The presence of tourist business can generate income that can be ploughed to improved local conditions such as roads, communications, and access to modern conveniences. Sustainable tourism will lead to employment diversification on a local level, which will reduce the vulnerability of the people's poverty. The tourism industry in East Africa has been one of the largest earners of foreign exchange. Of course, countries like Egypt, Morocco, Algeria and South Africa have invested relatively more on tourist industry; such that the sector has kept serving as one of the best foreign exchange earners for those countries.

Efforts exerted on tourist sector development in Africa need to be increased, especially when we take into account that it is gradually growing to be the leading sector for economic development of Africa. Countries that have shown signs of success in tourism are those that have satisfactory infrastructure and facilities. Certainly, infrastructure alone may not be enough due to the fact that tourists are not uniform; they are of different forms with different interests. For instance, tourism factors that can attract tourists could include environment at destination. Tourism is in its best form when the destination boasts of attractive conditions in the area including conducive climate. That is to say impacts of climate change may affect tourism demand directly, interfering with the choice of destination and the period of the trip, or indirectly affecting the quality of the experience, adverse perception after some extreme event and insecurity about the destination. Tourism is a service, which needs to be provided in such a way that it meets the test of various customers; this also meaning that it is an industry whose success will depend a lot on what is offered, how and when.

There is a lot that will need to go into promoting a destination – and most of it will sometimes be behind the scenes. The issues could include but not limited to development of good database including Websites. If possible, every local and regional tourism office will have to be advised to have a website. Guides; Press releases; Blogs; Social Media; Large activations, and Commercials that ought to be updated Constantly.

However, the basic question still is what exactly do we mean by tourist destination? We can attempt to define a destination as a place that attracts visitors for a temporary stay, and range from continents to regions, to countries, to states and provinces, to cities, to villages and to purpose built or developed resort areas. That is an all-embracing definition. It makes us get tempted to say further that Africa is a continent that is so rich of natural attractive sites that are so unique their promotion will make the continent to propel itself forward quite fast. African villages and activities in them are themselves tourist attractions to the rest of the world. But there are also great sites that are very unique. They only need to be earmarked, marketed, and promoted to enhance tourism in Africa.

5. POPULATION AND HUMAN RESOURCES DEVELOPMENT:

i) Population

Population is defined as a group of individuals living and interbreeding within a certain area, in this case the African continent. Every population pyramid is unique. Most can be categorized into three prototypical shapes: expansive (young and growing), constrictive (elderly and shrinking) and stationary (little or no population growth). Population can be a problem due to a number of factors. For instance, there can be unsustainable population growth and lack of access to productive health care. Those can put pressure on human communities, exacerbating food and water shortages, reducing resilience in the face of climate changes; and making it harder for most vulnerable communities to rise out of intergenerational poverty.

Population has many characteristics which could include the population size and density. Total size is generally expressed in the number of individuals in a population. There is also the issue of population age structure, natality (birthrates), and mortality rates (death rates). However, the factors that affect population size could include the birthrates and /or deathrates, immigrations, and emigrations. It is good also to say fast growth of population is not always bad. For instance, more people means more labour force, and wider markets. But population explosion can be very detrimental to development. It can prove difficult to feed the population and this can be worse at the low-income family level. Big families can be a big load to poor families in terms of their ability to provide basic needs such as education, health care, food, clothing's, and good shelter. So, family and even national policies should be cautious about decisions on the sizes of populations that are desirable.

However, population growth can be controlled. To do so a number of measures will need to be taken. The measures would include provision of education; especially to the people n the reproductive age that could be educated about the need for family planning. Deliberate national policy and legal provisions could also be taken to raise allowable marriage age; and there could also be introduced social or family incentives to people who decide to have small families.

A lot has been said above, but it has not been stated precisely why population development is considered to be of high priority. However, population is very important for a country's development because no country has ever reached high- income levels without enough population. Population growth increases density. A growing population will lead to an increase in total output. The sheer arithmetical increase in population impacts on output and productivity quite favourably. Low population growth in high-income countries is likely to create social and economic problems because production output may not reach its highest points because of shortage of labour. The results could be different where there is high population growth in low-income countries due to the fact that the economy cannot cope or even support the high growth. What all this means is that efforts in balancing the equation will have to be given a lot of emphasis. As the population increases the economy will benefit a lot from a bigger talent pool, economies of scale and greater specialization. Consequentially the country benefits from higher per capita incomes, which we have seen in major developed economies.

ii) Human Resources Development

Development is not possible without an adequate and desirable labour force. Labour is required in all productive and service sectors. However, labour could be divided into two major categories namely the skilled and the unskilled labour. Some skilled labour could be got through experience at the place of work, but what that method of skill acquisition cannot achieve are skill on new and more efficient ways of doing things. The fact that keeping the worker on doing the routine work on a specific task for years does not allow him/her to acquire new skills and hence not much in terms of increased productivity is realized. Workers are a great tool in enhancing production and the ultimate development. They need to be trained and re-trained. There is the on-the-job training, as well the formal training where a worker is given leave from work for a specified time to go and get involved in learning to acquire new skills. Human resources development is very important because it is an investment in employees that will ultimately result in a stronger and more effective workforce. Development of employees will strengthen assets and make employees even more valuable. A country which has technologically skilled and experienced employees has shown to have the potential to develop much faster than that without such important human resource.

iii) Urban Population:

All our efforts to plan are supposed to aim at enhancing the lives and welfare of the people. The Population is a factor that will have to call for a lot of attention in Africa. Urban population growth in particular is an issue that needs a special mention. African Cities have been growing at different rates, such that some have had very big populations while others have had relatively fewer people. The rate of growth has also varied from place to place within a country and from country to country, allowing the smaller ones to overtake the bigger ones and vice versa. Until 2010 the cities with the largest population in Africa included Lagos, Kinshasa, Cairo, and Nairobi. Today smaller cities have grown much faster. For instance, Dar es Salaam which was among the smallest some twenty years ago is today among the seven largest cities in Africa. African countries with the largest urban population as of 2021 are in the following order: Lagos (21million); Cairo (20.4 million); Kinshasa (13.3 million), Luanda (6.5 million), Johannesburg (5.6 million), Alexandria (5.3 million), Dar es Salaam (4.5 million), Nairobi 4.4 million), and Casablanca (3.7 million).

The trouble is that many of the mega cities in Africa have increased rapidly due to rural urban migration, which will continue to expand the number of megacities by 2030. Taking into account that urban area in Africa are generally plagued by environmental deterioration, inadequate housing, traffic congestion, social alienation slums, crime and homelessness, means that African countries have to take bold actions as soon as possible. Something will have to be done sooner rather than later, to avoid critical situations that seem to be on the offing often associated with the proliferation of cities. In other words, expansion of urban areas that are not matched with basic utility supply could lead to heightened inequality, less absolute poverty but poor housing manifested in the proliferation of slums, more traffic congestion and the absence of public transport, poorer environment conditions and run-down water and sewerage systems.

6. SCIENCE, TECHNOLOGY, AND ICT:

Necessarily Africa will have to embrace Science and Technology. That is necessary if it really wishes to catch up with the rest of the world, swiftly enough. Science capabilities along with development of merit-based processes, and institutions, are essential to the successful use of science, technology and innovation in Africa, and are fundamental to sound policy making, good governance and industrial development. The essence of how science and technology contributes to society is the creation of knew knowledge to boost the prosperity of human lives and to solve the various issues facing society.

At this juncture we come to the question, what is Information and communications technologies (ICT). In brief ICT incorporates electronic technologies and techniques used to manage information and knowledge, including information handling tools used to produce, store, process, and retrieve information. ICT plays a significant role in all aspects of modern society. ICT has helped to channel the way we communicate with each other, how we find needed information, work, conduct business, interact with government agencies, and how we manage social lives. ICT enables economic growth by broadening the reach of technologies such as highspeed internet, mobile broadband, and computing. Expanding these technologies itself creates growth, and the fact that technologies make it easier for people to interact and make workers more productive, creates more benefits.

The role of ICT in government is very great and significant. The advantages of the use of ICT could just be listed to include enhancing modes of communications and bringing about cost efficiencies in all productive or development activities. Application of ICT is paperless-it eliminates the large usage of paper and for teachers and students it serves as a better teaching and learning method. ICT is a good method for enhancement of data and information security, and what is more, it minimizes cost and serves a lot of time. ICT also brings automatic solutions to manual paper-based processes and procedures.

7. NATURAL RESOURCES EXPLOITATION:

Colonial nations exploited the natural resources of Africa for the benefit of their home countries and economies. In other words,

Africa gained nothing from the natural resources that were being exploited, which left Africa worse enlists. However, Africa is still well endowed with natural resources that if properly exploited they will take this continent further and faster than otherwise.

The natural resources included land that was used to produce agricultural products that were needed in Europe. Africa is rich in natural resources such as diamond, gold, salt, iron, cobalt, uranium, copper bauxite, silver, sugar, cocoa beans, tropical timber, tropical fruit, coal, tin and many others. Proved Petroleum reserves have been found has been found in quite a number of countries including, Libya, Nigeria, Algeria, Angola, and South Sudan, Egypt, Congo Brazzaville, Uganda, Gabon, Equatorial Guinea and Ghana. Libya is the richest country in oil deposits in Africa, accumulating 48.4 billion barrels of proved reserves. Other countries with proved reserves in billion barrels in bracket are as follows: Nigeria (37 billion barrels); Algeria(12.2 billion), Angola(7.8 billion), South Sudan(5 billion barrels),Egypt3.3 billion barrels), Congo Brazzaville (2.9billion barrels),Uganda(2.5 billion barrels), Gabon(2 billion barrels), Chad (1.5 billion barrels), Equatorial Guinea (1.1billionbarrels) and Ghana (0.7 billion barrels).

Related to oil reserves, Africa is also well endowed with natural gas deposits. We could begin by stating that almost half of Africa's 55 countries are known to have proven natural gas reserves, amounting to a total of more than800 trillion cubic feet. It is further estimated that the production of natural gas in Africa is likely to expand by 80% by the year 2035, which will contribute a great deal to a rise in Gross Domestic Product (GDP). Like we have asserted, almost 50% of the African countries have shown indications of having some natural gas deposits, which like oil can raise the economy of Africa to another level of developments. However the top ten most gas rich countries in Africa could be listed as follows: Nigeria has a proven gas deposits of 206.53 Trillion Cubic-feet. Others with Trillion cubic feet in bracket are Algeria (159.1), Senegal (120), Mozambique (100), Egypt (77.2), Tanzania (57.54), Libya (53.1), Angola (13.5), Congo (10.5), Equatorial Guinea (5), Cameroon (4.8) and Sudan (3).

Besides oils and gas deposits Africa is also very rich I minerals such as asbestos, antimony, chromium, bauxite, copper, cobalt, manganese, nickel, gold, lead, phosphate, platinum, palladium, titanium uranium, tin, iron, silver, tin and many more. Some minerals are more abundant in some countries than in others. Africa's two most profitable mineral resources are gold and diamond. Between the year 2007 and 2009 Africa produced close to 500 tons of gold annually which was a little more than 22% of the world's total production in South Africa accounts for almost 50 of Africa's gold production. Other big producers of gold in Africa are Ghana, Guinea, Mali, and Tanzania.

8.SAFETY AND SECURITY:

Safety and security are factors that should be given the importance they deserve in order to ensure that African countries acquire sustainable development. Safety and security have many facets. People need security in food supplies. Lack of food security will make the population scared and threatened especially during times of droughts, which lead to famine. A well-organized country with a good foresight will ensure that there is food security to sustain people's lives at all times.

Safety and security is also noticeable when a country is not assured of good defense against external threats. This explains why, besides having plans for economic development, issues of military defense against external as well as internal threats need to be given a lot of importance. A country which is unsafe from external threats, makes its citizens to remain unsafe. We could take the case of countries that have their people running for safety to neighbouring countries due to unassured safety in their own countries. The people stay away as refugees for unspecified periods. Production and per capita GDP do not grow because the citizens do not contribute to production because they are away as refugees.

Then there is the issue of safety and security of people's health. African countries have a role to establish hospitals at all levels of the community to ensure that their people are safe and healthy. African governments have been referring people with complicated diseases to places abroad. The treatments abroad are usually very expensive due to added transport costs and the need for payment in foreign exchange. That has made the majority of those who need to be treated abroad to be limited to only a few who have linkage with officials in government offices that grant those permissions. Health and education are areas that have to have good security measures. In the rural areas the situation could be worse due to absence of health facilities in remote places, where access roads are absent, thus creating great limitations to service provision even to mobile health deliveries. In rural dispensaries or health centres that can possibly be accessed there are no enough basic drugs and the medical personnel are not available or if they are, they lack incentives to perform their work efficiently.

Besides problems facing health service deliveries in the remote rural areas there are critical shortage of basic education facilities. Day schools can be closed for long periods during rainy seasons, (in some instances for the whole rainy season) due to the fact that children cannot get to school due to flooding rivers, or due to a washed away bridge or excessively slippery roads or other limiting factors. Some schools have dilapidated school buildings and in many cases children get crowded in one classroom due to over enrollments, making it impossible for teachers to fail to teach as expected. Cases have been seen of places in remote rural areas, where children have to get crowded under a tree, which serves as a classroom. In brief what is being underlined here is that African countries have an urgent duty to reorganize their priorities so that pressing issue such as these of health and education in the rural areas, where over 50% of the population lives, can be given deserving attention.

African countries have also seen the impact of terrorist elements in their countries or in countries that get invaded by terrorists. Countries with well- prepared security services have a chance of repulsing the terrorist elements. Those without enough preparedness have had many of their people and property destroyed, which deters development. Africa countries have a pressing need to prepare to move to the next level of development, meaning that they must do more in the area of safety and security.

9. YOUTH, WOMEN, ORPHANS AND THE AGED

i) The African Youth:

Almost 70%of the population of Africa is youth under the age of 30 years; and that over 40% of that youth is under the age of 15. Actually 20% of the youth in Africa are between the ages of 15 and 24. Such astoundingly high numbers could be an opportunity for the continent's growth and development. The disturbing thing is that the African youth is faced with a host of problems, which make their existence to look as a huge problem rather than an opportunity for Africa's development. The problems include unemployment, lack of information, (as information is power and lack of it is great weakness). Not only that, the number of African youth is growing in an environment of no bright future for it.

However, the two problems that have been listed are only among many others. The other problems can just be listed to include poor educational systems, lack of time management culture, involvement in drugs and substance abuses, crime, social media peer pressure, and wide spread females genital mutilations. The poor educational system and crime could further be elaborated on due to their unique nature. For instance, in the last two decades a lot of enrollment has been done for pupils in primary and secondary schools in Africa. That means dropout from the formal educational system has also been increasing. That has been so for those who complete primary schools, secondary schools and even collages and universities. Considering that the educational system that is there prepares a child only to know how to read and write and/or to finish the level of education he/she is, without any knowledge how to use it to further their future. Completing school has meant adding more educated to the ever-expanding army of unemployed population. Regarding crime, lack of employment at various levels has led to creating youth that is geared to seeking alternatives to enhancing their lives, thus falling into the trap of various types of crimes.

The crisis of the poor educational system in Africa is widespread. We can take the case that was undertaken in East Africa in 2018 as our basis for argument on this subject. The findings were that the East African region is experiencing a crisis in school learning. Despite the impressive and sustained improvement in enrolment that has been going on, it remains unclear how much students are actually leaning in the classrooms. The 2018 investigative evaluation done jointly and drawing experts from Ethiopia, Kenya, Tanzania and Uganda it came out clearly that, the crisis in learning is multidimensional and extends from primary level to post secondary school education. The experts noted that for a long time there have been problems of teacher absenteeism in schools, poor parental involvement in their children's conduct, outdated exam methods, and high- siloed disciplinary teaching. It was further noted that East African countries have been placing science, technology and knowledge economy at the centre of their development agendas; while the persistent challenges are hardly been addressed. The quality of graduates existing from the post - secondary programmes depend to a large degree on the type and quality of education they receive at the lower levels.

In conclusion, if primary and secondary education does not inculcate a genuine curiosity and love of learning in students, then the higher education system is unlikely to successfully produce the caliber of graduates necessary to engage in competitive global knowledge economy.

The number of Africa's youth is rising exponentially, but many African school qualifiers and University graduates are failing to find good jobs. African countries have been investing in vocational training across education institutions and industry. In that case there is expected immediate benefit that more apprenticeship could provide for young people and employers. In any case what needs to be filled to the brim in Africa is the workshop of the world with knowledgeable and highly skilled workforce that is able to propel the continent into the forth and fifth- industrial revolution.

Africa has started to plunge into the Forth industrial revolution. Just to save as a reminder, the fourth industrial revolution (4.0) is already here with us. By definition forth industrial revolution 4.0, is a way of describing the blurring of boundaries between the physical, digital, and biological worlds. It is the exponential growth of digital technologies, and the resulting impact on economic, political, and cultural systems. The technologies will in the future include artificial intelligence, robots, autonomous vehicles, nanotechnology, biotechnology, materials science, energy storage and quantum computing. That is where the world is heading to, and the African youth must be enabled to cope. Current education curriculum needs to be almost completely overhauled to enable the youth cope with what is now driving world development. The Africa youth must be groomed under education that will enable the youth to lead the way to economic growth and development. That will never be achieved under the current traditional educational systems that were designed for the First, Second and Third industrial revolution knowledge and technological needs.

Once again, the 4th industrial revolution is a fusion of advances in artificial intelligence (AI), robotics and other technologies. Fourth industrial revolution will change the way we live, work, and communicate. The 4.0 will reshape government, education, health, commerce and almost every aspect of life. Forth revolution could also change the things we value right now and bring new and more valuable ones. In the future technology will lead to a supply side miracle, with long term gains in efficiency and productivity; transportation and communication costs will drop, logistics and global supply chains will become more effective, and cost of trade will open new markets and drive economic growth. Africa partly saw the second and third industrial revolution, though it never became an effective participant due to impact of colonialisation and neo-colonialization. As we find ways of plunging fully into the 4.0 industrial revolution we ought to be mindful of the fact that the industrialized nations are already in the 5.0 industrial revolution, which means that Africa should also double up to struggle and jump into the band wagon.

ii) Women:

Generalists have defined African women as those who are from the continent of Africa. We can add that African women are those who are born, live and are from the continent of Africa. The culture, evolution and history of African women is related to the history of the African continent itself. However African women have been subjected to a host of challenges, which are related to economic exclusion and to financial systems that have been perpetuating women discrimination. African women find themselves subjected to limited participation in political and public life and lack of access to education. Other problems or challenges include those that are related to poor retention of girls in schools; subjection of women to gender posed violences; existence of harmful cultural practices and exclusion of women in peace negotiation processes. Depending on which African community the women hail from they generally suffer the lack of freedom of movement; that being in addition to intersectional feminism, gender inequality in decision making or in the distribution of income, sexual violence and harassment and workplace discrimination.

We wish to underline the issue of social and economic exclusion, which are alternatively called deprivation, and which are widely recognized as symptoms human poverty. All these have disabled effective use and allocation of resources, which constitute a significant hindrance for economic development of African countries. Issue of harmful cultural practices could include female genital mutilations, forced feeding of women, forced and early marriages, and various taboos and practices, which prevent women from controlling their own fertility, nutritional taboos, and traditional birth practices. In many African societies there are also problems related to 'son' preferences and their implications for the status of girls in the family. Harmful traditional practices are widespread and have made victims of the practices to suffer sexual and reproductive health consequences, including painful sex, forced and unwanted pregnancies, unsafe abortions, traumatic fistula, sexually transmitted infections such as HIVV/AIDS, and certainly countless deaths.

African women can be categorized in two groups, namely those who live in the urban areas, most of who have had some level of literacy and have been privileged to live some better life in homes accessed with utilities such as piped water, electricity, communication facilities such as roads, and communication gadgets such as telephone handsets. The other category is that of rural women, who happen to be the majority (almost 60%). They are generally poor, subsisting on what they can produce on the land. Many of the African rural women cannot read and/or write and the many of them are in the age group of above 35 years; owed to the fact that most of the younger ones have migrated to urban where apparently life is thought to be softer.

Like everywhere else African rural women must work extra hard to survive. They have to do with poor farming equipment. The situation is made more complex by the fact that most of the food consumed in the rural society is produced by rural African women. The further limiting factor is that women have no access to mechanized farming equipment. Other immediate challenges and issues that rural women face concern physical and mental health. There are also challenges related to education, improper health facilities, gender discrimination, and gender imbalance in the distribution of opportunities. Rural African women are further faced with problems of poor housing, significant fuel unavailability, poverty- an issue which has been threatening the wellbeing and sustainability of rural communities. Rural poverty is often a product of poor infrastructure that hinders mobility and development. There are no good roads that would increase access to agricultural inputs and markets. That has made the rural woman to be cut off from technological development and emerging markets in the ever-expanding urban areas. In summary the challenges facing women, especially the rural African women need a lot of attention now rather than later.

iii) Aged Population

Elderly people thank God that they have had the chance to grow to reach old age. To them, getting old is not a problem; but problems start to crop up when they find that their energies are starting to fail them and there is no readily available helping hand. Unlike in the developed countries, African nations are in general not best equipped to deal with the rise in numbers of older people. The most chronic problem that faces aged people in Africa include the absence of good nutrition and health care. Diseases that very commonly threaten the lives of the old people include arthritis, hypertension, hearing impairment, defective vision, diabetes, and varicose veins that tend to increase with age. The varicose veins are among the usual diseases that tend to occur more in women and tend to increase with age. The most critical problem is the low prioritization African governments accord to needs of aged people. African governments spend less on health care (especially on aged people) than most developed countries. For instance in 2005 48 of the 54 African countries spent an average of less than US $ 20 per capita in health care. Specifically Sub-Saharan countries spent 6.1 %

of its total GDP on health, far less than the 9.5 % of the GDP that the OECD countries spent on health.

In many instances people in Africa have to directly pay doctors and hospital bills- and that is for those who can afford to pay such bills (as over 75% of the people cannot do so). Such medical bills have posed many problems because even for the few ones such money has been difficult to find. The problem is compounded by the deterioration in traditional patterns of family support in Africa due mainly to urbanization and in some cases- the effects of HIV/AIDS. The HIV/AIDS pandemic became most marked from 1980s to the end of the first decade of the new millennium. In this period the medication for minimizing the intensity and impact of the disease had not been found. Many elderly persons, for a long time, found forced and/or burdened with childcare because of the HIV/AIDS related deaths of parents. More than 50% of orphans in Africa, especially in the years between 1980s and 2015 lived with their grandparents many on very limited and highly uncertain incomes. The health-care problem has been exacerbated by the long- term economic conditions associated with growing old such as heart diseases, cancer, respiratory disorders (including the COVID19), dementia, diabetes, blood pressure, and kidney disorders. These diseases are common throughout the world, but they have kept increasing faster in Africa where the system is less capable of dealing with them.

Many elderly people in Africa have as a rule a very small pension to rely on upon. The situation is worse in the rural areas where people are generally self-employed earning hardly enough to sustain their daily life. Actually, the problem of the aged population has been growing, thus exerting a lot more pressure on how to solve the general problem of unemployment to the youth, thus sidelining the crucial role of paying attention to the aged population. The situation is worsened by the fact that the youth is more vocal and visible than the elderly, and also because, governments find forced to pay more attention to the youth, largely due to the fear of social and political unrest that they can cause.

Solutions to problems facing the aged are not yet in sight in Africa. However, in some countries such as South Africa older persons receive free public primary healthcare and the beneficiaries who receive social assistance from the state in form of state pensions also receive free access to secondary and tertiary care. The start with other countries could borrow from South Africa and others who have started to move in that direction. Elderly people are always threatened by a variety of other problems, which increase as the age increases. So governments need to take more active move to minimize the problems of old age. The elderly are people who have done their duty of building their nations and thus they deserved to be handled better than now.

iv. Orphans:

With approximately 140 million orphans in the world in 2018/19, Africa was estimated to have about 52 million, which makes up more than 30% of them all. One of the major causes of children being orphaned is the HIV/AIDS epidemic. A child becomes an orphan when one or both parents die of the virus. The child may or may not have contracted the virus. In 2008 about 430,000 children got infected with HIV/AIDS virus. As of 2015 there was an estimate of 3.5 million orphans in South Africa alone. The South African statistics revealed that during the same period 812,000 and orphans had lost both parents; 2,13 of them had lost their fathers and 611,000 had lost their mothers.

However, in DRC there has been a high i.e. level of death rates. For instance, in year 2020 the death rate was at about 9.5 per thousand people and that was after it had fallen from 21 per thousand people in 1980s. Democratic Republic of Congo (DRC) was recently found to have approximately 5 million orphans, of which about 350,000 children had been orphaned due to HIV/AIDS alone.

General information in Angola has shown that there were a little over 1.5 million orphans and over 140,000 of those had been orphaned by HIV/AIDS. Angola has a very high mortality rate because of reasons such as malnutrition, which is actually widespread in that country, and is the main cause of deaths of small children. The other cause is the lack of enough drinkable water for the population of Angola, which has been a major cause of diseases such as diarrhea. The disease has been at the major contributor to the high mortality rates in that country. Despite great and exemplary economic performance of Angola (owing to production and export of oil) but observation in recent years continue to show that the life expectancy in Angola is still relatively low. The reasons for Angola's low life expectancy rate are complex and include a variety of factors such as widespread poverty, civil violence, food shortages, political unrest, and lack of enough medical services. Poverty is very widespread, especially in the rural areas.

Looking at Somalia we notice that it is a country with relatively small population. In 2020 the population was about 16 million. However, that country has an estimated number of 700,000 orphans with infant mortality rate of 146 infants per 1,000. Most of the deaths of children in Somalia are attributed to malnutrition, lack of safe drinking water, lack of proper sanitation, and absence of proper healthcare services in the country. Common diseases that cause deaths to children include Pneumonia, diarrhea, polio, measles, and neonatal disorders. These are the main contributors of the very high child mortality rates in Somalia.

The last place we wish to review briefly is South Sudan. South Sudan is a very young state, which makes it difficult to have very accurate estimate of its orphan population. However, both Sudan and South Sudan taken together are home for around 2 million orphans. The vast majority of them have been orphaned due to extreme poverty, ethnic conflicts, and HIV/AIDS. Not only that, over 82% of people in South Sudan are poor. We end this discussion on South Sudan by observing that thousands of children were separated from their parents by the war that was fought between North and South Sudan for many years. Actually, South Sudan fought the war for a period of not less than 22 years, leaving the country completely devastated.

We end the discussion in this section by observing that the examples that have been given above are enough to show how critical the state of orphans is in Africa today is. Actually, there are many orphans in all African countries. Some of the countries have started to take matters related to orphans in their plans and budgets, but in general the issue remains unattended to. Poverty, political unrest, civil wars, diseases, and pandemics have been the leading producers of orphans in the continent of Africa. The future of this continent will be very miserable if this issue is not taken with the seriousness it deserves by all African nations. The magnitude of the problem does not need to be found far from us. For those of us who live in major urban centres of Africa can witness swarms of young boys and girls loitering the streets begging. Many of these have had no parental care and no reliable source of their subsistence. Most such children are orphans with no future ahead of them. We should start imagining what type of Africa is being built under those circumstances. In brief time has come to have orphans and other needy children in our national policies, plans and budgets.

10 Constitutional Reforms

Most African countries still retain constitutions that were inherited from the colonial times, which were made to suit colonial interests including the management of colonial structures, the executive, legislature and judiciary. In the post independence times some minor constitutional amendments were made just to suit the interests of the new African regimes most of which did not really have much interest to bring true freedom to their citizens. This explains why it was easy for such autocratic governments to flourish and remain in power for as long as they wished. Most post-independence governments were autocratic, corrupt and hang on in power for undefined periods of time. The leaders ruled their citizens with high level of impunity. There are many examples of countries throughout the continent which never allowed political change since when they gained political independence some six decades ago. We can take a very simple example of countries like Tanzania, which forced its ruling party, CCM to keep on in power for 60 years since 1960. That is only an example; as there many such governments or countries, that have kept making some constitutional amendments that never made no impact in enabling people to have a say in serious matters that affected their daily lives. The changes that such governments have made to their constitutions have been geared to assisting those in power to rule without seeking for alternative ideas that could give more freedom to citizens.

To deal with this constitutional issues in a more appropriate manner, we first of all need to understand what constitutional reform means, especially for African countries. In brief, constitutional reform means the introduction of legislation to modify the rules and practices that determine the composition and functions of the organs of central as well as local governments in a state. There are many examples of constitutional changes some of which could include amendments to the existing constitution to make it take on board desired needs of reform in policies, political directions, operational procedures, and so on. Not all such changes are necessarily good for the nation and citizens, as some of them could be aimed to make the dictatorial regimes grow more muscles that can further suppress the citizens. Here is where a lot of care is needed for the people to know in precise terms what is intended to be achieved in constitutional reforms. The required reforms must be those that bring people to higher levels of democracy. Although any change in a constitution can be labeled "reform" the broad term "constitutional reform" is usually reserved for proposed amendments that will alter in some fundamental way the structure of government established by a nation's charter i.e. the organization of legislative, executive and judiciary.

There are various ways African countries can amend their constitutions, each according to the wishes and aspirations of their nations' citizens. This should nevertheless never preclude those aspirations outlined as pillars of the Africa's vision 2063.The possibilities for amending a constitution should aim at helping to ensure that certain weaknesses that are in the current constitutions- e.g., too much power vested in the head of state or lack of clauses that support democratic and inclusive processes, or issues that will lead to changes to strengthen people's participation in decision making. For instance, for over two decades i.e. since the closing of

1990s consensus has emerged and international organizations, governments, and civil society in Africa have agreed on the vital role that governance plays in economic and social development.

Democracy and good governance cannot flourish where the constitution is not designed to take citizens wishes on board. A constitution should be able to bringing accountability, transparency, participation and predictability and inclusiveness. Those ingredients will help to increase government efficiency and impact. Constitutional reform can serve as a vital tool to promote governance, by changing the rules to promote more accountability, transparency, participation, and predictability. A good constitution will define and protect people's rights from governmental abuse, it will limit and balance government power vis a vis other players and institutions. In that way it will safeguard minority rights. Properly constructed, a constitution is a touchstone for the legality of all other laws and will serve as a basis for reviewing executive and legislative actions.

If Africa wishes to build a strong basis for political, legal, and socio-economic development thus avoiding to build on the feeble democratic governance gains that have been achieved. The need is to design and adopt new democratic, down-to-earth constitutions. Most African countries need reformed constitutions. In countries such as South Africa, which has emerged from very suppressive racial government system, ultimately the oppressor and the oppressed in the new democracy are in agreement to live together as equals. In such situation the possibility and need of amending the constitution of such a country became necessary, because that action will certainly help to ensure that sustained harmony and development of all citizens is maintained. In order to build a nation that is founded in deep roots of democracy, equality, and equity we need a constitution that addresses the desired freedoms of the people.. A good democratic nation should be that which seeks for human dignity; equality and advancement of human rights and freedoms; with no-existence of racialism or sexism. Supremacy of the constitution and rule of law are values to be realized from sovereign and democratic state that has a down to earth people's interests and needs.

The norm in the western world is a liberal constitution that limits the power of the executive, that protects the human rights of all citizens, that provides for choosing leaders through free and fair elections and that is harder to change than ordinary laws. A constitution is a legal document that sets on the basic principles about the way a national state is ruled and governed. The political aspects of a constitution relate to the governance system, citizenship, election process, the provision and separation of power between the executive, the legislation and the judiciary, and the relation between central government and local and provincial (regional) state entities. While the social dimension would be related to the values within the state, the legal dimension on the other hand relates to the legislative process, the protection of human rights, and of citizens, independence of judiciary, and the way the constitution can be changed .

For African constitutional process to be well understood it may be necessary to know where African countries have come from and where they are at the moment. The fundamental tenets of the modern constitution are basically and theoretically that nobody regardless of his status is above the law. But like we have already put it, African countries and especially those with authoritarian leaders have been amending constitutions to keep themselves above the law.

However, constitutional reforms in Africa have come a long way. The constitution making in the continent could be traced in three phases. The first phase stated with independence in 1960s lasting to end of 1070s. The process in this phase was typically led by the colonial powers. The constitution that was built at that stage was part of the decolonialization process, but the thinking that went into them was basically colonial. The independence constitutions were as has been mentioned colonial legislations, which constituted the independent state.

The second phase of institution making in Africa was from 1980s to end of 1990s. During this phase constitution amendments were made to the independence constitutions, designed to concentrate power in the presidency. This became the birth period to authoritarian governments in the continent. Authorities managed their countries as their personal property, and citizens remained in the observer positions while the authorities managed the way they considered fit. This situation culminated into one party state systems of governance in Africa.

The third phase, which ran from the end of 1990s to second decade of the new Millennium, has got associated with the going global wave of democratization. During this phase, constitution making in Africa centred on the philosophy of rebuilding the political community as well as structures that had been distorted by political manipulations and violence during the era of authoritarian rule. However, in spite of the new awakening leaders still keep playing a lot of delaying tactics to enable them keep hanging on in power for as long as possible. They do so, while quite aware that they are doing wrong; but the fact that the un-reviewed constitution have provisions that allow them to do so, they use that weakness to keep pulling reform processes backward.

The third phase is further marked by promotion of participation of citizens in the affairs of their own countries and the accountability of governments. All the way, what has been needed in the constitution reviews is often that the constitution review process should entail the democratization needs, inclusiveness and peaceful settlement of conflicts. These are seen as a vehicle for national dialogue, good governance, and consolidation of peace.

All African countries have written constitutions, but they lack a culture of constitutionalism. African leaders love to lead and manage their nations the way they wished not the way they are guided by their constitutions. Things become worse when the African leaders decide to change the constitutions of their countries to suit their ulteriour motives of achieving personal gains. Many of them like to see constitutions changed to meet their evil desires such as holding on in power, getting justification to misuse their offices, corruption, and many other misdeeds. The citizens of Africa should take a lot of care when election periods come, and the people have to vote to get the leaders they want.

25

GOVERNANCE ISSUES IN AFRICA

In this chapter we are going to raise issues specifically related to governance challenges in Africa. It may be a bit difficult to understand how governance should be associated with future development of the continent. However, by now the reader will recollect what was said in the early chapters about what the leaders that took over from colonialists got involved in plundering the continent while crowning themselves as kings and other types of monarchies. Today, when there is drought, people must end up without water to drink, or without food, or with land to graze their cows. In the rural areas people have kept doing without electricity, reliable rural roads and without medicine. In the urban areas the slums that were left behind by colonialists are still there and are on the increase due to rising migrations to cities. Africa has a lot of land, but land cases keep increasing. Deforestation has reached unprecedented levels but look at who has been responsible for the plundering that has been going- you will find that that is done by people in leadership in their pursuit to get rich quickly. Workers in industries, in mining sector, and in all others are required to work harder every passing day but only people in leadership know why a wage for a countryman has remained without being raised for decades. While elsewhere, especially in keen societies people's welfare are taken with high level of importance, but not so much in Africa? We think only Africans and their leaders are supposed to answer those questions. That is the continent we wish to transform with a view of getting to our greatest tomorrow. The problem for all the listed problems and many more rests on the governance factor.

On the outset there is need to start by emphasizing that Africa is not poor, but its people are still very poor; and this is largely owed in one way or another to poor governance. Many of our leaders have failed as far as governance is concerned. Because of their failure in governance, they use extraordinary force to stay in power not to bring better life to their people, but to lavishly amass wealth for themselves and their families.

Africa has been independent for the last 60 plus years, but very little dent has been made to improve people's lives. The challenges arise from a number of factors including non-availability of information to the people, lack of accountability, poor management of the public sector and lack of appropriate legal frameworks to manage the other sectors. For instance, an informed citizenry is a prerequisite to maintaining the social contact between the established government and those governed by it. The people constitute nations, states, or localities. They require unimpeded access to information to continually assess and evaluate their requirements. There is also the issue of accountability, which in terms of ethics and governance, is equated with answerability, blameworthiness, liability, and the expectation of account-giving. In this aspect of governance, accountability is central to discussions or issues related to problems in the public sector, nonprofit and private and individual contexts; and in cases when it works well benefits everyone. It enables people to know how the government is doing, and how to gain redress when things go wrong. There is also the management of financial affairs and resources, which is usually the responsibility of the executive.

Weak governance is a driver of disaster risk and is linked to many other risk drivers such as poverty and inequality, poor planned urban development, and globalized economic development. There is the issue of an appropriate legal framework. In short, a good rule of law maintains good governance. As one of the characteristics of good governance, rule of law plays a pivoting role. Rule of law will provide legitimacy and authority to government; and that, the rules and regulations provide the framework for action and decision-making process.

Taking simple example of situation in East Africa e.g., Tanzania, Uganda, Sudan, and South Sudan, as well as Burundi and DRC during 2015 to 2022 period, improvement of governance was greatly constrained by an increasingly powerful executive branch, leading to closing civic space, violations of human rights, suppression of political competition and that of a still emerging civil society, low public accountability, and barriers to accessing information. Many other countries in West and Southern Africa found themselves in almost the same category. There was a general decline of level of good governance in the African continent as a whole and in the East and Southern African regions in particular. To cite only a couple of examples, Kenya got faced with a number of governance challenges including corruption at various levels, too much centralization of power and authority, criminalization of politics, cross violations of human rights and weak legislators with criminal records. The same happened in most of the other east, central, and southern African countries.

In the period between 2019 and 2021 the Ibrahim index of overall governance ranked Ethiopia as 31st out of 54 countries in Africa. That was not a good position at all. In balance between the four areas contributing to the index included safety and rule of law, participation and Human Rights, sustainable economic opportunity and Human Development. Uganda too kept performing rather badly when it came to issues of good governance. Tanzania was among the worst especially during 2015 to 2020 under the leadership of dictator John Magufuli. Regarding the state of governance in Sudan the situation has been very unsatisfactory for the last decade since 2010. For instance, following **a deadly civil war** and **genocide in Darfur, Sudan** was widely recognized as a **totalitarian state,** where all effective political power was held by President **Omar al-Bashir** and his **National Congress Party (NCP).** For a long time, Sudan has faced critical problems related to almost total absence of rule of law that has led to a very totalitarian government.

Regarding South Sudan that country is one of the world's most divided and unstable countries. Since achieving statehood in 2011, the country has plunged into civil war (2013-15) and become the scene of some of the worst human rights abuses on the African continent. Despite ongoing political turmoil, states and international institutions have pledged enormous resources to stabilize the country and shore up the current peace process but have had limited influence in dealing with the effects of rampant corruption and factionalism.

The most salient issues are those of lack of governance and have included suppression of people's voice and weak accountability; governing bodies refusing to listen to the voices of those they govern and also refusing to take accountability for their actions. Those have led to very bad governance record.

Like we said earlier, the governance problem is widespread and needs to be addressed sooner rather than later. But before we proceed there is a need now to define what governance really means. In simple terms it means the process of decision making and implementation in collective problems situation. Governance emphasizes not just routine implementation of policies and programmes but making the entire activity accountable. Governance is supposed to be democratic, participative, and responsive to people's needs. It further involves opening up of the arena of government to multiple actors, mobilizing the collective effort of government, civil society, private sector, and community.

There are many reasons why good governance should be fully exercised by governments, civil societies and even by companies and individuals in Africa. In short governance should aims to meet objectives such as: improvements in delivery of essential services to the citizens; empowerment of people through dissemination of information; transparency in government business and transactions; elimination of undesirable practices such as touts, speed money, deliberate delays, harassment, bogus documentation and of course corruption. Other objectives for good governance would include maintenance of broad based public awareness and participation in key areas of developmental effort; control over assets, revenues and expenditures; maintenance of better information base for decision making process; enhancement of productivity; efficiency of administrative functions; making the administration responsively friendly to citizens and ensuring accountability; establishing legitimacy and creditability of a government agency or department and safe-guarding interests of citizens in general.

The governance challenges facing Africa generally include dismal state of press freedom over the past decades especially between 1995 and 2021. During the period press freedom in Africa was seen to have the largest decline of any other fundamental freedoms. During the last decade (2010 to 2021) authoritarian governments emerged and continued to exert pressure on people's freedoms, imprisonments increased and many other types of harassment to suppress independent thinking, suppression of freedom of expression and reporting increased. Some media houses including reporters of prominent media houses including radio, TV, and Newspapers were banned from proceeding with their business because of one lame excuse or another. In Sub Sahara African countries during the 2010 to 2021 period, even the electronic media were put under very stressful surveillance. New laws were enacted and through those suppressive laws many people including journalists and editors were imprisoned or deported. The proliferation of restrictive laws also aimed to restrict activities of opposition parties, all with a view of eliminating opposition or expression of alternative ideas.

Taking into account the governance issues that have been outlined above and also the opinion of wide range of constitutional experts, almost all constitutions in Africa need some review or amendments; some of them needing very substantial changes, while others could be less so. The governance issues will need to feature very prominently in the constitutional reviews, as that is the only move which will enable Africa to make progress towards Africa that Africans aspire to have, as per African Vision 2063.

We should at this point say there are quite a number of positive notions that also ought to be made. In other words, it is very encouraging to note that in a span of just 10 years since 2012 Africa experienced some marginal change towards good governance though the remaining way to go is substantially long. The continent-wide mix of type of change of governments is what demands to be further addressed. During the period some countries sought for greater accountability and democracy. Today countries like Mauritius, Botswana, Cape Verde, Namibia, and Ghana rank relatively high as politically stable democratic countries in Africa. The other countries of Africa besides the five democracies listed above are at various stages towards good governance, although it is still quite difficult to predict when they will get to that level of envisaged democratic progress. That is so because there has been forward and backward motions depending on the type of new leaders that assume power after general elections. Movement to meaningful democracy has become a very challenging issue especially in Sub-Saharan Africa.

Looking closely at the five democratically stable countries it will be noted that there is a very close relationship between good governance and the rate of growth of a country. Economic transformation can have a strong destructive effect on political governance giving rise, for instance, to interest groups that push for accountable leaders and effective institutions.

As countries get richer, more effective institutions also become more affordable. Good governance means more efficient utilization of resources, better access to capital, better and high level of development, a sustained way of efficient domestic or regional capital markets. Furthermore, using the example of the five good performance countries, we note that good governance can promote accountability, transparency, efficiency and rule of law at all levels and will allow efficient management of human, natural, economic and financial resources for equitable and sustainable development, guaranteeing civil society participation in decision making, the human capability and choices in general. Health, knowledge, and skills are part of human development attracted to the many. Not only that but governance is also closely related to politics. The five democracies have proved to also be with stable governments with very articulate policies that have been developed in an inclusive way. So, in short, we should expect a lot more positive growth and development results from the five African democracies.

Governance has often been related to the functional way of institution, and human development, implied quality employment opportunities, and better chance of swift growth.

In spite of the good progress that was achieved until 2010 some African countries have had their revised laws and constitutions bringing a reverse outlook; and all that has depended on what inputs were put in the revision. Revisions may have been done to the constitutions and laws, but the revision may have not taken into account the need for development of sound constitutions, and laws including the need to have good electoral systems that takes the interests of citizens and general population into account. Closely observed constitutions and laws have been done with a view to keep leaders permanently in office.

Until 2014 more than 30 of the 54 African countries had held elections. The process to and the results of the elections had many faults, which deprived their citizens the right to choose or elect leaders of their choice. In such situations transparency in the election process has always been messed up. The result of the messing up is to bring the wrong people to power, and this happens even after some constitutions have been reviewed. What that means is that some new laws (or revisions) are put in place to ensure that democracy will never flourish. We could take the cases of national security laws, terrorist laws, anticorruption laws, and money laundering laws. In many cases the laws are good if they are genuinely designed to uproot the outlaws. But in many African countries such laws are aimed to suppress oppositions. Leaders and members of the opposition are arrested and imprisoned under those laws, so that the corrupt leaderships get ample time to fulfill their corrupt intentions.

In any case a good majority of African countries are basically dictatorship that manifest in form of tough democratic leadership. Those countries that at least have started on the road to sound democracy as well as other rising democracies across Africa, serve as encouragement to international partners that patients might pay and that stability could be achieved throughout the continent some day; and that is everybody's hope that it will happen within the shortest possible time; may be in the next ten or so years notwithstanding that the beautiful ones are not yet born.

Most African states are today, not ignorant of some of the challenges facing the continent. The African Union for example dedicated the entirety of 2018 to winning the battle against corruption and the consequences showed very encouraging results. The general feeling is that a lot can be achieved in this area of governance. However, we are not sure if the assessments or corruption reduction seen at the beginning of 2011 would be the same if it were to be redone in 2021 (it is doubtful if the results would be as good). That doubt arises from the fact that, from 2018 to 2022 there surfaced a lot of lack of seriousness in issues of governance. Most leaders involved in the battle have been talking politics but often they are over possessed by hypocrisy. For instance, external election observers have, without much exception, kept reporting positively on good governance; and they report that they have been witnessing good and fair elections. But in reality, that reporting has been very hypocritical. In as far as donor communities are concerned, they have never insisted on governance strongly enough. When policies failed, assistance has kept coming with a view to maintaining good relation with whatever regime that has been put in power. That has been happening because the foreign agencies have their own ulterior motives.

Some donors have till recently been raising the governance issue, linking it to assistance in order to ensure that the economy and clean politics are introduced. Increasingly, Africans are saying such conditions should be tied to policy performance, but not to a particular blueprint for democracy. This may explain why Africans should design their own approach to democracy, make a good-faith effort to govern well and to have programmes work in an efficient manner, and strive for the development of a culture of democracy between the rulers and the ruled, which is good idea, but some do not adhere to what they themselves pronounce were good for their people. In some situations, dictatorial approach is used to make the people of certain political cliques to convince the rest that there was democracy, thus suppressing the vocal groups in the same society.

It should be hoped in any case that improved governance policies and strategies including legal support blueprints should be taken into account before we moved on to meaningful fight for democracy. Africa is liberalizing, but it will take time, and one must be prepared to persevere for a long haul. The hope though is that soon rather than too late African governance and democratic system will come by to pave the way for the envisaged New-Africa in the not very many years to come. Surely after so many centuries and decades of Africa and African suppression by other nations and races, Africa should honestly aim to lead the way to a new world of peace, democracy, and love for all mankind and certainly, economic development should be the corner stone of everybody's thinking.

26

THE NEW PARTNERSHIP FOR AFRICA'S DEVELOPMENT (NEPAD)

In the previous Chapters we had a discussion about challenges that are facing the growth and development of the African continent. It was made clear that development was inevitable in order for Africa to catch up with the rest of the world. But growth and development needs articulate policies and strategies. It also needs prioritization of what should be implemented and target setting of the priority programmes and projects. However, there are many issues that have been constraining Africa, preventing it from moving forward as fast as it should. The issues include intrastate and interstate conflicts, terrorism, and unconstitutional changes of some governments, governance issues and so on. Actually, these remain the three of the biggest security issues in Africa. These are ongoing concerns and the continental responses, especially those of the AU Peace and Security Council (PSC) to these threats need to be closely observed.

Mindful of the need for African development to be properly coordinated and also the need for dealing with the key constraining issues, African Union established what is known as New Partnership for Africa's Development (NEPAD). This is a full-fledged development agency, charged primarily with coordinating and executing priority regional and continental projects outlined in Agenda 2063. The Agency is also mandated to mobilise the full range of resources required for the effective implementation of priority projects and to provide knowledge-based advisory services and technical assistance to AU Member States and Regional Economic Communities (RECs). Furthermore, NEPAD monitors and evaluates the implementation of programmes and projects and serves as the Continent's technical interface on policy development recommendation and implementation with partners and stakeholders.

NEPAD is a socio-economic flagship programme of the African Union (AU). Put in precise terms NEPAD is a pledge by African leaders to eliminate poverty and achieve sustainable path of growth and development on the continent. It is the place where governance issues are supposed to be handled. It is the Pan-African strategic framework for the socio-economic development of the continent.

NEPAD was officially adopted by the AU in 2002 as a primary mechanism to coordinate the peace and impact of Africa's development in the 21st century. The NEPAD was adopted by African Heads of state and government of OAU in 2001 and was ratified by the African Union (AU) in 2002 to address Africa's development problems within a new paradigm. Actually, what this means is that Millennium Africa Recovery Plan (MAP) and Omega Plan for Africa combined to give birth to a third initiative- the New African Initiative (NAI), which then led to the establishment of NEPAD in 2001. Institutionally, founding members of NEPAD included South Africa, Nigeria, Algeria, Egypt, and Senegal.

NEPAD is a holistic, comprehensive integrated strategic framework for the socio -economic development of Africa. It is there to provide a vision for Africa, a statement of the problems facing the continent and a programme of action to resolve these problems in order to reach the vision 2063. NEPAD is a plan that was and is conceived and developed by African leaders. As it is, it is a comprehensive integrated development plan that addresses social, economic, and political priorities in a coherent and balanced manner. It stands as a commitment the African leaders have been making to access the integration of Africa into a global economy. It is also seen as a framework for new partnership with the rest of the world; and stands as a call to the rest of the world to partner Africa in her own development on the basis of her own agenda and programme of action.

NEPAD has its priorities, which are set according to the development themes. Through those thematic priority areas, NEPAD gears to achieve specific targets, which include:

- Leveraging the demonstrated strengths of NEPAD with an enhanced operating model and clear mandate to sharpen its delivery capacity in complete alignment with continental and national priorities.

- Ensuring that policies and decisions are implemented in continental, regional and national spheres with a sound results-based approach.

- Playing a catalytic role to support capacity development of Member States and RECs.

- Mobilising resources for the accelerated and expanded implementation of development programmes across the Continent to achieve Agenda 2063.

- Ensuring horizontal linkages between RECs and Member States and vertical connections between stakeholders at continental, regional and national levels.

The NEPAD has three major goals, namely (i) to promote accelerated growth and sustainable development (ii) to eradicate widespread and severe poverty; and (iii) to halt the marginalization of Africa in the globalization process. These goals translate to some six sectoral priorities, which are to:

- Bridge infrastructure gap by building human resources to reduce poverty to

- Bridge education gap, reverse brain drains, and improve health.

- Develop a strong and sustainable agriculture.

- Ensure the safeguard and defense of environment.

- Spread and favour culture across the continent of Africa and

- Development of science and technology

Africa has many expectations from NEPAD. The expectations include the fact that when implemented it will bring about economic growth and development. It will also promote employment; and will lead to reduction in poverty and inequality. It will further lead to diversification of productive activities, enhance international competitiveness, and promote an increase in exports and finally increase integration of the African continent.

So far NEPAD has contributed a lot to the implementation to bring about growth and development, increased employment, reduction in poverty and inequality, diversification of productive activities, enhancement of international competition and increased exports and an increased integration of the African continent. NEPAD has been facilitating and coordinating the development of continent-wide programmes and projects, has mobilized resources and engaged the global community, Regional Economic Communities (RECs) and member states in the implementation of these programmes and projects.

NEPAD is in the current attempt to create an effective development strategy for the continent as a whole and has faced both praise and criticism for its efforts during the last 20years of its existence i.e., from 2002 to 2022. It constitutes the most important advance in Africa's development policy during the last four decades of Africa's independence. So, it is representing a real attempt by the continent to work together in creating an effective development programme. It has been promoting peace and stability, democracy, and sound economic development and has been assisting to cement ideas of the link between good governance and sustainable development.

Any powerful thing has also its weak points. NEPAD has also had its failures. Of the leading failure is the non-influence in member state internal affairs, and differences over the pace and objective of regional cooperation. The advocates of NEPAD have it that advancement of the idea of African Renaissance, translated to mean, shared African identity with shared suffering and desire to end it by reaffirming Africa's rise from ashes. The idea of renaissance is associated with the areas of encouragement of cultural exchange, the deepening and sustenance of economic development.

Like it has kept been emphasised since 2002 until 2022 NEPAD has had some very significant success stories which include the:

Adaptation of the African Peer Review Mechanism (APRM), which is designed to assess member country's most critical problems.

Identification of the needed actions and secure commitments from the country under review for fixing the problems and

Identification of the most critical problems through APRM and finding possible solutions and hence categorizing them.

As we start looking to the future of NEPAD, we should recognize its significance during the first two decades of its existence. The future of NEPAD lies in a number of factors some of which can be outlined to include its role in pushing the development initiatives available on an African scale. NEPAD has existed for the last 20 years, yielding conclusive results in areas such as science, technology, agriculture, and infrastructure. Its recent integration as a development agency in the African Union structure has lasted this long and relied on a formal, institutionalized framework such as this one, with a mandate focusing on issues of implementation.

As a flagship of African Union NEPAD will hopefully continue to be directly responsible, for some of the most important development strategies implemented in key areas such as agriculture, with the comprehensive Africa Agriculture Development Programme, which is among areas that are also deemed to be of the utmost priority. The fact that all African countries are expected to strive to implement the rules and norms of governance and disentanglement from poverty, strategies at the level of our continent will continue to serve as a great achievement.

Little is known regarding the African Peer Review Mechanism, whose goals must be implemented. This unique approach is about evaluating political or economic and governance in countries that are willing to be assessed. But as we move ahead such reviews should be extended to involve all countries. In other words, the action should not only affect the willing countries, but all; as long as they are members of the continental community.

Only Africa and Africans must carry high the banner of a good future for Africa avoiding what has often been coming from external media like CNN and others like it. Africa should avoid self-disparaging attitude, which only adds to enhancement of negative impact. We cannot afford to keep on offering our children a negative image of Africa. We need to put things into perspective. Take the instance of a country like Rwanda, which has made significant progress while reducing its reliance on foreign aid by mobilizing its own resources. Cape Verde too has succeeded in becoming a middle-income country. Judging from the design and implementation of its new constitution, Kenya is making significant progress in terms of governance. Botswana has been trying to refuse to appeal for foreign aid, with many other countries following its example.

Africa has been facing famine in various regions and places and the lack of political change, which has in many times resulted in revolution. What NEPAD can offer is to face up to these challenges which may also include the issues of political change and democratization.

27

THE AFRICAN INTEGRATION - THE SOLE VIABLE PATH

It is now time to say again that Africa has a role to double its efforts to get to the intended destination, which is described as the place of high level of economic emancipation. The place is in some way imaginary but refers to a place of high level of economic growth and development. The destination is properly defined in Africa Vision 2063 and is better spelt out in the Seven Africa's Aspirations, which form the pillars of the Vision 2063.

Africa's destination is thus further defined as the place that is governed by democracy and stability; characterized by both sound political and economic performance. The features could resemble those of what used to be First World, but it is not exactly so. The features that are to be found in that great destination are further stated to have high literacy rate, free enterprise, democracy and rule of law, high economic growth and development, high level of agricultural development, high level of industrial performance and innovations, equitable distribution of income, high average incomes (which could be measured by high level of GDP as well as the per capita GDP). The other features will include economic stability and freedom of entrepreneurship, private sector driven economy, peace and order, absence of poverty. It is like getting to the Garden of Eden if it could be rebuilt on the basis of the current or future technological developments which are likely to include artificial intelligence and machine learning, automation of robot processes, edge and quantum computing virtual as well as augmented reality, block chain, internet of things and getting to 5G and even 6G.

The objective of the OAU have always been to rid the continent of the remaining vestiges of colonization and apartheid to promote unity among African states; to coordinate and intensify cooperation for development; and to safeguard the sovereignty and territorial integrity of member states. The greatest thing OU has achieved is the African Union War established to empower African countries and ensure social economic and political development. What is desired now is to ensure there is a strategic framework that aims to drive its goals further for inclusive and sustainable development. The framework is a concrete manifestation of the Pan African drive for Unity, self determination, freedom, progress and collective responsibility, pursued under Pan Africanism and African Renaissance.

Africa is still trekking on rugged road full of economic, social, political, and even cultural and technological huddles; as the remaining road to be covered to achieve Vision 2063 is not far away. All Africans will have to fasten their seat belts as the continent keeps moving on the rugged road. Endurance, commitment, and solidarity are highly desirable as the continent keeps cruising through the political, terrorist, pandemics, poverty eradication, climate change and environmental hazards. In other words, the going will be very turbulent but hard work endurance, commitment, and the will to work as a united people will be factors that will enable the motion towards the destination of economic emancipation and development to be realized. It is time for Africa and Africans to build up a sense of determination to squeeze itself through the crowd to ultimately get space at the world economic development driver's seat. To get to that point is certainly not an easy task and has never been easy for anybody in such race due to the challenges that have been outlined in the various parts of this book. Those challenges and as stipulated in the Aspirations as outlined by African Pioneer leaders, must be addressed as shown in the re-dedication of African leaders in 2013.

Africa must grow and should be seen to be growing by others. It does not matter what others will gossip about Africa's ambition to move swiftly to destination and on to the driver's seat; but by all means the aim is to be ready for the safari. The saying has it that "it can be done as long as everybody plays his part". However, with Africa's Agenda 2063 blueprint and master plan for transforming it to the global powerhouse of the future, the landscape will certainly be very different from what we see today. Like has been hinted in 2013 African heads of state signed the 50th Anniversary Solemn Declaration to affirm their commitment to support Africa's new path for attaining inclusive and sustainable economic growth and development. That declaration (or- re-dedication) served as a testimony that Africa was still committed to achieving the goals set for Vision 2063. Once again, the declaration marked the re-dedication of Africa towards the attainment of the Pan- African Vision of the integrated, prosperous, and peaceful Africa, driven by its own citizens, representing a dynamic force in the international arena. On those grounds Agenda 2063 will thus continue to serve as the concrete manifestation of how the continent intends to achieve its Vision within the remaining period to 2063.

Reflecting a bit on historical perspectives we will note that Africa was home for the first man in the world. For thousands of years Africa and Africans accepted the responsibility to become nanny for those who came immediately after her; an act which also became monumental for the coming generations. Empires such as those of

Carthage, Libya, Egypt, Ethiopia including Axum, Ghana and many more, developed and disappeared. The lost empires also included Mesopotamia, which in those ancient days were black people African empires, that rose up between 2,300 and 539 BCE and which included the Akkadian empire, the Babylonian empire, the Assyrian empire, and the Neo-Babylonian Empire. According to physical anthropologists the Sumerians, Akkadians and Babylonians were a predominantly, Black African people's empires, just like were the Jews who at some stage spread to places in the Horn of Africa. Starting with the medieval times Africa fell prey of European nations, which enhanced slave trade, Imperialism, and colonialism, each in its own way aimed at perpetuating the plundering of African resources. This also brings up the issue of Africa as of where it is today.

In spite of past predicaments all the way to the end of the medieval period, Africa was leading the world. Until end of medieval time Africa was the powerhouse of the World, as it had got been entrusted to be the birthplace of human beings. Africa did the work of nursing the human species well and hopefully efficiently. It was from Africa many developments and civilizations were modeled as Africa kept sitting on the driver's seat of world development affairs. However, 16th century became the turning point to the hell life imposed on it and which survived until the end of colonialism and neo-colonialism.

The question now is why did things develop in that way and why this fuss about Africa getting to the driver's seat of the world development? Why the shout for Africa to become a Global Powerhouse of the future? The quick answer is that Africa has had enough of poverty, humiliation, discrimination, and has had Its natural resources plundered for over four centuries; and so, this is the right time when it should fight to permanently regain its integrity and glory. It is hoped if Africa will successively achieve the tenets of vision 2063, which should be realised by any means. Africa will get there as planned as long as it sticks to its commitment to move swiftly to Regional and to Continental economic integration- as stipulate in the re-dedication statement of the year 2013, and also planning well to speed up economic growth and development.

However, there is no need for Africa to be scared by what happened in the past. It is time to put on the boots and start moving on. For Africa to be strong politically, militarily, and economically the small states of Africa must keep getting together in regional economic communities, as already discussed, with a view of paving the way to a bigger community- the African Economic Community (AEC). Africa should not be happy unless it sees itself United. It is heartening to remember that that was the banner of OAU. Today, almost 70 years after the proposal to establish a strong African Union the real establishment is not on sight. Unfortunately, the current pace of globalization will give no choice to small developing countries, to get on smoothly without getting together. African nations must integrate into bigger markets; and that is possible only by having Africa as a single economic block.

OAU has already moved a step to African Union (AU), but that is only a name, the fathers of independent African nations hoped a lot more would have been done. However, one can walk a extra mile only after taking the first step. That first step has been made, but there is need to move faster to regional economic integrations and further on to real African Union. All these must be achieved in the remaining years till 2063.

So far the RECs are eight; they include eight sub regional bodies which are the building blocks of the African Economic Community established in the 1991 under Abuja Treaty, which provides the overarching framework for continental economic integration. The RECs are: the Arab Maghreb Union (UMA) in the north; the Economic Community of West African States (ECOWAS) in the west; the East African Community (EAC) in the east; the Inter - governmental Authority on Development (IGAD) also in the east; the Southern Africa Economic Community (SADC) in the south; the Common Market for Eastern and Southern Africa (COMESA) in the southeast; the Economic Community of Central African States (ECCAS) in the centre, and the Community of Sahel-Saharan (CENSAD) in the north.

The RECs do not only constitute key building blocks for economic integration in Africa but are also key actors working in collaboration with the AU, in ensuring peace and stability in their regions, and also serve as the implementing arms of the African Union (AU). However, the concern is on the speed at which the various RECS are committed to implementing the various benchmarks. Things have not been moving as quickly as one would envisage. That slow pace is at times breeding public thinking that despite the good intentions of establishing RECs, the African leaders that are responsible for making things happen have been exerting type of inertia for reasons that cannot be easily explained. This becomes even more critical issue when account is made of the fact that the RECs are highly essential and instrumental for the effective implementation, financing, monitoring and evaluation of Agenda 2063 and its flagship programmes, at particularly the regional levels.

African Union's 50-year structural transformation and development plan for realizing the Pan-African vision of an integrated, prosperous, and peaceful Africa, driven by its own citizens, and representing a dynamic force in the global arena, Agenda 2063 was enabled to provide a new impetus for enhanced engagement by the RECs. It is on those grounds this book proposes more commitments, and eager by African leaders to work practically harder towards regional and full continental integration.

www.ingramcontent.com/pod-product-compliance
Lightning Source LLC
LaVergne TN
LVHW021753060526
838201LV00058B/3080